外 国 人 实 用 汉 语 语 法

A PRACTICAL CHINESE
GRAMMAR FOR FOREIGNERS

by

Li Dejin   Cheng Meizhen

SINOLINGUA
BEIJING

First Edition	1988
Second Printing	1990
Third Printing	1994
Fourth Printing	1998
Fifth Printing	2003

ISBN 7-80052-067-6

Copyright 1988 by Sinolingua

Published by Sinolingua

24 Baiwanzhuang Road, Beijing 100037, China

Tel: (86) 10-68995871 / 68326333

Fax: (86) 10-68326333

E-mail: hyjx @263.net

Printed by Beijing Foreign Languages Printing House

Distributed by China International

Book Trading Corporation

35 Chegongzhuang Xilu, P.O. Box 399

Beijing 100044, China

说　明

　　我们根据三十年来教授外国学生基础汉语的经验，深感有必要为初学汉语的外国人编写这样一本浅近、实用的现代汉语语法入门书。

　　为了使外国读者通过本书能掌握汉语基本语法用于指导实践，准确运用现代汉语的基本语法规律进行会话和阅读，我们在编写时突出了以下几点：

　　1.编入最基本最常用的语法规则，简明扼要、通俗易懂地讲解理论，并提供大量例句或表格来说明。

　　2.着重介绍词和词组的分类及其用法特点。

　　3.针对外国人在学习、运用语法规则时可能出现的难点和问题，在每一章节里都提出若干注意事项。

　　4.例句用词绝大多数选自《外国人实用汉语常用词表》（北京语言学院1981年编），例句力求符合生活实际，学以致用。

　　5.每一章（或一节）后编有形式多样的练习材料。全书后附有语法术语表和练习答案。

　　在本书编写过程中，李景蕙、刘英林参加了编写计划和部分章节的起草和讨论。英文翻译：第一、二章张占一、张孝忠，第三—五章鲁健骥，第六—十章李长兰。袁鹤年审阅了第一、二章的译文，鲁健骥审阅了其他各章的译文。对此，我们表示衷心的感谢。

我们希望这本书能帮助初学者概括地了解现代汉语语法，正确运用语法规则，成为他们"入门"的良友。

编 著 者

李德津　程美珍

1982.6.于北京语言学院

FOREWORD

Thirty years of experience in teaching foreign students basic Chinese have brought to our attention the needs for a simple and practical modern Chinese grammar for beginners of Chinese as a foreign language.

In order to enable the users of this book to master the basic grammatical rules of Chinese and apply them to speaking and reading, we have emphasized the following points:

1. We have briefly dealt with the most frequently used grammatical rules and explained them theoretically in as non-technical a way as possible. To fascilitate their understanding, we have further illustrated them with many examples and tables.

2. We have highlighted the classification and features in the function of words and phrases.

3. A subheading is given in each section to enumberate the points that call for special attention in view of the difficulties foreigners may encounter and errors they are liable to make in learning Chinese.

4. We have tried to make the examples useful and realistic and most of the words used in them can be found in A PRACTICAL LIST OF COMMONLY USED CHINESE WORDS FOR FOREIGNERS (published by the Beijing Language Institute, 1981).

5. Various exercises are provided at the end of each sec-

tion/chapter and a list of grammatical terms as well as a key to all the exercises are given at the end of the book.

In the course of compilation, Li Jinghui and Liu Yinglin participated in discussing and making the first draft of the writing scheme and part of the content of this book. The English translators are: Zhang Zhanyi and Zhang Xiaozhong (Chapters I and II); Lu Jianji (Chapters III-V) and Li Changlan (Chapters VI-X). The compilers would like to express their sincere thanks to Professor Yuan Henian of the Beijing Foreign Language Institute who read and revised the English translation of Chapters I and II and Lu Jianji who read through the English translation of all the other chapters.

It is our hope that those who are learning Chinese as beginners will find the book a useful companion which gives them a general picture of modern Chinese grammar and guides them in applying the rules correctly.

Compiled by
Li Dejin, Cheng Meizhen
Beijing Language Institute
June, 1982

目　录
CONTENTS

6

9

第一章 导 言
Chapter One Introduction

一

  汉语是占中国人口百分之九十以上的汉民族的语言，也是中国各民族使用的共同语。汉语有非常悠久的历史，是世界上丰富发达的语言之一，也是国际通用的语言之一。

The Chinese language is the language of the Chinese Han nationality, which comprises over 90% of the total population of China, as well as being the common social language of all nationalities of China. It is also, with its long history, one of the most developed and wide-spread languages of the world.

  汉语存在着许多有严重分歧的方言。本书所研究的现代汉语是以北京语音为标准音、以北方话为基础方言、以典范的现代白话文著作为语法规范的普通话。

Chinese is a language with a great variety of dialects. The modern Chinese described in this book is the so-called *putonghua* (the common language) that takes Beijing speech sounds as its standard pronunciation, the Northern dialects as its basic dialect and standard modern vernacular literature as its grammatical model.

  语法是构成语言的要素之一。外国人学习现代汉语，除了必须掌握语音、汉字（汉语的书写符号）、词汇以外，还要很好地了解它的语法特点，才能掌握汉语用词造句的基本规律。

Grammar is one of the elements of a language. Foreigners learning modern Chinese must have a good understanding of the characteristics of its grammar, in addition to the command of pronunciation, Chinese characters (the written symbols of Chinese) and vocabulary, before they can acquire a mastery of the rules of sentence making and word usage.

<h1 style="text-align:center">二</h1>

为了便于学习并掌握现代汉语语法，我们先介绍一些基本概念。

To help students grasp modern Chinese grammar, some of the fundamental concepts concerned are introduced below.

（一）句子　Sentence

我们把在交际过程中能独立表达一个比较完整意思的语言单位叫作句子。汉语的句子可以分成单句和复句两大类，单句又可分成双部句和单部句两种。双部句包括主语部分和谓语部分，因此也叫主谓句。例如"我们学习汉语"这个句子里的主语部分是"我们"，"学习汉语"是谓语部分。而单部句是不同时具备主语和谓语两个部分的，如"来！""他呢？"这两个句子，单部句也叫非主谓句。汉语句子里的谓语可由实词直接充当，而不限于动词。

A sentence is a language unit which makes complete and independent sense in social communication. In the Chinese language, there are two kinds of sentences, the simple and the complex. Structurally, simple sentences can be classified into two different groups: the one-member sentence consisting of either the subject or the predicate, and the two-member sen-

2

tence consisting of both the subject and the predicate, which is also called the subject-predicate (S-P) sentence, e.g. in the sentence 我们学习汉语，我们 is the subject and 学习汉语 the predicate. In the sentence 来1，there is only the predicate, while in the sentence 他呢?，there is only the subject. Therefore the last two examples are called one-member sentences or non-subject-predicate sentences. One point which should be mentioned here is that in the Chinese language, not only verbs, but also other notional words, can function as the predicate.

（二）句子成分　Sentence elements

句子是由词或词组按照一定的语法关系组成的，构成句子的词或词组在句中担任的语法职务和所起的作用就叫句子成分。汉语句子一般有六种句子成分，即：主语、谓语、宾语、定语、状语和补语。例如在"我们学习汉语"一句里包含三种句子成分："我们"是主语，"学习"是谓语，"汉语"是宾语。在"我妹妹努力学习汉语"一句中包含五种句子成分：主语、谓语、宾语、定语和状语。请看下表：

A sentence is composed of various words or phrases arranged according to certain grammatical relationships. These words and phrases in a sentence with certain grammatical functions are called sentence elements. Generally speaking, there are six sentence elements in Chinese: subject, predicate, object, attributive, adverbial adjunct and complement. For instance, there are three elements in the sentence 我们学习汉语. 我们 is the subject, 学习 the predicate and 汉语 the object. In the sentence 我妹妹努力学习汉语，there are five elements: subject, predicate, object, attributive and adverbial adjunct.

The sentence elements are shown in the following table:

3

主　语　部　分 The subject section		谓　语　部　分 The predicate section		
	主语 Subject		谓语 Predicate	宾语 Object
定　语 Attributive		状　语 Abverbial Adjunct		
我	我　们 妹　妹	努　力	学　习 学　习	汉语。 汉语。

（三）词　Words

词是组成句子的最基本的语言单位。如"我们学习汉语"一句就是由"我们"、"学习"和"汉语"三个词组成的。"我妹妹努力学习汉语"一句是由"我"、"妹妹"和"努力"等五个词组成的。汉语的词按其意义和语法特点可以分成实词和虚词两大类。实词具有比较实在的意义，能单独充当句子成分，例如名词、代词等；上面两句中的六个词都是实词。虚词一般没有实在意义，一般不能单独充当句子成分，例如副词、助词等。

A word is the most basic unit in making up a sentence. The sentence 我们学习汉语 is composed of three words: 我们, 学习 and 汉语. In the sentence 我妹妹努力学习汉语, there are five words: 我，妹妹，努力，学习 and 汉语. Words in the Chinese language can be divided into two kinds, the notional word and the function word, according to meaning and grammatical function. Words which have concrete meaning and can function independently as sentence elements are called notional words, such as nouns, pronouns, etc. All of the words in the two sentences given above are notional words. Words without concrete meaning and which are unable to be used as

4

sentence elements by themselves, such as adverbs, particles, etc., are called function words.

（四）词组　Phrases

词组是词和词按照一定的语法规则组合起来的一组词。词组有主谓词组、动宾词组、偏正词组等。例如"我妹妹努力学习汉语"一句中主语部分"我妹妹"就是偏正词组。

A phrase is a combination of words arranged according to certain grammatical rules. There are the subject-predicate (S-P) phrase, the verb-object (V-O) phrase, the endocentric phrase, etc., e.g. in the sentence 我妹妹努力学习汉语， the subject section 我妹妹 is an endocentric phrase.

现将汉语句子的类型及其相互之间的关系简单地列表如下：

The types of Chinese sentences and the relationship between them are illustrated briefly in the following graph:

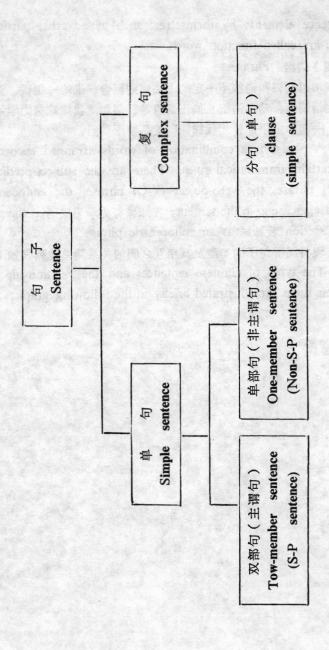

三

汉语里组词造句的最主要的语法手段一是词序，二是虚词的运用。

Grammatically, word order and the use of function words play the main role in the Chinese language.

词序在汉语里占有特别重要的地位，词和词的组合、句子成分在句子里的位置都有一定的排列次序。比如，汉语里的修饰成分（定语和状语）永远在被修饰的中心语前边。在"我也买"这个句子里，"也"是修饰成分（状语），"买"是中心语，绝不能把词序弄颠倒，如果说成"我买也"，就不能表达任何意义了。而在"我们都不去"和"我们不都去"这两个句子里，由于"都"和"不"的先后次序不同，意思也就不一样；前一句表示"我们"当中没人"去"，后一句表示"我们"中间有人"去"，有人"不去"。

Word order is extremely important since words and sentence elements in a sentence must be combined and placed according to a certain order. For instance, the modifier, be it attributive or adverbial, must be placed before the modified word. In the sentence 我也买，也 is the adverbial modifier, and 买 is the modified word. The order cannot be reversed to read 我买也，which does not make any sense in Chinese. The sentence 我们都不去 meaning "nobody is going" is quite different from the sentence 我们不都去，which means "not all of us are going" (some of us will go).

虚词指的是副词、介词、连词、助词等。这些词一般不表示具体的词汇意义，但在句子里起着极为重要的语法作用。比如："我书"不能表达明确的意思，而"我的书"表示"书属于我"

的意思。就是因为助词"的"起了作用。再如"我写一封信"表示"准备写",而"我写了一封信"中由于用了助词"了",就表示"已经写完了"。

The term "function word" refers to adverbs, prepositions, conjunctions and particles, etc., which do not express concrete lexical meaning but which grammatically plays a very important role. For example, 我书 does not make any sense, whereas 我的书 means "my book". This is only because of the use of the particle 的。The sentence 我写一封信 means "I am going to write a letter", while the sentence 我写了一封信 means "I have written a letter". The aspectual particle 了 expresses that the action of writing has been completed.

汉语里没有狭义的形态变化,因此,词序和虚词的运用更显得重要。

Word order and the use of function words are by far the most important since in the Chinese language there is no morphological change in the strict sense.

汉语的动词在任何情况下,也就是说,不论人称、性别、数量、时间等有什么差别,动词本身的形式都不改变。例如动词"是":

The form of a verb remains unchanged under all circumstances. Differences in person, gender, number or time do not require changes in the form of a verb. Let us take 是 for example:

1. 单数人称代词"我、你、她、他"虽然人称、性别不同,但后边的动词"是"都是同一个形式。例如:

Singular personal pronouns such as 我,你,她,他,are all followed by the same verb 是,in spite of their differences in person and gender. For example:

我是中国人。

8

你是中国人。

她是中国人。

他是中国人。

2．复数人称代词"我们、你们、她们、他们"虽然人称、性别不一样，但后边的"是"却永远不改变形式。例如：

Plural personal pronouns such as 我们，你们，她们，他们 are all followed by the same 是，which again has no change in form due to differences in person and gender. For example:

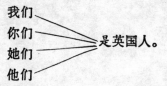

再如动词"学习"在表示不同时间的句子里形式不变。例如：

This can be illustrated by one further example. The form of the verb 学习 also remains unchanged with any time reference. For example:

我去年学习法语。——指过去 (Referring to the past)

我现在学习汉语。——指现在 (Referring to the present)

我明年学习日语。——指将来 (Referring to the future)

现代汉语语法还有一个特点。汉语里有丰富的量词，一件事物一个动作都有一定的计量单位，不能不用，又不能随便用。量词不但使用的范围广，而且错综复杂，外国人要特别注意每个量词的用法。

Measure words, which indicate the specific unit or measure of things or actions, are another feature of modern Chinese. Measure words, which are great in number and whose use is obligatory, extensive and complicated but not arbitrary, merit special attention.

总之，对外国人来说，要掌握一种主要靠词序和虚词进行组词造句的方法，是不容易的，但又是必要的。希望外国朋友能准确地抓住汉语语法的特点。

To sum up, for foreign learners to master a method of word formation and sentence construction which relies mainly on word order and function words is not easy, but it must be done. It is hoped foreign learners will strive hard to correctly grasp the characteristics of Chinese grammar.

第二章 词 类

Chapter Two Parts of Speech

一、词 Words

词是语言中有一定意义的能自由运用的最小单位，是表达思想的基本材料。汉语的词有单音节的、双音节的和多音节的。汉语里一个汉字代表一个音节，单音节词用一个汉字表示，双音节和多音节的词要用两个或两个以上的汉字表示。单音节词如：人、我、书、家，等等。双音节词如：汉语、客厅、沙发、同伴，等等。多音节词如：自行车、国际主义，等等。汉语里有的字不能单独成为有意义的词，必须和别的字结合在一起，例如"葡萄"的"葡"和"萄"，"枇杷"的"枇"和"杷"等。

A word is the smallest meaningful unit in a language, and is used as the basic material to express ideas. If a word is represented by a single syllable, we call it a monosyllabic word. If a word is represented by two syllables, we call it a dissyllabic word. Words composed of three or more syllables are called polysyllabic words. In writing, a syllable is a character. So a monosyllabic word is represented by one character, a dissyllabic word by two characters, and a polysyllabic one by more than two characters. For example: 人，我，书，家， etc. are monosyllabic words; 汉语，客厅，沙发，同伴， etc. are dissyllabic words; 自行车，国际主义， etc. are polysyllabic words. There are a few characters which are meaningless by themselves and they must be combined with other characters to make up words, e.g. in the word 葡萄 (grapes), neither 葡 nor 萄 carries any meaning by itself, and 枇 and 杷 in 枇杷 (loquate) are another example of such case.

二、词的分类　Classification of Words

　　汉语的词可以分成实词和虚词两大类。实词可以分为名词、动词、助动词、形容词、数词、量词和代词七类；虚词可以分为副词、介词、连词、助词、叹词和象声词六类。除了这十三类词以外，还有两个附类，就是词头和词尾两种构词成分。现列表如下：
（见第13—14页）

　　In Chinese, words can be divided into two kinds: notional words and function words. Nouns, verbs, auxiliary verbs, adjectives, numerals, measure words and pronouns belong to the notional word category; adverbs, prepositions, conjunctions, particles, interjections and onomatopes belong to the function word category. Besides, there are two kinds of affixes, namely, prefixes and suffixes. A table of parts of speech is given below: (P.13∼14)

三、词的兼类　Conversion of parts of speech

　　一般来说，每个词都分别属于一个词类。但有些词具备两类或两类以上的词的语法功能。例如"组织"一词，在"组织晚会"中是动词，表示通过安排使分散着的人或事物集中成一个"晚会"的形式。而"妇女组织"中的"组织"一词是名词，表示妇女们按照一定的宗旨和系统建立起来的集体。因此，"组织"一词兼属两个词类：动词和名词。又如"丰富"一词，在"内容丰富"里是形容词，表示种类多或数量大；而在"丰富内容"中是动词，是"使丰富"的意思。所以"丰富"一词也兼属两类：形容词和动词。另外，兼类词本身在形式上是没有什么区别的。

　　Normally a word belongs to a certain part of speech. But some words have the grammatical function of two or more parts of speech. Here are two examples:

汉 语 词 类 表
Chinese Parts of Speech

词 类 名 称 Names			例　词 Examples
实 词 Notional words		名　词 Nouns	中国　朋友　花　笔　风　**城市**　**年** 天　下　东
		动　词 Verbs	写　爱　去　坐　有　是　知道　给 会
		助 动 词 Auxiliary verbs	能　会　应该　要
		形 容 词 Adjectives	高　快　短　好　干净　伟大
		数　词 Numerals	一　二　三　十　百　千　万　两 零　半
	量　词 Measure words	名量词 Nominal	个　本　张　辆　只　公斤　点　毛
		动量词 Verbal	次　遍　回
	代　词 Pronouns	人称代词 Personal	你　我　他　她　我们　自己
		指示代词 Demonstrative	这　那儿　每
		疑问代词 Interrogative	谁　什么　哪　怎么样

词 类 名 称 Names			例 词 Examples
虚词 Function words	副 词 Adverbs		很 都 就 也 不 再 已经 又
	介 词 Prepositions		从 向 把 被 比 给 在
	连 词 Conjunctions		和 或者 并 但是 因为 只要
	助 词 Particles	结构助词 Structural	的 地 得
		动态助词 Aspectual	了 着 过
		语气助词 Modal	吗 吧 呢 了
	叹 词 Interjections		喂 哎呀 嗯
	象 声 词 Onomatopes		哗哗 乒乓
附类 Affixes	词 头 Prefixes		第 初 老
	词 尾 Suffixes		们 子 性 化 儿

In the phrase 组织晚会, which means "to hold (organize) an evening party", 组织 is a verb, while in the phrase 妇女组织, meaning "women's organization", it is a noun.

In the phrase 内容丰富, 丰富 is an adjective, meaning "rich", while in the phrase 丰富内容, 丰富 becomes a verb

14

meaning "to enrich". In this case, 丰富 belongs to two different parts of speech: adjective and verb. This is called conversion of parts of speech, i.e. they belong to different parts of speech without any change in form.

有些词虽然由于用在不同的地方，在句中作用也不同，但语法特点和意义没有什么变化，不列为兼类词。例如"我们学习"和"学习很重要"两句中的"学习"都是动词。

If the meaning of a word in different sentences remains unchanged, it is not considered conversion although it has different functions. For example: 我们学习 and 学习很重要，in both sentences, 学习 is a verb.

下面分节介绍每一种词类。

Now we shall deal with each part of speech separately.

第一节 名 词
Section I Nouns

一、名词的定义 Definition

表示人或事物名称的词叫名词。

A word denoting the name of a person or thing is called a noun.

根据名词的不同意义，又可分成以下各类：

Nouns can be grouped into the following kinds according to meaning:

专有名词（包括国名、地名、人名等）：

Proper nouns (including names of countries, places, persons, etc.). For example:

中国 北京 长江 庐山 孙中山 毛泽东

指人的名词：

Nouns of personal reference:

人　朋友　大夫　工人　同志

指动植物的名词：

Nouns of animate things:

鱼　羊　花　树

表示具体事物的名词：

Nouns of inanimate objects:

笔　车　山　风　楼　工厂　学校　城市

表示抽象事物的名词：

Nouns of abstract things:

友谊　汉语　经济　事　思想　行为

表示时间的名词：

Nouns of time:

年　月　日　钟点　早上　春天

表示方位的名词：

Nouns of locality:

上　下　前　里　东　南　左　上边　后面　西边
中间

二、名词的语法特点　Grammatical features

（一）　名词前边一般能加数词和量词。例如：

Generally a noun can be preceded by a numeral-measure word combination.　For example:

一个朋友　　　　一辆汽车

一支笔　　　　　一条鱼

（二）　一般不能受副词修饰。

A noun cannot be modified by adverbs.

（三）　少数单音节名词可以重叠，表示"每"的意思。例如：

Some monsyllabic nouns can be reduplicated to express

the meaning of "every". For example:

人人（每人）　　　事事（每件事）
天天（每天）

（四）　指人的名词后边可以加词尾"们"，表示复数。例如：

The suffix 们 can be added to a personal noun to express
the plural. For example:

朋友们　　　　　同志们
工人们　　　　　大夫们

（五）　有些名词是由名词或动词加上词尾"子"、"儿"或
"头"构成的。例如：

Some nouns are composed of a noun or verb with a
suffix 子，儿 or 头. For example:

桌子　　椅子　　杯子　　剪子
画儿　　活儿　　尖儿　　盆儿
石头　　木头　　指头　　舌头

三、名词的用途　Functions

一般的名词都可以在句子里作主语、宾语和定语。

Normally a noun can serve as subject, object and attributive in a sentence.

（一）　作主语。As the subject.

北京是中国的首都。　　　　冬天冷。
学生学习。　　　　　　　　东边有商店。

（二）　作宾语。As the object.

我看报。　　　　　　　　　现在是中午。
你画画儿。　　　　　　　　我们的学校在北边。
大家讨论问题。

（三）　作定语。As an attributive.

这是中国画。　　　　　　　我喜欢春天的早晨。
汉语语法不太难。　　　　　衣服在左边的箱子里。
姐姐的信在这儿。

17

（四） 作谓语。As the predicate.

今天晴天。

昨天星期日。

四、使用名词时需要注意的几个问题

Points that merit special attention

（一） 名词的复数和词尾"们"。

The plural form of nouns and the suffix 们.

汉语里名词本身的形式一般没有单复数的分别，表现复数的方式常见的有以下三种：

Usually the singular and plural forms of a noun are identical and the plural is expressed in three ways:

1.名词前边加数词和量词或其他表示复数的词。例如：

By premodifying numeral-measure words or other words implying the plural.　For example:

三支铅笔　　　　　很多水果

十七个孩子　　　　这些书

2.通过句子里其他成分来表示。例如：

By other elements in the sentence.　For example:

客人都来了。

东西全在桌子上。

3.加词尾"们"

By suffixing 们 to the noun.

指人的名词加"们"后就不能再用其他表示复数的词了。"们"读轻声。例如：（见第19页表）

By suffixing 们, which is pronounced in the neutral tone, to the noun.　When thus used, no other words expressing the plural number can be used.　For example: (table p.19)

（二） 关于时间词。Time nouns.

1.时间词是表示日期、时刻、季节等的名词。

Time nouns are nouns indicating dates, times of the clock, seasons, etc.

	正确的 Correct forms	错误的 Incorrect forms
朋友们	五个朋友	五个朋友们
	几个朋友	几个朋友们
	很多朋友	很多朋友们
	不少朋友	不少朋友们

2.时间词除了能作主语、宾语、定语和谓语外，还经常作状语，而一般名词不具有这个作用。例如：

Apart from serving as subject, object, attributive and predicate, time nouns can also serve as adverbial adjuncts, whereas nouns of other kinds cannot. For example:

你明天来。 　　　　他们后天到。

我晚上去。 　　　　图书馆上午开门。

（三） 关于方位词。Nouns of locality.

1.方位词是表示方向或位置的名词。方位词有单音节的、双音节的两种。举例如下：（见第20页表）

Nouns of locality are nouns showing direction and location. There are two kinds of them: the monosyllabic ones and the dissyllabic ones. Examples of nouns of locality are shown in the table: (table p.20)

2.方位词的用途。The function of nouns of locality.

单音节的方位词很少单独使用。双音节的方位词和一般名词用法基本相同，但除了能作主语、宾语和定语外，还可以作状语。例如：

Monosyllabic nouns of locality are seldom used by them-

单音节 Mono-syllabic	双 音 节 Dissyllabic				
	后面加"边" Followed by 边	后面加"面" Followed by 面	前面加"以" Preceded by 以	前面加"之" Preceded by 之	其 他 Miscel-laneous
上	上 边	上 面	以 上		上 下
下	下 边	下 面	以 下		底 下
前	前 边	前 面	以 前	之 前	前 后
后	后 边	后 面	以 后	之 后	
左	左 边	左 面	＼		左 右
右	右 边	右 面	＼		
里	里 边	里 面			
外	外 边	外 面	以 外		
中	＼	＼	＼		当 中
内	＼	＼	以 内		内 外
间	＼	＼	＼		中 间
旁	旁 边		＼		
东	东 边	东 面	以 东		东南，东北
南	南 边	南 面	以 南		
西	西 边	西 面	以 西		西南，西北
北	北 边	北 面	以 北		

selves. Dissyllabic nouns of locality can serve, roughly like ordinary nouns, as subject, object and attributive, only that they can function as adverbial adjuncts as well. For example:

您里边坐。

我们外边谈。

3. 注意事项：Points that merit special attention：

(1) 单音方位词"里"、"上"常用在名词后边。例如：

Monosyllabic noun of locality 里 and 上 are usually used after other nouns. For example:

> 屋子里　　院子里　　楼里
> 桌子上　　书架上　　树上

(2) "里（边）"的用法：The use of 里（边）：

当我们要表示"在…里边"的意思时，要注意"里（边）"的使用方法。

We should pay attention to the use of 里（边），when it is used to express the meaning of 在…里边。

A. 地理名词后边不用"里（边）"。例如：

里（边）cannot be used after nouns indicating geographical units. For example:

> 他在中国。
> 她在北京。

一定不能说"他在中国里（边）"，"她在北京里（边）"等。

We can never say 他在中国里（边），她在北京里（边），etc.

B. 表示物件的名词后边需要用"里（边）"。例如：

里（边）can be used after nouns indicating containers. For example:

> 书在抽屉里。
> 咖啡在杯子里。

一定不能说"书在书包"或"咖啡在杯子"等。

One can never say 书在书包，咖啡在杯子，etc.

(3) 方位词可以直接作句子成分，作主语或状语时前边都不用介词"在"。例如：

Nouns of locality can be used as various elements of a sentence. When a noun of locality serves as the subject or adverbial adjunct in a sentence, the preposition 在 is not used before it. For example:

里面有一架钢琴。

旁边是我的卧室。

不说"在里面有一架钢琴", "在旁边是我的卧室"。

There are no such forms as 在里面有一架钢琴, 在旁边是我的卧室, etc.

"您里边坐"是"请您到里边坐"的意思。不说"您在里边坐"。

您里边坐 means 请您到里边坐. One cannot say 您在里边坐.

(4) "以前"和"以后"的用法：

How to use 以前 and 以后：

方位词"以前"和"以后"一般只能表示时间。

The nouns of locality 以前 and 以后 are generally used to indicate time.

A. 作状语。As an adverbial adjunct.

我以前学英语，现在学汉语。

（在主语后谓语前）

(以前 is between the subject and the predicate.)

以后我再来。

（在句首，主语前）

(以后 is at the beginning of the sentence.)

B. 作定语。As attributive.

以前的房子不太好。

这是以后的计划。

(四) 名词作定语和结构助词"的 (de)"。

Nouns serving as attributives and the structural particle 的 (de)

1. 定语一定要放在被修饰的中心语（多为名词）前边。

例如：

The attributive must be placed before the modified word (normally a noun).   For example:

　　金老师是中国人。

　　　　（"金"、"中国"是名词，是定语；"老师"、
　　　　"人"是名词，是中心语。）

　　　　(金 and 中国 are nouns serving as attributive while 老师 and 人 are nouns used as modified words.)

　　这是纸花。

2．表示领属关系的名词定语后边要用助词"的"。例如：

The structural particle 的 should be used after an attributive composed of a noun indicating the possessive relation. For example:

　　老师的书在那儿。

　　姐姐的梳子是红的。

3．时间词、方位词作定语时一般要用助词"的"。例如：

When words of time or of locality serve as attributives, 的 is normally used.   For example:

　　这是星期一的票。

　　前边的楼是宿舍。

（五）名词作状语。Nouns used as adverbial adjuncts.

状语一定要放在被修饰的中心语（多为动词）前边。例如：

The adverbial adjunct must be placed before the modified word (normally a verb).   For example:

　　您明天来。

　　　　（"明天"是时间词，是状语；"来"是动词，
　　　　是中心语。'）

　　　　(明天 is a noun of time used as the adverbial adjunct and 来, a verb, is the modified word.)

我们里边谈。

（"里边"是方位词，是状语；"谈"是动词，
是中心语。）

（里边 is a noun of locality functioning as
adverbial adjunct modifying 谈, a verb used
as modified word.）

（六）少数名词可以直接作谓语，不需要加"是"等动词。
例如：

There are a few nouns which can serve as predicate
without using the verb 是. For example:

昨天阴天。

今天星期二。

明天元旦。

（七）单音节名词重叠后只能作主语或状语。例如：

The reduplication of monosyllabic nouns can only be
used as the subject or adverbial adjunct. For example:

人人有工作。 （作主语）

(As the subject)

事事顺利。 （作主语）

(As the subject)

他天天来。 （作状语）

(As the adverbial adjunct)

（八）名词"年"。The noun 年.

在汉语里，"年"只表示时间。例如：

In Chinese, 年 is only a measure of time. For example:

今年是一九八四年。

他一九八一年开始学习汉语。

练 习 一
Exercise 1

（一） 在下面正确的词组后边划"√"，错的后边划"×"。

Mark the correct phrases with a √ and the wrong ones with a ×.

1. 老师们　　（　　）　　2. 五个老师们　（　　）
3. 三个孩子们（　　）　　4. 孩子们　　　（　　）
5. 学生们　　（　　）　　6. 很多大夫们　（　　）
7. 不少裁判们（　　）　　8. 三个同学　　（　　）
9. 很多同志　（　　）　　10. 几个代表　　（　　）

（二） 填上适当的方位词。

Fill in the blanks with appropriate nouns of locality.

1. 院子_____有花。

2. 椅子在桌子_____。

3. 屋子_____热，屋子_____冷。

4. 电冰箱_____有牛奶。

5. 书_____是一本杂志。

6. 他在_____，我在_____，你在中间。

（三） 标出下列词中的名词。

Mark out the nouns among the following words.

1. 道路　2. 桥　3. 烫　4. 公民　5. 洗
6. 社会　7. 洒　8. 切　9. 码头　10. 摩托车
11. 从　12. 宇宙　13. 骂　14. 电　15. 雾
16. 喊　17. 税　18. 血　19. 舌头　20. 打字机

（四） 用横线标出下列句子里的名词。

Underline the nouns in the following sentences:

例如：

Example: 我是<u>研究生</u>。

1. 他是记者。
2. 教室里有黑板。
3. 那是银行。
4. 邮局在银行西边。
5. 我们去动物园。
6. 他在操场。
7. 这是我的地址。
8. 我买壶。
9. 她寄信。
10. 妹妹的头发很长。

第二节 动 词

Section II Verbs

一、动词的定义和种类 Definition and types of verbs

(一)表示动作、行为、心理活动、发展变化等的词叫动词。

例如：

Words indicating actions, behaviour, mental activities, changes and developments, etc. are called verbs. For example:

表示动作的：

Verbs indicating actions:

　　看　写　画　站　谈　听　走

表示行为的：

Verbs indicating behaviour:

　　表示　保卫　拥护　通过　禁止

表示心理活动的：

Verbs indicating mental activities:

　　爱　怕　想　喜欢　希望　知道

表示发展变化的：

Verbs indicating changes and developments:

　　生　死　生长　发展　变化　开始

表示判断、领有、存在的：

Verbs expressing judgement, possession, existence:

是　　有　　在

表示趋向的：

Verbs indicating direction:

上　下　进　出　起　过　回　来　去

(二)动词可以按能不能带宾语分为两类。

Verbs can be grouped into two kinds according to whether they take an object.

1．及物动词。Transitive verbs.

后边可以直接带宾语的动词叫及物动词。

Verbs which can be followed immediately by an object are called transitive verbs.

(1) 动词后边可以只带一个宾语。例如：

Verbs taking only one object.　For example:

动词 Verbs	宾语 Objects		
写	信	字	
看	电视	电影	朋友
听	音乐	报告	收音机
吃	饭	点心	药
骑	车	马	
穿	衣服	鞋	
研究	问题	数学	
保卫	祖国	家乡	
学习	外语	汉语	

（2）有的动词可以带两个宾语。例如：

Verbs taking two objects. For example:

动　词 Verbs	宾语1（指人） Object 1 (of personal reference)	宾语2（指事物） Object 2 (of non-personal reference)
给	我	书
教	朋友	汉语
问	老师	问题
告诉	她们	事情

2. 不及物动词。Intransitive verbs.

后边不能直接带宾语的动词叫不及物动词。例如：

Verbs which cannot immediately take an object are called intransitive verbs. For example:

单音动词：

Monosyllabic verbs:

活　病　醒　躺

双音动词：

Dissyllabic verbs:

休息　咳嗽　胜利　失败　出发　前进

二、动词的语法特点　Grammatical features

（一）多数动词后边可以带宾语。

Most verbs can have objects after them.

（二）动词后边一般可以加动态助词 "了(le)"、"着(zhe)"、"过 (guo)"。例如：

The aspectual particles 了 (le), 着 (zhe) and 过 (guo) can be suffixed to most verbs. For example:

吃了　　说了　　看了
吃着　　说着　　看着
吃过　　说过　　看过

(三)动词后边可以带各类补充成分。例如：

Various complements can occur after verbs. For example:

洗干净　　摘下　　走一趟　　呆一会儿
搬不动　　带来　　站起来　　起得很早

(四)动词前边可以加各类修饰成分。例如：

Verbs can be preceded by various modifiers. For example:

也看　　都有　　只是　　就去　　很尊重
明天来　　能讲　　努力学习　感谢地说　跟他握手

(五)否定形式是动词前边用否定副词"不"或"没(有)"。例如：

Verbs are negated by the negative adverbs 不 or 没 (有). For example:

我不去。　　他没有小说。　　他不在这儿。
他没(有)来。

(六)不少动词可以重叠。例如：

Many verbs can be used reduplicatively. For example:

说说　　看看　　研究研究　　整理整理

(七)能用正反式(即并列肯定形式和否定形式)表示提问。例如：

The affirmative-negative questions can be formed by putting the affirmative and negative forms together. For example:

看不看？　　洗不洗？
是不是？　　讨论不讨论？
有没有？

（八）有些名词、形容词后面可以加词尾"化"构成动词。例如：

Some nouns and adjectives can be turned into verbs by adding the suffix 化 to them. For example:

1.	名　词 Nouns	动　词 Verbs
	工业	工业化
	机械	机械化
	现代	现代化

2.	形容词 Adjectives	动　词 Verbs
	美	美化
	绿	绿化
	合理	合理化

三、动词的用途　Functions

（一）作谓语。As the predicate.

动词的主要用途是作谓语。例如：

Verbs mainly function as the predicate. For example:

我们去。　　　　　你骑自行车。

我有词典。　　　　我送他杂志。

（二）作主语。As the subject.

节约光荣。　　　　比赛开始。

分析很重要。　　　　讨论已经结束。

(三)作定语。As an attributive.

这是喝的水。　　　　买的书在这儿。

提的意见很正确。　　请的客人都来了。

(四)作宾语。As the object.

他喜欢游泳。　　　　她重视学习。

现在开始讨论。　　　我表示感谢。

(五)作补语。As a complement.

你拿走。　　　　　　我看得见。

大家没听懂。　　　　我们做不完。

(六)作状语。As an adverbial adjunct.

他注意地听着。

我钦佩地看着他。

四、使用动词时需要注意的几个问题

Points that merit special attention

（一）汉语里动词的形式是不变的，动词的形式不受人称、性别、单复数、时间等的影响。例如：

Chinese verbs have no morphological changes whatsoever resulting from person, gender, number, time, etc.. For example:

我买本子。　　　　　我们唱歌。

她们买本子。　　　　你再唱一个歌。

他昨天买了三本书。　姐姐不唱歌。

她喜欢妹妹。

你喜欢弟弟。

我喜欢你们。

（二）动词和动态助词"了 (le)、着 (zhe)、过 (guo)"。

Verbs and the aspectual particles 了 (le), 着 (zhe) and 过 (guo).

1. 动词后边加助词"了"，表示动作行为已经完成。例如：

The particle 了 is suffixed to a verb to emphasize a completed action. For example:

他写了一封信。　　（已经写完了）
　　　　　　　　　　(He has finished the letter.)

我们看了一个电影。　（已经看完了）
　　　　　　　　　　(We saw a film.)

2. 动词后边加助词"着"，表示动作正在进行或状态在持续。例如：

The particle 着 is suffixed to a verb to show a progressive action or continuous state. For example:

他吃着饭呢。　　（正在吃）
　　　　　　　　(He is having his meal.)

我们正开着会。　（正在开会）
　　　　　　　　(The meeting is going on.)

窗户关着呢。　　（处于"关"的状态）
　　　　　　　　(The window is in a closed state.)

3. 动词后边加助词"过"，表示动作曾经发生过或曾经有过某种经历。例如：

The particle 过 is suffixed to a verb to place special stress on a certain experience in the past. For example:

我看过这本小说。（所以，我知道这本小说的内容。）
　　　　　　　　　(so I know what it is about.)

昨天我去过你那儿。（但是，你不在。）
　　　　　　　　　(but you were not there.)

（三）动词"是"。The verb 是.

1. 动词"是"表示的意义。

The verb 是 has the following meanings.

（1）表示判断。例如：

To express judgement. For example:

32

我是北京人。　　　　　今天是星期日。

他是工程师。

（2）表示存在。例如：

To express existence.　For example:

楼前边是花园。　　　　那边是海关。

剧场旁边是商店。

（3）表示类别。例如：

To denote classification.　For example:

那是他的，这是你的。　　　他们是那个学校的。

那件上衣是兰的。

2．"是"的语法特点。Grammatical features.

（1）"是"本身不表示具体的动作，后边不能加动态助词"了、着、过"。

是 is not an action verb, therefore it cannot be followed by 了、着 or 过.

（2）"是"后边不能带补充成分。

No complement can be used after 是.

（3）"是"不能重叠。

是 cannot be reduplicated.

（4）"是"的否定形式是"不是"。例如：

The negative form of 是 is 不是.　For example:

我不是上海人。　　　　学校对面不是公园。

她不是工程师。

（四）动词"有"。The verb 有.

1．"有"的用途。Functions of the verb 有.

（1）表示领有。例如：

To express possession.　For example:

我有字典。　　　　她有时间。

他有中国画。

（2）表示存在。例如：

To express existence.   For example:

　　　　屋里有人。　　　　　　　　碗里有汤。

　　　　村子前边有一条小河。

（3） 表示列举。例如：

To give a list of things.   For example:

　　　　我的朋友有英国人、中国人、法国人、日本人。

　　　　屋子里有桌子，有椅子，有书架，有柜子。

（4）表示包含。例如：

To express inclusion.   For example:

　　　　一年有十二个月。　　　　一个星期有七天。

　　　　这本书有十章。

（5）表示达到（某个数量）。例如：

To express the meaning of reaching a certain quantity.
For example:

　　　　这些水果有三公斤。

　　　　盘子里的杯子有十个。

　　　　长江有六千三百多公里长。

　　　　珠穆朗玛峰有八千八百四十八米高。

2． "有"的语法特点。Grammatical features of the verb 有.

（1） "有"不能重叠。

有 cannot be reduplicated.

（2） "有"的否定形式是"没有"。例如：

The negative form of 有 is 没有. For example:

　　　　我没有字典。　　　　　　屋里没有人。

　　　　她没有时间。　　　　　　这些西红柿没有两公斤。

（五）动词 "在"。The verb 在.

1． "在"的意义。Functions of the verb 在.

动词 "在"表示存在。例如：

The verb 在 expresses existence.   For example:

　　　　老师在家。　　　　　同学们在体育馆。

钱在抽屉里。

2．"在"的语法特点。Grammatical features of the verb 在.

（1）"在"后边不能加动态助词"了、着、过"。

The aspectual particles 了, 着 or 过 cannot be used after 在.

（2）"在"不能重叠。

在 cannot be reduplicated.

（3）"在"的宾语一般指处所。例如：

The object of 在 generally indicates a place.　For example:

我在老师家。　　　　墨水在那儿。

他在房间。　　　　　钥匙在这儿。

指人的名词或代词不能单独充当"在"的宾语，后边一定要加上"这儿"或"那儿"。例如：

Nouns or pronouns of personal reference can not be used as objects of 在 unless 这儿 or 那儿 are added to them.　For example:

他在我这儿。

我在朋友那儿。

（六）关于动词和宾语。Verbs and objects.

1．及物动词可以带宾语，但并不是任何情况下都带宾语。例如：

Transitive verbs can take objects, but this is not necessarily always the case.　For example:

他学习汉语。（"汉语"是"学习"的宾语）

（汉语 is the object of 学习.)

学生学习。　（"学习"不带宾语）

（In this sentence, 学习 has no object.)

汉语必须带宾语的动词很少。

There are only a very small number of verbs in Chinese that must have an object.

2．动词和宾语在意义上要搭配得恰当。例如：

The collocation of a verb and its object must be logical.
For example:

我们喝水。

她收拾房间。

3．能带两个宾语的动词只限于"给、送、还、借、递、教、问、回答、告诉、通知"等少数动词。例如：

There are only a few verbs that can take two objects, among them are 给，送，还，借，递，教，问，回答，告诉，通知 etc.. For example:

她教我们英语。　　　他通知大家一件事。

我们回答老师问题。

（七）动词作主语时要有一定的条件，谓语需由形容词或表示"停止、开始、判断"一类的动词充当。例如：

A verb can be used as subject on condition that the predicate of the sentence must be an adjective or a verb expressing the ideas of "stop, start or judgement". For example:

工作紧张。　　　朗读是好方法。

表演开始。　　　锻炼可以增强体质。

（八）动词作定语或状语时后边要用助词"的"或"地"。例如：

的 or 地 must be added to a verb used as an attributive or adverbial adjunct. For example:

吃的东西很多。

我有休息的时间。

他关心地说："你休息吧"。

（九）表示心理活动等的动词可以受程度副词修饰。例如：

Verbs of mental activities can be modified by adverbs of degree. For example:

很喜欢　　　　　非常希望

多么爱　　　　　特别怕

（十）关于动词重叠。Reduplications of verbs

1．重叠形式和读音。

Formulas and pronunciation of the reduplicated verbs.

（1）单音节动词的重叠形式是：AA。例如：

The reduplicative formula for monosyllabic verbs is AA.
For example:

洗——洗洗　　　坐——坐坐

（2）双音动词的重叠形式是：ABAB。例如：

The reduplicative formula of dissyllabic verbs is ABAB.
For example:

学习——学习学习　　　检查——检查检查

（3）后面重叠的动词读轻声。

The reduplicated part is in the neutral tone.

2．哪些动词可以重叠，哪些动词不能重叠。

Verbs that can be reduplicated and verbs that cannot.

（1）表示动作、行为的动词可以重叠。例如：

Verbs of actions and behaviour can be reduplicated.
For example:

听——听听　　　讨论——讨论讨论

走——走走　　　打扫——打扫打扫

问——问问　　　收拾——收拾收拾

（2）含有积极思维活动的动词可以重叠。例如：

Verbs of positive thinking can be reduplicated. For
example:

想——想想　　　考虑——考虑考虑

启发——启发启发　分析——分析分析

（3）下面几类动词不能重叠。

The following kinds of verbs cannot be reduplicated。

37

A．表示心理活动的，如"怕、羡慕、喜欢"等。

Verbs expressing mental activities, such as 怕，羡慕，喜欢，etc.

B．表示发展变化的，如"生、发展、开始"等。

Verbs expressing change or developments, such as 生，发展，开始，etc.

C．表示存在、判断、领有的，如"在、是、象、有"等。

Verbs expressing existence, judgement, possession, etc., such as 在，是，象，有，etc.

D．表示趋向的，如"起、过、出、进"等。

Verbs showing directions, such as 起，过，出，进，etc.

3．动词重叠的附加意义。

Implications of reduplicated verbs.

（1）表示动作经历的时间短。例如：

The reduplication of a verb implies a short and quick action. For example:

　　　　您坐坐。　　　　这个问题需要思考思考。

　　　　我问问他。

（2）表示尝试。例如：

It expresses an attempt or trial. For example:

　　　　你尝尝，好吃吗？　　　你摸摸，热不热？

　　　　我找找。

（3）表示轻松。例如：

It expresses a sense of being light and relaxed. For example:

　　　　休息的时候，可以活动活动。

　　　　星期日，我写写信，洗洗衣服。

　　　　下班以后，他常常打打球、散散步。

4．注意事项：

Points that merit special attention:

（1） 动词后边如带宾语，只重叠动词，不能重叠宾语。例如：

In a verb-object construction, only the verb and not the object, can be reduplicated. For example:

　　　　我擦擦桌子，你扫扫地。

　　　　　（"桌子"和"地"是宾语，不能重叠）

　　　　　(桌子 and 地 are objects which can not be
　　　　　reduplicated.)

（2） 单音动词重叠，中间可以加"一"，意思不变。例如：

When monosyllabic verbs are reduplicated, — can be inserted between the two parts. For example:

　　　　　您说一说。

　　　　　我想一想。

双音动词重叠时，中间不能加"一"。不能说"活动一活动"等。

— cannot be inserted between the two parts of a reduplicated dissyllabic verb, so there is no such form as 活动一活动.

（3）如果要表示动作已完成，需用动态助词"了"，"了"要放在重叠动词中间。例如：

If the aspectual particle 了 is used to emphasize the completion of an action, 了 must be placed between the two parts of the reduplicated verb. For example:

　　　　他坐了坐。　　　　大家休息了休息。

　　　　我看了看。　　　　我们商量了商量。

不能说"看看了"、"看一看了"或"休息休息了"等。

One cannot say 看看了, 看一看了 or 休息休息了, etc.

练 习 2

Exercise 2

（一）从下列词里选出一个适当的名词填在动词后边。

Fill in the blanks with appropriate nouns chosen from the list below.

国家　　电视　　衣服　　祖国　　树　　脸

汉语　　饭　　英语　　代表　　问题　足球

家　　花

1. 学习_____　　　　2. 种_____

3. 吃_____　　　　　4. 看_____

5. 洗_____　　　　　6. 在_____

7. 建设_____　　　　8. 踢_____

9. 选_____　　　　　10. 讨论_____

（二）填上适当的动词。

Fill in the blanks with appropriate verbs.

1. 现在我们_____球。　2. 他以前_____汉语。

3. 她_____电影。　　　4. 明天他们_____颐和园。

5. 你_____茶。　　　　6. 我们_____房间。

7. 我_____画儿。　　　8. 她们_____广播。

9. 工人们_____机器。　10. 同学们_____博物馆。

（三）填上动词"是"、"有"或"在"。

Fill in the blanks with 是，有 or 在.

1. 我们_____大学生。　2. 他_____宿舍。

3. 我父亲_____医生。　4. 学校里_____树。

5. 他们_____英国人。　6. 邮局_____那边。

7. 我们_____汉语语法　8. 他前边_____他弟弟。
书。

9．本子＿＿＿＿＿老师那儿。10．研究所旁边＿＿＿＿＿＿植物园。

（四）改正下列病句。

Correct the following sentences.

1．他们是不工人。　　　2．我不有中文书。

3．她在朋友。　　　　　4．我们分析一分析。

5．他谈谈了意见。　　　6．学校前边在研究所。

7．他去了去图书馆。　　8．他在着朋友家。

9．我是了教师。　　　 10．你看一看了我的书房。

第三节　助　动　词

Section III　Auxiliary Verbs

一、助动词的定义　Definition

　　帮助动词表示需要、可能或愿望的词叫助动词。例如：

Verbs which "help" other verbs to express necessity, possibility and willingness are called auxiliary verbs.　For example:

　　表示有某种技能、能力的：

Those expressing capability:

　　　　能　　能够　　会

　　表示可能的：

Those expressing possibility:

　　　　能　　能够　　会　　可以　　可能

　　表示情理上需要的：

Those expressing necessity by reason:

　　　　应该　　应当　　该　　要

　　表示必要的：

Those expressing obligation:

　　　　必须　　得(děi)

表示主观愿望的：

Those expressing willingness:

要　　想　　愿意　　敢　　肯

二、助动词的语法特点　Grammatical features

（一）经常修饰动词（或形容词）。例如：

Auxiliary verbs are often used to modify verbs or adjectives. For example:

我会说英语。　　　　　　他肯来。

教室里应该安静。

（二）否定形式是在助动词前边用否定副词"不"。例如：

They are negated by 不. For example:

我不会说汉语。　　　我不能告诉你。

他不该去那儿。

（三）可以用正反式提问。例如：

The affirmative-negative question is formed by putting together the affirmative and negative forms of an auxiliary verb. For example:

你能不能来？　　　　　　他想不想学习？

我应该不应该去？

（四）能够单独回答问题。例如：

They can answer questions by themselves. For example:

你能不能来？　　能。

他愿意不愿意帮助你？　　愿意。

（五）不能重叠。

They cannot be reduplicated.

（六）后边不能加动态助词"了、着、过"。

The aspectual particles 了, 着 or 过 cannot be added to auxiliary verbs.

（七）后边不能直接带名词。

They cannot be immediately followed by a noun.

三、助动词的用途 Functions

助动词经常用在动词、形容词前边作状语。例如：

Auxiliary verbs are often used as adverbial adjuncts before verbs and adjectives. For example:

> 天气应该暖和了。　　我们得告诉他这件事。
>
> 病人要喝水。　　　　晚上我们可以去俱乐部。

四、使用助动词时需要注意以下几个问题

Points that merit special attention

（一）几个助动词的用法。

Usages of common auxiliary verbs.

1. "会"

（1）表示经过学习，掌握了某种技能。例如：

It expresses the grasp of a skill through learning. For example:

> 姐姐会织毛衣。
>
> 弟弟会打网球。

（2）表示有可能。例如：

It expresses possibility. For example:

> 她会来，您不要着急。
>
> 今天不会下雨。

2. "能"

（1）表示具备某种能力。例如：

It expresses capability. For example:

> 我能开汽车。　　　　张老师能教化学。
>
> 他能看中文小说。

（2）表示环境或情理上许可。例如：

It expresses possibility provided by circumstances or reason. For example:

> 圣诞节你能来吗？　　能。
>
> 他能参加运动会吗？　　不能。

星期天不能借书。

3．"可以"

（1）表示能够。例如：

It expresses the meaning of "can" or "be able to". For example:

锻炼可以增强体质。

我们可以帮助你。

（2）表示许可。例如：

It expresses permission. For example:

我可以抽烟吗？

现在你们可以走了。

4．"应该"

（1）表示情理上的需要。例如：

It expresses the meaning of "ought to". For example:

（天黑了，）我应该走了。

同学们应该积极发言。

你们应该表演节目。

（2）"应该"的否定形式是"不应该"或"不该"。例如：

不应该 and 不该 are the negative forms of 应该. For example:

你不（应）该去。

我们不（应）该这样做。

（3）口语里"应该"有时说成"该"。例如：

Sometimes 该 is used instead of 应该 in spoken Chinese. For example:

（十点了，）我该走了。

该上课了，（快走吧。）

5．"该"表示根据情理或者经验的推测，句尾常用语气助词"了"。例如：

It expresses a prediction by reason or experience. The

44

modal particle 了 is often used at the end of the sentence. For example:

明天该星期日了。

（天冷了，）你该加衣服了。

（晴天了，）该出太阳了。

6．"必须"

（1）表示事理上的需要。例如：

It expresses a reasonable requirement. For example:

干部必须严格要求自己。

学生必须带学生证。

大家必须团结（，才能取得胜利）。

（2）加强命令语气。例如：

It intensifies the imperative mood. For example:

后天你必须出席。　　　　你必须尊重别人的意见。

你们必须准备毕业论文。

7．"得(děi)"　口语里常用。

It is commonly used in spoken Chinese.

（1）表示做某件事的意志。例如：

To express a will or necessity to do something. For example:

他得想办法。　　　　我得谢谢你。

我们得商量商量。

（2）表示事实上的需要。例如：

To express an actual need. For example:

您得辅导我。　　　　妈妈的病得动手术。

你们得办理手续。

"得 (děi)" 的否定形式是 "不用"、"不要"。例如：

The negative form of 得 (děi) is 不用 or 不要. For example:

您不用辅导我。

你们不用办理手续。

妈妈的病不要动手术。

不能说"不得(děi)"。

One cannot say 不得(děi).

8．"要"

（1）表示做某件事的愿望。例如：

It expresses a desire to do something.　For example:

她要报名。　　　　　客人要走。

病人要出院。

否定形式是"不想"。例如：

In this sense the negative form is 不想.　For example:

她不想报名。

（2）表示事实上的需要。例如：

It expresses an actual need.　For example:

你要注意发音。　　　（路滑，）要小心。

大家要努力工作。

否定形式是"不用"，表示事实上没有必要。例如：

In this sense, the negative form of 要 is 不用 (need not) rather than 不要.　For example:

你们不用着急。

他不用替我。

（3）"不要"常用在动词前边作状语，表示禁止、劝阻，口语里常用"别"。例如：

不要 or 别, which is more preferable in spoken Chinese, is used as an adverbial adjunct expressing prohibition or dissuasion.　For example:

不要粗心。　（别粗心。）

不要大声喊。（别大声喊。）

不要浪费。　（别浪费。）

9．"想" 有"打算"、"希望"的意思。例如：

It has the meaning of "plan" or "want".　For example:

他想学艺术。　　　　我们想去中国。

外国朋友想看杂技。

（二）用正反式提问时，只能并列助动词的肯定和否定形式。例如：

The affirmative-negative question can only be formed by putting together the affirmative and negative forms of the auxiliary verb. For example:

你愿意不愿意去？　　　你会不会下棋？

他们能不能作诗？

（三）助动词不能直接用在名词前边。只有兼属动词的才能带名词宾语。例如：

Auxiliary verbs cannot be immediately followed by nouns unless they function as the main verb as well, which can take an object. For example:

我会法语。　　　　她想妈妈。

他要红毛衣。

这里的"会、要、想"都是动词，不是助动词。

In the examples, 会，要 and 想 are main verbs, not auxiliary verbs.

练 习 3

Exercise 3

（一）用横线标出下边句子里的助动词。

Underline the auxiliary verbs in the following sentences.

例如：

Example:　　学生应该努力学习。

1．我会写汉字。

2．孩子们想去公园。

3．奶奶要买眼镜。

4．爷爷要围围巾。

5．我们应该改正错误。

6．他会说英语，不会说法语。

7．她肯帮助我们。

8．你得告诉我。

9．我可以接受他的建议。

10．你敢爬山吗？

（二）填上适当的助动词。

Fill in the blanks with appropriate auxiliary verbs.

1．他下午_____回家吗？

2．（阴天了，）_____下雨了。

3．我们_____按时完成任务。

4．弟弟不_____说汉语。

5．我们_____承认事实。

6．你不_____立刻去。

7．大家_____保持安静。

8．（太晚了，）她不_____去了。

9．你_____解释解释这些句子吗？

10．我们一定_____保证安全。

（三）把下列句子改成否定式。

Make the following sentences negative.

1．明天他要请客。

2．我们能做这个试验。

3．我想请教他。

4．我们应该选他。

5．领导可能表扬他。

6．他愿意发表声明。

7．我们得限制时间。

8. 大家该相信他。

9. 我哥哥会开飞机。

10. 他们肯参加。

第四节 形 容 词
Section IV   Adjectives

一、形容词的定义 Definition

表示人、事物的形状、性质或者动作、行为等的状态的词叫形容词。例如：

Words that describe the shape or property of a person or thing, or the state of a movement or action, are called adjectives. For example:

表示人或事物的形状的：

Describing shape:

<blockquote>
大   小   高   矮   红   绿   整齐   美丽
</blockquote>

表示人或事物的性质的：

Describing property or quality:

<blockquote>
好   坏   冷   热   对   错   正确   伟大

优秀 严重
</blockquote>

表示动作或行为等的状态的：

Describing the state of a movement or action:

<blockquote>
快   慢   紧张   流利   认真   熟练   残酷
</blockquote>

二、形容词的语法特点 Grammatical features

（一）大部分形容词前边可以用程度副词修饰。例如：

Most adjectives can be modified by adverbs of degree.
For example:

<blockquote>
很对   最好
</blockquote>

特别大　　　　　非常干净

（二）否定式是在形容词前用否定副词"不"。

The negative adverb 不 is placed before an adjective for the negative form.

（三）可以用正反式提问。例如：

The affirmative-negative question can be formed by putting together the affirmative and negative forms of the adjective.　For example:

对不对?　　　　　干净不干净?

长不长?

（四）有些形容词可以重叠，表示程度加深。例如：

Some adjectives can be reduplicated for intensification.　For example:

长长　　　　　高高

整整齐齐　　　　安安静静

（五）后边不能带宾语。

Adjectives do not take objects.

（六）后边可以带补充成分。例如：

Adjectives can be followed by complements.　For example:

聪明极了　漂亮得很　快三秒钟　好多了

三、形容词的用途　Functions

（一）作定语。

As an attributive.

形容词最主要的用途是修饰中心语。例如：

Adjectives are mainly used as modifying attributives.

For example:

兰帽子　　　　　旧杂志

漂亮的布　　　　美好的生活

（二）作谓语。

As the predicate.

任务紧急。　　　　　这朵花好看。

他很诚恳。　　　　　他很着急。

（三）作状语。

As an adverbial adjunct.

形容词的一个重要用途是在动词前作状语。例如：

One of the important uses of adjectives is to be put before a verb as an adverbial adjunct. For example:

快走!　　　　　　　少买点儿吧!

主人热情地接待我们。　你应该严肃地处理这件事。

（四）作补语。

As the complement.

形容词常作谓语动词的补语。例如：

Adjectives often serve as complements to predicate verbs. For example:

衣服晒干了。　　　　玻璃没擦干净。

晚饭准备好了。　　　我没看清楚。

（五）作主语。

As the subject.

骄傲不好。　　　　　光荣属于大家。

谦虚是好品德。

（六）作宾语。

As the object.

他喜欢安静　　　　　现在你需要休息。

女孩子爱漂亮。

四、使用形容词时需要注意的几个问题

Points that merit special attention

（一）形容词作定语和结构助词 "的 (de)"。

The attributive use of adjectives and the structural particle 的 (de)

定语一定要放在中心语前边。

The attributive must precede the word it modifies.

1. 单音形容词可以直接修饰中心语。例如：

A monosyllabic adjective can modify directly. For example:

> 新书——"新"是单音形容词，是定语；"书"是
> 名词，是中心语。
>
> 新，a monosyllabic adjective, is the attri-
> butive and 书 is a noun and the modified
> word.

> 白床单
>
> 凉开水

如要强调修饰性，可以在单音形容词和中心语之间用助词"的"。例如：

When we wish to stress the modification, 的 can be used between the monosyllabic adjective and the modified word. For example:

> 新的书　　　　　白的床单
>
> 凉的开水

2. 双音形容词修饰单音名词，要用助词"的"。例如：

When a dissyllabic adjective is used to modify a monosyllabic noun, 的 must be placed between them. For example:

> 勇敢的人　　　　好看的画
>
> 重要的事

双音形容词修饰双音名词，用不用助词"的"都可以。例如：

If both the adjective and the modified word are dissyllabic, 的 is optional. For example:

> 伟大（的）祖国　　　干净（的）窗帘
>
> 幸福（的）老人

3. 形容词重叠后作定语，要用"的"。例如：

When the attributive is a reduplicated adjective, 的 is used. For example:

> 小华红红的脸、大大的眼睛真可爱。
>
> 孩子们在暖暖和和的房子里做功课。

（二）形容词作状语和结构助词"地(de)"。

The adverbial use of adjectives and the structural particle 地 (de).

状语一定要放在中心语前边。

The adverbial adjunct must be put before the word it modifies.

1. 单音形容词作状语可以直接修饰中心语。常见的有：

A monosyllabic adjective used as an adverbial adjunct can directly precede the modified word. Following are the common monosyllabic adjectives:

> 要学好外语，必须多听、多说、多读、多写。
>
> ——"多"是单音形容词，是状语；"听"、
> "说"、"读"、"写"是动词，是中心语。
>
> 多 is a monosyllabic adjective as an adverbial adjunct and 听, 说, 读 and 写 are verbs used as modified words.
>
> 他每天早出晚归。
>
> 我们快走吧。

2. 双音形容词作状语，用不用助词"地"都可以。要强调修饰性时，常用"地"。例如：

When the adverbial adjunct is a dissyllabic adjective, 地 is optional. But when we wish to stress the modification, 地 is usually used. For example:

> 老同学热情（地）欢迎新同学。
>
> 他们努力（地）钻研业务。

3. 兼属动词的形容词作状语，一定要用助词"地"。例如：

地 must be used after the adverbial modifier composed of an adjective which is converted from a verb. For example:

他清楚地回答了我们的问题。

大家高兴地唱起歌来。

4．双音形容词重叠后作状语，一定要用助词"地"。例如：

地 must be used after an adverbial modifier which is the reduplication of a dissyllabic adjective. For example:

她们高高兴兴地谈着。

他每天都在紧紧张张地工作。

单音形容词重叠后作状语，用不用助词"地"都可以。例如：

However, 地 is optional when the adverbial adjunct is the reduplication of a monosyllabic adjective. For example:

母亲紧紧（地）抱着自己的孩子。

天气慢慢（地）暖和了。

他们早早（地）出发了。

（三）关于形容词重叠。Reduplication of adjectives.

1．重叠形式。

Formulas of reduplication.

（1）单音形容词的重叠形式是：ＡＡ。例如：

The reduplicative formula for monosyllabic adjectives is AA. For example:

大——大大　　　　快——快快

红——红红　　　　慢——慢慢

（2）双音形容词的重叠形式是：ＡＡＢＢ。例如：

The reduplicative formula for dissyllabic adjectives is AABB. For example:

干净——干干净净　　凉快——凉凉快快

清楚——清清楚楚　　痛快——痛痛快快

2．有的形容词兼属动词，也可以按动词的重叠方式重叠。

例如：

Some adjectives can be converted into verbs, in which case they can be reduplicated in the formula for reduplicating verbs. For example:

今年丰收，大家应该高兴高兴。

大家休息休息，在树下边凉快凉快。

（四）汉语里形容词可以直接充当谓语，前边不用动词"是"。例如：

是 is not used before an adjective which functions as the predicate. For example:

他高。（不说"他是高"）

形容词作谓语时，前边常用副词"很"，但表示程度的成分很弱。例如：

When an adjective functions as the predicate, a weakened adverb of degree 很 is often used. For example:

他很高。

有些形容词重叠后可以作谓语，后边必须用助词"的"。例如：

Some reduplicated adjectives can act as the predicate and the particle 的 must be used after them. For example:

他的脸红红的。

屋子里暖暖和和的。

（五）形容词作主语常表示被判断的对象，谓语多由形容词或表示判断的动词充当。例如：

The adjective serving as the subject in a sentence is often the object of a judgement expressed by the predicate which is generally composed of an adjective or a linking verb. For exampie:

勤劳很重要。

骄傲是不好的。

（六）形容词不能带宾语，但少数形容词兼属动词可以带宾语。这种兼类词带宾语时含有"使"的意思。例如：

Adjectives can not take objects except for a few of them when they are converted into verbs with the meaning 使 (to make). For example:

形、动兼类词 Adjectives and their verbal conversions	形容词用法 Used as adjective	动词用法 Used as verb
丰　富	内容丰富	丰富内容
严　格	纪律严格	严格纪律
壮　大	队伍壮大	壮大队伍
繁　荣	经济繁荣	繁荣经济
密　切	关系密切	密切关系

又如：

Here are two more examples:

这篇文章的内容很丰富。

再丰富一下内容，这篇文章就更好了。

（七）形容词"多"和"少"。

The adjectives 多 and 少.

"多、少"作定语修饰名词时，前边必须用"很"和"不"构成"很多"和"不少"，后边一般不用助词"的"。例如：

多 and 少 must be combined with 很 or 不 to serve as attributives modifying nouns, and it is not necessary to use 的 after 很多 and 不少. For example:

公园里有很多人。

很多城市都有这种设备。

不少同学买了这种书包。

今天我解决了不少问题。

这里的"很"并不强调程度深。一定不能说"公园里有多人"、"少同学买了这种书包"等。

Here 很 does not express a high degree. One can not say 公园里有多人，少同学买了这种书包， etc.

（八）形容词"男、女、正、副、公共、共同"等一般不能作谓语，只能作定语。例如：

Adjectives such as 男，女，正，副，公共，共同，etc., generally can only function as attributive, but not predicate. For example:

男孩子　　女孩子　　正经理　　副经理
公共汽车

又如：

Here is another example:

张先生有一个男孩子和一个女孩子。

"公、母、雌、雄"一般用来形容动植物。例如：

The adjectives 公，母，雌 and 雄 are normally used with animals and plants. For example:

公鸡　cock　　　　　　母兔　female rabbit (doe)
雌花　pistillate flower　雄蕊　androecium

这类形容词后边不带名词时，就要用助词"的"。例如：

When the noun is absent, the particle 的 must be used after this kind of adjectives. For example:

男的　　　　　　整的
正义的　　　　　唯一的

又如：

Here is another example:

那个班有九名学生，五名是男的，四名是女的。

一定不能说"五名是男，四名是女"。

One never says 五名是男，四名是女.

练 习 4

Exercise 4

（一）在下边正确的词组后边划 "√"。

Mark the correct phrases with "√" in the brackets.

1．多地方　（　　）　　　2．很多水　（　　）

3．很多村子（　　）　　　4．少饭　　（　　）

5．不少商店（　　）　　　6．很多动物（　　）

7．少经验　（　　）　　　8．不少节目（　　）

9．多工程师（　　）　　　10．不少日子（　　）

（二）在下列各名词前填上一个适当的形容词。

Fill in the proper adjectives before the nouns.

1．＿＿绸子，　　　＿＿绸子

2．＿＿汽车，　　　＿＿汽车

3．＿＿线，　　　　＿＿线

4．＿＿鱼，　　　　＿＿鱼

5．＿＿消息，　　　＿＿消息

6．＿＿毛巾，　　　＿＿毛巾

7．＿＿墨水，　　　＿＿墨水

8．＿＿肉，　　　　＿＿肉

9．＿＿现象，　　　＿＿现象

10．＿＿本子，　　　＿＿本子

（三）在下列各动词前填上一个适当的形容词。

Add an adjective before each of the following verbs.

1．＿＿来，　　　　＿＿来

2．＿＿学习，　　　＿＿学习

3．＿＿说，　　　　＿＿说

4. ___走, 　　　　___走
5. ___支持, 　　　___支持
6. ___观察, 　　　___观察
7. ___解决, 　　　___解决
8. ___欢迎, 　　　___欢迎
9. ___准备, 　　　___准备
10. ___买, 　　　　___买

第五节 数 词
Section V Numerals

一、数词的定义　Definition

表示数目的词叫数词。基本的数词有：

Words representing numbers are called numerals. Following are the basic ones:

一（1） 二（2） 三（3） 四（4） 五（5）

六（6） 七（7） 八（8） 九（9） 十（10）

百 　　千 　　万 　　亿

零（〇） 两

二、数词的语法特点　Grammatical features

（一）基本的数词可以和某些词连在一起表示各种数。

The above basic numerals can be combined with some words to represent various kinds of numbers.

1. 整数　Whole numbers

基本的数词可以互相组合起来表示其他整数。例如：

The basic numerals can be combined to represent whole numbers. For example:

十一（11） 　　十六（16） 　　三十（30）

一百四十五（145）

三千零七十（3 070）

一万五千三百二十（15 320）

2．序数 Ordinal numbers

（1）数词前边加上词头"第"可以表示顺序。例如：

Ordinal numbers can be formed by placing the prefix 第 before numerals. For example:

第一　　第二　　第十二　　第一百零八

（2）数词后边可以直接带名词表示序数。常见的有：

However numerals can be put directly before nouns to act as ordinal numbers. Following are some common instances:

二哥　　一月　　三楼

3．倍数 Multiple numbers

数词后边加量词"倍"字表示倍数。例如：

Multiple numbers are formed by adding the measure word 倍 after numerals. For example:

一倍　　五倍　　二十倍

4．小数 Decimals

数词可以用在"…点…"这一格式里表示小数。前面的数字是整数，后面的数字是小数。例如：

Decimals are shown by the formula "...点..." The number before 点 is the whole number and the figures after 点 are the decimal places. For example:

零点三（0.3）

三点一四一六（3.1416）

二十点七五（20.75）

5．分数 Fractions

数词可以用在"…分之…"这一格式里表示分数。前边的数字是分母，后边的数字是分子。例如：

We use "...分之..." to indicate fractions. The

denominator is placed before the numerator.　For example:

$$三分之二 \left(\frac{2}{3} \right) \qquad\qquad 百分之六十 \left(\frac{60}{100},\ 60\% \right)$$

$$十分之七 \left(\frac{7}{10} \right) \qquad\qquad 千分之一 \left(\frac{1}{1000} \right)$$

6.　概数　Approximate numbers

表示概数的方法，常用的有以下几种：

There are different ways of indicating approximate numbers.　Here we introduce only the most common ones:

（1）邻近的两个数词连用。例如：

Using two adjacent numerals together.　For example:

一两个	七八个	十五六
三四十	四五百	

（2）数词"几"可以表示1—9之间的概数。"几"常用在"十、百、千、万、亿"前面或"十"后面。例如：

Using the numeral 几 (several) which can be substituted for the numbers from one to nine.　几 is often put before 十，百，千，万，亿 or after 十. For example:

我有几本中文书。　　　　屋子里有十几个人。

阅览室有几百种杂志。

（3）数词"多"用在"十、百、千、万"等数词后边表示多于前边的数目。例如：

Adding the numeral 多 after 十，百，千，万，etc. to indicate a number bigger than the given one. For example:

我们班一共十多个同学。　　　他买了三十多张票。

这个公社种了一万多棵树。

（4）数词"十、百、千、万"等后边常加"来"表示接近前边的数目。例如：

Putting 来 after 十，百，千，万，etc. to show a number near the quantity indicated by the given figure.　For example:

这儿有三十来把椅子。

（5）数词后边可以加"左右、上下"表示概数。例如：

Adding 左右 or 上下 after a numeral. For example:

十五左右　　　　三十左右　　　　五千左右
八十上下　　　　六百上下　　　　两万上下

（二）在现代汉语中，数词和名词之间要用一个适当的量词（如"个、条、辆、本、支"等）。例如：

In modern Chinese, there is always a measure word (such as 个，条，辆，本，支，etc.) between the numeral and the noun it modifies. For example:

一个学生　　　　三条鱼
六辆汽车　　　　四本画报

三、数词的用途　Functions

（一）作主语。

As the subject.

九是三的三倍。

二等于四的二分之一。

（二）作宾语。

As the object.

这是十　　　　　　　　十的一半是五。

三三得九

（三）作定语。

As an attributive.

他有一本中文书。　　　十的五分之一是二。

三的五倍是十五。

（四）作谓语。

As the predicate.

三七二十一

五八四十

四、使用数词时需要注意的一些问题

62

Points that merit special attention

（一）称数法。

Enumeration.

1.一百以下的数目，汉语里用"十进位法"表示。

In Chinese, the decimal system is used for counting numbers below one hundred.

（1）1—10是：

One to ten:

一（1）　二（2）　三（3）　四（4）　五（5）

六（6）　七（7）　八（8）　九（9）　十（10）

（2）11—19是："十"加后面的个位数字。即：

The numbers from eleven to nineteen are formed by adding 十 before the units. Here are they:

十一（11）　十二（12）　十三（13）　十四（14）

十五（15）　十六（16）　十七（17）　十八（18）

十九（19）

（3）"20—90"中个位数是"〇"的，一律按 "十位数的数字"加"十"的格式来表示。例如：

The tens are formed by adding 十 after the digit of the tenth's place. For example:

20 是 二十　　30 是 三十

70 是 七十　　90 是 九十

（4）其他数目用"十位数的数字"加"十"加"个位数的数字"的格式来表示。例如：

Numerals between the tens are formed by the formula "the tenth's place 十 the unit". For example:

21 是 二十一　　32 是 三十二

54 是 五十四　　67 是 六十七

98 是 九十八

2. 一百以上的数目，汉语里用下面九个"位"来表示。即

按下面 "位" 的顺序说出每一个数字来。例如:

There may be nine digit places in all in a big number and one reads it in this order:

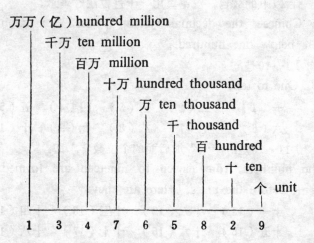

应说成:一万万(或:一亿)三千四百七十六万五千八百二十九。

It should be read: 一万万(or一亿)三千四百七十六万五千八百二十九.

九个 "位" 中以 "万万、万、个" 为基本单位。例如: "1 500" 是 "一千五(百)",不能说成 "十五百"; "15 000" 是 "一万五(千)",不能说成 "十五千"。

Of the nine digit places, 万万, 万 and 个 are the basic ones, e.g. 1 500 is read 一千五(百), not 十五百; 15 000 一万五(千), not 十五千.

为了便于准确地说出多位数,常先从个位数开始,由右往左,按上述顺序倒着数,即:个、十、百、千、万、十万、百万、千万、万万,确定第一个数字的 "位" 后就能说出多位数了。例如:

In order to read a big number correctly, one first determines the place of the first digit by counting all the

·places from right to left in tnis order: 个，十，百，千，
万，十万，百万，千万，万万．For example:

353   三位数字，个、十、百

        三百五十三

The three digit places in it are 个，十 and 百 and it is read 三百五十三．

1 500   四位数字，个、十、百、千

        一千五（百）

The four digit places in it are 个，十，百 and 千 and it is read 一千五（百）

4 678   四位数字，个、十、百、千

        四千六百七十八

The four digit places in it are 个，十，百 and 千 and it is read 四千六百七十八．

81 943   五位数字，个、十、百、千、万

        八万一千九百四十三

The five digit places in it are 个，十，百，千 and 万 and it is read 八万一千九百四十三．

156 749   六位数字，个、十、百、千、万、十万

        十五万六千七百四十九

The six digit places in it are 个，十，百，千，万 and 十万 and it is read 十五万六千七百四十九．

1 458 367   七位数字，个、十、百、千、万、十万、百万

        一百四十五万八千三百六十七

The seven digit places in it are 个，十，百，千，万，十万 and 百万 and

it is read 一百四十五万八千三百
六十七.

123 456 789　九位数字

一亿（或：万万）二千三百四十五万
六千七百八十九

There are nine digit places in it and it
is read 一亿 （or 万万）二千三
百四十五万六千七百八十九.

3. 用多位数字表示年代、船只、车辆、房间、电话等号码
时，常直接读出数字，不说"位"。例如：

Serial numbers, such as the name of a year or the
number of a ship, vehicle, room or telephone are read
out figure by figure. For example:

他住五楼三二一。　　　　　　　　（321）
这辆汽车的号码是九三四五七六。（934576）
我的电话是二七七五三一一。（277531）

（二）"0"的表示法。

The way to read "0" (zero).

1. 单独的"0"读作"零"。例如：

"0" as a unit is read *líng*. For example:

二减二等于零。

2. 多位数中的"十"位数是"0"时，一定要读出"零"
来。例如：

When "0" occupies the place of 十, we must also read
it *líng*. For example:

308 是 三百零八。
不能说成"三百八"或"三百零十八"。
308 should be read 三百零八 not 三百八 or 三
百零十八.

509 是 五百零九。

509 should be read 五百零九.

701 是 七百零一。

701 should be read 七百零一.

如果"0"在"千"位"万"位上，可以不说出"零"。例如：

When "0" occupies the place of 千 or 万, it is not necessary to read it out. For example:

40 602 是 四万（零）六百零二。

3. 多位数中有两个或两个以上的"0"连在一起时，只读一次"零"。例如：

When there are two or more zero places in succession in a big number, one reads out *líng* only once. For example:

90 086 是 九万零八十六。

90 086 is read 九万零八十六.

900 086 是 九十万零八十六。

900 086 is read 九十万零八十六.

9 000 086 是 九百万零八十六。

9 000 086 is read 九百万零八十六.

4. "0"在多位数的末尾时，不管是一个还是几个连用，一律不读"零"。例如：

The zero place(s) at the end of a big number is (are) not read out. For example:

120 是 一百二（十）。

120 is read 一百二（十）.

12 000 是一万二（千）。

12 000 is read 一万二（千）.

如果这样的多位数后边有量词，就要把"0"前边的"位"读出来。例如：

If the big number is followed by a measure word, the

place just before the zero place should be read out. For example:

> 120张电影票，要说成：一百二十张电影票。

> > 120张电影票 should be read一百二十张电影票.

> 12 000 个观众，要说成：一万二千个观众。

> > 12 000 个观众 should be read 一万二千个观众.

5.车辆、船只、电话等号码需要直接读出数字时，每个 "0" 都要读出来。例如：

Every "0" should be read out when one gives a serial number. For example:

> 车号是900501。

> > 应该读成：车号是九零零五零一。

> > This should be read: 车号是九零零五零一.

（三） "1" 在多位数中的表示法。

The way to read "1" in a big number.

"1" 在 "十" 位数上，也应当读 "一十"。例如：

When "1" occurs at the place of 十， one reads it as 一十。 For example:

> 215 是 二百一十五，不说 "二百十五"。

> > 215 is read 二百一十五， not 二百十五.

> 3 418 是 三千四百一十八,不说 "三千四百十八"。

> > 3 418 is read 三千四百一十八,not 三千四百十八.

> 61 119 是 六万一千一百一十九。

> > 61 119 is read 六万一千一百一十九.

（四） "2" 的表示法。

The way to read "2".

1. 汉语里， "2" 可以用 "二" 或 "两" 来表示。 "二" 可以单说， "两" 不能单独使用。例如：

Although the number "2" can be represented by 二 or 两 in Chinese, the two are different in that 二 can be

68

used in isolation, whereas 两 can not.   For example:

一, 二, 三。

这是二。

不能说 "一、两、三"，"这是两"。

One can not say 一，两，三；这是两.

2.直接读出数字时读 "二"。例如：

In a serial number, "2" is read 二. For example:

324 ——三二四

5 230——五二三零

3．在多位数中的 "十" 位数和 "个" 位数上，一定要读 "二"。例如：

When it occupies the place 十 or 个，"2" is read 二. For example:

28　是　二十八

28 is read 二十八.

752　是　七百五十二

752 is read 七百五十二.

8 722　是　八千七百二十二

8 722　is read 八千七百二十二.

4．表示序数的 "2" 读 "二"。例如：

In ordinal numbers, "2" is read 二. For example:

第二　　　　第二排

二姐　　　　二层

5．在分数中，读 "二"。例如：

In fractions, "2" is read 二. For example:

$\frac{2}{5}$　是　五分之二

2/5 is read 五分之二.

$\frac{1}{2}$　是　二分之一

1/2 is read 二分之一.

6． 在量词前边一般要说"两"。例如：

"2" is read 两，when followed by a measure word. For example:

> 2只兔子——两只兔子
> 2块手表——两块手表
> 2个小时——两个小时
> 2张报——两张报
> 去2次——去两次

一定不能说"二只兔子"、"二块手表"等。

One never says 二只兔子，二块手表，etc.

但在度量衡单位量词前边的"2"可以说成"二"或"两"。例如：

But when it precedes a measure word of length, capacity or weight, "2" can either be read 二 or 两。 For example:

> 2米布——二米布，两米布
> 2公斤糖——二公斤糖，两公斤糖

（五）数词作定语和结构助词"的 (de)"。

Numerals used as attributives and the structural particle 的 (de).

1． 数词常直接用在量词前作定语。例如：

Numerals are often used as attributives immediately before a measure word. For example:

> 我是一个学生。　　　　他有一支红圆珠笔。
> 我买三套纪念邮票。　　那是十张世界地图。

不能说"一学生"、"一红圆珠笔"、"三纪念邮票"、"十世界地图"。

One can never say 一学生，一红圆珠笔，三纪念邮票，十世界地图.

2． 数词在其他数目前作定语时，要用助词"的"。例如：

When a numeral is used as an attributive modifying another numeral, the particle 的 should be used. For example:

三的五倍是十五。

五是二十五的五分之一。

一百的四分之三等于七十五。

（六）数词直接用在名词前表示序数时，多属下列情况：

Under the following conditions, the numeral followed immediately by a noun is an ordinal number:

1. 表示亲属称呼的。例如：

Used in a vocative for a family member. For example:

二叔　　　　三姐　　　　四弟

2. 表示年、月、日的。例如：

Used in the names of the year, month or date. For example:

一九八〇年　　一九八一年　　一二〇〇年

二月　　　　六月　　　　十二月

十一号　　　　二十号　　　　二十八号

3. 表示事物等级和类别的。例如：

Used to show grades and catagories. For example:

一级　　　　二层

一年级　　　　三班

（七）表示概数时一定要连用两个邻近的数词，而且要按次序先说小的数字，不能随意连用。例如：

The small one of the two adjacent numbers in an approximate number is always followed by the bigger one. For example:

六七十

不能说成"五七十"等。

There is no such form as 五七十, etc.

十三四

不能说成"十三五"等。

There is no such form as 十三五, etc.

但有个别的例外，有时说"三五个"或"三两次"。

But there are a few exceptions, like 三五个，三两次，etc.

（八）"半"的用法。

The use of 半

"半"是一个特殊的数词，它的数量等于二分之一，但用法和一般数词不完全相同。

半, meaning "half", is a special numeral which is not always used in the same way as an ordinary numeral.

1．"半"不能单独使用。

It can not be used in isolation.

2．"半"常用在量词前边。例如：

It is often put before a measure word. For example:

半碗（饭）　　　　（½碗）

半张（纸）　　　　（½张）

半瓶（牛奶）　　　（½瓶）

3．"半"常用在整数和量词后边。例如：

It often follows a "whole number ＋ measure word" sequence. For example:

一天半　　　　　（1½天）

三张半　　　　　（3½张）

五公斤半　　　　（5½公斤）

（九）倍数是用来表示增加的，如要表示数量减少，只能用分数。例如：

Multiple numbers are used to show increases. When we wish to express a decrease, we use fractions. For example:

工作效率提高了两倍，时间却缩短了二分之一。

不能说"时间缩短了一倍"。

One can never say 时间缩短了一倍.

这个工厂今年的产量比去年减少了百分之二十。

不能说"减少百分之二百（或：两倍）"。

There is no such form as 减少了百分之二百
（or 两倍）

（十）提问数目时，常用"几"和"十、百、千、万"等连用的方法。例如：

几 is often combined with 十，百，千，万，etc. to ask about amount or quantity. For example:

今年你弟弟十几（岁）？

门前停着几十辆汽车？

那个礼堂能坐几百人？

你们生产队种了几千棵树？

这本书有几万字？

也常用"多少"提问。例如：

多少 is also often used in questions like:

这是多少？

你这个月工作了多少天？

（十一）表示分数时，必须先说分母，后说分子，绝不能颠倒。例如½只能说"二分之一"，不能说成"一分之二"

In reading a fraction, the denominator always precedes the numerator, as ½ is read 二分之一, not 一分之二.

练 习 5

Exercise 5

（一）用汉字写出下边的数目。

Put the following numbers into Chinese characters.

例如：

Example: 3 856——三千八百五十六

1. 2——
2. 22——
3. 115——
4. 3 478——
5. 10——
6. 61 912——
7. 308——
8. 7 005——
9. 50 490——
10. 380 000——
11. $\frac{2}{5}$——
12. $\frac{7}{9}$——
13. $\frac{80}{100}$——
14. $\frac{29}{100}$——
15. $\frac{5}{1000}$——

（二）用汉字直接写出下列数字。

Write the following serial numbers in Chinese characters.

例如：

Example: 329——三二九

1. 8——
2. 28——
3. 228——
4. 9607——
5. 9001——
6. 10002——
7. 56430——
8. 899922——
9. 12050——
10. 504030——

（三）用汉字写出下列数目。

Write the numerals in Chinese characters.

1. （ 2 ）____支笔
2. （ 2 ）____本字典
3. （ 2 ）____块面包
4. （ 12 ）____瓶汽水
5. （ 20 ）____把勺子
6. （ 22 ）____盘点心
7. （ 62 ）____户人家
8. （120）____名战士
9. （222）____页书
10. （182）____天

第六节 量 词

Section VI Measure Words

一、量词的定义　Definition

表示计算单位的词叫量词。量词可以分成两类：

Words indicating counting units are called measure words. There are two kinds of them:

（一）名量词。

Nominal measure words.

表示人、事物单位的词叫名量词。例如：

Nominal measure words are those indicating units of persons or things, such as:

度量衡单位：

Measure units:

厘米　　分米　　　公尺（米）

克　　公斤　　吨

货币单位：

Monetary units:

元（块）　　　角（毛）　　　分

时间单位：

Time units:

点　　分　　秒　　刻

个体单位：

Individual units:

个　　条　　辆　　本　　支

集体单位：

Mass units:

对　　双　　副　　套　　批

不定量单位：

Indefinite units:

点　　些

复合单位：

Compound units:

人次　架次

（二）动量词。

Verbal measure words.

表示动作单位的词叫动量词。例如：

Verbal measure words are those indicating the frequency of an action, such as:

次　　遍　　回　　趟　　下儿

二、量词的语法特点　Grammatical features

（一）量词不能单独使用。

Measure words cannot be used by themselves.

（二）量词要用在数词或指示代词后面。例如：

Measure words are used after numerals or demonstrative pronouns.　For example:

一个　　　一条　　　一斤　　　一次

三张　　　四项　　　五米　　　七下儿

这个　　　这条　　　这把　　　这趟

那件　　　那支　　　那双　　　那回

（三）量词可以重叠。

Measure words can be used reduplicatively.

单音量词一般可以重叠，有“每”的意思。例如：

The reduplication of monosyllabic measure words has the meaning of "every".　For example:

个个（每个）　　　　件件（每件）

条条（每条）　　　　次次（每次）

张张（每张）

三、量词的用途　Functions

（一）量词不能单独作句子成分。

Measure words can not serve as sentence elements by themselves.

（二）量词总是跟在数词或指示代词后边结合成数量词组等充当句子成分。例如：

Measure words are always preceded by numerals or demonstrative pronouns (Such combinations are called numeral-measure word phrases.) to function as sentence elements. For example:

他买了一个杯子。　　（作定语）
　　　　　　　　　　(As the attributive)

我得去一趟。　　　　（作补语）
　　　　　　　　　　(As the complement)

黄教授一次讲不完。　（作状语）
　　　　　　　　　　(As the adverbial adjunct)

一件多少钱？　　　　（作主语）
　　　　　　　　　　(As the subject)

我想买两支。　　　　（作宾语）
　　　　　　　　　　(As the object)

四、使用量词时需要注意的几个问题

Points that merit special attention

（一）关于名量词。Nominal measure words.

汉语里有丰富的量词。很多事物都可以计量，而且都有自己特定的量词，不能乱用。因此需要记住每个量词的用法，这是外国人学习汉语时不可忽视的。

In Chinese, there are a large number of measure words. Everything can be "measured" and that measure is represented by a specific measure word. Therefore it is imperative for foreign learners of Chinese to learn every noun with its matching measure word.

现将常用的量词和名词的搭配情况举例如下：

Here is a list of commonly used measure words with some of the nouns matching them:

名 量 词 Nominal measure words	可以和量词搭配的名词 Matching nouns
把	刀子　尺　牙刷　梳子　钥匙　伞　椅子
杯	水　牛奶　咖啡　茶　酒
本	书　杂志　画报　字典　词典　小说　地图
册	书
层	楼　台阶　灰　奶油　皮（儿）
打	纸
滴	水　油　酒　眼泪
点	水　酒　东西　事
顶	帽子
段	路　时间　文章　话
堆	东西　粮食　草　木头　煤
队	战士
对	花瓶　沙发　枕头
吨	钢　煤　大米　花生
朵	花　云
封	信　电报
副	手套　眼镜
个	人　学生　朋友　同志　学校　医院　国家 书架　面包　杯子　碗　汉字　符号

名 量 词 Nominal measure words	可以和量词搭配的名词 Matching nouns
根	竹子　棍子　针
公尺	布
公斤	水　石油
公里	路
行	字
户	人家
架	机器　飞机
间	屋子　房子　病房
件	衣服　毛衣　衬衫　大衣　上衣　行李　事情
届	会
克	糖　水果　点心　金子
句	话　汉语　英语
棵	树　草　白菜
颗	星　心　子弹
课	书　课文
口	人　井　猪
块	钱　糖　面包　点心　手表　手绢　肥皂 黑板
类	人　问题　事情
里	路
粒	米　粮食　种子　子弹
列	火车
辆	车　汽车　自行车　摩托车　坦克
米	布

名 量 词 Nominal measure words	可以和量词搭配的名词 Matching nouns
面	镜子
名	学生　记者
平方公里	地　土地
幕	剧　话剧　歌剧
排	人　树　房子
批	货　产品
匹	马　布　绸子
篇	文章　论文
片	肉　面包　药　草地　树林
瓶	啤酒　香水
公顷	土地　地
群	孩子　羊　鸭
首	歌　诗
双	鞋　袜子　筷子　手
所	学校　医院
台	机器　打字机
套	衣服　房子　家具　房间
条	鱼　狗　黄瓜　毛巾　床单　船　路　裙子 腿　裤子
筒	牙膏　鞋油
头	牛　骆驼
位	老人　先生　专家　英雄　模范　朋友　客人
项	任务　建议　工程
样	点心　东西

名 量 词 Nominal measure words	可以和量词搭配的名词 Matching nouns
页	书　纸
张	纸　报　画儿　票　邮票　照片　桌子　床 嘴　脸
支	笔　钢笔　毛笔　铅笔　圆珠笔　粉笔　枪 歌
只	猫　狼　鸡　鸽子　眼睛　耳朵　箱子　手 脚
种	布　锻子　水果　蔬菜　事情　东西　人 意见
幢	房子
座	山　楼　城市　桥　宫殿　庙　塔　宾馆

1. "个"是应用最广的名量词。

个 is the most common and multi-purpose nominal measure word.

2 "位"用于指人的名词表示敬意。但不能直接作"人"的量词，不能说"一位人"。

位 is used with nouns of personal reference in a polite manner with the exception of 人. Therefore there is no such form as 一位人.

3."点、些"都是不定量词，前面只能用"一"，不能用其他数词。例如：

点 and 些 are indefinite measure words which can only be placed before the numeral 一. For example:

一点水　　　　　　　一点礼物

一些香蕉　　　　　　　一些朋友

"一点"表示少量，只能用于事物，不能用于人，不能说"一点人"，"一点小朋友"等。

一点（儿）which means a small quantity can only modify nouns of non-personal reference. One cannot say 一点人，一点小朋友, etc.

"点、些"也常用在代词"这、那、哪"后边。例如：

点 and 些 are also often used after the pronouns 这，那 and 哪. For example:

　　　　这点东西　　　那点糖　　　那点事
　　　　这些客人　　　那些花　　　哪些地方

4．本身带有量词性的名词前边不能再用量词。例如：

Measure words cannot be used with nouns of quantity. For example:

　　　　一年　不能说成"一个年"
　　　　　　　One cannot say 一个年.

　　　　一天　不能说成"一个天"
　　　　　　　One cannot say 一个天.

常见的还有"岁、课"等。

Other examples are 岁，课，etc.

5．有些度量衡单位量词可以连用。例如：

Some measure words of units of length, capacity and weights can be used in succession. For example:

　　　　公斤·米/秒　表示每秒钟移动一米的公斤数
　　　　　　　　　　　It means kilogram-metre per second.

但一般名量词不能连用。绝不能说"一个本画报"、"一张篇论文"、"一个朵花"等。

But ordinary nominal measure words cannot be used this way, e.g. one can never say 一个本画报，一张篇论文，一个朵花, etc.

6. 名量词重叠后常作主语或主语的定语。例如：

The reduplicated form of nominal measure words often serve as subjects or attributives modifying the subject. For example:

  条条（道路）都可到那儿。 （作主语）

  (As the subject)

  本本画报都很有意思。 （作定语）

  (As the attributive)

谓语前边一般用"都"。

都 is generally used before the predicate.

（二）关于动量词。Verbal measure words.

汉语里很多动作也可以计量。现将常见的动量词和动词的搭配情况举例如下：

The frequency of actions can be counted. Here is a list of the commonly used verbal measure words and some verbs matching them. For example:

动 量 词 Verbal measure words	可以和量搭词配的动词 Matching verbs
次	去　找　来　参　观
遍	看　说　写　念　听　抄　翻译
下儿	打　敲　摇　想　玩　讨论
趟	去　来
回	看　送
场	下（雨）　打（球）
阵	刮（风）
顿	吃　打　骂

1. 动量词大多用在动词后边作补语，表示数量。例如：

Most verbal measure words are used as complements of verbs to indicate the frequency of actions. For example:

我们讨论两次。

我去一趟。

动量词也可以放在动词前边作状语，一般表示强调在若干次数内完成或进行某动作。例如：

Verbal measure words can also be used before verbs as adverbial adjuncts emphasizing that the action is carried out or completed within a certain number of times. For example:

我们两趟就搬完了。

他要一次写好。

2. "遍"指从头到尾的完整过程。例如：

遍 indicates the complete duration of an action from beginning to end. For example:

这篇文章你再看一遍吧。

3 "下儿"有两种含义。

下儿 has the following two meanings:

（1）表示具体的动作单位。例如：

Indicating the number of times sth. happens. For example:

钟敲六下儿。　　　　（六点钟）

主席摇两下儿铃。　　（铃响两声）

（2）"下儿"前边用"一"，表示动作经历的时间短，作用和动词重叠一样。例如：

一 is used before 下儿 to show that an action lasts for a very short time. 一下儿 functions as a verbal reduplication. For example:

我得去一下儿。

对不起，您等一下儿。

4.动量词重叠后常用在动词前作状语。例如：

Reduplicated verbal measure words are used before verbs as adverbial adjuncts. For example:

他次次都来。

5.有的动量词可用在名量词后边表示人或事物和动作数量的总和。例如：

There are some combinations of "Nominal measure word + Verbal measure word" which indicate the total number of times of an action done by a certain number of agents (persons or things). For example:

架次　　　综合表示飞机的架数和飞行的次数。

The total number of flights made by a certain number of aeroplanes.

人次　　　综合表示人数和次数。

The total number of times of an action done by a certain number of people.

（三）量词和数词"半"连用时的位置。

Position of the measure word when used with the numeral 半.

1.　量词在"半"的后边，表示数量是二分之一。例如：

Followed by a measure word, 半 means "half of the total quantity or amount". For exrmple:

（1）"半"——量词——（名词）

半　+ measure word + (noun)

半个（桔子）　　　半张（纸）

半瓶（酒）　　　半只（鸡）

半公斤（苹果）　　　半个（钟头）

（2）"半"——带量词性的名词

半　+ noun of quantity

半年　　　半天

85

2.量词前边有整数时，"半"要放在量词后边，表示还有二分之一。例如：

半 occurring after a measure word preceded by a whole number expresses the meaning of "...and a half", as in:

（1）整数——量词——"半"——（名词）

Whole number + measure word + 半 + (noun). Examples:

　　　　我只要一张半（纸）。

　　　　他们打了一个半小时（球）。

又如：

Here are some more examples:

　　　　三瓶半（酒）　　　　五块半（肥皂）

　　　　两斤半（羊肉）　　　　两个半（桃儿）

（2）整数——带量词性的名词——"半"

Whole number + noun of quantify + 半

　　　一课半　　　两岁半

这时"半"不能放在量词前边。一定不能说"我只要一半张（纸）"、"他们打了一半个小时（球）"等。

Note that in this case 半 can never precede the measure word. One cannot say 一半张纸, 一半个钟头, etc.

（四）量词和数词"多"连用时的位置。

Position of the measure word when used with the numeral 多.

量词和表示超过某数的"多"连用时要注意两点：

Two points should be noted when the measure word is used in combination with 多 (...and more):

1. 表示多于"十、百、千、万"等的概数时，"多"紧接在整数后边，用在量词或本身带量词性的名词前边。例如：

多 immediately follows the whole number 十, 百, 千, 万, etc. and precedes the measure word or noun of quantity, as in:

86

（1）整数（个位数为"〇"）——"多"——量词——（名词）

Whole number (the unit place is "0") + 多 + measure word + (noun)

这双皮鞋要三十多块（钱）。

今天食堂买了三百多公斤（肉）。

又如：

Here are two more examples:

一千多吨（煤）　　　一万三千多个（人）

不能说成"这双皮鞋要三十块多（钱）"，"今天食堂买了三百公斤多（肉）"等。

One can never say 这双皮鞋要三十块多（钱），今天食堂买了三百公斤多（肉）， etc.

（2）整数（个位数为"〇"）——"多"——带量词性的名词

Whole number (the unit place is "0" + 多 + noun of quantity

马丽二十多岁了。　　　我们三十多年没见面了。

又如：

Here are two more examples:

三百多天　　　六十多课

绝不能说成"玛丽二十岁多了"、"我们三十年多没见面了"等。

One can never say 玛丽二十岁多了，我们三十年多没见面了, etc.

2. 表示不满"一"的概数时，量词要放在整数和"多"之间。例如：

In order to express an approximate number below 一, the measure word should be placed between the whole number and 多, as in:

（1）整数（个位数为1—9）——量词——"多"——（名词）

Whole number (the unit place is a number from 1 to 9) + measure word +多 + (noun)

他们走了两个多小时。

十二点多钟他才到家。

又如：

Here are some more examples:

五分多（钟）　　　　一个多（月）

三公斤多（西红柿）　　二十三块多（钱）

不能说成"他们走了两多个小时"，"十二多点钟他才到家"等。

One can not say 两多个小时，十二多点钟, etc.

（2）整数（个位数为1—9）——带量词性的名词——"多"

Whole number (the unit place is a number from 1 to 9) + noun of quantity + 多

我工作两年多了。

今年小明八岁多。

又如：　Here are some more examples:

五天多　　　　四课多

不能说成"我工作两多年了"或"今年小明八多岁"等。

One can not say 我工作两多年了，or 今年小明八多岁，etc.

（五）"一点儿"的用法。

The use of 一点儿.

1. 可在名词前作定语。例如：

It is used before a noun as an attributive. For example:

我想查一点儿资料。

他会一点儿英语。

2. 可在形容词后作补语。例如：

It can be used after an adjective as a complement. For example:

88

她的病好一点儿。

今天暖和一点儿了。

3．"一点儿"用在动词或形容词后边时，"一"可以省去，只说"点儿"。例如：

When preceded by a verb or an adjective, 一 in 一点儿 can be omitted. For example:

我想查点儿资料。

今天暖和点儿了。

4．不能用在形容词（或动词）前作状语。不能说"昨天一点儿冷"，"老师一点儿不舒服"，"他一点儿发烧"等。

It can not be used as an adverbial adjunct to premodify an adjective (or verb), e.g. one never says 昨天一点儿冷，老师一点儿不舒服，他一点儿发烧，etc.

（六）钱的表示法。

Counting Chinese money.

1．中国钱币是人民币。人民币的计算单位是"元、角、分"或"块、毛、分"。

The Chinese currency *Renminbi* (RMB) has three units: 元，角 and 分 or 块，毛 and 分.

2．用阿拉伯数字写出来的钱数，后边的单位量词一定要用"元"。例如：

元 is always used after an amount of money written in Arabic numerals. For example:

0.01元　是　一分（钱）

0.20元　是　两角（钱）

6.75元　是　六元七角五分（钱）

8.00元　是　八元（钱）

53.49元　是　五十三元四角九分（钱）

钱数后边的名词是"钱"，口语里常不用。

In spoken Chinese, 钱 in the above examples is often

omitted.

3. 口语里多用"块、毛、分",还常省去最后一个量词不说。例如:

The units 块, 毛 and 分 are more preferable in spoken Chinese, and the last one is often omitted. For example:

        1.20元　是　一块二（毛）

        3.50元　是　三块五（毛）

        2.22元　是　两块两毛二（分）

        5.35元　是　五块三毛五（分）

        9.50元　是　九块五（毛）

注意不能把"0.20元"说成"两毛分"或"二十分";不能把"3.00元"说成"三块零毛零分"或把"5.50元"说成"五块半"等。

Note that 0.20元 can not be spoken as 两毛分 or 二十分; 3.00元 can not be spoken as 三块零毛零分 and 5.50元 as 五块半.

（七）时间的表示法。

Expressions of time.

1.年、月、日的时点表示法。

The expressions of the year, month and date.

（1）年:序数——"年"。例如:

Ordinal number + 年。For example:

    1980 A.D.　是　公元一九八零年

（2）月:序数——"月"。

Ordinal number + 月.

一年有十二个月,这十二个月的名称是:

The twelve months in a year are:

一月,二月,三月,……十月,十一月,十二月

（3）日:序数——"日"或"号"。

Ordinal number + 日 or 号.

每个月的第一天叫"一日"或"一号"，第二天叫"二日"或"二号"，以此类推，一直到"十号"，……"二十号"，……"二十九号"，"三十号"，"三十一号"。例如：

The first day of a month is 一日 or 一号; the second day, 二日 or 二号 and accordingly we can say 十号,…二十号,…二十九号，三十号 and 三十一号. See this example:

今天是二月二十八号。

口语里多用"号"。表示时点不能用"天"，不能说"今天是二月二十八天"。

号 is more common in spoken Chinese. Note that 天 can never be used with "date" as a point of time, e.g. we cannot say 今天是二月二十八天。

（4）星期：一个星期有七天，这七天的名字叫作：

The names of the seven days of the week are:

星期一　　星期二　　星期三　　星期四

星期五　　星期六　　星期日（or "星期天"）

（5）汉语里表示年、月、日的顺序是：年——月——日——星期。例如：

If the year, month, and date are given at the same time, follow this order: Year — month — date — day of the week. For example:

一九八零年十月二日星期四

1980年10月2日（号）星期四

1980.10.2.

注意不能写成：2.10，1980。

One can not write as 2.10, 1980.

2．年、月、日的时段表示法。

Year, month and day as periods of time.

（1）年：基数——"年"

Numeral ＋ 年.

　　　　　　5年——五年　　　　　他学五年汉语。

　　　　　　12年——十二年　　　他工作十二年了。

　（2）月：基数——量词"个"——"月"

Numeral ＋ measure word 个＋月.

　　　　　　三个月

　　　　　　六个月——半年

　　　　　　十二个月——一年　　　一年有十二个月。

　（3）日：基数——"天"（或"日"）

Numeral ＋ 天 (or日).

　　　　　　一个月有三十天。

　　　　　　一年有三百六十五天。

　　　　　　他病了两天。

　（4）星期：基数——量词"个"——"星期"

Numeral ＋ measure word 个＋星期

　　　　　　两个星期（14天）　　　　三个星期（21天）

　　　　　　八个星期（56天）

　　　　　　一个星期有七天。

　（5）"上午、下午、晚上"等表示时点的名词，也可以用在基数和量词"个"后边作为时段的单位。例如：

Nouns expressing points of time such as 上午，下午，晚上，etc., can also be used after numerals and measure word 个 as units of periods of time.　For example:

　　　　　　一个上午　　　　三个下午

　　　　　　两个晚上

3　钟点的表示法。

Expression of times of the clock.

（1）"点"、表示时点。

点 means "o'clock".

数词（1—12）——量词"点"——（名词"钟"）

Numeral (1 — 12) ＋ measure word 点 ＋ (noun 钟)

1:00	是	一点（钟）
2:00	是	两点
3:00	是	三点
10:00	是	十点
12:00	是	十二点

"点"后边的名词"钟"。口语里一般不说。

钟 is often left out in spoken Chinese.

（2）"分"，比"点"小的单位，表示时点。

分 means "minute" indicating a point of time.

数词（1—59）——量词"分"——（名词"钟"）

Numeral (1 — 59) + measure word 分 + (noun 钟)

1:01	一点（零）一分，	一点过一分
1:05	一点（零）五分，	一点过五分
1:09	一点（零）九分，	一点过九分
1:10	一点十分，	一点过十分
1:15	一点十五分，	一点一刻
1:30	一点三十分，	一点半
1:45	一点四十五分，	一点三刻
1:55	一点五十五分，	差五分两点
1:59	一点五十九分，	差一分两点

十五分钟时，常说"一刻"；四十五分时，常说"三刻"。例如：

一刻 is often substituted for 十五分钟 and 三刻 for
四十五分钟. For example:

2:15	两点一刻（钟）	
6:15	六点一刻	
9:15	九点一刻	
3:45	三点三刻，	差一刻四点
7:45	七点三刻，	差一刻八点
12:45	十二点三刻，	差一刻一点

三十分钟时，常说：数词——量词"点"——"半"。例如：

For 三十分钟, we use this formula: Numeral + measure word 点 + 半. For example:

   2:30 两点半（钟）

   5:30 五点半

   11:30 十一点半

不能说"两刻"或"四刻"。

There are no such forms as 两刻 or 四刻.

（3）"秒"，比"分"小的单位，表示时点。

秒 meaning "second" is a unit smaller than 分, indicating a point of time.

  数词（1—59）——量词"秒"——（名词"钟"）

  Numeral (1 — 59) + measure word 秒 + (noun钟)

   一点三分十秒   三点七分六秒

4．"小时"等表示时段。

小时 (hour), etc. indicating periods of time.

（1）"小时"、"钟头"

一天有二十四个小时。汉语里用"小时"或"钟头"表示时段。例如：

There are 24 hours in a day. In Chinese, 小时 or 钟头 is used for "hour". For example:

   一个小时 （60分钟）

   三个小时 （180分钟）

   半个钟头 （30分钟）

   两个钟头 （120分钟）

   一个半小时 （90分钟）

   两个半钟头 （150分钟）

用"钟头"时，数词和"钟头"之间一定要用量词"个"；用"小时"时，数词和"小时"之间可以不用量词"个"。例如，可以说"一小时"，不能说一钟头"。

The measure word 个 must be used between the numeral

and 钟头, whereas 个 is optional when 小时 is used instead of 钟头, e.g. 一小时, but not 一钟头.

（2）"分"、"秒"

一小时有60分钟，一分钟有60秒钟。例如：

There are 60 minutes in an hour and 60 seconds in a minute. For example:

五分（钟）——300秒（钟）

十秒（钟）

（3）"刻"

一刻钟　　　（15分钟）

三刻钟　　　（45分钟）

练 习 6
Exercise 6

（一）用汉字写出（　　）中的 "2"。

Write the numeral 2 in Chinese characters.

1．（2）____本小说　　　2．（2）____张照片

3．（2）____块手表　　　4．（2）____斤桔子

5．（2）____条手绢　　　6．（2）____件衬衫

7．（2）____位教授　　　8．（2）____瓶墨水

9．（2）____对花瓶　　　10．（2）____套房间

（二）填上适当的量词。

Fill in the blanks with appropriate measure words.

1．一____飞机　　　2．一____信

3．三____毛衣　　　4．一____山

5．五____朋友　　　6．两____钱

7．六____糖　　　8．八____布

9．一____眼镜　　　10．一____针

（三）用汉字写出下列钱数。

Write the following amounts of money in Chinese characters.

1. 1.00元   2. 2.22元
3. 4.50元   4. 9.90元
5. 3.35元   6. 7.86元
7. 10.05元   8. 32.31元
9. 100.50元   10. 121.12元

（四）用汉字写出下列时间。

Write the times of the clock in Chinese characters.

1. 1:48   2. 2:20
3. 9:30   4. 3:45
5. 4:05   6. 6:10
7. 10:15   8. 8:37
9. 7:01   10. 5:59

（五）把下列各组词译成中文。

Translate the following dates into Chinese.

1. Thursday, 25th December 1980
2. 1st October 1949
3. 10th May 1964
4. Sunday, 8th March 1981
5. 7th June 1972

第七节　代　词

Section VII Pronouns

一、代词的定义和种类　Definition and types of pronouns

代替名词、动词、形容词、数词或副词的词叫代词。代词可

96

以分成三类。

A pronoun is a word which can take the place of a noun, a verb, an adjective, a numeral or an adverb. Pronouns can be divided into three kinds.

（一）人称代词。Personal pronouns.

代替人或事物的代词叫人称代词。例如：

A pronoun which refers to persons or things is called a personal pronoun. Here are some examples:

单　数 Singular	复　数 Plural
我	我们　咱们
你	你们
您	
他	他们
她	她们
它	它们
自己　　别人	大家

（二）指示代词。Demonstrative pronouns.

区别人或事物的代词叫指示代词。例如：

A pronoun which is used to distinguish people or things is called a demonstrative pronoun. For example:

这　　这里　这儿　这么　这样
那　　那里　那儿　那么　那样
每　　各

（三）疑问代词。 Interrogative pronouns.

表示疑问的代词叫疑问代词。例如：

A pronoun which is used to indicate interrogation is called an interrogative pronoun. For example:

谁　什么　哪　　哪里　哪儿

几　多少　怎么　怎样　怎么样

二、代词的语法特点　Grammatical features

（一）不能重叠。

Personal pronouns cannot be reduplicated.

（二）人称代词前边一般不能受别类词修饰。

Personal pronouns cannot take words of other parts of speech as pre-positioned modifiers.

（三）部分人称代词有复数形式。

Some personal pronouns have plural forms.

三、代词的用途　Functions

代词和它所代替的词类的作用基本相同。

Pronouns serve basically the same function as the words which they substitute.

（一）作主语。As the subject.

她是技术员。	那里不安全。
咱们下盘棋。	哪儿卖邮票?
这是银行。	什么最好吃?

（二）作宾语。As the object.

王教授请您。	她在那儿。
他常照顾别人。	那位先生是谁?
我们住这里。	你要多少?

（三）作定语。As an attributive.

他的身体比较弱。	这样的竹子很多。
你的箱子真漂亮。	你买几瓶汽水?
那块毛巾是我的。	哪种照相机好?

（四）作状语。As an adverbial adjunct.

咱们应该这么做。	你怎么翻译?
我不该那样说。	这件事怎样处理?

（五）作谓语。As the predicate.

这个剧场怎么样？

你哪里？　（只用于打电话）

　　　　　(Used only in telephone calls)

（六）作补语。As a complement.

她们唱得怎么样？

他写得怎么样？

四、使用代词时需要注意的几个问题

Points that merit special attention

（一）代词的复数形式。The plural forms of pronouns.

1. 人称代词"我们、你们、他们、她们"都是复数形式，是由表示单数的人称代词"我、你、他、她"后边加词尾"们"构成的。因此，使用人称代词时要分别使用单、复数形式。例如：

The personal pronouns 我们，你们，他们 and 她们 are all plural in form. They are formed by adding the suffix 们 to the singular forms of pronouns 我，你，他，and 她. So pronouns should be used either in the singular or in the plural according to circumstances. For example:

我是英国人。

他们是中国人。

人称代词作主语、宾语时，无论是单数还是复数，形式都不变。例如：

The form of a personal pronoun, whether in the singular or plural, remains unchanged when it is used as an object. For example:

她看我们。

我们找她。

2. "您"表示尊敬，口语中不用复数形式，有时在书面语中用复数。

Generally, the pronoun 您, a respectful form of adress, is not used in the plural.

3．"它"是指人以外的事物的，"它"和词尾"们"也可以构成复数形式"它们"，"它"、"它们"在读音上是和"他"、"他们"一样的，所以只用于书面语。

它 refers to things rather than human beings. With the suffix 们, it becomes the plural form 它们 which, however, appears only in written Chinese, because 它 and 他，or 它们 and 他们 are the same in pronunciation.

4．"大家"表示复数，而"自己"和"别人"表示单数或复数都可以，要根据语言环境确定。例如：

大家 indicates plural while 自己 and 别人 may express either singular or plural. The number shown by 自己 or 别人 depends on the context. For example:

　　　　他自己知道。　　（单数）

　　　　　　　　　　　(singular)

　　　　我们要靠自己。　（复数）

　　　　　　　　　　　(plural)

5．指示代词"这、那"和疑问代词"哪"后边可以加"些"表示复数。例如：

The demonstrative pronouns 这，那 and the interrogative pronoun 哪 can indicate the plural with 些 added to them. For example:

　　　　这些是他的书。（作主语）

　　　　　　　　　　(as the subject)

　　　　那些东西不好。（作定语）

　　　　　　　　　　(as an attributive modifier)

　　　　哪些画儿好看？（作定语）

　　　　　　　　　　(as an attributive modifier)

（二）人称代词的性别。The gender of personal pronouns.

在书面语里，"他"指男性，"她、她们"指女性，但在口语里由于读音一样，没有这种区别。

100

In written Chinese 他 refers to a male person and 她 or 她们 female, but the difference is lost when spoken because of their same pronunciation.

"他们" 一般指男性，也可以包括女性。例如：

他们 generally refers to the male but may also include the female. For example:

他们（姐姐和弟弟）回来了。

王老师教他们（男同学和女同学）。

（三）代词和句子成分。pronouns and sentence elements.

1. 三类代词都能作主语、宾语和定语。

The three kinds of pronouns can all serve as subject, object or attributive modifier.

2. 有的指示代词和疑问代词还能作状语。例如：

Some of the demonstrative pronouns and interrogative pronouns can also serve as adverbial adjuncts. For example:

你不应该那样写。

这句话怎样解释？

疑问代词"谁"、"什么"不能作状语，不能说"这个字什么念"或"他什么说"等。

The interrogative pronouns 谁 and 什么 cannot be used as adverbial adjuncts, so one can not say 字什么念 or 他什么说, etc.

3. 只有疑问代词"怎么样"能作谓语和程度补语。例如：

Of all pronouns the interrogative pronoun 怎么样 is the only one that can be used as the predicate or as a complement of degree of a sentence. For example:

这个话剧怎么样？　　（作谓语）

（as the predicate)

演员们跳得怎么样？　　（作补语）

（as a complement)

"怎么"不能作补语，不能说"他学得怎么"。

Note that the word 怎么 cannot serve as a complement, so one do not say 他学得怎么.

（四）代词作定语和结构助词"的 (de)"。

A pronoun used as an attributive modifier and the structural particle 的 (de).

1.人称代词和指人的疑问代词"谁"作定语，而中心语是表示亲属关系或集体单位的名词时，后边一般不用助词"的"。例如：

Usually 的 is not used after a persona! pronoun or 谁, an interrogative pronoun referring to person, used attributively modifying a noun of kinship or institution.　For example:

我妈妈是医生。　　　　我校有两千多学生。

谁弟弟病了？　　　　　我国在亚洲。

而表示领属关系时要用"的"。例如：

However, when they express possession, 的 is obligatory. For example:

他们的衣服在柜子里。

这是谁的练习本？

2.指示代词"这、那"和疑问代词"哪"用在数词或量词前作定语时，一律不用"的"。例如：

When the demonstrative pronouns 这, 那 and the interrogative pronoun 哪 serve as attributive modifiers of numerals or measure words, 的 is not used at all. For example:

这三支钢笔很好用。　　　哪座楼是办公楼？

那张床太小。

其他指示代词作定语时，一般要用"的"。例如：

When other demonstrative pronouns are used as attributive modifiers, 的 is usually required.　For example:

这儿的风景真好!

我不买那样的缎子。

3.疑问代词"什么"、"多少",总是直接用在名词前边作定语,不用"的"。例如:

The interrogative pronouns 什么 and 多少, when used as attributive modifiers, always go directly in front of noun. For example:

这是什么地方?

多少人参加晚会?

(五)疑问代词"多少"和"几"。

The interrogative pronouns 多少 and 几.

1."多少"代表的数目可大可小;"几"常代表1—9的数字。例如:

The number expressed by 多少 may be great or small; 几 often indicates numbers from 1 to 9. For example:

这个大学有多少(个)学生?

那个城市有多少(个)人?

你有多少(本)中文书?

你家有几口人?

他买几双鞋?

这儿有十几本中文书?

2."多少"和名词可以直接联系,中间可不用量词;"几"和名词之间一定要用量词。例如:

There must be a measure word between 几 and a noun while 多少 can be directly linked to a noun. For example:

你们班有多少同学?　　　你要几双筷子?

你有多少中文书?　　　　你学几种语言?

你们上午有几节课?　　　他买几条鱼?

一定不能说"他买几鞋"、"你有几本子"、"你住几房间"、"这是几衣服"等。

In no case should one say 他买几鞋，你有几本子，你住几房间 or 这是几衣服， etc.

（六）指示代词"每"。

The demonstrative pronoun 每

1．"每"指全体中的任何一个。"每"一般用在量词或带量词性质的名词前作定语，后面常用副词"都"，表示"全部是这样"。例如：

每 refers to any one of the whole, generally placed as an attributive modifier before a measure word or a noun with the quality of a measure word. It is often accompanied by 都, meaning "all". For example:

他每天都来这儿。　　　　每个菜都很好吃。

我每年都去上海。　　　　每种词典都很贵。

2．"每"和"常"不能同时出现在一个句子里。不能说"他每天常来这里"，"每天下午我们常打球"等。

每 and 常 can not occur together in the same sentence, therefore we cannot say 他每天常来这里 or 每天下午我们常打球, etc.

（七）人称代词"我们"和"咱们"。

The personal pronouns 我们 and 咱们.

1．"我们"指包括说话人在内的若干人，一般 不 包括对方（听话的人）。例如：

我们 generally stands for a number of people including the speaker except the other party (the people spoken to). For example:

我们都是教师。

我们还有事（你可以先走）。

2．"咱们"包括说话人（"我"或"我们"）和对方（"你"或"你们"）。例如：

咱们 includes both the speaker（我 or 我们）and the other

104

party（你 or 你们）. For example:

> 咱们都是一个单位的。
>
> （您快来，）咱们一起商量。
>
> 咱们确定一下旅行的路线。

练 习 7
Exercise 7

（一）填上适当的疑问代词。

Fill in the blanks with the proper interrogative pronouns.

1. 你住____?
2. 他姓____?
3. ____是你们的外语老师?
4. 她是____国人?
5. 这位老人的身体____?
6. 这个词____翻译?

（二）标出下列代词分属哪一类。

Mark what type each of the following pronouns belongs to.

例如：他们（人称代词）

1. 他　（　　　）　2. 这样　（　　　　）
3. 哪儿（　　　）　4. 怎么样（　　　　）
5. 您　（　　　）　6. 这里　（　　　　）

（三）写出下列代词的复数形式。

Write out the plural forms of the following pronouns.

例如：他——他们

1. 我——　　　　　2. 她——
3. 这——　　　　　4. 哪——
5. 那——　　　　　6. 你——

（四）填上适当的量词。

Put in the missing measure words.

    1．他买几____碗？

    2．你有几____汉语语法书？

    3．他们住几____房间？

    4．你问他几____问题？

    5．你借几____自行车？

    6．桌子上有几____钱？

（五）把下面的句子翻译成中文。

Translate the following into Chinese.

    1．Where are you (pl.) going?

    2．What is this?

    3．Who has a Chinese-English dictionary?

    4．How is this flat?

    5．How would you answer his question?

    6．How do you analyse this sentence?

第八节 副 词

Section VIII Adverbs

一、副词的定义 Definition

　　一般用在动词、形容词前面表示时间、程度、范围、重复、否定、可能、语气等的词叫副词。例如：

A word generally used in front of a verb or an adjective to express time, degree, scope, repetition, negation, possibility or tone of speech, etc. is called an adverb. For example:

　　表示时间的： Adverbs expressing time:

　　　　才　　就　　刚　　已经　　常常　　正在

表示程度的： Adverbs expressing degree:

很　太　更　非常　特别　真　多（么）

表示范围的： Adverbs expressing scope:

都　只　一共　一起　全

表示重复的： Adverbs expressing repetition:

又　再　还　也

表示否定的： Adverbs expressing negation:

不　没有　别　不用

表示估计的： Adverbs expressing estimation:

大概　也许

表示语气的： Adverbs expressing tone of speech:

可　却　倒　究竟　到底

表示疑问的： Adverb expressing inquiry:

多

二、副词的语法特点　Grammaticle features

（一）不能重叠。

They cannot be reduplicated.

（二）大部分不能单独回答问题。

Most of them cannot be used alone to answer a question.

（三）一般不能修饰、限制名词。

They cannot be used as a modifier of a noun.

（四）部分副词能起关联作用。例如：

Some adverbs can function as link words. For example:

他打完球就走。

小朋友们又唱又跳。

只有共产党，才能救中国。

三、副词的用途　Functions

副词的基本用途是作状语。例如：

The basic use of an adverb is to serve as adverbial adjunct.

For example:

> 战士们已经出发了。　　我们都参加晚会。
>
> 这个姑娘真英勇。　　你再唱一个歌。
>
> 他今天特别高兴。　　我不会吸烟。

四、使用副词时需要注意的一些问题

Points that merit special attention

（一）副词总是在动词、形容词前边作状语，不能放在动词、形容词后边。例如：

As an adverbial adjunct, the adverb is always placed before a verb or an adjective and not after them. For example:

> 他们一直在这儿。
>
> 我们也祝贺你。

一定不能说成"他们在这儿一直"，"我们祝贺你也"。

In no case should one say 他们在这儿一直，我们祝贺你也.

少数副词可以放在主语前边，而"都、也、就、又、才、再"等一定不能放在主语前边。例如：

A few of the adverbs may precede the subject. However, 都，也，就，又，才，再，etc. can never be placed before the subject. For example:

> 他也许已经走了。（也可以说：也许他已经走了。）
>
> 你们到底去不去？（也可以说：到底你们去不去？）
>
> 同学们都喜欢这种方法。（不能说成"都同学们…"）
>
> 吃了饭我就去。（不能说成"…就我去"）

（二）副词"都"。The adverb 都.

1．经常总括"都"前边的成分。例如：

都 is often used to sum up the preceding elements. For example:

> 运动员们都刻苦锻炼。　　我每天都听汉语广播。

108

大夫们都认真负责。

2．和"也"连用时，"也"要放在"都"的前边。例如：

When 都 and 也 are used together, 也 comes first. For example:

这些青年是大学生，那些青年也都是大学生。

他们喜欢体育活动，我们也都喜欢体育活动。

（三）"不"和"没"。不 and 没.

"不"和"没"都是表示否定的副词，具体用法不同。

Both 不 and 没 are adverbs indicating negation. However, they are used differently.

1．"不"用来否定：

不 is used to negate:

（1）表示思想活动的动词。例如：

Verbs expressing mental activity. For example:

我不了解这个情况。　　　她不认识这个人。

他不知道。

（2）经常的习惯的动作。例如：

Frequent or habitual actions. For example:

他从来不喝酒。　　　我们常常不睡午觉。

那个商店不卖瓷器。

（3）现在或未来的动作。例如：

Actions at the moment or in the future. For example:

现在不开会。　　　明年他不准备回国。

今天不休息。

（4）助动词。例如：

Auxiliary verbs. For example:

我们不应该这么处理。　　　明天不会太热。

你不要乱扔果皮。

（5）"是、象、在、存在"等表示判断、存在的动词。例如：

Verbs expressing judgement or existence, such as 是，象，在，存在, etc. For example:

> 他伯父不是专家。　　　目前这里不存在浪费现象。
>
> 她不象她妈妈。

（6）表示性质、状态的形容词。例如：

Adjectives expressing character or state.　For example:

> 那条公路不长。
>
> 这个答案不对。

（7）表示程度的副词。例如：

Adverbs expressing degree.　For example:

> 那个湖不太大。　　　那里的交通不十分方便。
>
> 这些老树不很粗。

（8）表示范围的副词。例如：

Adverbs expressing scope.　For example:

> 大家不一起走。
>
> 他们不都是英国人。
>
> 他们不全掌握这个地方的情况。

2．"没" 用来否定：

没 is used to negate:

（1）表示领有、存在的动词 "有"。例如：

The verb 有 expressing possession and existence.　For example:

> 现在我们没有时间。　　　屋子里没（有）人。
>
> 她没有《汉英词典》。

（2）表示动作发生或完成的动词。例如：

Verbs expressing occurence or completion of an action. For example:

> 昨天没举行排球比赛。　　　他没参加宴会。
>
> 刚才他们没来这儿。

（四）"没" 和 "没有"。　没 and 没有.

1．这两个副词都可以作状语修饰动词，否定动作的发生或完成。例如：

Both the adverbs 没 and 没有 can serve as adverbial adjuncts to qualify verbs. They are used to negate the occurence or the completion of the action expressed by the verb. For example:

她没有参加招待会。

也可以说：她没参加招待会。

We can also say: 她没参加招待会.

昨天我们没有考试。

也可以说：昨天我们没考试。

We can also say: 昨天我们没考试.

2．"有"的否定形式是"没有"。例如：

The negative form of 有 is 没有. For example:

我没有中文报。

院子里没有果树。

"有"带宾语时，也可以只说"没"。例如：

When 有 takes an object, 没 alone can express the negation. For example:

我没中文报。

院子里没果树。

但不能说"我没有有中文报"。

However, do not say 我没有有中文报.

（五）副词"不"和副词"都"、"全"或"很"等连用时，"不"的位置可以在"都"等的前边或后边，但表示的意义不同。

The adverb 不, when used with the adverbs 都, 全 or 很, may come either before the adverbs or after them, but with different meanings.

1．"不"在"都"等前边。例如：

不 comes in front of 都 etc. For example:

我们不都坐车。

（指整体中的每一个不完全一样，有的坐车，有
的不坐。）

(This means that people in the same group are
different, some will take a bus and some will
not.)

我们不全坐车。

这个办法不很好。

（"不"否定"很好"，表示没达到"很好"的
程度。）

(不 negates 很好, meaning that something has
not yet reached the extent of 很好.)

2．"不"在"都"等后边。例如：

不 comes after 都, etc. For example:

我们都不坐车。

（指整体中的任何一个完全一样。）

(This means that people in the same group are
the same.)

我们全不坐车。

这个办法很不好。

（"不"否定"好"，"很"强调"不好"的程度。）

(不 negates 好, while 很 intensifies the degree
of 不好.)

（六）"又"和"再"。 又 and 再.

这两个副词都表示动作的重复，但用法不同。

Both 又 and 再 are used to express the repetition of an
action, but with different meanings.

1．"又"表示动作、情况已经重复。例如：

又 indicates that the action or situation has repeated.

For example:

上午他去了图书馆，下午又去了。

昨天很冷，今天又很冷。

他上星期没来，这星期又没来。

2．"再"表示动作将要重复。例如：

再 indicates that the action is going to recur. For example:

我再反映一下大家的要求。

您再安慰安慰老人。

我不想再看见他了。

（七）表示程度的副词"多（么）"和"很、非常、特别、太、真"等其他程度副词的异同。

Similarities and dissimilarities between the adverb 多（么）and other adverbs of degree 很，非常，特别，太，真，etc.

1．相同处：这些程度副词都可以直接修饰部分形容词和某些动词，强调程度深。例如：

Similarities: These adverbs of degree can all stress a great degree by qualifying directly some adjectives or verbs. For example:

多（么）难	很难
多（么）美丽	非常美丽
多（么）希望	特别希望
多（么）有水平	真有水平

2．不同处："多（么）"用在感叹句里表示感叹，句尾常用助词"啊"和感叹号；"很"等要用在陈述句里，句尾常用句号。例如：

Dissimilarities: 多（么）, used in an exclamatory sentence, expresses exclamation and the sentence usually ends with a modal particle 啊 and a exclamation mark; 很, etc. are used in a statement and there is usually a full stop at the end of the sentence. For example:

那个同志多（么）坚强啊！ 这个地方的名胜古迹多（么） 　　吸引人啊！	那个同志太坚强了。 这个地方的名胜古迹真 　　吸引人。

"多（么）"不能跟其他程度副词连用。不能说"那个同志多（么）很坚强啊"。

多（么） can not be used together with other adverbs of degree. Therefore one can not say 那个同志多么很坚强啊.

（八）副词和助动词连用时，副词通常是在助动词前边。例如：

When an adverb is used together with an auxiliary verb, the adverb usually precedes the auxiliary verb. For example:

　　钱先生也许能来。　　　　我们已经会说汉语了。

　　你不应该提那件事。

（九）表示时间和范围的一些副词可以在数量词前作状语。例如：

Some adverbs of time or degree can be placed before a numeral-measure word as an adverbial modifier. For example:

　　已经九点了。　　　　　一共三十七块六毛五（分钱）。

　　才一个人。

（十）个别副词可以单独回答问题，如"不，没有，大概，也许，可能"。

A few adverbs can stand for an answer by themselves, such as 不，没有，大概，也许，可能, etc.

（十一）只有个别副词可以作补语。如副词"极"加上"了(le)"，或"很"在助词"得(de)"后边，可以作形容词（或能

114

表示程度的动词）的补语。例如：

Only one or two adverbs can serve as a complement. For example, the adverb 极 followed by 了 (le), or 很 preceded by the structural particle 得 (de) can be used as a complement of an adjective (or a verb denoing degree). For example:

　　　　这次旅游累极了。

　　　　这个地方我们喜欢极了。

　　　　现在西瓜便宜得很。

（十二）表示关联作用的副词有下面几种情况。

The uses of the correlative adverbs are as follows:

1．单独用的。例如：

To be used independently. For example:

　　　　他说了一遍又一遍。 （"又"表示重复）

　　　　　　　　　　　　　（又 indicates repetition)

　　　　看了电影才回家。 （"才"表示动作发生得晚）

　　　　　　　　　　　　　（才 indicates late occurence of

　　　　　　　　　　　　　　the action)

2．前后配合使用的。例如：

To be used as correlatives. For example:

　　　　风越刮越大。

　　　　他一听就明白。

练 习 8
Exercise 8

（一）选用适当的副词填空。

Fill in the blanks with proper adverbs.

　　都　也　就　特别　常常　不　马上　永远

　　1．大家＿＿想买那种新式上衣。

2. 他＿＿＿说汉语。

3. 她是记者，我＿＿＿是记者。

4. 我＿＿＿喜欢运动。

5. 今天他＿＿＿高兴。

6. 我＿＿＿就来。

（二）把（ ）中的副词放在下列句中的适当位置上。

Put the adverbs in the brackets in their proper places.

1. 我的兴趣广泛。　　　　（ 很 ）

2. 他的理想实现了。　　　（ 终于 ）

3. 这件事给我的印象深。　（ 非常 ）

4. 他能完成这项工作。　　（ 按时 ）

5. 你可以来我的办公室。　（ 随时 ）

6. 最近下了三天雨。　　　（ 一连 ）

（三）把下面的句子改成否定式。

Make the following sentences negative.

1. 他也许来。

2. 他可能接见我们。

3. 我们也准备出席。

4. 他们常组织晚会。

5. 这些孩子很瘦。

6. 他的技术太熟练了。

（四）改正下列各句中副词的位置。

Put right the misplaced adverbs in the following sentences.

1. 他们都也参加谈判。

2. 这件事公布已经了。

3. 我反对这种作法一直。

4. 都我们从事文艺工作。

5. 多么他今天激动啊。

6. 我明天搞再。

（五）用下边各组词组句（注意副词"都、也、就、常常、不"

116

的位置）。

Make sentences with each of the following word groups, paying special attention to the position of the adverbs 都，也，就，常常，不.

1. 都　大家　买
2. 也　作家　是　他
3. 就　我　来
4. 常常　她　锻炼
5. 不　她们　唱

第九节　介词
Section IX　Prepositions

一、介词的定义　Definition

加在名词、代词前边构成介词结构，表示动作的时间、处所、方向、对象、原因、方式、被动、比较或排除等意义的词，叫介词。例如：

A word, which can be put before a noun or a pronoun to form a prepositional phrase indicating time, place, direction, object, reason, manner, the passive, comparison, or exclusion, etc. is called a preposition. For example:

表示时间、处所、方向的有：
Indicating time, place, direction:

在　从　向　往

表示对象的有：
Indicating object:

跟　对　给　对于　关于　把　连

表示原因的有：

Indicating reason:

          为   为了   由于

表示方式的有：

Indicating manner:

           按照   根据

表示被动的有：

Indicating the passive:

          被   叫   让

表示比较的有：

Indicating comparison:

          比

表示排除的有：

Indicating exclusion:

          除   除了

二、介词的语法特点　Grammatical features

（一）不能单独使用。

They can not be used alone.

（二）不能重叠。

They can not be reduplicated.

（三）一般不能加动态助词"了、着、过"。

They can not normally take aspectual particles 了, 着, 过.

（四）一般不能用正反式提问。

They can not normally be turned into an affirmative + negative question.

三、介词的用途　Functions

（一）介词一般不能单独充当句子成分。

Generally speaking, a preposition cannot be an element of a sentence by itself!

（二）绝大多数介词后面总是带着名词、代词构成介词结构充当状语、补语和定语。例如：

118

Most of the prepositions have to take a noun or a pronoun to form a prepositional phrase to serve as an adverbial adjunct, complement or attributive. For example:

他从北方来。　　　　（作状语）

(as an adverbial adjunct)

这是关于月亮的传说。（作定语）

(as an attributive)

这列火车开往上海。（作补语）

(as a complement)

四、使用介词时要注意的几个问题

Points that merit special attention

（一）几个介词的用法。

Usage of several prepositions.

1．"在"和宾语：　在 and its object：

（1）介词"在"的宾语多表示处所。例如：

The objects of the preposition 在 usually indicate locality. For example:

在北京学习　　　在球场比赛

在他家玩　　　　在学生宿舍休息

（2）指人的名词或代词，不能单独充当介词"在"的宾语表示处所，后边一定要加上"这儿"或者"那儿"。例如：

Nouns or pronouns denoting persons can not be used independently as the object of the preposition 在 to show locality. They must take 这儿 or 那儿. For example:

在我这儿看电视

在朋友那儿跳舞

不能说"在我"或"在朋友"等。

One can not say 在我 or 在朋友, etc.

2．"从"和宾语：　从 and its object：

（1）"从"后边的宾语可以是表示处所的词。例如：

The objects of the preposition 从 may be words denoting locality. For example:

　　从家走

　　从学校出发

（2）指人的名词或代词，不能单独充当介词"从"的宾语，表示处所，后边一定要加上"这儿"或"那儿"。例如：

The nouns or pronouns denoting persons can not be used independently as the object of the preposition 从 to show locality. They must take 这儿 or 那儿. For example:

　　　从我这儿去

　　　从我叔叔那儿来

不能说"从我去"或"从我叔叔来"等。

One can not say 从我 or 从我叔叔, etc.

3．"对于"和"对"：　对于 and 对：

（1）"对于"和"对"都可以加上宾语构成介词结构，引出对象。例如：

Both 对于 and 对 with an object can form a prepositional phrase to introduce the object. For example:

　　　对于他的行为　　　　对他的行为

　　　对于这个问题　　　　对这个问题

　　　对于身体　　　　　　对身体

但"对"的动作性比"对于"强些。

However, the preposition 对 is more motional than 对于.

（2）"对"可以有"向"、"朝"的意思。例如：

对 may carry the meaning of 向 or 朝. For example:

　　　对病人说　　　　对学生讲

　　　对我笑

这时不能说"对于病人（说）"，"对于我笑"等。

In such cases one can not say 对于病人（说）or 对于我笑, etc.

（3）"对"可以有"对待"的意思。例如：

对 may have the meaning of 对待. For example:

> 对我好
>
> 对人诚恳

4. "跟"：

（1）介词"跟"常引出动作的对象，表示"同…一起"进行某动作。例如：

The preposition 很, meaning to engage in an action together with someone else, often introduces the partner(s) or opponent(s). For example:

> 我想跟你练习发音。
>
> 他们队跟很多队赛篮球。

（2）"跟"可以有"对、向"的意思。例如：

The preposition 跟 may have the meaning of 对, 向. For example:

> 你的主意好，快跟同学们说说。
>
> 妈妈跟我说："早一点休息。"

5. "给"：

（1）介词"给"可引出动作服务的对象，有"为、替"的意思。例如：

The preposition 给 may introduce the object of an action and has the meaning of "for" (为, 替). For example:

> 她给我们当翻译。
>
> 他给我们介绍经验。
>
> 你给我寄（一）封信，可以吗？

（2）"给"可以引出动作的对象，有"朝、向、对"的意思。例如：

The preposition 给 may introduce the object of an action and has the meaning of 朝, 向, 对. For example:

> 孩子们给老师敬礼。
>
> 校长给全体学生讲话。

我要给玛丽小姐打电话。

（3）"给"可以引出动作者表示被动。例如：

给 can be used to introduce the agent to express the passive. For example:

衣服给雨水淋湿了。

小树给大风刮倒了。

那本书给人借走了。

（二）只有个别介词，如"被"和表示被动的"给"在一定条件下可以单独作状语。例如：

Only one or two prepositions, such as 被 and the passive 给, can independently serve under certain circumstances as an adverbial adjunct. For example:

他被打伤了。

自行车给骑走了。

（三）汉语里的介词大部分是由古汉语动词演变而来的，有的介词和动词的界限很清楚，如"从、被、对于、关于、由于"等；但有的兼属动词，如"在、给、比"等。例如：

Most of the prepositions in the Chinese language come from verbs that have lost their original meanings in classical Chinese. As a result, there are prepositions such as 在，给，比, etc., which are at the same time verbs. Such words as 从，被，对于，关于，由于, etc. however, are distinctively prepositions. For example:

动词 Verbs	介词 Prepositions
他在家。	他在家写文章。
我给他。	我给他倒茶。
咱们比比。	你比我小。
这都为你。	我们要为人民服务。

练 习 9
Exercise 9

（一）填上适当的介词。

Fill in the blanks with proper prepositions.

1. 他们＿＿＿美国来。

2. 您＿＿＿我们讲讲。

3. 他＿＿＿我说："最近忙极了。"

4. 同学们＿＿＿张中家吃饭。

5. 我们＿＿＿朋友那儿来。

6. 那些护士＿＿＿病人非常关心。

7. 我们家＿＿＿那个公园不远。

8. 你＿＿＿前看。

9. ＿＿＿他，我们都准备参加毕业考试。

10. 团长＿＿＿团员们说一件事。

11. 高教授＿＿＿学生非常严格。

12. 我们都＿＿＿他高兴。

13. 他＿＿＿大家介绍这里的情况。

14. 今天我们＿＿＿岸边散步。

15. 客人们＿＿＿那边走了。

16. 大家＿＿＿新同学很照顾。

17. 牛＿＿＿草地上吃草。

18. 明天早上八点＿＿＿学校出发。

19. 你别＿＿＿这儿唱歌。

20. 晚上我们＿＿＿他那儿看画报。

（二）把下面的词组翻译成中文（注意用上适当的介词）。

Turn the following phrases into Chinese (using proper prepositions).

1. to take a walk in the garden
2. to come from one's friend's home
3. to walk to the west
4. to act according to principles
5. to be warm towards people
6. to listen to music at the teacher's home
7. to work for others
8. to discuss with me
9. to give a lecture to the students
10. to talk with the athletes

第十节 连 词

Section X Conjunctions

一、连词的定义　　Definition

连接两个词、词组或句子，表示并列、因果、条件、假设等语法关系的词叫连词。例如：

A conjunction is a word, which can join two words, phrases or sentences to indicate the grammatical relation of coordination, causality, condition, supposition, etc. For example:

表示并列的有：

Indicating coordination:

　　和　　跟　　同　　与　　及　　并　　而

表示因果的有：

Indicating causality:

　　因为　　　所以　　　因此

表示条件的有：

Indicating condition:

只要　只有　不管

表示假设的有：

Indicating supposition:

如果　要是

表示推论判断的有：

Indicating inference:

既然　这样　那么

表示转折的有：

Indicating transition:

虽然　但是　可是　不过

表示让步的有：

Indicating concession:

即使　就是

表示选择的有：

Indicating alternative:

还是　或者

表示列举的有：

Indicating enumeration:

例如　比如

表示紧接相承的有：

Indicating succession:

接着　于是　然后

表示进一步的有：

Indicating progression:

甚至　至于　而且

二、连词的语法特点　Grammatical features

（一）不能单独使用，不能单独回答问题。

Conjunctions can not be used by themselves, and they can not be used alone to answer questions.

（二）不能重叠。

125

They can not be reduplicated.

（三）没有修饰作用，只有连接作用，表示各种意义上的语法关系。

They are only connectives expressing different grammatical relationships and can never serve as modifiers.

三、连词的用途　Functions

（一）不能单独充当句子成分。

Conjunctions can not serve as any sentence element.

（二）连接词、词组或句子，表示一定的语法意义。例如：

They are used to connect words, phrases or sentences to give certain grammatical senses.　For example:

医生和护士工作都很认真。

（连接名词）

（Connecting two nouns）

我们讨论并（且）通过了这个改革方案。

（连接动词）

（Connecting two verbs）

打排球或者踢足球，他都喜欢。

（连接词组）

（Connecting two phrases）

要是你不能走路，就坐车。

（连接句子）

（Connecting two sentences）

他不但喜欢画画儿，而且喜欢养花。

（连接句子）

（Ditto）

四、使用连词时要注意的几个问题

Points that merit special attention

（一）连词表示语法关系的种类。

Conjunctions show types of grammatical relations.

126

1. 并列关系　Coordination

被连接的两个词、词组是平等的，不分主次，有时前后位置可以互换，但意义不变。

The two joined words or phrases are equal to each other with neither being primary or secondary. Sometimes the order of the two parts can be reversed, though the meaning expressed remains the same.

（1）连接名词、代词或名词性词组的连词有"和、跟、同、与、及"。

Conjunctions joining nouns, pronouns or nominal phrases are 和，跟，同，与 and 及.

A．"和、跟"多用于口语。例如：

和，跟 are commonly used in spoken Chinese. For example:

> 工程师和技术员都到了。
>
> （名词）
>
> （Joining nouns）
>
> 我跟你不需要参加这次考试。
>
> （代词）
>
> （Joining pronouns）
>
> 英文报和法文报都没订。
>
> （名词性词组）
>
> （Joining nominal phrases）

B．"同、与、及"多用于书面语。例如：

同，与，及 are chiefly used in written Chinese. For example:

> 国家大力发展工业与农业。
>
> （名词）
>
> （Joining nouns）
>
> 这个小卖部不卖笔、墨、纸及其他文具。
>
> （名词）
>
> （Joining nouns）

127

（2）连接动词、词组或分句的连词"并且"，也可以说成"并"。例如：

Conjunction 并且 joins verbs, phrases or clauses. It is also known as 并. For example:

新事物不断发生并（且）发展。

（动词）

（Joining verbs）

代表们热烈讨论并（且）一致通过了这个草案。

（词组）

（Joining phrases）

我们应该并（且）能够完成这个任务。

（助动词）

（Joining auxiliary verbs）

（3）连接形容词或形容词性词组的连词有"而、而且"。例如：

Conjunctions joining adjectives or adjective phrases are 而, 而且. For example:

她是一位朴素而美丽的姑娘。

这个运动员迅速而且准确地完成了每一个动作。

（4）可以连接各类词或词组的连词有"或者"。例如：

或者 can be used to join all kinds of words or phrases. For example:

你们或者打球，或者跑步，或者打太极拳，都行。

2．偏正关系　Subordination

被连接的词、词组或句子之间的关系是一偏一正，有主次之分。常用的连词有"如果、不但、因为、即使、但是"等等。有的连词常两个配合使用。例如：

The conjunctions 如果, 不但, 因为, 即使, 但是, etc. are frequently used if the relationship between the joined words or phrases is that of subordination. Some of these conjunctions are often used in pairs.

我因为忙，所以没去。

今天虽然有风，但是不冷。

有的连词要跟别的副词配合使用。例如：

Some of these conjunctions are often used together with other
adverbs. For example:

只要努力，就能取得好的成绩。

既然来了，就多坐坐。

（二）几个连词的用法。

Usage of several conjunctions.

1.“和”：

（1）“和”除了常连接名词、名词性词组和代词外，还可
以连接动词、形容词和动词性词组。例如：

The conjunction 和 is often used to join nouns, pronouns,
nominal phrases as well as verbs, adjectives and verbal phrases.
For example:

讨论和通过　　巩固和发展

（动词）

（Connecting two verbs）

幸福和愉快　　勤劳和勇敢

（形容词）

（Connecting two adjectives）

划船、游泳和爬山

（词组）

（Connecting two phrases）

积极恢复和努力发展

（词组）

（Ditto）

（2）用“和”连接的成分是并列的，在意义上往往是同类
的。“和”一般不连接分句。例如：

The elements joined by 和 are coordinate and they often belong to the same kind. Generally, it is not used to join clauses. For example:

我现在复习生词和念课文。

这种钢笔多少钱一支？墨水多少钱一瓶？

大夫给我一些药并且说："要按时吃药、多喝水，注意休息"。

不能说成"我现在复习生词和我念课文"，"这种钢笔多少钱一支和墨水多少钱一瓶"，"大夫给我一些药和说：'要按时吃药……'"。

One can not say 我现在复习生词和我念课文；这种钢笔多少钱一支和墨水多少钱一瓶；大夫给我一些药和说："要按时吃药……"。

（3）用"和"连接三个或更多的词或词组时，"和"一般用在最后的词或词组前边。例如：

When 和 is used to join three or even more than three words or phrases, it is usually put in front of the last. For example:

桌子上有书、本子、钢笔和墨水。

也可以用顿号"、"代表连词"和"。例如：

A slight-pause mark can be used to stand for the conjunction 和. For example:

桌子上有书、本子、钢笔、墨水。

但不说"…有书、本子和钢笔、墨水"。

But one can not say …有书、本子和钢笔、墨水.

2．"及"：

"及"只用于书面语，只能连接名词。"及"所连接的事物如在意义上有主次的分别，主要的放在"及"前面。例如：

The preposition 及 is only used in written Chinese to join nouns. The primary part, if it can be differentiated from

130

what is secondary in the joined parts, should be placed before 及. For example:

这个商店卖布、绸、缎及其他商品。

3．"并且"：

"并且"常用在两个动词或动词性词组之间，表示两个动作同时或先后进行。例如：

并且 is often used between two verbs or verbal phrases and indicates that two actions are in progress simultaneously or sucessively. For example:

大会热烈讨论并且一致通过了决议。

我们商量并且决定明天去拜访一位经济专家。

4．"还是"和"或者"：

这两个连词都表示选择，但用法不同。

Both 还是 and 或者 indicate alternative. However, they have different uses.

（1）"还是"主要用于疑问句或用在陈述句里表示不能确定的意思。例如：

还是 is mainly used in an interrogative sentence or in a declarative sentence with the implication of uncertainty. For example:

你去还是他去？
我不知道上午还是下午。

（2）"或者"一般都用于陈述句。例如：

或者 is usually used in a declarative sentence. For example:

今天或者明天都行。
你带一支钢笔或者圆珠笔。

练 习 10
Exercise 10

（一）填上适当的连词。

Put in the proper conjunctions.

1．数学____物理　　2．咱们____他们

3．整齐____清洁　　4．继承____发扬

5．检查____治疗　　6．钢笔、铅笔____毛笔

7．光荣____伟大　　8．吃苹果____吃桔子？

9．画画儿____雕刻　10．欣赏音乐____做游戏？

（二）把（　　）里的连词放在下面句子里适当的位置上。

Put each of the conjunctions in its proper position in the following sentences.

1．白粉笔、彩色粉笔都在黑板旁边。　　　　（和）

2．主人、客人都进了客厅。　　　　　　　　（跟）

3．他这个月搜集、整理这些资料。　　　　　（并）

4．我们应该迅速、准确地完成这个计算任务。（而）

5．他要进行全面、详细、深入的分析。　　　（和）

6．主任要了解情况解决困难。　　　　　　　（并且）

7．我打排球打乒乓球。　　　　　　　　　　（或者）

8．他们去长城去十三陵？　　　　　　　　　（还是）

（三）把下列各组词翻译成中文（注意用上适当的连词）。

Turn the following phrases into Chinese (that proper conjunctions are used).

1．science and art

2．you and I

3．industrious and brave

4．realize and correct one's mistake

132

5. read carefully and analyse
6. quantity and quality
7. simple and clear
8. invention and creation
9. strong or weak?
10. whether the conditions are ripe or not?

第十一节 助 词
Section XI Particles

一、助词的定义和种类 Definition and types of particles

附在词、词组或句子后边，表示各种附加意义、语法关系或
语气的词叫助词。助词可以分成三类。

A word which is added to another word, a phrase or a
sentence to indicate various supplementary meanings, grammatical relations or mood is called a particle. The particles
can be divided into three kinds.

（一）结构助词 The structural particles

附在词或词组后边表示语法关系的助词叫结构助词。结构助
词有：

Particles added to words or phrases to indicate grammatical
relations are called structural particles. The structural particles
are:

的 (de)　　　地 (de)　　　得 (de)

（二）动态助词 The aspectual particles

附在动词后边表示附加意义的助词叫动态助词。动态助词
有：

Particles added to verbs to indicate a supplementary

meaning are called aspectual particles. The aspectual particles are:

了 (le)　　着 (zhe)　　过 (guo)

（三）语气助词　The modal particles

附在句子末尾表示各种语气的助词叫语气助词。语气助词有：

Particles used at the end of a sentence to express moods are called modal particles. The modal particles are:

吗 (ma)　　呢 (ne)　　吧 (ba)　　了 (le)　　啊 (a)

二、助词的语法特点　Grammatical features

（一）没有实在意义。

They do not have any concrete meaning.

（二）不能单独使用。

They can not be used alone.

（三）读轻声。

They are read in the neutral tone.

三、助词的用途　Functions

（一）助词不能单独充当句子成分。

Particles can not be used alone as sentence elements.

（二）助词总是附在别的词、词组后边一起充当句子成分，或附在句末。例如：

In a sentence element, particles always occur after other words or phrases or at the end of a sentence. For example:

奶奶的眼镜　　　　（附在名词后边）
　　　　　　　　　(Attached to a noun)

十分兴奋地谈论　　（附在词组后边）
　　　　　　　　　(Attached to a phrase)

说得流利　　　　　（附在动词后边）
　　　　　　　　　(Attached to a verb)

保卫着祖国　　　　（附在动词后边）
　　　　　　　　　(Ditto)

他来吗？	（附在句尾）
	(Attached to a sentence)
快走啊！	（附在句尾）
	(Ditto)

四、使用助词时要注意以下几个问题

Points that merit special attention

（一）结构助词"的、地、得"的写法。

Writing of the structural particles 的，地 and 得.

这三个结构助词音调完全一样，都是轻声"de"，但在书面语里分别写为"的、地、得"，不能写错。

With the neutral tone "de", the pronounciation of the three structural particles is exactly the same. However, they are respectively written as 的，地 and 得 in written Chinese.

（二）三个结构助词的用法。

Usage of the three structural particles.

1．"的"是专门附在定语后边的助词。例如：

Structural particle 的 only occurs after an attributive modifier. For example:

妹妹的眼镜很漂亮。	（名词作定语）
	(Noun as attributive)
她的眼镜配得不错。	（代词作定语）
	(Pronoun as attributive)
新的眼镜在这儿。	（形容词作定语）
	(Adjective as attributive)
配的眼镜取回来了。	（动词作定语）
	(Verb as attributive)
这是昨天配的眼镜吗？	（词组作定语）
	(Phrase as attributive)
他配的眼镜很贵。	（词组作定语）
	(Ditto)

135

2．"地"是专门附在状语后边的助词。例如：

The structural particle 地 only occurs after an adverbial adjunct. For example:

大家都热烈地欢迎外国朋友。

（形容词作状语）

(Adjective as adverbial adjunct)

我们刻苦地钻研。 （形容词作状语）

(Ditto)

妈妈很关心地问："你最近身体怎么样？"

（词组作状语）

(Phrase as adverbial adjunct)

汉字要一笔一笔地写。（词组作状语）

(Ditto)

3．"得"是专门附在动词、形容词后边、补语前边的助词。例如：

The structural particle 得 only occurs in between a verb or an adjective and a complement. For example:

来得早 （附在动词后边）

(Attached to a verb)

跑得快 （附在动词后边）

(Ditto)

做得完 （附在动词后边）

(Ditto)

吃得下 （附在动词后边）

(Ditto)

快得很 （附在形容词后边）

(Attached to an adjective)

（三）动态助词和动词。Aspectual particles and verbs.

汉语的动词没有形态变化。动词后边常用助词"了、着、过"来表示各种附加意义。但并不是所有的动词都能附加"了、着"。

Chinese verbs do not have inflection in form. A verb often takes after it the particles 了, 着 and 过 to indicate various additional meanings. However, not every verb can take 了 and 着.

1. 下面几类动词不能带助词"着"。

Verbs of the following kinds can not take the particle 着.

（1）本身不能表示持续行为的，如"是、在、等于、结束、完、逝世、消灭、塌、逃、进、出、去"等。

Verbs which can not by themselves express a continuous aspect such as 是，在，等于，结束，完，逝世，消灭，塌，逃，进，出，去, etc.

（2）本身含有持续动作的，如"恨、怕、知道、象、需要、认识、拥护、赞成、同意"等。

Verbs which contain a continuous aspect such as 恨，怕，知道，象，需要，认识，拥护，赞成，同意, etc.

（3）前边有助动词的，如"能说"、"会写"、"想买"等。

Verbs which take before them an auxiliary verb such as 能说，会写，想买, etc.

（4）含有动补关系的，如"打倒、打败、推翻、说明"等。

Verbs which take after them a complement such as 打倒，打败，推翻，说明, etc.

2. 下面几类动词不能带助词"了"。

Verbs of the following kinds can not take the particle 了.

（1）表示的动作不是短时间内能够完成的。如"爱、恨、企图、羡慕、想念、反对"等。

Verbs which express an action not to be completed in a short time such as 爱，恨，企图，羡慕，想念，反对, etc.

（2）动作性不强的。如"象、是、在、姓、叫作"等。

Verbs which do not express an actural action such as 象，是，在，姓，叫作, etc.

（3）前边有助动词的。

Verbs which take before them an auxiliary verb.

（四）动态助词和副词。Aspectual particles and adverbs.

每个动态助词都能跟特定的副词配合使用。

Each aspectual particle can be used together with a certain adverb.

1．动态助词"了"常跟"已经"呼应。例如：

The aspectual particle 了 is often accompanied by 已经. For example:

> 他已经回了两次家。

> 我已经写了信了。

2．动态助词"着"常跟"正…（呢）"、"在…（呢）"配合使用。例如：

The aspectual particle 着 is often used together with 正…（呢），在…（呢）. For example:

> 他进来的时候，我们正说着话（呢）。

> 他在写着信呢，我们不要打搅他。

3．动态助词"过"常跟"曾经"呼应。例如：

The aspectual particle 过 is often accompanied by 曾经. For example:

> 她曾经到过那里。

> 我们曾经商量过这件事。

（五）后附动态助词的动词的否定形式是：（见第139页表）

The negative forms of verbs taking an aspectual particle after them are as follows: (P.139)

（六）三个动态助词的用法。

Usage of the three aspectual particles.

1．"着"附在动词后边，表示动作和行为在某特定时间内还在进行或处于某种状态，或某种状态在持续。例如：

When added to a verb, 着 indicates that an action or a conduct is in progress or in a certain state at a certain time, or a certain state continues.   For example:

他们正谈着。　　　　　（动作正在进行）
　　　　　　　　　　　（The action is in progress）

她正弹着钢琴。　　　　（Ditto）

门开着，灯亮着。　　　（状态在持续）
　　　　　　　　　　　（The state continues）

我们坐着喝茶。　　　　（处于某种状态）
　　　　　　　　　　　（To be in a certain state）

肯定形式 Affirmative form	否定形式 Negative form
大门开了	大门没开。　（不能说"没开了"） （One can not say没开了）
大门开着	大门没开着。（要保留"着"） （Keep 着 in the sentence）
大门开过	大门没开过。（要保留"过"） （Keep 过 in the sentence）

2．"了"附在动词后边，表示动作已经完成。例如：

When preceded by a verb, 了 indicates that an action has already been completed. For example:

我买了一本《汉英词典》。　（动作已经完成）
　　　　　　　　　　　　　（The action has already been completed）

他去了。　　　　　　　　　（Ditto）

我下了班，就来你这儿。　　（动作将来完成）
　　　　　　　　　　　　　（The action will·be com-

pleted in the future)

她收拾了东西就走。　　　(Ditto)

3．"过"附在动词后边，表示动作已成过去，有的兼表经历、阅历。例如：

When preceded by a verb, 过 indicates that an action took place in the past. Some phrases of this kind may show experience as well. For example:

他吃过中餐。　　　她学过法语。

我去过上海。　　　我们当过工人。

（七）几个语气助词的用法。

Usage of some modal particles.

1．"吗"

"吗"是表示疑问的语气助词。表示问话人不知道，希望得到回答时，可在陈述句末尾加上"吗"。例如：

吗 is a modal particle showing interrogation. When not knowing something and expecting an answer, the speaker can put 吗 at the end of a statement. For example:

窗户关着吗？

那里的风景美吗？

那是一个著名的城市吗？

2．"呢"

（1）"呢"可用在正反式疑问句末尾，表示不肯定的语气。例如：

呢 can be used at the end of an affirmative + negative sentence to indicate a tone of uncertainty. For example:

他是不是留学生呢？

您买不买世界地图呢？

我们能不能这样回答呢？

（2）"呢"可用在有疑问代词问句的末尾，表示猜测的语气。例如：

140

呢 can be used at the end of a question with an interrogative pronoun to indicate a tone of conjecture. For example:

那是谁的手套呢?

道理在哪儿呢?

这个字怎么念呢?

（3）"呢" 可以用在选择式问句末尾，表示疑问语气。例如：

呢 can be used at the end of an alternative question to indicate a tone of interrogation. For example:

这种点心是甜的，还是咸的呢?

你学文学还是学艺术呢?

她喜欢红衬衫还是绿衬衫呢?

（4）"呢" 可以在名词、代词等后边构成单部问句，问"在哪儿"或"怎么样"。例如：

To ask "where" or "how", 呢 can be used after a noun or a pronoun to form a one-member question. For example:

现在我去办公室，你呢? （你去哪儿？）

马上就要出发，他呢? （他怎么还没来？）

这是她的箱子，我的呢? （我的箱子在哪儿？）

（5）"呢" 可用在陈述句末尾，表示动作或情况还在进行或持续。例如：

呢 can be used at the end of a statement to show that an action or a state is in progress or continuation. For example:

别走了，下雨呢! 小王叫你呢!

他们做实验呢!

3. "吧"

（1）"吧" 可用在陈述句末尾，表示请求、命令、商量或提议。例如：

吧 can be used at the end of a statement to express request, command, consultation or proposal. For example:

咱们一起走吧！　　　　　您再思考思考吧！

帮帮忙吧！

（2）"吧"可用在陈述句末尾，表示同意。例如：

吧 can be used at the end of a statement to show agreement.
For example:

好吧，我答应你的要求。

大家就这样干吧！

（3）"吧"可用在陈述句末尾，表示说话人对某事有估计，
但不能完全肯定。这时句末常用问号，语气比较缓和。例如：

吧 can be used at the end of a statement to indicate that
the speaker has an estimate of something but is not very
certain. There is usually a question mark at the end of
such a sentence indicating a mild tone. For example:

那个钟停了吧？　　　　　您大概忘了吧？

他们不来了吧？　　　　　这是你的吧？

4."啊"

（1）"啊"可用在陈述句末尾，表示感叹。例如：

啊 can be used at the end of a statement to show exclamation.
For example:

多糟糕啊！汽车坏了。　　　　　字写得真漂亮啊！

日子过得真快啊！

（2）"啊"可用在陈述句末尾，表示肯定、催促、嘱咐等
语气。例如：

啊 can be used at the end of a statement to indicate a
tone of certainty, urging or exhortation, etc. For example:

是啊，已经决定了。　　　　　你一定要小心啊！

快跑啊！

（3）"啊"可用在正反式问句、选择式问句或用疑问代词
的问句末尾，表示疑问。例如：

啊 can be used at the end of an affirmative + negative

question, an alternative question or a question with an interrogative pronoun to indicate interrogation. For example:

> 你表演不表演这个节目啊？
>
> 你唱歌还是跳舞啊？
>
> 你参加哪儿的联欢啊？

5. "了"

（1）"了"可用在陈述句末尾，表示出现新的情况。例如：

了 can be used at the end of a statement to show emergence of a new situation. For example:

> 春天了。 天黑了。
>
> 花开了。 现在他是国家干部了。

（2）"了"可用在陈述句末尾，表示认识、主张、想法、行动等有变化。例如：

了 can be used at the end of a statement to show a change in understanding, opinion, ideas, or action, etc. For example:

> 我明白你的意思了。
>
> 我现在还有事，不能去俱乐部了。
>
> 他可以不参加这次贸易谈判了。

（3）"了"可用在句尾，表示催促、劝告或提醒。例如：

了 can be used at the end of a sentence to express urging, advice or reminder. For example:

> 走了，走了，不能再等了。
>
> 好了，不要再说了。
>
> 别喊了，大家正在休息。
>
> 上课了，快进教室吧。
>
> 吃饭了，别写了。

（八）语气助词 "吗" 和疑问句。

The modal particle 吗 in a question.

每个语气助词都要在一定的句式里表示一定的语气。"吗" 只能用在陈述句末尾构成疑问句，而不能用在其他疑问句后边。

例如：

Each modal particle must be used in a certain kind of sentence to express a certain mood. The modal particle 吗 can only be used at the end of a statement to form a question, not after other kinds of interrogative constructions. For example:

他是裁判吗？ 或者 （or） 谁是裁判？

（不能说成"谁是裁判吗？"）

（One can not say 谁是裁判吗？）

指挥来吗？ 或者 （or） 指挥来不来？

（不能说成"指挥来不来吗？"）

（One can not say 指挥来不来吗？）

你作翻译吗？ 或者 （or）你作翻译还是他作翻译？

（不能说成"你作翻译还是他作翻译吗？"）

（One can not say 你作翻译还是他翻译吗？）

练 习 11
Exercise 11

（一）填上适当的结构助词（ "的"、"地"或"得"）。

Fill in the blanks with proper structural particles (的，地 or 得).

1. 重要____事情
2. 姑娘____理想
3. 高兴____笑
4. 说____对
5. 翻译____文章
6. 爷爷____围巾
7. 作____好
8. 明确____告诉
9. 总统____贵宾
10. 麻烦____很

（二）填上适当的语气助词。

Fill in the blanks with proper modal particles.

1. 他是护士____？

2．天气多（么）好____!

3．这支笔是谁的____?

4．好____，我一定去。

5．已经七点二十了，快走____。

6．他看电影，你____?

7．她是演员还是记者____?

8．他打太极拳不打太极拳____?

9．现在表决____。

10．我们能说服他____?

（三）把（ ）里的动态助词放在句中适当的位置上。

Put the aspectual particles in the brackets in their proper places.

1．他正喝凉开水。 （着）

2．他对大家点点头。 （了）

3．他们曾经安装这种机器。 （过）

4．她翻译一本小说。 （了）

5．昨天我买三套明信片。 （了）

6．我在朋友那儿听那支歌。 （过）

7．父亲正穿大衣。 （着）

8．孩子嘴里含糖。 （着）

9．我们村子里没发生这类事情。 （过）

10．这张画儿存在不少毛病。 （着）

第十二节 叹 词

Section XII Interjections

一、叹词的定义 Definition

表示感叹或者呼唤应答的词叫叹词。例如：

An interjection is a word which can express an exclamation, a call or a response. For example:

　　　　喂 (wèi)　嗯 (ń)　啊 (à)　哎呀 (āiyā)　噢 (ō)　哦 (ò)

二、叹词的语法特点　Grammatical features

（一）没有实在的意义，只表示一种感情或一种使人注意的声音。

No interjection has a concrete meaning. It only indicates a kind of feeling or a sound that draws attention.

（二）独立性非常强，和句子其他部分没有结构上的关系。

Interjections are quite independent and have no grammatical relationships with other parts of the sentence.

（三）一般出现在句子前边。

Interjections usually occur at the beginning of a sentence.

三、叹词的用途　Functions

（一）不充当句子成分。

They can not be used as a sentence element.

（二）独立于句子之外，表示呼唤、应答、惊讶或赞叹等。例如：

They are separated from the sentence, and indicate a call, a response, surprise or admiration, etc. For example:

　　　　喂！你是张明吗？　　（表示呼唤）
　　　　　　　　　　　　　　　(A call)

　　　　嗯！我知道了。　　　（表示答应）
　　　　　　　　　　　　　　　(A response)

　　　　哎呀，我的帽子呢？　（表示惊讶）
　　　　　　　　　　　　　　　(Indicating surprise)

　　　　啊！伟大的祖国！　　（表示赞叹）
　　　　　　　　　　　　　　　(Indicating admiration)

四、使用叹词时要注意的几个问题

Points that merit special attention

（一）每个叹词都表示一定的感情或声音，不能随便使用。

Each interjection expresses a certain feeling or imitates a certain sound, so it can not be used indiscriminately.

（二）几个叹词的用法。

Usage of some interjections.

1．"喂"表示呼唤。例如：

喂 indicates greeting. For example:

> 喂！你去哪儿啊？　　　　　喂，该起床了。
>
> 喂，快来吧。

2．"嗯、唉"表示答应。例如：

嗯，唉 indicates response. For example:

> 嗯，我懂了。　　　　唉，我来了。
>
> 嗯，您放心。　　　　唉，我马上就回来。

3．"哎呀"表示惊讶。例如：

哎呀 indicates surprise. For example:

> 哎呀！那儿有一条蛇！　　　　哎呀！太晚了！
>
> 哎呀！我的录音机坏了！

4．"啊（à）"表示赞叹。例如：

啊（à）indicates admiration. For example:

> 啊！这里的风景太好了！
>
> 啊！今年的庄稼长得真好！

5．"哦（ò）"表示领会、醒悟。例如：

哦（ò）indicates realization or awakening. For example:

> 哦，原来是这样。　　　　哦，我想起来了。
>
> 哦，我清楚了。

6．"噢、喔（ō）"表示了解。例如：

噢、喔（ō）indicates understanding. For example:

> 噢，你来了！　　　喔，是叫我啊！
>
> 噢，原来是他！

（三）同一个叹词由于声调不同，表示的感情也不同。例如：

The same interjection can express different feelings on account of its different tones. For example:

1．"欸"

（1）读"ế"时，表示招呼、提醒。例如：

When pronounced as ế, 欸 indicates a greeting or a reminder. For example:

　　欸，你到底去不去？

（2）读"é（或éi）"时，表示奇怪、惊异。例如：

When pronounced as é or éi, 欸 indicates curiosity or astonishment. For example:

　　欸，你怎么了？

（3）"读ě（或ěi）"时，表示不以为然。例如：

When pronounced as ě or ěi, 欸 inticates disapproval. For example:

　　欸，怎么能这样做呢？

（4）"读è（或èi）"时，表示同意、答应。例如：

When pronounced as è or èi, 欸 indicates agreement or response. For example:

　　欸，我听见了。

2．"啊"

（1）读ā时，表示惊异、赞叹。例如：

When pronounced as ā, 啊 indicates astonishment or admiration. For example:

　　啊，天晴了。

（2）读a时，表示追问。例如：

When pronounced as á, 啊 indicates a further inquiry. For example:

　　啊，你怎么还不走？

　　啊，你说什么啊？

（3）读 à 时，表示答应、赞叹。例如：

When pronounced as à, 啊 indicates response or admiration. For example:

啊，好吧。　　　（答应）
　　　　　　　　　（Response）

啊，太热了。　　　（赞叹）
　　　　　　　　　（Admiration）

第十三节　象声词

Section XIII　Onomatopes

一、象声词的定义　Definition

摹拟、表示物体或动作声音的词叫象声词。例如：

An onomatopoeic word is one which imitates the sound of a thing or an action.　For example:

哗哗　（流水声）
　　　（Sound of water flowing）

哈哈　（笑声）
　　　（Sound of laughter）

叮当　（金属、瓷器碰撞的声音）
　　　（Clink of metal or porcelain ware）

轰隆　（雷声、机器声、炮声）
　　　（Sound of thunder, machine or artillery）

呼呼　（刮风声）
　　　（Sound of wind）

乒乓　（枪声、打乒乓球的声音）
　　　（Sound of gun fire or a ping-pong ball）

扑通　（重物落水的声音）

(Sound of a big weight falling into water)

二、象声词的语法特点 Grammatical features

（一）没有实在意义，只表示一种声音。

No onomatope has concrete meaning, it only indicates a sound.

（二）可以修饰名词或动词。

An onomatope can modify a noun or a verb.

（三）可以和数量词连在一起用。

An onomatope can work together with numerals.

三、象声词的用途 Functions

（一）独立在句子外边。例如：

It can be separated from the sentence. For example:

哈哈，我猜对了。

哗哗，水从山上流下来。

轰隆轰隆，打雷了。

（二）作状语。 As an adverbial adjunct.

水哗哗地流着。

老人哈哈地笑了。

铃叮当叮当地响着。

（三）作定语。 As an attributive.

他扑通一声跳进了水里。

呼呼的北风吹得人真冷。

我在外边就听见乒乓的声音了。

四、使用象声词时要注意的问题

Points that merit special attention

（一）象声词作状语时一般要用助词"地"。象声词常和数量词一起作状语，后面不用"地"。例如：

When an onomatope is used as an adverbial adjunct, the particle 地 should be used. However, when an onomatope works together with a numeral, the particle 地 is not necessary.

For example:

北风呼呼地刮着。

什么东西扑通一声掉到水里去了?

（二）象声词作名词的定语时要用助词"的"，但在数量词
前一般不用"的"。例如：

When an onomatope serves as a modifier of a noun, the
particle 的 should be used. But 的 is generally unnecessary
when an onomatope procedes a numeral. For example:

外边轰隆轰隆的响声，可怕极了。

附表一：词类和句子成分的关系
Table 1: Relationships Between the Parts of Speech and the Elements of a Sentence

词类 Parts of Speech	句子成分 Sentence Elements					
	主语 S	谓语 P	宾语 O	定语 Attrib.	状语 Adv. adjunct	补语 Compl.
名词 N	✓	(✓)	✓	✓	时间词 Time words 方位词 N's of locality	
动词 V	✓	✓	✓	✓	✓	✓
助动词 Aux. V					✓	
形容词 Adj.	✓	✓	✓	✓	✓	✓
数词 Num.	✓	✓	✓	✓		
代词 Pron. 人称代词 Personal	✓		✓	✓		\
代词 Pron. 指示代词 Demonstrative	✓		✓	✓	✓	
代词 Pron. 疑问代词 Interrog. Pron.	✓	(✓)	✓	✓	✓	(✓)
副词 Adv.					✓	(✓)
介词 Prep.					(✓)	

"✓"表示该词类可以充当某种句子成分。

"✓" indicates that the word can serve as a certain element of the sentence.

"(✓)"表示个别词可以充当某种句子成分。

"(✓)" indicates that only one or two words can serve as a certain element of the sentence.

第三章　词　组

Chapter Three　Phrases

一、词组　Phrases

句子是由词和词组构成的。词组是词和词按照一定的语法关系组合起来的一组词。词组的作用跟词一样,可以充当句子成分。有些词组也可以自己形成句子。"词组"也可以叫作"结构"。

A sentence is composed of words and phrases. Phrases are combinations of grammatically related words, and like words, function as sentence elements. Some phrases can also stand alone as a sentence. Phrases are sometimes called constructions.

二、词组的种类　Classification of phrases

汉语里有很多种词组,常见的有以下十一种:

There are a variety of phrases in Chinese, of which the following 11 are the commonly used ones:

1. 联合词组

The coordinative phrase

2. 主谓词组

The subject-predicate (S-P) phrase

3. 动宾词组

The verb-object (V-O) phrase

4. 偏正词组

The endocentric phrase

5．数量词组

The numeral-measure phrase

6．补充词组

The complementary phrase word (N-Mw) phrase

7．方位词组

The locality phrase

8．同位词组

The appositive phrase

9．固定词组

The set phrase

10．介词结构

The prepositional phrase

11．"的"字结构

The 的 -phrase

三、词组分类的依据　The basis for classifying phrases

我们可以从以下几个方面来区别不同词组的特点：

We distinguish the various phrases according to the following features:

1．词组是由什么词类充当的，以及表达什么样的语法关系和意义。

In terms of the parts of speech, grammatical relations and meanings of their constituents.

2．词组内部的词序是否固定。

In terms of whether their constituents are arranged in a fixed order.

3．词和词之间用不用虚词以及用什么虚词连接。

In terms of the ways in which their constituents are connected, ie. whether conjunctions are employed and if so what kind of conjunctions.

4．词组前后能否带其他成分以及能带什么样的成分。

In terms of whether the phrase can be preceded or followed by other elements and of what kind these elements are.

下面分节介绍各种词组的构成和用途。

The formations and functions of the various kinds of phrases are introduced respectively in the following sections.

第一节 联 合 词 组
Section I The Coordinative Phrase

一、联合词组的定义 Definition

联合词组一般是由同类的两个或两个以上的词组合起来表示并列关系的一组词。例如:

A coordinative phrase is one formed by two or more words of the same part of speech in coordinative relation. For example:

老师学生　　　("老师"、"学生" 都是名词)
　　　　　　　(Both 老师 and 学生 are nouns.)

他和我　　　　("他"、"我" 都是代词)
　　　　　　　(Both 他 and 我 are pronouns.)

参观访问　　　("参观"、"访问" 都是动词)
　　　　　　　(Both 参观 and 访问 are verbs.)

积极努力　　　("积极"、"努力" 都是形容词)
　　　　　　　(Both 积极 and 努力 are adjectives.)

耐心地温和地　("耐心"、"温和" 都是形容词)
　　　　　　　(Both 耐心 and 温和 are adjectives.)

二、联合词组的语法特点 Grammatical features

（一）联合词组里词和词的次序一般可以调换,不影响意思。

The order of the two constituents is not fixed. Reversion

155

of the order does not affect the meaning.

（二）联合词组一般由名词、代词、动词或形容词构成。

A coordinative phrase is usually composed of nouns, pronouns, verbs or adjectives.

（三）联合词组里词和词之间可以用虚词连接。例如：

The constituents can be connected by a conjunction. For example:

笔和纸	上午或者下午
你们和他们	光荣而伟大
参观并讨论	又高又瘦

（四）联合词组前边可以带修饰成分。

It can take a premodifier.

（五）动词性联合词组后边可以带宾语、补语或动态助词。

A verbal coordinative phrase can be followed by an object, a complement or an aspectual particle.

三、联合词组的用途 Functions

（一）作主语。

As the subject.

被子、褥子都在这儿。

工人农民都是体力劳动者。

苏州、杭州都是中国有名的旅游城市。

他们和我们都学习汉语。

滑冰和游泳都是很有意义的体育运动。

勤劳勇敢是我国人民的优良品质。

（二）作谓语。

As the predicate.

他也要恋爱结婚。	这个电影真实、有意思。
大家又唱又跳。	孩子们真活泼可爱。
大家很同情和关心他们。	这间屋子高而且大。

（三）作宾语。

As the object.

> 这里有许多松树和柏树。
>
> 我找你和张文。
>
> 副总理下午接待外国大使和专家。
>
> 他们经常得到朋友们的支持和援助。
>
> 感谢你们的欢迎和接待。
>
> 那个城市的特点是清洁、美丽。

（四）作定语。

As an attributive.

> 父亲母亲的工作都很忙。
>
> 你和他的球票在我这儿。
>
> 她有一对大而亮的眼睛。
>
> 他是一个聪明诚实的人。
>
> 宴会充满了亲切友好的气氛。
>
> 吃和喝的东西都有。

（五）作状语。

As an adverbial adjunct.

> 每天他们都紧张、愉快地工作。
>
> 那个小孩天真、顽皮地跑着。
>
> 她又严肃又柔和地说。
>
> 他又感激又信任地看着我。
>
> 弟弟又蹦又跳地过来了。
>
> 我放心满意地走了。

（六）作补语。

As a complement.

> 他画得真实生动。
>
> 汉字他写得清楚、好看。
>
> 这张桌子做得又笨又重。
>
> 这个房间，他布置得又整齐又好看。
>
> 这几个菜，她做得又好看又好吃。

她织毛衣织得快而且好。

四、使用联合词组时需要注意的问题

Points that merit special attention

（一）联合词组和句子成分。

The coordinative phrase and sentence elements.

1. 联合词组可以直接充当句子成分，本身没有特别标记。

A coordinative phrase can serve as a sentence element without any particular marker.

2. 联合词组是由哪类词构成的，就具有哪类词的某些特点和用途，可以叫作哪类词性的联合词组。

A coordinative phrase is characterized and functions according to its constituents, therefore we can name a coordinative phrase after the names of its constituents' parts of speech.

（1）各类实词构成的联合词组都可以作主语、宾语和定语。例如：

The notional coordinative phrase can function as subject, object or attributive. For example:

煤和石油都是燃料。

（名词性联合词组作主语）

(A nominal coordinative phrase as the subject)

我喜欢猫和狗。

（名词性联合词组作宾语）

(A nominal coordinative phrase as the object)

她是一个又聪明又漂亮的姑娘。

（形容词性联合词组作定语）

(An adjectival coordinative phrase as the attributive)

（2）动词性和形容词性的联合词组还可以作谓语和状语。例如：

Verbal and adjectival coordinative phrases can also function

158

as predicate or adverbial adjunct. For example:

大家又鼓掌又欢呼。

（动词性联合词组作谓语）

（A verbal coordinative phrase as the predicate）

我悲痛而遗憾地离开了那儿。

（形容词性联合词组作状语）

（An adjectival coordinative phrase as an adverbial adjunct.)

（3）只有形容词性联合词组能作补语，而且只能作程度补语。例如：

The adjectival coordinative phrase is the only one among the various phrases that can serve as the complement of degree. For example:

他介绍得简单、全面。

我们谈得又亲切又热烈。

（二）联合词组和结构助词。

The coordinative phrase and structural particles.

1. 联合词组作定语时，要用助词"的"。例如：

When a coordinative phrase functions as the attributive, the structural particle 的 should be used. For example:

我和他的友谊很深。

听和说的能力都应该提高。

2. 动词性或形容词性的联合词组作状语时,要用助词"地"。例如：

When a verbal or adjectival coordinative phrase serves as an adverbial adjunct the structural particle 地 should be used. For example:

我羡慕、钦佩地看着他。

他迅速而细心地检查机器。

有时联合词组内两个形容词后边各带一个助词"地"。例如：

In some cases, each of the adjectives is followed by 地.
For example:

　　　　他们强烈地愤怒地抗议这种残酷行动。

　　　　那个病人吃力地痛苦地躺在病床上。

　　3．形容词性联合词组作补语时，联合词组与中心语之间一定要用助词"得"。例如：

When the adjectival coordinative phrase is used as the complement (of degree), the structural particle 得 should be used. For example:

　　　　我们完成得又快又好。

　　　　他跑得又累又渴。

　　（三）不用虚词连接的联合词组常用顿号"、"表示词和词之间联合关系。例如：

The pause mark (、) can be substituted for the conjunction to express the coordination of the constituents of a coordinative phrase. For example:

　　　　伯父、伯母都很爱我。

　　　　我们下午复习、预习。

　　　　他热情、友好地向我们招手。

　　（四）三个或三个以上的词联合时，连词用在最后一个词前边。例如：

When there are three or more constituents in the coordinative phrase, the conjunction precedes the last one. For example:

　　　　哥哥、姐姐和我都在北京上学。

　　　　桌子上有笔、墨水、纸和尺。

　　（五）一般来说，联合词组中两个词的前后次序改变后意思不变；但有些词组根据意义或习惯说法，词序比较固定。例如：

Generally speaking, the order of the two constituents is reversible, but if the phrase is an idiomatic expression or one where the reversion is not permitted in terms of meaning, the order is fixed. For example:

桌子椅子　（很少说 "椅子桌子"）
(One seldom says 椅子桌子)

爸爸妈妈　（很少说 "妈妈爸爸）
(One seldom says 妈妈爸爸)

讨论并修改（指先讨论后修改）
(Discussion usually precedes revision.)

（六）联合词组前边有定语时，定语后边要用结构助词 "的"。例如：

The structural particle 的 must be used after the premodifying attributive of a coordinative phrase. For example:

这个孩子的父亲母亲都是国家干部。

我的老师和同学都在这儿。

他穿着黑色的上衣和裤子。

这是讨论的题目和文章。

（七）形容词性联合词组前边有状语时，状语后边不用助词 "地"。例如：

The structural particle 地 is not used after the premodifying adverbial adjunct of an adjectival coordinative phrase. For example:

他十分勇敢、坚定。

我实在又饿又困。

（八）动词性联合词组后边可以带一个宾语。例如：

A verbal coordinative phrase can take an object after it. For example:

我们下午收拾布置那个房间。

如果联合词组后边还有动态助词 "了"，宾语要放在 "了" 后边。例如：

The object follows the aspectual particle 了 which is

suffixed to the coordinative phrase. For example:

我们已经收拾布置了那个房间。

动词性联合词组后边还可以带各种补语。例如：

A verbal coordinative phrase can also be followed by a complement of any kind. For example:

他们已经收拾布置好了那个房间。

（结果补语）

(Complement of result)

他们收拾布置得很好。

（程度补语，用"得"）

(Complement of degree with 得)

我们讨论修改了两次。

（数量补语）

(Complement of frequency)

练 习 12
Exercise 12

（一）标出联合词组中实词的词类。

Mark the notional constituents in the following phrases and give their parts of speech.

1. 风雨	2. 老大爷和小孙子
3. 关心和照顾	4. 好而便宜
5. 物理化学	6. 过去、现在和将来
7. 短而粗	8. 继承并发扬
9. 启发教育	10. 规章制度
11. 姓名年龄	12. 先进和落后
13. 我和他们	14. 雷电
15. 又长又细	16. 他们跟咱们

17. 爷爷奶奶   18. 称赞并奖励

（二）标出句中的联合词组，并填上适当的结构助词（"的"、
　　　"地" 或 "得" ）。

Mark the coordinative phrases in the following sentences
and fill in each blank with an appropriate structural particle
(的，地 or 得).

　　1. 七月、八月＿＿天气比较热。
　　2. 他们要研究棉花和花生＿＿生长规律。
　　3. 他能正确而流利＿＿说汉语。
　　4. 他们安排＿＿又舒服又周到。
　　5. 他又安静又慈祥＿＿睡了。
　　6. 我简单而明确＿＿答复了他。
　　7. 我们有成功和失败＿＿经验。
　　8. 她穿＿＿又朴素又好看。
　　9. 我们要提高听和说＿＿能力。
　　10. 那棵树长＿＿又高又大。

第二节　主　谓　词　组

Section II The Subject-Predicate Phrase

一、主谓词组的定义 Definition

　　按照陈述和被陈述的关系组合起来的一组词，叫主谓词组。
例如：

A subject-predicate (S-P) phrase is one in which the constituents are combined in the S-P relation. For example:

　　　　　　头发长（"头发"是"主"，"长"是"谓"）

　　　　　　　　（头发 is the subject and 长 the predicate.）

　　　　　　他描写（"他"是"主"，"描写"是"谓"）

(他 is the subject and 描写 the predicate.)

二、主谓词组的语法特点 Grammatical features

（一）主谓词组的词序是固定的，前边是"主"，后边是"谓"。

The order of the two constituents is fixed with the subject preceding the predicate.

（二）前边是"主"，是被陈述的对象，经常由名词、代词充当；后边的是"谓"，是陈述"主"的，常由动词、形容词充当。例如：

The first constituent of a S-P phrase is usually a noun or pronoun serving as a topic or the subject, and the second one, usually a verb or an adjective, is the predicate describing the subject. For example:

　　　　　我看　（"我"是代词，是"主"；"看"是动词，是"谓"）

　　　　　　　　（The pronoun 我 is the subject and 看, a verb, the predicate.)

　　　　　目的明确（"目的"是名词,是"主"；"明确"是形容词，是"谓"）

　　　　　　　　（The noun 目的 is the subject and 明确, an adjective, the predicate.)

（三）两个词之间不用任何虚词连接。

No function word whatsoever is used between the two constituents.

（四）主谓词组的重音一般在后一个词上。

The second constituent is normally stressed in pronunciation.

三、主谓词组的用途 Functions

（一）作主语。

As the subject.

张教授来太好了。　　　　　　理论联系实际很重要。

他这样做不对。

（二）作谓语。

As the predicate.

　　他头疼。　　　　　　　　　电影票我买两张。

　　他手指破了。

（三）作宾语。

As the object.

　　我希望你成功。　　　　　　我知道他已经出发了。

　　我相信我们还会见面。

（四）作定语。

As an attributive.

　　留学生住的地方在那边。　　这是我们游览的日程。

　　您提的意见很正确。

（五）作状语。

As an adverbial adjunct.

　　妈妈心疼地看着女儿。

　　他态度激昂地表示反对。

（六）作补语。

As a complement.

　　他说得大家全笑了。　　　　他热得脸都红了。

　　我笑得肚子都疼了。

四、使用主谓词组时需要注意的问题

Points that merit special attention

（一）主谓词组的词序不能颠倒，否则结构和意思就都变了。例如"他描写"是表示"他"进行"描写"这个动作，"描写"的对象可以是人、事物或风景等；如果颠倒成"描写他"，就变成了动宾关系，表示"描写"的对象是"他"。

The order of the two constituents in a S-P phrase cannot be reversed, for the reversion of order will bring about a change

both in structure and in meaning. For example, the phrase
他描写 means "he describes". The object of the verb 描写
may be a person, thing or scene. If we put it as 描写他, the
phrase will turn to one of a V-O relationship, meaning "to
describe him".

（二）主谓词组可以直接充当主语、宾语或定语等句子成
分，不需要用代词连接。例如：

A S-P phrase can function as subject, object or attributive without being introduced by a pronoun. For
example:

<blockquote>

天气热是这里的特点。　　（作主语）

(As the subject)

气温下降会影响农业生产。

他说他不会。　　（作宾语）

(As the object)

我怕资料太少。

这是他写的小说。　　（作定语）

(As an attributive)

我们搜集的资料很充分。

</blockquote>

（三）主谓词组和结构助词。

A S-P phrase and structural particles.

1. 主谓词组作定语时一定要用助词"的"。例如：

The structural particle 的 must be used after a S-P
phrase which serves as an attributive. For example:

<blockquote>

他看的小说是中文的。

他补充的意见太宝贵了。

</blockquote>

如果不用"的"，结构和意思就变了。如第一句中"小说"
是中心语，如果说成"他看小说"，"小说"就成了"看"的宾
语，这句话就不通了。

Without 的, both the meaning and structure of the phrase

will be changed. For instance, if, instead of 他看的小说, as in the first sentence above, in which 小说 is the modified word, we say 他看小说, with 的 after 看 omitted, 小说 will become the object of 看 and the whole sentence will be grammatically unsound.

2. 主谓词组作状词时一定要用助词"地"。例如：

When a S-P phrase serves as an adverbial adjunct, the structural particle 地 must be used after it. For example:

> 我们精神饱满地工作着。

> 同学们意见一致地鼓了鼓掌。

3. 主谓词组作补语时一定要用助词"得"。例如：

When a S-P phrase serves as a complement, the structural particle 得 must be used before it. For example:

> 他笑得嘴都合不上了。

> 太阳晒得地都热了。

（四）主谓词组作谓语时要具备一定的条件。

Only under the following conditions, can a S-P phrase serve as the predicate of a sentence.

1. 主谓词组中的"主"和全句主语一般有领属关系，后者常是属于前者的。例如：

The subject in a S-P·phrase is related to the subject of the whole sentence with the latter as a part of the former. For example:

> 他们工厂生产自动化了。　我身体很健康。

> 那儿树砍了。　　　　　　那姑娘头发真黑。

如果在全句主语和主谓词组的"主"之间加上结构助词"的"，就变成定语和中心语的关系了，意思也有些变化。

The subject of the sentence will become the attributive of the (S-P) phrase subject if the structural particle 的 is inserted between them and the meaning of the sentence will change slightly.

2. 主谓词组中动词可带宾语，这宾语是全句主语的一部分。例如：

The predicate verb in a S-P phrase can have an object indicating a thing which is a part of what is indicated by the subject of the sentence. For example:

  衬衫他买了两件。

  牛奶我喝了一杯。

（五）主谓词组只能在有限的一些动词后边充当宾语。例如：

Only a very limited number of verbs can take a S-P phrase as its object. For example:

  我盼望他今天就来。

  他相信这件事是真的。

（六）主谓词组只能作程度补语，不能作其他补语。例如：

A S-P phrase can only function as a complement of degree. For example:

  他笑得眼泪都流下来了。

  屋子里热得人很不舒服。

练 习 13
Exercise 13

（一）标出下列主谓词组中的词和词类。

Break up the following S-P phrases into words and give their parts of speech.

  1. 变化小   2. 老虎叫

  3. 颜色深   4. 命令取消

  5. 技术交流 6. 路窄

168

7. 记者报道　　8. 距离大

9. 他设计　　10. 我们反对

11. 心好　　12. 座位远

13. 答案正确　　14. 这里安静

15. 情绪稳定　　16. 衣服薄

17. 关系密切　　18. 效果怎么样

19. 基础好　　20. 皮肤白

（二）标出句中的主谓词组。

Mark the S-P phrases in the following sentences.

1. 我怕外边冷。

2. 他讨厌猫叫。

3. 我觉得他很糊涂。

4. 他反对没关系。

5. 阳光充足对孩子很有好处。

6. 身体健康可以提高工作效率。

（三）标出句中主谓词组，并填上适当的结构助词（的、地、得）。

Mark the S-P phrases in the following sentences and fill in each blank with the appropriate structural particle (的，地 or 得).

1. 我们爬____山叫万寿山。

2. 他态度坚决____表示反对。

3. 他急____满头大汗。

4. 学校邀请____专家来了。

5. 暖水瓶里是我们刚打____开水。

6. 我心急____找着。

7. 他们都是我请____客人。

8. 他语气柔和____给我们解释。

9. 家乡变____我都快不认识了。

10. 他意志坚强____克服了许多困难。

第三节 动宾词组

Section III The Verb-Object Phrase

一、动宾词组的定义 Definition

按照支配和被支配的关系组合起来的一组词，叫动宾词组。例如：

A verb-object (V-O) phrase is one in which the constituents are combined in the V-O relation. For example:

吃饭 （ "吃" 是动词； "饭" 是名词，是宾语 ）
(吃 is a verb and 饭 a noun functioning as the object.)

写汉字 （ "写" 是动词； "汉字" 是名词，是宾语 ）
(写 is a verb and 汉字 a noun serving as the object.)

二、动宾词组的语法特点 Grammatical features

（一）动宾词组的词序是固定的，动词一定在前边。

The order of constituents of a V-O phrase is fixed: the verb precedes the object.

（二）前一个词是及物动词，表示动作、行为；后一个词是表示受前边动作行为的影响或支配的人或事物。

The first constituent of a V-O phrase is a transitive verb indicating an action or behavior, while the second refers to the person or thing affected by the action.

（三）动词后边直接带宾语，中间不需要用虚词。

No function word is used between the verb and its object.

（四）动宾词组的重音一般在后一个词上。

Normally the stress of a V-O phrase falls on the second

constituent in pronunciation.

（五）动宾词组中动词后边可以带动态助词或补语。

An aspectual particle or complement can be used after the verb of a V-O phrase.

三、动宾词组的用途　Functions

（一）作主语。

As the subject.

　　　　学习汉语要注意方法。　　听音乐是一种休息。

　　　　检查质量很重要。

（二）作宾语。

As the object.

　　　　她喜欢学习汉语。　　　　他最爱爬山。

　　　　我的任务是检查质量。

（三）作定语。

As an attributive.

　　　　她要订一个学习汉语的计划。

　　　　他有检查质量的经验。

　　　　学过汉语的人都认识这个字。

（四）作状语。

As an adverbial adjunct.

　　　　大家充满信心地迎接新的战斗。

　　　　他没有目的地走着。

　　　　他低着头走路。

（五）作补语。

As a complement.

　　　　他冷得发抖。

　　　　他感动得说不出话。

四、使用动宾词组时需要注意的问题

Points that merit special attention

（一）动宾词组的词序不能颠倒，否则结构和意思就变了，有时甚至是错误的。例如"吃鸡"，一般是指人或其他动物"吃"的对象是"鸡"；如果说成"鸡吃"就变成了主谓关系，指"鸡""吃"别的东西。如果把动宾词组"吃饭"的词序颠倒为"饭吃"，那就不成话了。

The order of the constituents in a V-O phrase cannot be changed, for the change of order will lead to the change of structure and meaning or even make the phrase logically or grammatically unsound. For instance, 吃鸡 means "to eat chicken", but if we put it as 鸡吃, the meaning of the phrase becomes "a chicken eats" and it is in an S-P relation. If we change the order of 吃饭 to 饭吃, it becomes meaningless.

（二）动宾词组可以直接充当主语、宾语或定语等句子成分，不需要用代词或介词等表示。例如：

A V-O phrase can serve as a subject, object or attributive, etc. without the indication of any pronoun or preposition. For example:

> 访问中国是我的愿望。　　（作主语）
> (As the subject)
> 我希望访问中国。　　　　（作宾语）
> (As the object)
> 我有一个访问中国的计划。（作定语）
> (As the attributive)

（三）动宾词组和结构助词。

The V-O phrase and structural particles.

1. 动宾词组作定语时一定要用助词"的"。例如：

The structural particle 的 must be used when a V-O phrase serves as an attributive. For example:

> 开会的人都到了。
> 外边都是打听消息的人。

2. 动宾词组作补语时一定要用助词"得"。例如：

The structural particle 得 has to be used when a V-O phrase serves as a complement.   For example:

　　大家高兴得跳起舞来了。

　　他困得睁不开眼。

（四）动宾词组常作状语表示动作的方式。例如：

V-O phrases are often used as adverbial adjuncts indicating manner of action.   For example:

　　她晒着太阳织毛衣。

　　父亲戴着眼镜看报。

（五）动宾词组作定语或状语时，动词后边有时带动态助词。例如：

An aspectual particle is sometimes used after the verb in a V-O phrase which functions as an attributive or an adverbial adjunct.   For example:

　　看过这本小说的人很多。　　他抬着头看墙上的画。

　　这是一件变了颜色的衣服。　　我点了点头说："好吧。"

（六）动宾词组"有一点儿"。

The V-O phrase 有一点儿.

　　"有一点儿"可以在形容词（或某些动词）前边作状语，表示轻微的程度，多指不太如意的事。例如：

有一点儿 serves as an adverbial adjunct before adjectives (or certain verbs), showing sth. slightly dissatisfying.   For example:

　　昨天有一点儿冷。　　　　　他有一点儿发烧。

　　老师有一点儿不舒服。

　　这几句中的"有一点儿"都不能说成"一点儿"。"一点儿"只能用在名词前边作定语，或者用在形容词后边作补语。例如：

有 in 有一点儿 in the above examples can not be omitted, since 一点儿 can only be used attributively before nouns, or as a complement after adjectives. For example:

我想买一点儿东西。（"一点儿"作定语）

快一点儿，车来了。（"一点儿"作补语）

练　习　14
Exercise　14

（一）标出下列动宾词组的宾语，并指出宾语的词类。

Mark the objects of the following V-O phrases and state what part of speech each object is.

1. 找谁	2. 有差别
3. 感到为难	4. 睡觉
5. 记日记	6. 进行辩论
7. 接受批评	8. 谈话
9. 骑马	10. 开始表演
11. 掌握语法	12. 逛商场
13. 尊敬老人	14. 说服大家
15. 希望参观	16. 游览长城
17. 善于学习	18. 出汗
19. 接见我们	20. 保持安静

（二）标出句中的动宾词组，并指出作什么句子成分。

Mark the V-O phrases in the following sentences, and state what sentence elements they function as.

1. 买机床的人真多。

2. 他喜欢吃中国饭。

3. 缺乏经验是一件遗憾的事。

4. 他伤心得流眼泪了。

5. 我同意个别交换意见的办法。

6. 参加晚会的人很多。

7. 现在开始表演节目。

8. 他谈得符合实际。

9. 我用左手写字。

10. 大家喝着茶谈话。

11. 老师有计划地安排了这次活动。

12. 锻炼身体十分重要。

13. 完成任务的人已经走了。

14. 他做得符合标准。

15. 她含着眼泪送我们。

（三）填上"有一点（儿）"或者"一点（儿）"。

Fill in the blanks with 有一点（儿） or 一点（儿）.

1. 我要买_____水果。

2. 地上有_____水。

3. 我今天_____疲倦。

4. 屋子里_____热。

5. 我想延长_____时间。

6. 这个菜_____辣。

7. 昨天我喝了_____酒。

8. 他最近_____悲观。

9. 他需要_____帮助。

10. 我_____后悔。

第四节 偏正词组

Section IV The Endocentric Phrase

一、偏正词组的定义 Definition

按照修饰、限制和被修饰、限制的关系组合起来的一组词，叫偏正词组。

An endocentric phrase is one in which the constituents are combined go that the first one modifies the second.

偏正词组一般可分为两类：

An endocentric phrase can be divided into two types:

（一）名词性偏正词组，也就是后一部分由名词充当的偏正词组。例如：

The nominal endocentric phrase, in which the second constituent is a noun. For example:

> 沙漠地带（"沙漠"是"偏"，是定语；"地带"是"正"，是中心语）
>
> > (沙漠 is the premodifying attributive of the noun 地带, which is the modified word.)
>
> 劳动人民（"劳动"是"偏"，是定语；"人民"是"正"，是中心语）
>
> > (劳动 is the premodifying attributive of the noun 人民, which is the modified word.)

（二）动词性偏正词组和形容词性偏正词组，也就是后一部分为动词或形容词的偏正词组。例如：

Verbal and adjectival endocentric phrases, in which the second constituent is a verb or an adjective respectively. For example:

> 详细解释（"详细"是"偏"，是状语；"解释"是"正"，是中心语）
>
> > (详细 is the premodifying adverbial adjunct of the modified word 解释.)
>
> 很结实　（"很"是"偏"，是状语；"结实"是"正"，是中心语）
>
> > (很 is the premodifying adverbial adjunct of the modified word 结实.)

二、偏正词组的语法特点　Grammatical features

（一）偏正词组的词序是固定的。前边是"偏"，后边是"正"。前一部分是修饰、限制后一部分的。例如：

The order of the two constituents in an endocentric phrase is fixed: the modifying word precedes the modified word. For example:

一本书	会做
两个小时	多么繁荣
他叔叔	高兴地说
用的东西	不缺
可怜的人	多听多说
蓝蓝的天空	非常乐观

（二）偏正词组的后一部分由名词、动词或形容词构成，前一部分可由各类修饰成分充当。

The second constituent of an endocentric phrase is either a noun, a verb or an adjective while the first one can be a premodifier of any kind.

（三）偏正词组中"偏"和"正"之间有时要用虚词连接。例如：

Sometimes, a function word is used to connect the two constituents. For example:

安静的环境	严肃地宣布
他的声音	客观地分析

（四）偏正词组的重音常在前边的修饰部分上。

The stress of an endocentric phrase falls on the first constituent in pronunciation.

三、偏正词组的用途　Functions

（一）作主语。

As the subject.

　　　　严格要求是做好工作的重要条件。

　　　　认真分析十分必要。

（二）作谓语。

As the predicate.

  那天大风天。

  林先生北京人。

（三）作宾语。

As the object.

  我觉得很合适。

  他怕太晚。

（四）作定语。

As an attributive.

  那件球衣的颜色很漂亮。

  很多运动员的衣服都湿了。

  运动员都有一个很结实的身体。

  刚走的那个同志是谁？

（五）作状语。

As an adverbial adjunct.

  八月的一天，我和朋友去公园了。

  一天晚上，我忽然感到不舒服。

  他很诚恳地谈了自己的看法。

  他十分关心地问了每个人的情况。

（六）作补语。

As a complement.

  他们观察了三个小时。

  他们讨论得很热烈。

  这块绸子你买得真便宜。

四、使用偏正词组时需要注意的问题

Points that merit special attention

（一）偏正词组的词序不能颠倒。汉语里的修饰成分（定语和状语）永远在被修饰成分（中心语）的前边；否则结构和意思就变了，有时甚至是错误的。例如：

The order of the two constituents in an endocentric

phrase can not be reversed, since, in the Chinese language modifiers (attributive and adverbial) are always placed before the modified words. The reversion of order will lead to a change both in structure and in meaning, or even make the phrase logically or grammatically unsound. For example:

他哥哥　　　　我的书

劳动人民　　　很高兴

严格要求

"他哥哥"是指"他"的"哥哥"，不是别人的哥哥，如果说成"哥哥他"，结构就变成同位关系，意思也变为指"哥哥"自己了，这里的"他"就是"哥哥"。

他哥哥, meaning "his elder brother", can not be changed into 哥哥他, which is in the appositive relation, meaning "he who is my elder brother".

"劳动人民"是指"靠劳动生活的人"。如果说成"人民劳动"，就变成主谓词组，表示"人民"在"劳动"了。

劳动人民 means "working people", while 人民劳动, a S-P phrase, means "people work".

"严格要求"如果说成"要求严格"，就变成主谓词组了。

The endocentric phrase 严格要求 if changed into 要求严格, will become a S-P phrase.

而"我的书"和"很高兴"，如果说成"书的我"和"高兴很"就完全不成话。另如"北京人"、"吃的东西"、"马上去"和"公开号召"等也绝不能倒过来说。

If we change 我的书 into 书的我 or 很高兴 into 高兴很, they will become grammatically unsound. Similarly, we can not change the order of the two constituents in 北京人, 吃的东西, 马上去, 公开号召, etc.

（二）有的偏正词组可以直接充当主语、宾语和谓语，不需要任何标记。例如：

Some endocentric phrase can be used as the subject, object or predicate without any particular marker. For example:

> 经常锻炼有好处。
>
> （动词性偏正词组，作主语）
>
> (A verbal endocentric phrase as the subject.)
>
> 我觉得很累。
>
> （形容词性偏正词组，作宾语）
>
> (An adjectival endocentric phrase as the object.)
>
> 这个孩子五岁。
>
> （名词性偏正词组，作谓语）
>
> (A nominal endocentric phrase as the predicate.)

（三）偏正词组作定语和结构助词"的"。

The attributive endocentric phrase and the structural particle 的.

1． 偏正词组作定语，一般都要用助词"的"。例如：

When an endocentric phrase is used attributively, the structural particle 的 is usually used after it. For example:

> 这是他弟弟的排球。
>
> 刚买的花瓶是白色的。
>
> 这是一个最好的游泳池。
>
> 他发明了一种非常科学的方法。

2． 形容词性偏正词组"很多"、"不少"作定语时，一般不用助词"的"。例如：

When the adjectival endocentric phrases 很多 and 不少 are used as the attributive, the structural particle 的 is not usually used. For example:

> 星期天很多同学去游览长城。
>
> 不少书没买到。

（四）偏正词组作状语和结构助词"地"。

The adverbial endocentric phrase and the structural

particle 地.

1. 名词性偏正词组作状语，常表示时间、处所，后面不用助词"地"。例如：

The structural particle 地 is not used with a nominal endocentric phrase serving as an adverbial adjunct of time or place. For example:

　　　　他两个上午就翻译完那篇文章了。

　　　　你们屋里坐。

2. 动词性或形容词性的偏正词组作状词时，一定要用助词"地"。例如：

The structural particle 地 must be used after a verbal or adjectival endocentric phrase functioning as an adverbial adjunct. For example:

　　　　他很耐心地帮助我。

　　　　他不满意地走了。

　　　　大家十分吃惊地听着。

　　　　她非常坚决地说："我不去！"

　　　　她很自然地笑了笑。

（五）偏正词组前边还可以有修饰成分。例如：

The endocentric phrase can be qualified by modifiers. For example:

　　　　他有一件深灰色的大衣。　他说得的确十分有意思。

　　　　他的那本书丢了。　　　　那张画挂得实在太高。

练　习　15
Exercise　15

标出下列偏正词组里的修饰成分。

Underline the modifying constituent in each of the

following endocentric phrases.

1.	大河	2.	这只黑熊
3.	后天去	4.	三个月
5.	儿童时期	6.	及时处理
7.	很主观	8.	外交关系
9.	狡猾的狐狸	10.	临时决定
11.	绿叶	12.	很多动物
13.	山洞	14.	真奇怪
15.	熟练工人	16.	祖国的山河
17.	公开宣布	18.	白鸽子
19.	突然发现	20.	那些评论
21.	圆镜子	22.	个别解决
23.	必要的研究	24.	关键问题
25.	十分为难	26.	怎么办
27.	非常全面	28.	一切希望
29.	全国人民	30.	村子的东边

第五节　数　量　词　组

Section V　The Numeral-Measure Word Phrase

一，**数量词组的定义**　Definition

由数词和量词组合而成的一组词，叫数量词组。

A phrase which is the combination of a numeral and a measure word is called a numeral-measure word (N-Mw) phrase.

数量词组一般可分为两类：

There are two kinds:

（一）由数词和名量词构成的。例如：

That consisting of a numeral and a nominal measure

word. For example:

　　　　一张　　（"一"是数词，"张"是名量词）

　　　　　　　　(一 is a numeral and 张 a nominal measure
　　　　　　　　word.)

　　　　三支　　（"三"是数词，"支"是名量词）

　　　　　　　　(三 is a numeral and 支 a nominal measure
　　　　　　　　word.)

　　　　五个　　七本　　两公斤　　六块

　　　　九盒　　一只　　五米　　十二点

（二）由数词和动量词构成的。例如：

That consisting of a numeral and a verbal measure word.
For example:

　　　　两趟　　（"两"是数词，"趟"是动量词）

　　　　　　　　(两 is a numeral and 趟 a verbal measure
　　　　　　　　word.)

　　　　一次　　（"一"是数词，"次"是动量词）

　　　　　　　　(一 is a numeral and 次 a verbal measure word.)

　　　　一顿　　两遍　　四回　　五下儿

二、数量词组的语法特点　Grammatical features

（一）数词总在量词前边，起限制作用。

In the N-Mw phrase the qualifying numeral always
precedes the measure word.

（二）数词和量词之间不需要用任何虚词连接。

No function word is used between the numeral and the
measure word in an N-Mw phrase.

（三）数量词组一般可以重叠。

An N-Mw phrase can be reduplicated when necessary.

（四）数量词组的重音一般在前边的数词上。

The stress of an N-Mw phrase normally falls on the
numeral in pronunciation.

（五）数量词组前边可有修饰成分。

An N-Mw phrase can take a modifier before it.

三、数量词组的用途　Functions

（一）作定语。

As an attributive.

一间屋子里住两个人。

这是三本地图。

他家有两辆汽车。

我买一筒牙膏、一双筷子、一根绳子。

我们每天吃三顿饭。

一阵风把窗户吹开了。

一场电影需要一个半小时。

（二）作补语。

As a complement.

今天他来了两趟。　　　他比我大一些。

我念三遍。　　　　　　那件衣服长一点儿。

我跟他说一下儿。

（三）作状语。

As an adverbial adjunct.

他们八点出发。　　　　他一顿吃两个面包。

我一次只能拿十本。　　我一遍记不住。

（四）作主语。

As the subject.

一公斤等于一千克。　　三公斤太多。

一米就是一百厘米。　　两毛（五）一个。

（五）作宾语。

As the object.

那种钢笔，我有一支。

那些花瓶真好看，我要买两对。

一年有三百六十五天。

（六）作谓语。

As the predicate.

这个本子三毛。

今天三十一号。

四、使用数量词组时需要注意的问题

Points that merits special attention

（一）数量词组的词序是固定的。数词一定要用在量词前边，不能颠倒。例如：

The order of the two constituents in an N-Mw phrase is fixed: the numeral always precedes the measure word. This order can not be reversed. For example:

一个	三本	两支	三张
五块	一种	八条	十米
一次	三回	五遍	两趟

绝不能颠倒次序说成"个一、本三、支两、次一"等。

Under no circumstances can one put them in the reverse order as 个一，本三，支两，次一， etc.

数量词组一定要用在名词前边作修饰成分。例如：

An N-Mw phrase acting as a modifier always comes before a noun. For example:

一个人	三本书
两支笔	三张床

只有在统计时才说"书十本，本子二十个，铅笔两支"等。

However, one can say 书十本，本子二十个，铅笔两支， etc. in statistics.

（二）数量词组和结构助词"的"。

The N-Mw phrase and the structural particle 的.

1. 由名量词构成的数量词组的主要作用是修饰名词。数量词组和名词中心语之间不能用助词"的"。例如：

The nominal N-Mw phrase is mainly used to modify

a noun. The structural particle 的 is not used between the N-Mw phrase and the modified word. For example:

一个人	三座山
两辆汽车	一只鸡
五支铅笔	三把椅子
一张桌子	一张纸
两个本子	两件衣服
一块钱	三公斤白糖
两米布	一盆花
一封信	七位客人
三个苹果	一杯茶
两条鱼	一条裙子
一双鞋	六双筷子

少数动量词构成的数量词组也可以这样用。例如：

Some verbal N-Mw phrases can also function this way. For example:

一场电影

一次参观

绝不能说成"一个的人"、"三座的山"、"两辆的汽车"或"一场的电影"等。

It is entirely wrong to say 一个的人, 三座的山, 两辆的汽车, 一场的电影, etc.

2. 中心语所代表的事物跟量词不一致不能搭配时，数量词组后面要用助词"的"。例如：

The structural particle 的 should be used between the N-Mw phrase and the modified word when the measure word and the noun are not the usual match. For example:

一公斤的书 （书有一公斤重）

　　　　　(The book(s) weigh(s) 1 kg.)

三件的钱 （买三件衣服的钱）

186

(The cost for three pieces of clothes.)

一场的时间　（看一场电影或打一场球的时间）

(The duration of a film show or a ball game.)

3．有的名词可以用在数词"一"后边作临时量词，表示数量多，有描写修饰作用；"一"有"满"的意思。后面可以用助词"的"。例如：

Some nouns can be borrowed as temporary measure words, functioning after the numeral — as a modifier and showing sth. in great quantity. Here the numeral — means "full of", and can be followed by the structural particle 的. For example:

一地的水　　　一桌子的书
一屋子的人

（三）数量词组作补语。

The N-Mw phrase serving as a complement.

1．由动量词构成的数量词组的主要作用是在动词后边作补语，表示动作的次数。数量词组和动词之间一律不用助词"得"。例如：

Verbal N-Mw phrases mainly function as complements after verbs, showing the frequency of an action. But with this kind of complement, the structural particle 得 is not used. For example:

我再念一遍。
你来一趟吧。

2．名量词构成的数量词组可以在形容词后边作补语，表示具体的长度、高度、深度等。例如：

Nominal N-Mw phrases can be used as complements of adjectives to show specific length, height, depth, etc. For example：

这块布长八米。

这件衣服的颜色深一些。

这张桌子比那张桌子高一厘米。

慢一点！别摔了。

（四）名量词构成的数量词组作宾语时，它所指的人或事物是前边已经提到过的。例如：

When used as the object, a nominal N-Mw phrase refers to the person(s) or thing(s) of earlier mention. For example:

（这种花布）我买六米。

（这种点心）你尝一块。

数词"一"构成的数量词组在宾语前作定语时， "一"可以省去不说。例如：

— is optional when it is the numeral in a N-Mw phrase used as the attributive of an object. For example:

我写一封信。 ——>我写封信。

他有一辆汽车。 ——>他有辆汽车。

她是一位科学家。 ——>她是位科学家。

（五）关于数量词组的重叠。

Reduplication of an N-Mw phrase.

1．重叠形式。Formulas of reduplication.

（1）数词和量词都重复：ＡＢＡＢ。例如：

An N-Mw phrase is reduplicated in the formula ABAB. For example:

一个———一个一个 三辆——三辆三辆

两张——两张两张 一次———一次一次

（2）数词是"一"时，可以只重复量词：ＡＢＢ。例如：

But when the numeral is —, the phrase can be reduplicated in the formula ABB, i.e. only the measure word is reduplicated. For example:

一个———一个个

一条———一条条

一趟———一趟趟

2. 表示的意义和用途。

Meanings and functions of reduplicated N-Mw phrases.

（1）作定语。

As an attributive.

数词"一"和名量词构成的数量词组重叠后作定语，表示事物很多，而且强调集体中有个体。这种定语后面要用结构助词"的"。例如：

A reduplicated nominal N-Mw phrase consisting of the numeral — and a measure word used attributively shows something in great quantity, emphasizing the individuals contained in a mass. The structural particle 的 should be used after this kind of attributive. For example:

书架上摆着一本一本的词典，都是外文的。

玛丽说："一个一个的汉字都跟画儿一样。"

（2）作状语。

As an adverbial adjunct.

名量词构成的数量词组重叠后作状语，表示动作的方式，表示事物有秩序地罗列或动作是按次序进行的。这种状语后边要用结构助词"地"。例如：

Reduplicated nominal N-Mw phrases are used adverbially to show things set out in order or actions happening in a particular sequence. The structural particle 地 must be used after this kind of adverbial adjunct. For example:

他把那些花一盆一盆地都摆在院子里了。

你们两个两个地进来。

数词"一"和动量词构成的数量词组重叠后作状语，表示动作次数多而且连续发生。例如：

A reduplicated verbal N-Mw phrase in which the numeral

is 一 can be used as an adverbial adjunct to indicate that an action happens frequently and continuously.   For example:

他一次一次地来过五六次了。

我们一趟一趟地去请你，你为什么不来？

（六）数量词组常用在指示代词"这、那"和疑问代词"哪"的后边。例如：

A N-Mw phrase is often preceded by the demonstrative pronouns 这，那 or the interrogative pronoun 哪. For example:

这两张报是昨天的。   教你们汉语的是哪一位老师？

那三本画报是借的。   哪几位同学要买电影票？

如果"这、那、哪"后边的数词是"一"，"一"可以省去不说。例如：

If the numeral after 这，那 or 哪 is 一, 一 can be omitted.   For example:

这一间——这间   这一块——这块

那一包——那包   哪一本——哪本

这一块肥皂一块钱。

我想看那一本小说。

词序是：

Here is the word order:

指示代词——数词——量词——名词

Demonstrative Pronoun + Numeral + Measure Word + Noun

这——两——间——屋子

练　习　16
Exercise　16

（一）标出句中的数量词组。

Mark the N-Mw phrases in the following sentences.

1．一年有十二个月。

2．大屋子我们打扫了一间。

3．一米等于一百厘米。

4．今天三月二十五号。

5．你再去一次。

6．这种收音机才八十块钱。

7．商店里摆着一双一双的皮鞋。

8．孩子们一个一个地表演节目。

9．他十分钟能写完。

10．他这一趟游览了不少名胜古迹。

（二）在对的词组后边划"√"；错的后边划"×"，并改正。

Mark the correct phrases with a "√" and the wrong ones with a "×".

1．一座山	2．五条的裤子
3．一瓶一瓶的汽水	4．一张一张地挂
5．两架飞机	6．一篇一篇阅读
7．一支一支笔	8．这四把椅子
9．那个书架	10．那位两先生
11．哪三个房间	12．三本的字典
13．一件外衣	14．两把的剪子
15．这次	16．那一杯

第六节　补充词组

Section VI The Complementary Phrase

一、补充词组的定义　Definition

按照补充关系组合起来的一组词，叫补充词组。

A complementary phrase is one in which the constituents

are combined in a complementary relationship.

补充词组一般可分成两类：

A complementary phrase can generally be divided into two subclasses:

（一）动补词组，是由动词和补充成分组成的。例如：

The verb-complement (V-C) phrase, which is formed by a verb and its complement. For example:

> 洗干净 （"洗"是动词，是中心语；"干净"是形容词，是补充成分）
>
> (The verb 洗 is the modified word and the adjective 干净 the complement.)
>
> 选出 （"选"是动词，是中心语；"出"是动词，是补充成分）
>
> (The verb 选 is the modified word and the verb 出 the complement.)

（二）形补词组，是由形容词和补充成分组成的。例如：

The adjective-complement (A-C) phrase which is made up of an adjective and its complement. For example:

> 高得很 （"高"是形容词，是中心语；"很"是副词，是补充成分）
>
> (The adjective 高 is the modified word and the adverb 很 the complement.)
>
> 少一点儿 （"少"是形容词，是中心语；"一点儿"是数量词组，是补充成分）
>
> (The adjective 少 is the modified word and the N-Mw phrase 一点儿 the complement.)

二、补充词组的语法特点 Grammatical features

（一）补充词组的词序是固定的，补充成分一定在中心语后面。例如：

192

The order of the two constituents in a complementary phrase is fixed: the modified word is always followed by the complement. For example:

整理好　　听懂　　念三遍　　休息一会儿

（二）补充词组里的中心语和补充成分之间有时要用结构助词"得"或"不"连接。例如：

Sometimes the modified word and its complement in a complementary phrase are connected by the structural particle 得 or the adverb 不 for the negative. For example:

睡得早　　起得晚　　修不好　　看不见

（三）补充成分可由动词、形容词、个别副词或词组充当。

The complement may be a verb, an adjective, and in a few cases, an adverb or a phrase.

（四）补充词组的重音一般在后边的补充成分上。

The stress of a complementary phrase usually falls on the second constituent or the complement.

三、补充词组的用途　Functions

（一）作主语。

As the subject.

说清楚就行了。　　　　起得太早也不好。

睡得太晚会影响健康。　多一点儿没关系。

（二）作宾语。

As the object.

我认为画得不错。　　　今天我看抄不完。

我计划去两次。　　　　他觉得累极了。

（三）作定语。

As an attributive.

整理好的资料都在这儿。　来得晚的人坐后边。

柜子里有洗干净的毛巾。　这是借来的杂志。

（四）作补语。

As a complement.

他写得快得很。　　　　他高兴得跳起来了。

哥哥跑得快多了。　　　　我比他起得晚一点。

他唱得好极了。

四、使用补充词组时需要注意的问题

Points that merit special attention

（一）补充词组的词序不能颠倒，否则结构和意思就变了。例如"整理好"是指经过"整理"达到"好"的结果；如果说成"好整理"就变成了偏正词组，表示"容易整理"的意思了。再如"休息一会儿"是指"休息"的时间不长，如果说成"一会儿休息"就表示"过一会儿"再开始"休息"的意思了。有的补充词组颠倒过来就不能表达任何意思了，例如"接触到"、"少一点儿"都不能倒过来说。

The order of the two constituents in a complementary phrase can not be reversed, because the reversion of order will bring about a change both in structure and in meaning. For instance, 整理好 means "to put sth. in good order" whereas the 好整理, an endocentric phrase, means "easy to put sth. in order". 休息一会儿 means "to rest for a while" whereas 一会儿休息 means "will have a rest in a moment". Some complementary phrases such as 接触到, 少一点儿, etc. would make no sense if their constituents were arranged in the reverse order.

（二）补充成分的种类很多，常见的有以下几种。

Apart from some others, the following kinds of words and phrases can often be used as the complement in a complementary phrase.

1．形容词、动词、个别副词，数量、主谓、动宾、偏正等词组都可以用在动词后边作补充成分。例如：

Adjectives, verbs, some adverbs, N-Mw phrases, S-P

194

phrases, V-O phrases, endocentric phrases, etc. can all serve as complement in a V-C phrase.　For example:

写对	摔坏	画得好	看得清楚
买来	睁开	捡起	做得完
抄一遍	去两次	差十分	笑得肚子疼
笑得直不起腰		哭得很伤心	

2.　数量词组、形容词"多（了）"和副词"很"、"极（了）"可以用在形容词后边作补充成分。例如：

N-Mw phrases, the adjective 多（了） and the adverbs 很 and 极（了） can all be used as the complement in an A-C phrase.　For example:

瘦一点	麻烦一些	宽半米	早五分钟
快多了	大多了	亮多了	多多了
顺利极了	危险极了	可惜得很	普通得很

（三）补充词组和结构助词"得"。

The complementary phrase and the structural particle 得.

1.　有的补充成分直接与动词（或形容词）组成补充词组，中间不用助词"得"。例如：

Some complementary phrases are formed by putting the complement constituent immediately after the verb or the adjective, i.e. the two constituents are not introduced by the structural particle 得.　For example:

表示动作结果的形容词、动词——学会、学好

Resultant adjectives and verbs as in 学会，学好 etc.

表示动作时间、次数的数量词组——学一遍、差三分

N-Mw phrases indicating the duration or frequency of an action, as in 学一遍，差三分，etc.

表示程度的副词"极（了）"——恨极了、潮湿极了

The degree adverb 极（了） as in 恨极了，潮湿极了, etc.

表示长度、宽度、高度等的数量词组——远一点、高一米

N-Mw phrases of length, width, height, etc. as in 远一点，
高一米， etc.

表示动作趋向的动词——拿来、放进、挂起来

Verbs of direction such as 拿来，放进，挂起来， etc.

2．有的补充成分不能直接与动词（或形容词）组成补充词
组，中间要用助词"得"。例如：

In some complementary phrases, the two constituents
must be introduced by the structural particle. In other words,
the verb or adjective in a complementary phrase can not be
immediately followed by the complement. For example:

表示动作进行的程度的形容词和词组——学得好、写得非常
整齐，等等。

Degree adjectives and phrases, such as 学得好、写得非常
整齐， etc.

表示程度的副词"很"——好得很、关心得很，等等。

The degree adverb 很 as in 好得很，关心得很， etc.

表示动作可能达到某种结果或情况的动词、形容词：

Verbs and adjectives expressing the possibility of achieving
a result or reaching a certain situation such as:

看得见　　听得懂　　洗得干净　　搬得进去

（四）补充词组可以直接充当句子成分，不需要用代词或介
词等。例如：

Complementary phrases can serve as sentence elements
without being introduced by a pronoun or a preposition. For
example:

念三遍不够。　　　　　（作主语）

(As the subject)

他说保存得不好。　　　（作宾语）

(As the object)

选出的代表已经去了。　（作定语）

(As the attributive)

她唱得好听极了。　　　　　（作补语）

(As the complement)

（五）补充词组作定语、补语和结构助词。

The attributive and complement use of the complementary phrase and structural particles.

1．补充词组作定语时，补充词组和后边的中心语之间一定要用助词"的"。例如：

A complementary phrase must be followed by the structural particle 的, when it acts as an attributive. For example:

送去的礼物都收到了。

听不懂的地方可以问老师。

如果不用"的"，有的就变成动宾关系了，例如"选出代表"，意思也完全变了。

If 的 is absent, some of the phrases will be in the V-O relationship, e.g. when 选出的代表 becomes 选出代表, the meaning will change completely.

2．补充词组作补语时，补充词组和前边的中心语之间一定要用助词"得"。例如：

The structural particle 得 must be used before a complementary phrase acting as a complement. For example:

他跑得快得很。　　　　　他兴奋得欢呼起来。

我们玩得高兴极了。

不能说成"他跑快得很"等。

It is wrong to say 他跑快得很, etc.

练 习 17
Exercise 17

（一）标出下列词组中的补充成分，并注明哪些是词、哪些是词组。

Mark the complement in each phrase and state whether it is a word or a phrase.

1.	安排妥当	2.	填平
3.	安全得很	4.	容易极了
5.	解释清楚	6.	睁开
7.	装满	8.	抄写三遍
9.	记录半小时	10.	掏出来
11.	煮熟	12.	对准
13.	领来	14.	跳得很高
15.	麻烦得很	16.	歇一天
17.	存进去	18.	烫极了
19.	分析得很正确	20.	打伤

（二）标出句中的补充词组，并指出中心语的词类（动词还是形容词）。

Mark the complementary phrases in the following sentences and state whether the modified word in each phrase is a verb or an adjective.

1. 我看得清楚极了。
2. 听完的磁带在那儿。
3. 这是刚织好的毛衣。
4. 这件行李捆得结实得很。
5. 休息一天够了。
6. 我感到幸福得很。

7. 他认为挑选得很合适。

8. 吃得太饱对胃不好。

9. 这些是写得很有水平的论文。

10. 我相信学得会。

第七节 方位词组

Section VII The Phrase of Locality

一、方位词组的定义 Definition

由方位词作中心语构成的，表示处所、时间或数量的一组词，叫方位词组。例如：

A phrase of locality is one where the noun of locality is a modified word indicating place or position, time or quantity. For example:

表示处所 Indicating position：

城东　路南　校外　屋里　桌子上　学校前面

他左边

表示时间 Indicating time：

夜里　晚上　三天前　饭后　一个星期左右

一个月以前

表示数量 Indicating quantity：

三十岁以上　四十里以外　五十个左右　四十岁上下

二、方位词组的语法特点 Grammatical features

（一）方位词组的词序是固定的，前一部分是修饰后边的方位词的。

The order of the two constituents in a phrase of locality is fixed: the noun of locality is preceded or premodified by the first constituent.

（二）方位词组的前一部分可以是名词、代词、时间词、动词或词组后一部分是方位词。

The first constituent of a phrase of locality may be a noun, a pronoun, a time noun, a verb or a phrase while the second is a noun of locality.

三、方位词组的用途　Functions

（一）作主语。

As the subject.

图书馆东边是教学楼。

大使馆前边有一条很宽的马路。

他左边是王方。

我后边没有人。

屋子里边暖和。

（二）作宾语。

As the object.

奖学金在抽屉里。

你们看墙上边。

他看着窗户外边。

你坐桌子这边，他坐桌子那边。

我们扫扫门外边。

（三）作定语。

As an attributive.

黑板上的字是老师写的。

书下边的报是今天的。

我看见抽屉里的奖学金了。

那是三天前的事。

三十岁以上的人都知道。

（四）作状语。

As an adverbial adjunct.

你饭后再来吧。

我们一个星期以后再见。

咱们院子里坐坐。

楼旁边种着很多花。

您屋里喝茶。

四、使用方位词组需要注意的问题

Points that merit special attention

（一）方位词组的词序不能颠倒，否则意思就变了。例如：

The order of the two constituents can not be reversed, for the reversion will lead to a change of meaning. For example:

三天前——指"三天以前"
            (three days ago)
前三天——指"特定时间以前的三天"
            (three days before a certain time)

屋里——指"屋子里边"
            (in a room)
里屋——指"里边的屋子"
            (the inner room)

城东——指"城市的东边"
            (to the east of a city)
东城——指"城市的东部地区"
            (the eastern part of a city)

（二）方位词组和结构助词"的"。

The phrase of locality and the structural particle 的.

1．方位词组中单音方位词和前边的名词、代词之间不能用助词"的"。不能说"城的东"、"夜的里"、"柜子的前"、"她的右"、"我们的后"等。

的 can not be used between the premodifying noun or pronoun and the monosyllabic noun of locality, e.g. one can not say 城的东，夜的里，柜子的前，她的右，我们的后，etc.

2．"上下、左右"和带"以、之"的双音方位词和名词之间也不能用助词"的"。不能说"一千公斤的上下"，"五十个的左右"，"两个星期的以前"，"四十公里的以外"等。

的 is not used between the premodifying noun and the disyllabic nouns of locality 上下，左右 or those with 以 or 之, e.g. there are no such forms as 一千斤公的上下，五十个的左右，两个星期的以前，四十公里的以外, etc.

3．带"边、面"的双音方位词和名词之间有时可以用助词"的"。例如：

的 is sometimes used between the premodifying noun and the disyllabic locality nouns with 边 or 面. For example:

他的左边　　张文的旁边　　宿舍的前面

（三）方位词组和句子成分。

The phrase of locality and its functions as a sentence element.

1．表示处所的方位词组可以充当主语、宾语、定语和状语，不能作谓语和补语。例如：

A phrase of locality of place or position can act as a subject, object, attributive, or adverbial adjunct, but not a predicate or complement. For example:

山上有很多树。　　　　（作主语）
　　　　　　　　　　　　(As the subject)

本子在桌子上。　　　　（作宾语）
　　　　　　　　　　　　(As the object)

书架上的书都是他的。（作定语）
　　　　　　　　　　　　(As the attributive)

你们门外边玩。　　　　（作状语）
　　　　　　　　　　　　(As the adverbial adjunct)

2．表示时间的方位词组可以充当定语和状语，有时也作主语和宾语。例如：

A phrase of locality of time can function as an attributive, adverbial adjunct and sometimes as the subject or object. For example:

这是两个星期以内的参观计划。（作定语）
(As the attributive)

三点以前他们不会来。（作状语）
(As the adverbial adjunct)

七点以后比较合适。（作主语）
(As the subject)

晚会的时间是八点以后。（作宾语）
(As the object)

3．表示数量的方位词组一般可以作主语、谓语和定语。例如：

A phrase of locality of quantity usually serves as a subject, predicate or attributive. For example:

五千块以内也是一个不小的数目。（作主语）
(As the subject)

他二十岁左右。（作谓语）
(As the predicate)

他到三十里以外的地方去了。（作定语）
(As the attributive)

4．方位词组充当句子成分时，不需要用代词或介词表示。

A phrase of locality can serve as a sentence element without being introduced by a pronoun or preposition.

（四）方位词组作定语时，后边一般要用结构助词"的"。例如：

The structural particle 的 is usually necessary when a phrase of locality is used attributively. For example:

院子里的花真香！（表示处所）

(Indicating position)

三年以前的事他都记得。　　（表示时间）

(Indicating time)

那个人有四十岁上下的年纪。　（表示数量）

(Indicating quantity)

（五）单音方位词"上"和"下"，"左"和"右"常结合在一起，构成复合方位词"上下"和"左右"，用在数词或数量词组后边表示概数。例如：

The compound locality nouns 上下 and 左右 are the combinations of the simple nouns of locality 上 and 下，左 and 右. These are preceded by numerals or N-Mw phrases to indicate an approximate number.　For example:

三点左右我一定来。

那些水果有二百公斤上下。

"前"和"后"常结合成"前后"，用在名词、数量词组后面表示时间或处所。例如：

前后, the combination of 前 and 后, is often used after a noun or an N-Mw phrase to indicate time or position.　For example:

新年前后我要回家。　　　（表示时间）

(Indicating time)

五号前后我们就要见面了。

我们家前后都有院子。　　（表示处所）

(Indicating position)

（六）方位词组"…以前"和"…以后"。

The phrases of locality ... 以前 and ... 以后.

1．"…以前"和"…以后"一般只表示时间。

Usually ... 以前 and ... 以后 are used only with a time reference.

2．"以前"和"以后"的前边可以是名词、动词或者数量、动宾、偏正、主谓等词组。

In these two phrases, 以前 or 以后 may be preceded by a noun, a verb or an N-Mw phrase, a V-O phrase, an endocentric phrase or a S-P phrase.

3．用途：Functions:

（1）作状语。

As an adverbial adjunct.

> 元旦以前我在北京。
> 春节以后他就开始旅游。
> 我动身以前一定去你那儿。
> 十号以后我就离开首都了。
> 离开首都以后我一定给你写信。
> 我三天以前收到了这封信。
> 我回来以后你再走。

（2）作定语。后边一定要用结构助词"的"。例如：

As an attributive, the structural particle 的 must be suffixed to 以前 or 以后. For example:

> 这是五号以前的消息。
> 放假以前的工作都安排好了。
> 圣诞节以后的计划在这儿。
> 他毕业以后的工作已经找到了。

4．"以前"用在动词、动宾词组、动词性偏正词组或主谓词组后边作状语时，其中动词可以是肯定形式或者否定形式，句子的意思不变。例如：

Both the affirmative and the negative forms of the verb or the verb in a V-O phrase, a verbal endocentric phrase or a S-P phrase preceding 以前 mean the same a negative sense when 以前 is used as adverbial adjunct. For example:

> { 他来以前，你不要离开这儿。
> { 他没来以前，你不要离开这儿。

$$\left\{\begin{array}{l}\text{我走以前一定告诉你。}\\\text{我没走以前一定告诉你。}\end{array}\right.$$

但"以后"没有这种否定形式的用法。

But 以后, the opposite of 以前, doesn't function like this.

练 习 18
Exercise 18

（一）指出下列方位词组表示的意义（时间、处所或数量）。

Give the meanings (time, place or position, or quantity) of the following phrases of locality:

1. 一个星期以后	2. 二十左右
3. 中国北部	4. 邮局南边
5. 两点前后	6. 他旁边
7. 三十岁以上	8. 鼻子上
9. 盒子里	10. 两公斤以下
11. 门后边	12. 一年以前
13. 路北	14. 我们前面
15. 椅子上	16. 三号左右
17. 五岁以后	18. 树下边
19. 五十个上下	20. 十天以内

（二）改正下列方位词组。

Correct the mistakes in the following phrases of locality.

1. 两天的以后	2. 手的上
3. 路的东	4. 圣诞节的以前
5. 箱子的里	6. 墙的上
7. 三个月的以内	8. 一个星期的左右
9. 他的右	10. 十二点的左右
11. 五百公斤的以上	12. 六十岁的上下

第八节 同位词组

Section VIII The Appositive Phrase

一、同位词组的定义 Definition

两个词从不同角度指出同一个人或事物并互相说明，这样组合起来的一组词叫同位词组。例如：

A combination of two words which refer to the same person or thing from different aspects, and where each adds some information to the other is called an appositive phrase. Here are some examples:

> 张平同志（"张平"是一个人的"姓名"，"同志"是称呼；意思是这个"同志"是名叫"张平"的人）
>
> (张平 is a personal name and 同志 a vocative. The phrase means "This comrade is the man named 张平.")
>
> 张平他们（"张平"是一个人的姓名，"他们"是第三人称复数代词；意思是"他们"指的"张平"和"跟张平一起"的人）
>
> (张平 is a personal name and 他们 a third person plural. The phrase means "他们 refers to 张平 and others".)

二、同位词组的语法特点 Grammatical features

（一）同位词组的词序一般是固定的，表达的重点一般在后边。

The order of the two constituents is fixed, with the emphasis on the second one.

（二）有的同位词组前一部分指具体人或事物，后一部分指一般性的人或事物。重音一般在前一部分上。例如：

In some appositive phrases, the first constituent refers to a specific person or thing, while the second has a generic reference. The stress is on the first one in pronunciation. For example:

　　姐姐她们

　　圣诞节那天

有的则相反，前一部分是概括性的，后一部分表示具体的意义。重音一般在后一部分上。例如：

In some other cases, the first one has a generic reference and the second one, with the stress on it, has a specific reference. For example:

　　我的朋友张京　　　　他们海军战士

　　我们青年人

（三）同位词组中前一部分对后一部分常起限制作用，两部分之间不用虚词连接。例如：

The first constituent restricts the second one and no function word is used between them. For example:

　　中国首都北京　　　　你们三个人

　　他自己　　　　　　　我们大家

三、同位词组的用途　Functions

（一）作主语。

As the subject.

　　方雷他们明天去美国。　咱们大家都应该帮他的忙。

　　中国首都北京到了。　　琼斯先生是教授。

（二）作宾语。

As the object.

　　我们都很尊敬刘文教授。　这件事只能怪他自己。

　　同学们都欢迎你们两位。　这是我姐姐玛利。

208

（三）作定语。

As an attributive.

唱歌跳舞是你们年轻人的爱好。

春秋两季的天气最好。

你参加他们俩的结婚典礼了吗？

你们几个人的学习都不错。

四、使用同位词组时需要注意的问题

Points that merit special attention

（一）同位词组的词序不能随意改变。有的如果改变了词序，结构和意义就变了。例如：

The order of the constituents in an appositive phrase can not always be reversed, for with some appositive phrases, the reversion will lead to a change in structure and meaning. For example:

姐姐她——同位词组，"姐姐"和"她"是一个人

This is an appositive phrase in which 姐姐 and 她 refer to the same person.

她姐姐——偏正词组，"她"和"姐姐"是两个人

This is an endocentric phrase in which 她 and 姐姐 (in the possessive) refer to two persons.

有的如果改变了词序就不成话，不能表达任何意思了。例如：

With some others, the reversion of order will make the phrase grammatically unsound or completely meaningless. For example:

咱们大家——不能说成"大家咱们"

大家咱们 is ungrammatical.

张平自己——不能说成"自己张平"

自己张平 is ungrammatical.

（二）同位词组中两个部分之间不能用结构助词"的"。例

如，不能说"咱们的大家"、"张平的自己"等。

The structural particle 的 can not be inserted between the two constituents, e.g. we can not say 咱们的大家，张平的自己, etc.

（三）同位词组多数由名词或代词等构成，具有名词、代词的某些作用。可以充当主语、宾语或定语，不能作谓语、状语和补语。

Appositive phrases have some of the functions of a noun and pronoun since most of them are composed of nouns or pronouns, namely, they function as the subject, object or an attributive, but not as the predicate, an adverbial adjunct or a complement.

（四）同位词组可以直接充当句子成分，本身无任何标记。

An appositive phrase functions as a sentence element without any marker.

（五）同位词组作定语时，同位词组和中心语之间一般要用结构助词"的"。例如：

When an appositive phrase is used attributively, the structural particle 的 should usually be used between it and that which it modifies. For example:

他自己的意见是住家里。

这是你们三个人的飞机票。

练　习　19
Exercise 19

（一）标出下列句中的同位词组，并指出作什么句子成分。

Mark the appositive phrases in the following sentences and state what their functions are.

1. 我们学校北京语言学院在北京西郊。
2. 我要订一份杂志《旅游》。
3. 小马他的意见怎么样？
4. 第一、第二两本的内容不难。
5. 你请张文、谢明两位老师了吗？
6. 我们自己组织这次活动。
7. 大家都想见见你们俩。
8. 这是钱民同学的电报。
9. 我们大家一起跳舞吧。
10. 我的朋友王刚昨天去上海了。

（二）选填合适的词，构成同位词组。

Fill in each blank with a word in apposition with the preceding one.

1. 他们＿＿＿（自己、同学）
2. 弟弟＿＿＿（大家，他们）
3. 张平＿＿＿（张明，先生）
4. 新年＿＿＿（一天，那天）
5. 我的老师＿＿＿（张文，一个人）
6. 你们＿＿＿（俩，弟弟）

第九节 固定词组
Section IX The Set Phrase

一、固定词组的定义 Definition

由某些词组成的固定格式，表示一个特定的概念，并作为一个整体来使用的词组，叫固定词组，如专名、术语或成语等。例如：

A set phrase, such as a proper noun, a technical term, an

idiom, etc. is one which is composed of fixed constituents to express a specific concept and is used as a whole.　For example:

全国 人民 代表 大 会　　　　　（五个词）
The National People's Congress　　（Composed of 5
　　　　　　　　　　　　　　　　constituents)

人民 英雄 纪念 碑　　　　　　（四个词）
Monument to the People's Heroes （Composed of 4
　　　　　　　　　　　　　　　　constituents)

有 始 有 终
Carry sth. through to the end

坐 井 观 天
Look at the sky from the bottom
　　　of a well — have a very
　　　narrow view

中华 人民 共和国　　　　　　（三个词）
The People's Republic of China （Composed of three
　　　　　　　　　　　　　　　constituents)

北京 语言 学院
The Beijing Language Institute

中国 人　　　　　　　　　　（两个词）
A Chinese　　　　　　　　　（Composed of two
　　　　　　　　　　　　　　 constituents)

二、固定词组的语法特点　Grammatical features

（一）固定词组的词和词序都是固定的。

None of the constituents in a set phrase can be substituted and they are arranged in a fixed order.

（二）固定词组一般由两个或两个以上的词，按一定的语法关系组合而成，表示一个固定的意思。

The two or more constituents in a set phrase are combined in a certain grammatical relation to express fixed and specific meaning.

（三）固定词组在句中的作用相当于一个词。

The set phrase acts as a single word in a sentence.

三、固定词组的用途　Functions

（一）作主语。

As the subject.

人民英雄纪念碑在天安门广场中央。

北京语言学院有许多外国留学生。

康藏公路 (the Xikang-Tibet Highway) 是解放以后建
成的。

（二）作宾语。

As the object.

我的汉语老师是中国人。

我们学习汉语普通话 (the common speech of the
Chinese language)。

他最近得了半身不遂 (paralysis of one side —hemi-
plegia)。

（三）作定语。

As an attributive.

这是中华人民共和国的地图。

北京图书馆 (the Beijing Library) 的地址在北海大桥
西边。

他是一个多才多艺 (gifted in many ways) 的人。

（四）作谓语。

As the predicate.

这篇文章短小精悍 (terse and forceful)。

我们应该言行一致 (one's actions accord with one's
words)。

他对这里的情况了如指掌 (to know sth. like the
palm of one's hand)。

（五）作状语。

As an adverbial adjunct.

他们千方百计 (in a thousand and one ways) 地完成
了这项设计任务。

我们俩应该开诚布公 (to speak frankly and sincerely)
地谈一谈。

他小心翼翼 (with great care) 地在旁边站着。

（六）作补语。

As a complement.

她们姐妹俩长得一模一样 (exactly alike)。

他讲得头头是道 (clear and logical)。

他被大家说得不知所措 (at a loss as to what to do)。

四、使用固定词组时需要注意的问题

Points that merit special attention

（一）固定词组的词和词序都是固定的，不能改动。

In a set phrase both the constituents and their order are
fixed.

例如"北京语言学院"、"北京大学"等都是专名；"言
行一致"、"头头是道"等都是成语，"电子计算机"、"高速
公路"等都是术语；这些都不能改动。

For example, under no circumstances can you make any
change to the proper nouns 北京语言学院，北京大学, etc.; to
the idioms 言行一致，头头是道, etc. or to the technical terms
电子计算机 (electronic computer)， 高速公路 (expressway),
etc.

不能随意增减字数。例如：

One can not make addition or reduction to the number
of constituents of the set phrase at will. For example:

中国人——不能说成"中国的人"。

Not 中国的人。

普通话——不能说成"普通的话"。

        Not 普通的话.

人民日报 (the People's Daily)

        ——不能说成"人民的日报"。

        Not 人民的日报.

公共汽车 (public bus)

        ——不能说成"公共的汽车"。

        Not 公共的汽车.

不能随意调换词序。例如：

The order of constituents can not be changed. For example:

三番五次 (again and again)

        ——不能说成"三次五番"。

        Neither 四番六次 nor 三次五番 is possible.

千方百计

        ——不能说成"百计千方"或"百方千计"。

        One can not say 百计千方 nor can one say 百方千计.

（二）较长的专名或术语常有简称，简称也是固定的，不能随意改变。例如：

Abbreviated forms, especially for longer proper nouns and technical terms, are also fixed.　For example:

北京大学——北大　(Beijing University)

清华大学附属中学

        ——清华附中 (the Middle School attached to Qinghua University)

第四届全国人民代表大会

        ——四届人大　(the Fourth National People's Congress)

（三）固定词组和结构助词。

The set phrase and the structural particles.

1．固定词组作定语，一般要用助词"的"。例如：

Used attributively, the set phrase is usually followed by the structural particle 的. For example:

世界上没有十全十美 (perfect) 的人。

2．固定词组作状语，一般要用助词"地"。例如：

Used adverbially, the set phrase is usually followed by the structural particle 地. For example:

我们恋恋不舍 (reluctant to part with) 地离开了首都。

3．固定词组一般只能作程度补语，前边一定要用助词"得"。例如：

The set phrase can serve as complement of degree only and it must be preceded by the structural particle 得.   For example:

他高兴得手舞足蹈 (dance for joy)。

第十节　介词结构
Section X　The Prepositional Phrase

一、介词结构的定义　Definition

介词带着宾语构成的词组叫介词结构（也叫介宾词组）。介词结构可以表示动作的方向、处所、时间、对象、目的、原因、方式、被动、比较、处置、排除等等。例如：

The prepositional phrase (or the preposition-object phrase) is formed by a preposition and its object.   It refers to directions, place or position, time, the object, purpose, reason, or manner of an action, and expresses passiveness, comparison, disposal or exclusion etc..   For example:

朝南　（方向）　(direction)

（"朝"是介词；"南"是方位词，是"朝"的宾

語）

(朝 is a preposition and its object is the
locality noun 南.).

在草地上　（处所）(place)

（"在"是介词；"草地上"是方位词组，是
"在"的宾语）

(在 is a preposition and its object is 草地上
which is a locality phrase.)

从八点	（时间）	(time)
向英雄模范	（对象）	(object)
为人民	（目的）	(purpose)
由于他	（原因）	(reason)
按照这个方法	（方式）	(manner)
被姐姐	（被动）	(passiveness)
比别人	（比较）	(comparison)
把这本画报	（处置）	(disposal)
除了这个城市	（排除）	(exclusion)

二、介词结构的语法特点 Grammatical features

（一）介词结构的词序是固定的，介词永远在它宾语的前
边。

The word order of a prepositional phrase is fixed: the
preposition always precedes its object.

（二）介词的宾语可以是名词、代词、数量词组、方位词、
方位词组、时间词或名词性偏正词组。

Nouns, pronouns, N-Mw phrases, nouns and phrases of
locality, time nouns or nominal endocentric phrases can serve
as prepositions' objects.

（三）介词和宾语之间不需要别的虚词连接。

No other function word is used to connect the preposition
and its object.

217

（四）重音一般在介词后边的宾语上。

The stress of a prepositional phrase is on the object rather than the preposition.

三、介词结构的用途　Functions

（一）作状语。

As an adverbial adjunct.

介词结构的主要作用是在句子里充当状语。例如：

A prepositional phrase is chiefly used as the adverbial adjunct in a sentence.　For example:

> 他们在北京语言学院学习。
>
> 那位女老师给我们讲汉语语法。
>
> 他对人很热情。
>
> 我们应该向他们表示感谢。
>
> 他们从下月开始准备考试。
>
> 他从公园回来了。
>
> 我从哥哥那儿来。
>
> 你朝东看。
>
> 往南走吧。
>
> 我把那本小说给朋友了。
>
> 他的自行车被妹妹骑走了。
>
> 弟弟比哥哥高一点。
>
> 服务员对游览的人很热情。
>
> 由于他，我们没赶上十点的火车。
>
> 关于印刷方面的问题，我不太了解。

（二）作定语。

As an attributive.

> 他提了不少对教材工作的建议。
>
> 他住朝南的那座楼上。
>
> 关于他的消息，我已经听说了。

（三）作补语。

As a complement.

> 这列火车开往北京。
>
> 我们充满希望地走向胜利。

四、使用介词结构时需要注意的问题

Points that merit special attention

（一）介词结构直接充当句子成分，不需要任何标记。例如：

A prepositional phrase is used as a sentence element without any particular marker.　For example:

> 农民在地里劳动。　　　　（作状语）
>
> 爷爷给小孙子讲故事。　　（As an adverbial adjunct)
>
> 你把窗户打开。
>
> 他对于这类事的兴趣不高。（作定语）
>
> 　　　　　　　　　　　　（As an attributive)
>
> 时针正指向十二点。　　　（作补语）
>
> 　　　　　　　　　　　　（As a complement)

（二）介词结构经常在主语后、动词谓语前作状语；有时也在形容词谓语前作状语。后边一律不用结构助词"地"。例如：

The prepositional phrase often acts as an adverbial adjunct between a subject and verbal predicate or before an adjectival predicate.　The structural particle 地 is not used in either case.　For example:

> 作者根据读者的意见修改。（在动词前）
>
> 　　　　　　　　　　　　（Before the verb)
>
> 侵略军被我们打败了。　　（在动词前）
>
> 　　　　　　　　　　　　（Before the verb)
>
> 他比我大。　　　　　　　（在形容词前）
>
> 　　　　　　　　　　　　（Before the adjective)

介词结构作状语时，一定不能放在动词或形容词后边。不能说"农民劳动在地里"，"他来从北方"，"我们吃饭在食堂"，"我高比弟弟"等。

As an adverbial adjunct, a prepositional phrase never occurs after a verb or an adjective, e.g. one can not say 农民劳动在地里，他来从北方，我们吃饭在食堂，我高比弟弟，etc.

有的介词结构可以放在句首，表示突出、强调，语气上常有语音停顿，书面上常用逗号"，"表示。例如：

To give prominence or emphasis, some prepositional phrases can be placed at the beginning of a sentence. There is usually a pause after the phrase in pronunciation, whereas in writing the pause is indicated by a comma "，" For example:

> 对于这个问题，代表们的意见很一致。
>
> 关于这件事，我们以后谈。
>
> 由于种种原因，他不能出席这个会了。
>
> 按照实际情况，你们处理吧。
>
> 为了人类的进步，科学家们努力地工作着。

（三）介词结构作定语时，一定要放在被修饰的中心语前边，后边要用结构助词"的"。例如：

As an attributive, a prepositional phrase must be placed before the word it modifies and the structural particle 的 should be suffixed to it. For example:

> 马主任作了关于技术革新的报告。
>
> 中国有不少关于月亮和太阳的传说。

（四）只有极少数介词（"往、向"等）构成的介词结构可以在动词后边作补语，表示动作进行的结果所达到的方向或终点。例如：

Only in a very few cases, can a prepositional phrase, such as one with the preposition 往，向， etc., be used as the complement to a verb to indicate the direction in which the action proceeds or the destination it arrives at. For example:

> 这些拖拉机都要运往农场。
>
> 我们一定要勇敢地奔向前方。

（五）几个常见的介词结构。

Some commonly used prepositional phrases.

1．"在…上"

（1）"在…上"表示动作进行或状态存在的场所，意思是
"在…上边"，经常作状语。例如：

在 . . . 上, meaning 在 . . . 上边, is used as an adverbial
adjunct to indicate the place where an action takes place or a
state exists.　For example:

　　　　他在床上躺着。

　　　　她在沙发上坐着。

　　　　我在本子上写字。

"在"和"上"中间多为名词或名词性偏正词组。

Between 在 and 上 there is often a noun or a nominal
endocentric phrase.

（2）"在…上"表示范围或方面，"在"和"上"中间多
为表示抽象意义的名词或动词。例如：

在 . . . 上 indicates a certain scope or aspect when an
abstract noun or verb is inserted.　For example:

　　　　这类事在历史上是不少的。

　　　　他在原则上已经同意了。

　　　　他在会上发表了很好的意见。

　　　　他们在学习上有明显的进步。

　　　　我们在科研上要取得显著成绩。

又如：

Here are some other phrases:

　　　　在工作上　　在生活上　　在专业上　　在思想上

这种用法经常作状语，有时用在句首表示强调。例如：

These phrases are often used adverbially and they sometimes
occur at the beginning of a sentence to express emphasis.　For
example:

在学习上，他们有明显的进步。

在生活上，我们经常互相照顾。

2．"在…下"

（1）"在…下"可表示具体的场所，意思是"在…下边"。例如：

在 . . . 下 means 在 . . . 下边, indicating a concrete place or position. For example:

我在山下等你们。

他在树下休息。

（2）"在…下"常表示条件、情况，中间多为名词性偏正词组。例如：

在 . . . 下 indicates a condition or a state of affairs when a nominal endocentric phrase is used between 在 and 下. For example:

在共产党的领导下，中国人民得到了解放。

在老师的帮助下，同学们都有很大变化。

在朋友的鼓励下，他接受了这个任务。

还可以说：

Other such phrases are:

在…的教育下　　　　在…的努力下

在…（的）条件下　　在…（的）情况下

3．"在…中"表示范围，中间可以是名词或名词性偏正词组。作状语。例如：

When a noun or nominal endocentric phrase is used between 在 and 中, the phrase indicates scope and it is used as an adverbial adjunct. For example:

在同学中，我最喜欢他。

在我的朋友中，他最聪明。

"在…中"中间也可以是动词，表示"在某个动作进行的过程中"。例如：

Verbs may also be inserted to express an action in progress. For example:

> 他们在讨论中，又发现了新问题。
>
> 大家在学习中都有很多收获。

4. "从…起" 是一个表示时间或空间的方式，表示 "从…开始" 的意思，常用在主语后谓语动词前作状语。例如：

从 ... 起 indicates time or space, meaning 从 ... 开始. The phrase acts as an adverbial adjunct between the subject and the predicate verb. For example.

> 这个工厂从本月起生产电冰箱。
>
> 我们从下月一号起放暑假。
>
> 他从参加这项工作起，搜集了不少资料。

"从…起" 也可以用在句首。例如：

It also occurs at the beginning of a sentence.   For example:

> 从本月起，这个工厂生产电冰箱。
>
> 从下月一号起，我们放暑假。

5. "从…到…" 也是一个常用的表示时间和空间的方式。例如：

从 ... 到 ... is another common structure indicating time and space.   For example:

> 我每天上午从八点到十二点有课。
>
> （作状语）
>
> (As an adverbial adjunct)
>
> 他从一九五〇年八月到一九五八年在日本工作。
>
> 从北京到上海可以坐飞机。
>
> 从我家到学校有三公里。
>
> （作主语）
>
> (As the subject)

6. "对于…" 和 "对…"

（1）用 "对于" 引出对象，介词结构 "对于…" 可以在动词、形容词前作状语。例如：

对于 introduces a target and the prepositional phrase thus functions as an adverbial adjunct before a verb or an adjective. For example:

> 大家对于他的行为不太满意。
> 我们对于这个问题要进一步研究。
> 抽烟对于身体没有好处。

为了突出"对于"的宾语，"对于…"也可以放在句首、主语前边。例如：

To give prominence to the object of 对于, the phrase can also be placed at the beginning of a sentence before the subject. For example:

> 对于这个问题，我们要进一步研究。

以上用"对于"的句子都可以换用"对"。但是介词"对"的动作性比较强。以下用"对"的地方不能用"对于"代替。

对于 in the above examples can be substituted by 对. However they are not interchangeable in the following examples, as here 对 behaves more like a verb.

（2）"对"可以有"向、朝"的意思。例如：

对 has the meaning of 向 or 朝. For example:

> 大夫对病人说："一定要按时吃药，注意休息。"
> 老师对学生讲："你们应该充满信心。"
> 老大娘对我笑了笑。

可以带双宾语的动词"问、告诉"等前不能用"对…"；不能说"大夫对病人问"、"团长对团员们告诉"等。

A phrase using 对 can not be used with verbs taking two objects such as 问, 告诉, etc. so one can not say 大夫对病人问，团长对团员们告诉, etc.

224

练　习　20

Exercise　20

填上适当的介词。

Fill in the blanks with appropriate prepositions.

1. 他们____体育馆练球。

2. 她们____中国来。

3. 大夫____病人看病。

4. 我们____东走。

5. 他____我说："谢谢！"

6. 你____我大一岁。

7. 大家七点____小王家集合。

8. 我刚____朋友那儿回来。

9. 标语____大风刮坏了。

10. ____老高（以外），我们都不知道。

11. 南方____北方暖和。

12. 他____大家讲长城的历史。

13. 他们____咖啡馆喝咖啡。

14. 我们俩____张文那儿去剧场。

15. 我们____您请教一件事。

16. 你____那边看。

17. 他们____我们很客气。

18. 我们都应该____人民做好事。

19. 我____八点开始工作。

20. ____他（以外），同学们都来了。

第十一节 "的"字结构

Section XI The 的-phrase

一、"的"字结构的定义 Definition

由结构助词"的"附在实词或词组后边组合而成的词组，叫"的"字结构。这样的结构有表示人或事物名称的作用。例如：

The 的-phrase is one in which the structual particle 的 is attached to a notional word or phrase which refers to a person or thing. For example:

这些画报是哥哥的。——"的"在名词后边
的 is suffixed to a noun.

这些笔记是我的。—— "的"在代词后边
的 is suffixed to a pronoun.

红的做衣服。—— "的"在形容词后边
的 is suffixed to an adjective.

参观的有二百人。—— "的"在动词后边
的 is suffixed to a verb.

参加晚会的都来了。——"的"在动宾词组后边
的 is suffixed to a V-O pharse.

我买的在这儿。—— "的"在主谓词组后边
的 is suffixed to a S-P phrase.

二、"的"字结构的语法特点 Grammatical features

（一）"的"字结构的"的"一定附在其他词或词组后边，词序是固定的。

In a 的-phrase, as a rule, 的 must be suffixed to the other

constituent (a word or a phrase).

（二）"的"字结构中间不用其他虚词连接。

No other function word is used between 的 and the other constituent.

（三）"的"字结构在句中的作用相当于一个名词。

The 的-phrase functions as a noun in a sentence.

三、"的"字结构的用途 Functions

只作主语和宾语。

The 的-phrase acts only as the subject and the object.

（一）作主语。

As the subject.

> 表演的是有名的演员。
>
> 参加运动会的有各国留学生。
>
> 送报的来了。
>
> 他给我的是一张节目表。

（二）作宾语。

As the object.

> 我要买新的。
>
> 那封介绍信是他的。
>
> 我告诉我们班的同学，你告诉你们班的。
>
> 那位艺术家是我们请来的。

四、使用"的"字结构时需要注意的问题

Points that merit special attention

（一）"的"字结构中的"的"一定不能省略。例如：

的 can in no circumstances be omitted from the phrase. For example:

> 这项帽子是他的。 这项帽子是刚买的。
>
> 这项帽子是老师的。 这项帽子是他买的。
>
> 这项帽子是黑的。

绝不能说成"这项帽子是他"等。

One never says 这顶帽子是他, etc.

（二）"的"字结构经常在下列情况下代替名词。

Under the following circumstances the 的-phrase can be subsituted for a noun.

1."的"字结构泛指人或具体事物。例如：

When it refers to people in general or concrete things. For example:

> 参加招待会的都在客厅里。
>
> （指"参加招待会的人）
>
> (Referring to all who attended the reception.)
>
> 跟我一起来的是李大夫。
>
> （指"跟我一起来"的人）
>
> (Referring to the person coming with me.)
>
> 这个礼物是我送你的。
>
> （指"我送你"的礼物）
>
> (Referring to the gift I gave you.)
>
> 你拿的是什么？
>
> （指"你拿"的东西）
>
> (Referring to what you have got with you.)

2."的"字结构中的修饰语是指从事的某种工作。例如：

When the modifier in a 的-phrase refers to the occupation, profession, etc., that a person is engaged in. For example:

> 他哥哥是教书的。
>
> （"教书的"指教员）
>
> (教书的 means "teacher")
>
> 今天送信的来过了。
>
> （"送信的"指邮递员）
>
> (送信的 means "postman".)
>
> 我每天坐这辆车，开车的和卖票的都认识我。
>
> （"开车的"指司机，"卖票的"指售票员）

（开车的 means the "driver" and 卖票的 "the conductor.")

需要说明的是，直接称呼对方时，为了表示尊重，应用"老师"、"邮递员同志"、"司机同志"和"售票员同志"，或只称"同志"。

What should be noted is that when one speaks to a person directly, to be more polite, one should use the vocative such as 老师，邮递员同志，司机同志，售票员同志， or only 同志.

3．"的"字结构中的修饰语是限制性或分类性的。例如：

When the modifier in a 的-phrase is restrictive in nature or denotes a class . For example:

　　　我用坏的，你用好的。
　　　这两双袜子，黑的三块钱，蓝的两块八。
　　　这件灰色的怎么样？

练　习　21

Exercise 21

（一）标出句中的 "的"字结构， 并指出作句子的什么成分。

Mark the 的-phrases in the following sentences and state what their functions are.

　　1．那所大学是新建立的。
　　2．这本画报是你的，他的在抽屉里。
　　3．他买的电视机是彩色的，我买的是黑白的。
　　4．现在他吃的、穿的都不错。
　　5．公园门口的狮子是石头的。
　　6．这件毛衣是我自己织的，不是买的。
　　7．他拿的是一本新杂志。

8. 你认识那位戴眼镜的吗？

9. 这两个孩子，男的十岁，女的六岁。

10. 这是今天的，昨天的报在那儿。

（二）指出"的"字结构所代替的名词。

Which nouns are the 的-phrases subsituting in the following sentences?

1. 我送你的是一条围巾。

2. 那个穿花裙子的是我妹妹。

3. 那些书有中文的，有英文的。

4. （这种毛衣的样子不错，）我喜欢蓝的。

5. 操场上有很多跑步的。

附表二： 词组和句子成分的关系

Table 2: Phrases and Their Functions

词 组 Phrases		句 子 成 分 Functions					
		主语 S	谓语 P	宾语 O	定语 Attri.	状语 Adv. adjunct	补语 Compl.
联合词组 Coordinative phrase		✓	✓	✓	✓	✓	✓
主谓词组 S-P phrase		✓	✓	✓	✓	✓	✓
动宾词组 V-O phrase		✓		✓	✓		✓
偏正词组 Endocentric phrase	名词性 Nominal	✓	✓	✓	✓	✓	✓
	动词、形容词性 Verbal or adjectival	✓		✓	✓	✓	✓

N-Mw phrase 数量词组	用名量词 Nominal	✓	✓	✓	✓	✓	✓
	用动量词 Verbal				✓	✓	✓
Complementary phrase 补充词组	动补 V-C	✓		✓	✓		✓
	形补 Adj. -C	✓		✓	✓		✓
方位词组 Locality phrase		✓		✓	✓	✓	
同位词组 Appositive phrase		✓		✓	✓		
固定词组 Set phrase		✓	✓	✓	✓		✓
介词结构 Prepositional phrase					✓	✓	✓
"的"字结构 的 -phrase		✓		✓			

"✓" 表示该词组可以充当某种句子成分。

The mark ✓ indicates the phrase can function as that element.

第四章 句 子 成 分
Chapter Four Sentence Elements

　　句子是进行交际时能独立表达意思的最小的语言单位。句子是由词和词组按照一定的语法关系构成的，句子中的词和词组按照它们在句子中担任的职务和所起的作用可划分为若干个句子成分。汉语里的句子一般可有六种成分。请看下表：

A sentence is the smallest language unit of communication which can be used by itself to express an idea. Sentences are composed of words and phreses arranged according to certain grammatical relationships which can be analysed into several sentence elements in line with their syntax functions. Generally speaking, there are six sentence elements, which are shown in the following table:

句子成分　Elements	例　子　Examples
1.主　语　Subject	哥哥听音乐。
2.谓　语　Predicate	哥哥看小说。
3.宾　语　Object	他们听音乐。
4.定　语　Attributive	我哥哥看外文小说。
5.状　语　Adverbial adjunct	他专心地写文章。
6.补　语　Complement	他写完毕业论文了。

　　句子成分都是由词或词组充当的。例如：

Words or phrases can act as sentence elements. For example:

我的 朋友　　都　　　写 完　　毕业.论文 了。

1. 主语部分			谓 语 部 分			
The subject section			The predicate section			
2. 主语			谓 语		宾 语	
Subject			Predicate		Object	
定 语		状 语	补 语		定 语	
Attributive		Adverbial adjunct	Complement		Attributive	
3. 偏正词组			动补词组		偏正词组	
Endocentric phrase			V-C phrase		Endocentric phrase	
4. 代 助	名	副	动	动	动	名 助
词 词	词	词	词	词	词	词 词
Particle Pronoun	Noun	Adverb	Verb	Verb	Verb	Noun Particle

第一节　主　语
Section I　The Subject

一、什么叫主语　Definition

　　汉语里大多数句子是由两个部分——主语部分和谓语部分——组成的。主语部分里主要的词（也叫中心语）就叫主语。例如：

Most Chinese sentences are composed of two sections: the subject section and the predicate section. The main word (or key word) in the subject section is named the subject. For example:

我姐姐去。　　　　　这个同志是作家。

她的裙子很漂亮。

"我姐姐"、"她的裙子"、"这个同志"是主语部分，"姐姐"、"裙子"、"同志"是主语部分里主要的词，也就是主语。

In the above examples, 我姐姐, 她的裙子 and 这个同志 are the subject sections in which 姐姐, 裙子 and 同志 are the subjects or the key words in the subject sections.

主语部分只有一个词时，这个词就是主语。例如：

The subject section may be a single word. In that case the subject section and the subject are identical. For example:

他来。

孩子们可爱。

我是医生。

主语是陈述的对象，指出谓语说的是"谁"或是"什么"等。

The subject is the theme of a statement pointing out "who" or "what" the predicate is about.

二、主语的语法特点　Grammatical features

（一）一般来说，主语在谓语前边。

The subject normally precedes the predicate.

（二）主语多由名词、代词或名词性的词组充当，也可以由其他各类词或词组充当。

Most subjects are nouns, pronouns or nominal phrases, though words of other parts of speech and other phrases can also function as the subject.

（三）主语前边可有表示修饰或限制的词和词组充当的定语。

The subject can be premodified by attributives composed of words or phrases.

三、可以充当主语的词和词组

Words and phrases which can serve as the subject

（一）名词。

Nouns.

中国在亚洲东部。	明天（是）星期日。
老师讲语法。	外边不热。
天气很暖和。	礼堂在那边。

（二）代词。

Pronouns.

他很热情。	那儿是操场。
我们爱旅行。	谁在院子里？
这是五块钱。	

（三）动词。

Verbs.

学习很重要。	失败是成功之母。
旅行是一种有意义的活动。	演出已经开始了。

（四）形容词。

Adjectives.

艰苦可以锻炼人。	细心是他的特点。
消极是不对的。	

（五）数词。

Numerals.

六是二的三倍。

一百等于五个二十。

（六）量词重叠。

Reduplicated measure words.

（他们班的同学，）个个都是好青年。

（你看那些衬衫）件件都很好看。

（七）联合词组。

Coordinative phrases.

我和琼斯都是美国人。

铁路、公路都提前修建成功了。

这样、那样都行。

参观访问可以增长知识。

踏实、刻苦是应该受到鼓励的。

（八）主谓词组。

Subject-predicate (S-P) phrases.

我们明天去比较合适。　　你也去太好了。

他写比我写好。　　头疼是很讨厌的。

（九）动宾词组。

Verb-object (V-O) phrases.

爬山对身体很有好处。

洗衣服非常方便。

骑自行车要注意安全。

听录音可以提高听、说能力。

（十）偏正词组。

Endocentric phrases.

能去最好，不去也没关系。

早睡早起是个好习惯。

（十一）数量词组。

Numeral-measure word (N-Mw) phrases.

（这种衬衫很好，）一件多少钱？

（他送我两本杂志，）一本是《中国建设》，一本是
《中国妇女》。

（这儿有三张票，）两张给你，一张给他。

（十二）补充词组。

Complementary phrases.

捆得太紧不好。

厚一点更好。

（十三）方位词组。

Locality phrases.

> 学校里有个游泳池。　　　　门旁边没有树。

> 公园中间是一个湖。

（十四）同位词组。

Appositive phrases.

> 解放军战士谢刚走了。

> 《中国建设》这本杂志很有意思。

> 你们的老师张先生要见你们。

（十五）固定词组。

Set phrases.

> 南京长江大桥是中国人造的。

> 北京语言学院在北京西北郊。

（十六）"的"字结构。

的 -phrases.

> 红的最好看。　　　　　开门的是位女同志。

> 他讲的都是新鲜事。　　修理缝纫机的来了。

四、需要注意的问题　Points that merit special attention

（一）汉语里的主语是由它在句中的位置和表达的意义决定的。主语一般都在句首、在谓语前边，表示要陈述的对象。例如：

In Chinese, the subject of a sentence is determined by its position and meaning. Usually the subject, which is the theme of a statement, occurs at the beginning of a sentence before the predicate. For example:

> 他聪明。　　　　　外祖父是工程师。

> 我买。　　　　　　明天哥哥休息。

（二）汉语里当动词和形容词或动词性的词组代表一种事物时也可以充当主语，不过谓语有一定的限制，多是用来描写、判断主语的。例如：

Verbs, adjectives or verbal phrases can serve as the

subject only when they refer to a thing or a state, and the predicate is limited to one describing or identifying the subject.

比赛很精彩。　　　　马虎不好。

犹豫没用。　　　　　懒是不行的。

实现这个计划是不难的。

（三）表示时间、处所的词或词组作主语时，谓语多由动词"是"、形容词或名词充当。例如：

When a noun or phrase of time or place is used as the subject, the predicate is usually the verb 是, an adjective or a noun. For example:

后天是新年。　　　　今天晴天。

花园里很安静。

（四）汉语里主语本身没有任何标记，词和词组都是直接充当主语的。动词或动词性的词组作主语也同样不需要代词等表示，动词形态不变。这一点很重要。例如：

Another important feature is that there is not any particular marker for the subject in Chinese. Words or phrases can serve as subjects without any change in form, even verbs or verbal phrases functioning as subject are not marked by any words such as pronouns etc., and the form of the verbs will remain unchanged. For example:

问候是一种礼节。

推广汉语普通话很有必要。

互相帮助可以加强友谊。

（五）受事主语。

Subjects which are receivers of actions.

汉语里主语大部分是施事者，是谓语动词的发出者。但有些表示事物的主语本身是不能发出任何动作行为的，而是意义上的被动者，动作的受事者。例如：

In Chinese, subjects in most sentences are doers of

actions, but there are some cases in which the subjects refer to the receivers rather than the doers of actions. For example:

药吃了。　　　　　屋子打扫干净了。

铁路建成了。　　　　苍蝇打死了。

练　习　22
Exercise 22

（一）用横线标出句中的主语部分。

Underline the subject sections in the following sentences.

例：

Model: 我们的计划完成了。

1．这个词是名词。

2．风停了。

3．工人们在劳动。

4．月亮出来了。

5．咱们大家小心一点儿。

6．五的五倍是二十五。

7．这样做很妥当。

8．访问中国是他的愿望。

9．明天星期日。

10．汽车准备好了。

11．骆驼和象都可以骑。

12．客厅的灯亮了。

13．呼吸新鲜空气很有好处。

14．生活幸福是大家希望的。

（二）用横线标出句中的主语，并指出是哪类词或词组。

Underline the subject (or the key word in the subject section) in each sentence and state what kind of word or phrase it is.

例：

Model： 我们和邻居的<u>关系</u>很和睦。（名词 Noun）

1. 今天十月十四号。 （　　　）
2. 模仿是儿童学话的重要方法。（　　　）
3. 很多儿童参加了少年先锋队。（　　　）
4. 对这件事要加以调查。 （　　　）
5. 经理告诉我们明天休息 （　　　）
6. 师傅对徒弟的印象相当不 。（　　　）
7. 听新闻广播是我的一种爱好。（　　　）
8. 我弟弟十七（岁）。 （　　　）
9. 那种颜色太好了。 （　　　）
10. 那几位文学家精神都很饱满。（　　　）
11. 损失很大。 （　　　）
12. 赞成或者反对都要说明理由。（　　　）
13. 治病救人是医生的责任。 （　　　）
14. 电灯和电扇都开着。 （　　　）
15. 遵守交通规则是非常要紧的。（　　　）

第二节　谓　语

Section II　The predicate

一、什么叫谓语　Definition

一个句子的谓语部分里只有主要的词（也叫中心语）才叫谓语。例如：

The predicate is the main word (or key word) of the predicate section in a sentence. For example:

他是经理。　　　小王会唱歌。

大家一起研究。

"是经理"、一起研究"、"会唱歌"是谓语部分，"是"、
"研究"，"唱"是谓语部分里主要的词，也就是谓语。

In the above examples, 是经理, 一起研究 and 会唱歌 are
the predicate sections. 是，研究 and 唱 are the predicates
which are the main words (or key words) in the predicate
sections.

谓语部分只有一个实词时，这个词就是谓语。例如：

When it is a single notional word, the predicate section is
identical with the predicate. For example:

你来。 你们商量商量。

树叶黄了。

谓语是陈述主语的，说明主语是什么人或事物，说明主语作
什么、怎么样等。

The predicate tells who or what the subject is, what it does
and how it is, etc.

二、谓语的语法特点 Grammatical features

（一）一般来说，谓语都在主语的后边。

The predicate is normally preceded by the subject.

（二）谓语可由各类实词和多数词组直接充当，不需要任何
标记。

All notional words and most phrases can serve as predicate without any particular marker.

（三）汉语里大量句子的谓语是由动词担任的，谓语动词没
有形态变化。

Most predicates are verbs and it should be noted that,
in Chinese, verbs have no morphological changes.

（四）由动词充当的谓语后边可以带宾语、补语和动态助
词。

A verb predicate can have objects, complements and aspectual particles after it.

（五）形容词充当的谓语后边可以带补语。

An adjectival predicate can be followed by a complement.

（六）谓语前边可以有各类表示修饰、限制的状语。

The predicate can be modified or qualified by various adverbial adjuncts.

三、可以充当谓语的词和词组

Words and phrases which can function as the predicate

（一）动词。

Verbs.

老师教，学生学。　　　　　窗户开着。

我们的理想实现了。　　　　这位太太有一只小狗。

她是我大姨。　　　　　　　炮弹、炸弹都挖出来了。

颐和园在北京的西北郊。　　那个孩子长得很漂亮。

那张画撕了。　　　　　　　昨天代表团团长来过。

那位贵宾赠送市长一件礼物。

（二）形容词。

Adjectives.

北京的夏天很凉快。　　　　他的发音非常准确。

这个青年战士特别勇敢。　　这里的风景美极了。

那个故事很可笑。

（三）名词。

Nouns.

明天新年。

今天阴天。

（四）数词。

Numerals.

他三十。

昨天十一，今天十二。

（五）代词。

Pronouns.

他的发音怎么样？　　　　　　　事情已经这样了。

你怎么了？

（六）联合词组。

Coordinative phrases.

我们已经复习、预习了。

那个孩子活泼可爱。

（七）主谓词组。

Subject-predicate phrases.

她眼睛很大。　　　　　　　病人伤口发炎了。

他态度温和。　　　　　　　毛衣他穿了两件。

（八）偏正词组。

Endocentric phrases.

他北京人。

今天晴天。

（九）数量词组。

Numeral-measure word phrases.

这件毛衣三十块。

现在四点。

（十）固定词组。

Set phrases.

他对朋友一视同仁。

我们应该助人为乐。

四、需要注意的问题 Points that merit special attention

（一）主语和谓语的关系。

Relationships between the subject and the predicate.

主语和谓语的关系有很多种。从意义和作用来看，主语可以是谓语的动作、行为的发出者，也可以是谓语动作的对象；谓语可以表示主语发出或接受动作、行为，也可以对主语进行描写、说明、判断等。例如：

The relationships between the subject and the predicate are

various. In terms of meaning and function, the subject may be either the doer or the receiver of an action indicated by the predicate. The predicate indicates an action done or received by the subject, or describes, explains or makes a judgement of the subject. For example:

他们搬走了屋子里的箱子。

（谓语动作是主语发出的）

(The action indicated by the predicate is done by the subject.)

箱子搬走了。

（谓语动作不是主语发出的，而是由主语接受的）

(The action indicated by the predicate is received rather than done by the subject.)

我们都是青年人。

（谓语对主语进行判断）

(The predicate makes a judgement of the subject.)

这些作家很谦虚。

（谓语对主语进行描写）

(The predicate describes the subject.)

战士们练习投弹。

（谓语对主语的行为进行说明）

(The predicate explains the subject.)

（二）动词作谓语。

Verbs serving as predicate.

1. 动词充当谓语时没有形态变化。无论主语是第几人称、是单数还是复数，是什么性别，是什么词或词组，谓语动词的形式都不变。这一点要特别注意。例如：

The predicate verbs have no morphological changes due to the person, number, gender, word class or phrase class of the subject. For example:

她去南方。　　　　　　我去外国。

你们去吗？

这三个句子的人称、性别和数量都不同，而谓语动词都是"去"。

Although the subjects of the above sentences are different in person, gender and number, the form of the verb 去 is the same.

2. 动词谓语后边可以带宾语。例如：

A predicate verb can have one or two objects after it. For example:

> 我们种花。　　　　　（一个宾语）
> 　　　　　　　　　　（One object）
>
> 他们下棋。
> 他给我两张票。　　　（两个宾语）
> 　　　　　　　　　　（Two objects）
>
> 我教他汉语。

3. 谓语前边可以带各类状语。例如：

A verb predicate can be modified by various adverbial adjuncts. For example:

> 他明天出国。　　　　（时间词）
> 　　　　　　　　　　（Time noun）
>
> 你们里边坐。　　　　（方位词）
> 　　　　　　　　　　（Locality noun）
>
> 那位教授很年轻。　　（副　词）
> 　　　　　　　　　　（Adverb）
>
> 高工程师能参加，　　（助动词）
> 　　　　　　　　　　（Auxiliary）
>
> 小心，慢走！　　　　（形容词）
> 　　　　　　　　　　（Adjective）
>
> 我们一次拿不了。　　（数量词组）

他怎么说？　　　　　　　（ 代　词 ）
　　　　　　　　　　　　　(Pronoun)
我对这种工作很有兴趣。　（ 介词结构 ）
　　　　　　　　　　　　　(Prepositional phrase)

4．动词谓语后边可以带各类补语。例如：

A verb predicate can have various complements after it.
For example:

我听懂了。　　　　　　　（ 结果补语 ）
　　　　　　　　　　　　　(Resultant complement)
他只休息十分钟。　　　　（ 数量补语 ）
　　　　　　　　　　　　　(Quantitative
　　　　　　　　　　　　　complement)

您再讲一遍吧。
你们下来。　　　　　　　（ 趋向补语 ）
　　　　　　　　　　　　　(Directional
　　　　　　　　　　　　　complement)

他跑下来了。
她唱得真好听。　　　　　（ 程度补语 ）
　　　　　　　　　　　　　(Degree complement)
这只箱子太重，我搬不动。（ 可能补语 ）
　　　　　　　　　　　　　(Potential complement)

5．动词谓语后边还可以带动态助词"了、着、过"。例如：

The aspectual particles 了，着 or 过 can be suffixed to a
predicate verb.　For example:

他朋友送了他一束花。　　　　他上星期来过。
我们都坐着。

（三）形容词作谓语。

Adjectives serving as predicate.

1．汉语里，形容词可直接充当谓语，形容词谓语和主语之间不用动词"是"来连接。例如：

In Chinese, an adjective can function as predicate, and the subject and the adjectival predicate are not linked by the verb 是. For example:

（这件衣服长，）那件衣服短。

这种花香，（那种花不香）。

不说"（这件衣服是长，）那件衣服是短"，"这种花是香…"等。

One does not say（这件衣服是长，）那件衣服是短, 这种花是香…, etc.

2．形容词谓语前边一般要用副词"很"，否则就有对比的意思（如上面两个例句）。例如：

The adverb 很 is normally put before an adjective predicate. Without 很, the sentence has an implication of comparison (like the above two examples). For example:

他很高兴。

我们很健康。

3．形容词谓语后边可以带补语。例如：

An adjective predicate can have a complement after it. For example:

这儿的人多极了。　　　（结果补语）
　　　　　　　　　　　　（Resultant complement）

他快五秒钟。　　　　　（数量补语）
　　　　　　　　　　　　（Quantitative complement）

这个公园大得很。　　　（程度补语）
　　　　　　　　　　　　（Degree complement）

他高兴得唱起来了。

（四）名词作谓语。

Nouns serving as predicate.

名词、数词、名词性偏正词组或数量词组作谓语的情况比较少，一般只限于说明主语的职业、籍贯、日期、天气或年龄。例如：

Nouns, numerals, endocentric nominal phrases or nume-ral-measure word phrases function as predicate only to indicate occupation, nationality, date, weather or age. For example:

我大学生。　　　　今天二十二号。

她十八。　　　　　今天晴天。

他上海人。

（五）主谓词组作谓语。

Subject-predicate phrases serving as the predicate.

主谓词组作谓语时，它和全句主语之间一般不能用动词"是"连接。例如：

The verb 是 can not be used between the sentence subject and the predicate which is a subject-predicate phrase. For example:

这孩子头发很少。　　　（孩子的头发少）

那种苹果我买两公斤。　　（我买两公斤苹果）

一般不说"这孩子是头发很少"或"那种苹果是我买两公斤"。

Usually we don't say 这孩子是头发很少 or 那种苹果是我买两公斤

练　习　23
Exercise 23

（一）用横线标出下列句子的谓语部分。

Underline the predicate sections in the following sen-tences:

例：

Model: 社员们<u>觉得这个办法好</u>。

1．他舍不得离开这儿。

2．他们是石油工人。

3．那位戴眼镜的老师很关心同学。

4．我们全体同学都想参观那个画展。

5．这些句子包括主语部分和谓语部分。

6．他送我们许多礼物。

7．这条新闻引起了广大群众的注意。

8．大声朗读课文是十分必要的。

9．那个小男孩哭得真伤心。

10．我们今天请的客人都是老朋友。

（二）用横线标出下列句子的谓语，并指出是哪类词或词组。

Underline the predicates in the following sentences and explain what kind of words or phrases they are.

例：

Model: 我们都<u>热爱</u>自己的祖国。（动词Verb）

1．这里的交通很方便。　　　　　（　　　　　）

2．他是人民群众的领袖。　　　　（　　　　　）

3．我给他一张报纸。　　　　　　（　　　　　）

4．他的考试成绩很好。　　　　　（　　　　　）

5．星星、月亮都出来了。　　　　（　　　　　）

6．他说他傍晚来。　　　　　　　（　　　　　）

7．每个人都应该谦虚谨慎。　　　（　　　　　）

8．她们两个人意见一致。　　　　（　　　　　）

9．一公斤虾两块钱。　　　　　　（　　　　　）

10．这个问题还没解决。　　　　　（　　　　　）

第三节　宾　语

Section III　The object

一、什么叫宾语 Definition

　　动词谓语后边可以有一种连带成分，表示动作的对象、产生的结果，或表示动作达到的处所、动作所用的工具等等，这样的连带成分叫宾语。例如：

The object is a sentence element following the predicate verb indicating the target or result of an action, the place where the action reaches, or the instrument with which the action is done.　For example:

动词谓语　——　宾语

Predicate verb ＋ object

看　　　　　电视

织　　　　　毛衣

参观　　　　学校

讲　　　　　故事

他写信。

工人打井。

代表们去礼堂。

他们用剪子。

二、宾语的语法特点 Grammatical features

（一）宾语一般在动词谓语后边。

An object is usually preceded by the predicate verb.

（二）宾语多由名词、代词充当，也可由其他词和词组充当，不需要任何标记。

Objects are mainly nouns and pronouns, but may also be words of other parts of speech or phrases without any particular marker.

（三）宾语前边可以带各类表示修饰和限制的词和词组作定语。

The object can be premodified by attributive words or phrases.

三、可以充当宾语的词和词组

Words or phrases which can serve as the object

（一）名词。
Nouns.

他每天自学汉语。　　　　　我们参观故宫博物院。

我明天去大使馆。　　　　　我送妹妹一对枕头。

他们看足球比赛。　　　　　他告诉我一件事。

我想买点东西。

（二）代词。
Pronouns.

昨天我看见他了。　　　　　麻烦您了。

我去过那儿。　　　　　　　酱油在这儿。

这件事教育了大家。　　　　他给我一张歌剧票。

（三）动词。
Verbs.

他特别喜欢旅游。

他每天早上坚持锻炼。

一九四九年中国人民获得了解放。

吃米饭是南方人的习惯。

（四）形容词。
Adjectives.

他不怕苦，不怕累。　　　　那儿有没有危险？

劳动的时候要注意安全。

（五）数词。
Numerals.

九加二等于十一。　　　　　他的房间号是三一七。

四的两倍是八。

（六）联合词组。
Coordinative phrases.

我有梳子和镜子。

他找你和我。

出席这次大会的都是劳动模范和战斗英雄。

我们应该不断地总结经验和教训。

这首诗反映了人们的愿望和要求。

（七）主谓词组。

Subject-predicate phrases.

他发现这里也有这种细菌。 这是我第一次来中国。

我知道他出国了。 我认为你比他热情。

（八）动宾词组。

Verb-object phrases.

她喜欢开玩笑。 他爱观察各种自然现象。

她最讨厌抽烟。 我们开始写汉字吧。

（九）偏正词组。

Endocentric phrases.

他觉得不太舒服。

他表示非常了解。

（十）数量词组。

Numeral-measure word phrases.

（这种梨）我想买三公斤。 （这些礼物）你挑几件吧。

（那本小说）我才看了两页。

（十一）补充词组。

Complementary phrases.

他感到高兴极了。 她怕买多了。

我觉得饿得很。

（十二）方位词组。

Locality phrases.

他在我左边儿。 那件大衣在衣柜里。

你的信在桌子上。

（十三）同位词组。

Appositive phrases.

我看马方他们。

这个消息已经通知他们俩了。

我们要去的地方是中国最美丽的城市杭州。

（十四）固定词组。

Set phrases.

我去过万里长城。

他想参观北京大学。

（十五）"的"字结构。

的-phrases.

这些都是铁的。　　　　他买吃的。

我要绿的。　　　　　　你用我的。

四、需要注意的问题 Points that merit special attention

（一）宾语和动词谓语的关系。

Relationships between the object and the verbal predicate.

宾语和动词谓语的关系有很多种。从意义和作用来看，宾语可以是接受谓语动作的对象或发出者，也可以是动作产生的结果、影响，也可以是动作达到的处所或动作所用的工具等。例如：

The relationships between the object and the verb predicate are various. In terms of meaning and function, the object can be the doer or receiver of an action, the result or influence of an action, the destination of an action, or the instrument with which an action is done. For example:

他们踢足球。

（"足球"是动作的对象）

（足球 is the receiver of the action 踢.）

外边来了一个人。

（"一个人"是动作的发出者）

（一个人 is the doer of the action 来.）

她织了一件毛衣。

（"一件毛衣"是动作的结果）

（一件毛衣 is the result of the action 织.）

他去上海。

（"上海"是动作达到的处所）

（上海 is the destination of the action 去.）

（二）汉语里宾语本身没有任何标记，词和词组都是直接充当宾语的。动词、动宾词组、动词性联合、偏正词组、动补词组或主谓词组作宾语时，也不需要用介词或代词等，而且动词形态不变。这一点很重要。例如：

Words or phrases are used as objects without any morphological marker. When verbs, V-O phrases, coordinative or endocentric verbal phrases, V-C phrases or S-P phrases function as the object, no preposition or pronoun is required to go with them and the verb in these phrases remains unchanged in form. This point is very important. For example:

我们需要休息。　　　我需要休息一会儿。

他需要要喝水。　　　他决定去一次。

我们需要计划安排。　我们听说他住院了。

他需要多休息。

绝不能说成"我们听说那件事他住院了"等。

One can never say 我们听说那件事他住院了, etc.

（三）当动词和形容词代表一种事物时，也可以充当宾语，不过谓语有一定的限制。例如：

In Chinese, verbs and adjectives can also function as the object when they refer to things. But they only go with the following kinds of predicate verbs:

1．表示心理活动或感知性的动词作谓语。

Verbs denoting mental activities and senses.

他不怕冷，怕热。　　我认为应该警惕。

大家感到满意。　　　他知道怎样走。

2．表示开始、持续、终结的动词作谓语。

Verbs indicating beginning, continuation or ending.

这儿又开始热闹了。　　　　他们俩常常进行辩论。

我们继续钻研。　　　　　　那里已经停止战斗。

3．表示得、失、增、减一类意义的动词作谓语。

Verbs indicating gain or loss, addition or reduction.

他遭到了不幸。　　　　　这样做能减少损失。

这种机床已经得到改进。　对不起，给您添麻烦了。

（四）表示处所的名词、代词可以作宾语。要表示与人或事物有关的处所时，宾语需由方位词组担任，或在指人或事物的名词、代词后边加上指示代词"这儿"或"那儿"。例如：

Place nouns and pronouns can be used as objects. To refer to a place relevant to a person or thing, the object must be a locality noun phrase or a noun (personal or non-personal reference) plus the demonstrative pronoun 这儿 or 那儿. For example:

我们去老师那儿。　　　　球在椅子那儿。

今天的报在我这儿。

绝不能说成"我们去老师"，"报在我"或"球在椅子"等。

One can never say 我们去老师, 报在我 or 球在椅子, etc.

（五）数量词组作宾语时，它所指的事物在前边提到过或语言环境很清楚。例如：

Wher acting as an object, a N-Mw phrase must be one referring to sth. mentioned earlier or understood by the context. For example:

这些点心你吃几块吧。

（你买桔子吗？）我买六个。

（这种蛋很好）我要两公斤半。

（六）单宾语和双宾语。

Single objects and double objects.

1.汉语里，及物动词后边可以带宾语，也可以不带宾语。例如：

In Chinese, a transitive verb can take an object and it can go without one. For example:

我们听写。 （不带宾语）
（Without an object)

我们听写汉字。 （带宾语"汉字"）
（With 汉字 as the object)

带一个宾语时，叫单宾语。例如：

When there is only one object, it is called a single object. For example:

他喝啤酒。 我炒菜。

她们烤面包。

2.少数及物动词后边还可以带两个宾语，叫双宾语。前一个叫间接宾语，多由指人的名词、代词充当。后一个叫直接宾语，多由指事物的名词或词组充当。例如：

Some transitive verbs take two objects, which are called double objects. The first one, mostly a personal noun or pronoun, is called an indirect object and the second one, mostly a noun or phrase of non-personal reference, is named the direct object. For example:

（主语——）谓语（及物动词）——间接宾语（指人）——直接宾语（指事物）

(Subject +) Predicate (Transitive Verb) + Indirect Object (Referring to a thing) + Direct Object (Referring to a person)

（中国教师——）教——我们——汉语。

（他——）送——外国朋友——一件礼物。

两个宾语之间不需要任何虚词连接。但两个宾语的次序是固定的，指人的间接宾语一定要放在指事物的直接宾语前边，不能弄错。例如：

No function word is used between the two objects, but their order is fixed: the indirect object (referring to person) is followed by the direct object (of non-personal reference). For example:

他还朋友一本地图。

哥哥给我一个足球。

不能说成"他还一本地图朋友","哥哥给一个足球我"等。

One can not say 他还一本地图朋友, 哥哥给一个足球我, etc.

可以带双宾语的动词很少。（见第二章动词一节）

Verbs which can have double objects are very few in number. (See Section I, Chapter Two.)

（七）主谓词组作宾语。

Subject-predicate phrases serving as objects.

少数表示心理活动、感知性等的动词作谓语时，后边可以带主谓词组充当的宾语。例如：

Verbs denoting mental activities and cognition can take S-P phrases as objects, but they are very few in number. For example:

他说他明天回信。

我想他明天一定来。

我觉得他很为难。

这样的动词还有：

Other verbs of this category are:

认为、记得、知道、发现、相信、希望、盼望、看见、听见、听说、答应、记住、忘了、忘记、怕。

（八）前置宾语。

The fronted object.

为了强调、对比，或使句子简洁起见，有时宾语也可以放在动词谓语或主语前边，这样的宾语叫前置宾语。前置宾语在形式上没有任何标记；从意义上看，一般应是动词谓语能支配的对象，而且可以移到动词谓语后边；从结构上看，谓语前边或后边常带状语或补语等。

The object can be moved to the front of the predicate verb or the subject for emphasis, comparison or terseness. This is known as the fronted object. The fronted object is not marked morphologically, but notionally it must be the target which can be affected by the predicate verb and, moreover, it can be placed at the normal post-position. Structurally, the predicate is usually preceded by an adverbial adjunct or followed by a complement.

1. 前置宾语在主语后谓语前。例如：

The fronted object coming between the subject and the predicate. For example:

　　　　我这些文章能看懂。

　　　　　　（我能看懂这些文章。）

　　　　我上海去过，南京也去过。

　　　　　　（我去过上海，也去过南京。）

　　　　他们那个展览会已经参观了。

　　　　　　（他们已经参观了那个展览会。）

　　　　他英语、汉语说得都很好。

　　　　　　（他说英语、汉语说得都很好。）

2. 前置宾语在主语前。例如：

The fronted object coming before the subject. For example:

　　　　那个问题我们解决了。

　　　　　　（我们解决了那个问题。）

　　　　那样的裙子她买来了。

　　　　　　（她买来了那样的裙子。）

258

杭州、广州他都住过。

　　　　（他住过杭州、广州。）

你寄来的信我收到了。

　　　　（我收到了你寄来的信。）

　　前置宾语在主语前的句子和主谓词组作谓语的句子不同。带前置宾语的句子中谓语后边不能再带别的宾语，说话时重音在前置宾语上；而在主谓词组作谓语的句子中，主谓词组里的动词后边常带数量词组充当的宾语，而且是属于全句主语的一部分，说话时重音在谓语上。例如：

Note that a sentence with the object before the subject is different from that with a S-P phrase as predicate. In the first case, the predicate can not have another object after it, and the fronted object should be stressed in pronunciation. But in the second case, the verb of the S-P phrase usually has a N-Mw phrase as its object, which is also a part of the sentence subject, and the stress falls on the predicate verb in pronunciation. For example:

　　　　这件衬衫我洗干净了。　　（前置宾语）
　　　　　　　　　　　　　　　　　(Fronted object)

　　　　那几位委员我不认得。
　　　　他的眼镜腿摔坏了一条。　（主谓词组作谓语）
　　　　　　　　　　　　　　　　　(S-P phrase as predicate)

　　　　那些馒头我炸了两个。

练 习 24
Exercise 24

（一）用横线标出下列句子的宾语，并指出是哪类词或词组。

Underline the objects in the following sentences and

explain what kind of words or phrases they are.

例：

Model：我很喜欢<u>晒太阳</u>。 （动宾词组） (V-O phrases)

1．这块大石头象<u>一只狮子</u>。
2．我们叫<u>一辆出租汽车</u>吧。
3．每个民族都有<u>自己的风俗习惯</u>。
4．客人对主人表示<u>祝贺</u>。
5．我听说<u>那个城市不太大</u>。
6．一年有<u>十二个月</u>。
7．我的朋友琼斯排球篮球都打得很好。
8．上星期六我们请来了<u>几位作家</u>。
9．每个人都应该爱护<u>自己的眼睛</u>。
10．你送我的那支钢笔我很喜欢。

（二）用横线标出下列句子的<u>主语</u>和<u>宾语</u>，并指出宾语是哪类词或词组。

Draw a double line under the subject and a single line under the object in each sentence and explain what kind of a word or phrase the object is.

例：

Model：<u>这</u>是<u>竹子</u>。（名词） (Noun)

1．他妹妹是护士。
2．那台拖拉机是人民公社的。
3．他们工厂需要请一位医生。
4．看病是他的职业。
5．那位优秀售货员介绍了自己的经验。
6．光线太强对眼睛没有好处。
7．每个人都应该学习一些科学常识。
8．他答应下星期比赛。
9．他发现同学们已经出发了。
10．我忘了他妹妹是护士。

第四节 定 语

Section IV The Attributive

一、什么叫定语 Definition

修饰、限制主语或宾语的词或词组叫定语，被修饰的词叫中心语。定语是表示中心语的性状、质料、数量、所属、处所、时间、范围等的前加成分。例如：

A word or phrase which modifies or restricts the subject or object is called an attributive and the word modified by the attributive is called the head word. In other words, the attributive is the premodifier showing the property, quality, quantity, category, place, time or scope of what is denoted by the head word. For example:

在主语前边的定语：

Attributives preceding the subject:

定语——中心语（主语）——谓语——（宾语）

Attributive + head word (subject) + predicate + (object)

他朋友是一个演员。	这套衣服是我的。
我的汉语老师是中国人。	下月的计划在抽屉里。
我们小组去英国。	休息的地方很多。
石头房子很结实。	衣柜里边没有大衣。

在宾语前边的定语：

Attributives preceding the object:

主语——谓语——定语——中心语（宾语）

Subject + predicate + attributive + modified word
                                    (object)

教我们世界历史的老师是英国人。

我要买两顶帽子。

他们在花园里。

参观的人都住南边的楼上。

这是晚上七点的歌剧票。

我想听一个钟头的音乐。

今天下午我们听他的报告。

我喜欢白颜色。

你参加周末（跳）舞（晚）会吗？

二、定语的语法特点 Grammatical features

（一）定语一定在中心语前边。

The attributive always precedes the head word.

（二）定语可由各类实词或词组充当。

All notional words or phrases can serve as attributives.

（三）定语后边常带结助构词"的 (de)"。

The structural particle 的 (de) is often attached to the attributive.

三、可以充当定语的词和词组

Words or phrases which can serve as attributive:

（一）名词。

Nouns.

厂长的办公室在二层。　　那是经理的帽子。

去年的画报都给别人了。　　这是爷爷的袜子。

旁边的房间是空的。

（二）代词。

Pronouns.

我父亲不吸烟。　　我参加了他们的婚礼。

我们学校在郊区。　　我很喜欢这儿的天气。

我的老师对工作十分认真。

（三）形容词。

Adjectives.

他喜欢圆桌子。　　　　　　　大家走进了庄严的会场。

这座楼里有许多空房间。

（四）动词。

Verbs.

我看见过游行队伍。　　　　旅行的人都走了。

请的客人都到了。

（五）数词。

Numerals.

三的二十倍是六十。

这个书架一共有五层。

（六）联合词组。

Coordinative phrases.

父亲答应了我和弟弟的要求。

我接到了父亲、母亲的回信。

大家用信任和谅解的眼光看着他。

这是积极而可靠的办法。

（七）主谓词组。

Subject-predicate phrases.

他热爱他从事的工作。

我们参观的工厂在郊区。

我新买的那件上衣是浅绿的。

他就是我说的那个人。

（八）动宾词组。

Verb-object phrases.

参加比赛的运动员来到了体育馆。

交流经验的座谈会明天开。

看武术的人坐这辆汽车。

我想认识几个说普通话的中国朋友。

（九）偏正词组。

Endocentric phrases.

他是音乐老师的好朋友。

刚成立的研究小组有五个人。

这儿有很高级的家具。

那本语法书的封面上有他的名字。

（十）数量词组。

Numeral-measure word phrases.

这是一所医院。　　　　那是一幢新楼

草原上有一群羊。　　　　他买了两件大衣。

（十一）补充词组。

Complementary phrases.

洗好的照片在这个盒子里。

学得好的同学都得到了奖励。

进来的这个人是我哥哥的朋友。

看完的书应该放回原来的地方。

（十二）方位词组。

Locality phrases.

书架上的花瓶倒了。

他写了一万字以上的论文。

这位三十岁左右的同志是新来的职员。

我要查查十二号前后的报纸。

（十三）同位词组。

Appositive phrases.

他们俩的友谊特别深。　她自己能处理好她自己的事。

我去姐姐她们那儿。　　琼斯他们的汉语水平很高。

（十四）固定词组。

Set phrases.

你有中华人民共和国的地图吗？

他是一个多才多艺的人。

（十五）介词结构。

Prepositional phrases.

我们已经完成了对这个问题的调查。

关于这个题目的论文他写了一篇。

我谈谈对于妇女地位的看法。

四、需要注意的问题 Points that merit special attention

（一）定语的位置。The position of the attributive.

定语一定要放在被修饰、限制的中心语前边，不能颠倒，否则结构和意思就会完全改变，甚至不能表达任何意思。这一点要特别注意。例如：

It must be noted that the attributive must be placed before the head word it modifies and this order can not be reversed, for the reversion of order will lead to a change of structure and meaning and will even make the phrase senseless.   For example:

前边的路

（"路的前边"的中心语是"前边"，"路"是定语）

(In the phrase 路的前边, 前边 is the head word and 路 the attributive of 前边.)

左面的山真美。

（"山的左面"的中心语是"左面"，"山"是定语）

(In the phrase 山的左面, 左面 is the head word and 山 the attributive of 左面.)

旁边的箱子

（"箱子的旁边"的中心语是"旁边"，"箱子"是定语）

(In the phrase 箱子的旁边, 旁边 is the head word and 箱子 the attributive of 旁边.)

你妹妹

（指"你的妹妹"——"她"）

(你妹妹 means "your younger sister". It refers to a third person.)

（"妹妹你"是同位词组）

(妹妹你 is an appositive phrase.)

厚棉衣

（"棉衣厚"是主谓词组）

(棉衣厚 is a S-P phrase.)

取得的成绩

（"成绩的取得"的中心语是"取得"，定语是
"成绩"）

(In the phrase 成绩的取得, the head word is
取得 and 成绩 the attributive.)

木头桌子

（不能说"桌子木头"）

(桌子木头 is ungrammatical.)

厂长的办公室

（不能说成"办公室的厂长"）

(办公室的厂长 is not logical.)

大使的汽车

（不能说成"汽车的大使"）

（汽车的大使 makes no sense.)

今天的《人民日报》

（不能说成"《人民日报》的今天"）

（《人民日报》的今天 means sth. else.)

去年的《中国建设》

（不能说成"《中国建设》的去年"）

（《中国建设》的去年 is senseless.)

我们的教室

（不能说成"教室的我们"）

(There is no such form as 教室的我们.)

大家的主意

（不能说成"主意的大家"）

（One can not say 主意的大家.)

    人家的行李

（不能说成"行李的人家"）

（One can not say 行李的人家.)

（二）定语和结构助词"的"。

Attributives and the structural particle 的.

有些定语后边需要用助词"的"，有的不能用"的"，有的用不用"的"都可以。定语后边用不用"的"，一般规律可归纳如下：

Some attributives must be followed by 的, others must not and with still others 的 is optional. The general rules for the use of 的 are as follows:

1. 下列情况都需要用"的"：

的 must be used in the following circumstances:

定 语 Attributives	举 例 Examples
名词：表示领属关系 Nouns: Possessive nouns	病人的心脏
表示时间 Time nouns	今天的活动安排
表示处所 Place nouns	中间的座位
代词：表示领属关系 Pronouns: Possessive pronouns	你的信
表示处所 Place pronouns	这儿的风俗
表示方式、式样等 Pronouns of manner or type	这样的的做法 那样的房子

形容词：强调修饰性的单音词
Adjectives:
    Monosyllables emphasizing
      modification
	新的杂志

修饰单音词的双音词
    Dissyllables modifying
      monosyllables
	快乐的歌

重叠形式 The reduplicated forms	绿绿的庄稼 整整齐齐的队伍
数　词：在数目前边 Numerals preceding a number	十的二分之一
动　词 Verbs	讨论的题目
联合词组 Coordinative phrases	儿子和女儿的事 学习和工作的内容
主谓词组 S-P phrases	留学生住的房间 他讲的话
动宾词组 V-O phrases	看话剧的观众 游览长城的人
偏正词组 Endocentric phrases	一个衣柜的价钱 很快的速度 三点开的火车

补充词组 Complementary phrases	洗干净的毛巾 看不清楚的字 寄来的东西 跳得非常好的舞蹈演员 短一点的绳子
方位词组 Locality phrases	树上的叶子 一年以内的打算 五十上下的年纪
同位词组 Appositive phrases	我自己的意见 玛丽她们的汽车
固定词组 Set phrases	天安门广场的面积
介词结构 Prepositional phrases	关于太阳的传说 朝南的屋子

2．下列情况不用"的"：
的 is not used under the following circumstances:

定　语 Attributives	举　例 Examples
名　词：表示人或事物的性质 Nouns: Nouns denoting the 　　　quality of a person or 　　　thing	玻璃杯 金戒指
固定组合 　Fixed combinations	北京机场

代　词：表示亲属关系 Pronouns: Pronouns indicating family relationships	我母亲 她哥哥
在表示集体单位的名词前 Pronouns used before nouns referring to names of collectives or units	我们学校 我国
"这、那"在数词、量词前这 or 那 preceding a numeral or a measure word	这三本 那张
"什么、多少"在名词前 什么 or 多少 preceding a noun	什么地方 多少时间
形容词：单音词 Adjectives: Monosyllables	大游泳池 薄毛衣
双音词的固定组合 Dissyllabic adjectives in fixed combinations	老实人 要紧事
量　词：重叠形式 Measure words: Reduplicated forms	件件礼物 门门课程
动　词：表示人或事物的性质 Verbs: Verbs denoting the quality of a person or thing	劳动人民 庆祝活动
数量词组：在名词前 N-Mw phrases: Before nouns	一架飞机 三座山
在动词前 Before verbs	一场争论

3.下列情况用不用"的"都可以：

的 is optional in the following circumstances:

定 语 Attributives	举 例 Examples
代 词：双音词修饰表示集体单 位的单音名词 Pronouns: Dissyllables modify- ing monosyllables refe- rring to names of coll- ectives or units	你们（的）班 他们（的）组
形容词：双音词修饰双音词 Adjectives: Dissyllables modifyi¯ ng dissyllables	幸福（的）生活 痛苦（的）回忆
数量词组：数词"一"和借用名 词，表示"量多" N-Mw phrases: "Numeral 一 + Noun of Measure" indicating a great quantity 重叠形式 The reduplicated form[s]	一头（的）汗 一屋子（的）人 一辆一辆（的）汽车
偏正词组"很多"、不少 The endocentric phrases 很多 and 不少	很多（的）问题 不少（的）人

（三）定语的排列次序。

Order of attributives.

主语或宾语前边可以有各种表示修饰、限制的词和词组充当的定语，有些可以同时使用。这些并用的词和词组一般按下列次序排列。

The subject or object can have various attributives, i.e. words or phrases premodifying them. Sometimes the attributives can be used simultaneously and they are arranged according to the following order.

表示领属关系的名词、代词——指示代词——数量词组——表示修饰关系的形容词或名词——（中心语：指人或事物）

Possessive noun or pronoun + demonstrative pronoun +Numeral-Measure word phrase +Descriptive adjective or noun + (head word of personal or non-personal reference)

例如：

For example:

你——这——三本——新——（杂志）

我朋友——那——（一）架——长城牌——（照相机）

他——那——（一）个——好——（朋友）

我——这——四位——老——（领导）

练 习 25
Exercise 25

（一）用横线标出下列句子的定语，并指出中心语是主语还是宾语。

Underline the attributives in the following sentences and state whether the head words are subjects or objects.

例：

Model:　这是他借来的汉英词典。（宾语）(Object)

1. 中国是一个多民族的国家。

2. 我和他的想法一样。

3. 哪间屋子是厨房？

4. 他买到了新出版的《中国青年》了。

5. 人民的利益最重要。

6. 雄伟壮观的长城到了。

7. 爱好美术的同学都在这儿。

8. 那些高大的建筑是一个研究所的。

9. 为人民牺牲的英雄们永远值得纪念。

10. 我们都听到了这个鼓舞人的消息。

（二）在下列句子中适当的地方加上结构助词"的"。

Put the structural particle 的 in the following sentences whenever necessary.

1. 你看看挂在墙上照片。

2. 这座楼是学生吃饭地方。

3. 去上海旅客从这边上车。

4. 刚才来客人是我叔叔。

5. 这巳经是三年前事了。

6. 那座大楼是研究环境保护地方。

7. 我刚接到朋友寄来信。

8. 人们都穿着干干净净衣服。

9. 我买了三张下星期三电影票。

10. 他真是一个很热情人。

第五节 状 语
Section V   Adverbial Adjuncts

一、什么叫状语 Definition

修饰、限制谓语的词或词组叫状语，被修饰的词叫中心语。

状语是表示中心语的时间、处所、程度、范围、情态、肯定否定、重复、主动被动、对象、原因等的前加成分。例如：

A word or phrase modifying or restricting the predicate is called an adverbial adjunct and the word it modifies is the head word. In other words, the adverbial adjunct is the pre-modifying element denoting the time, place, degree, scope, aspect, affirmation or negation, repetition, activeness or passiveness, target, reason, etc. of the head word. For example:

在动词谓语前边的状语：

Adverbial adjuncts premodifying the verb predicate:

状语——中心语（动词谓语）

Adverbial adjunct ＋ modified word (verb predicate)

他昨天参加了一个招待会。

我们那边看看。

他很关心大家的健康。

我只有一本汉语语法书。

她们不肯来。

今天他又打了一个电话。

工人们都熟练地工作着。

小弟弟顽皮地笑了。

他的汉语书被朋友借去了。

小王为做实验准备了一个星期。

在形容词谓语前边的状语：

Adverbial adjuncts premodifying adjective predicate:

状语——中心语（形容词谓语）

Adverbial adjunct ＋ Head word (adjective predicate)

他非常谨慎。

他对人很热情。

他说话的声音不大。

在其他谓语前边的状语

274

Adverbial adjuncts premodifying other types of predicates:

他已经二十八岁了。

今天大概十七号。

二、状语的语法特点 Grammatical features

（一）状语一定要在中心语前边。

The adverbial adjunct always precedes the head word.

（二）状语可由各类词或词组充当。

All kinds of words or phrases can act as an adverbial adjunct.

（三）状语后边常带结构助词"地 (de)"。

The structural particle 地 (de) is often attached to the adverbial adjunct.

三、可以充当状语的词和词组

Words or phrases which can serve as adverbial adjuncts

（一）副词。副词的基本作用就是作状语。例如：

Adverbs. Adverbs function basicly as adverbial adjuncts. For example:

他很喜欢这种花。　　　　他始终是我的好朋友。

他曾经来过这个城市。　　这棵树相当高。

他刚离开我这儿。　　　　他再三表示感谢。

他经常去市图书馆。　　　观众陆续走进了剧场。

我们赶快走吧。　　　　　他们大约六点半到。

他一向尊重别人。　　　　你们到底赞成不赞成？

（二）介词结构。介词结构的主要作用是作状语。例如：

Prepositional phrases. Prepositional phrases are mainly used as adverbial adjuncts. For example:

客人们从这边走。　　　这次报告会凭票入场。

这件事由他负责。　　　这篇论文的内容比那篇丰富。

他们家离旅馆不太远。

（三）名词（时间词、方位词）。

Nouns (including nouns of time and locality).

我们后年毕业。　　　　　　我们外边散散步吧。

星期四学校举行联欢晚会。　你里边坐一会儿。

他每天下午练钢琴。

（四）助动词。助动词的主要作用是作状语。例如：

Auxiliary verbs: Auxiliary verbs mainly function as adverbial adjuncts. For example:

他会煎鸡蛋。　　　　　　你能适应这儿的气候吗？

我们应该提高效率。　　　他要解答读者的问题。

他敢跟你比赛。

（五）动词。

Verbs.

他尊敬地说："谢谢！"　　我明确地答复了她。

他称赞地点了点头。

（六）形容词。

Adjectives.

这个字要重读。

桌子上的资料你们不要乱动。

这些困难都顺利地克服了。

这次科学大会圆满地闭幕了。

（七）代词。

Pronouns.

你们这样抄。

这个汉字怎么写？

（八）联合词组。

Coordinative phrases.

朋友们耐心亲切地安慰我。

他具体生动地叙述了一遍。

他小心冷静地处理着这个事件。

他又失望又后悔地哭了。

（九）主谓词组。

Subject-predicate phrases.

大家都心情舒畅地交谈着。

他语气肯定地说明了情况。

她心疼地吻了吻自己的小儿子。

我心急地等着他的答复。

（十）偏正词组。

Endocentric phrases.

他三点钟会见代表团成员。

我们一个月组织了两个展览。

同学们十分诚恳地劝他。

他不同意地摇摇头。

（十一）数量词组。

Numeral-measure word phrases.

他三天只睡了八小时。　　宴会八点点始。

我们这遍念得快一些。　　我一趟拿得了。

（十二）方位词组。

Locality phrases.

我们花园里走走。　　我两点以前在公园门口等你。

你们屋里谈吧。　　参加旅游的人十天以后回来。

（十三）固定词组。

Set phrases.

他不知所措地看着我们俩。

大家实事求是地总结了前一段的工作。

四、需要注意的问题　Points that merit special attention

（一）状语的位置。

The position of the adverbial adjunct.

状语一定要放在被修饰、限制的中心语前边，而不能在后面。这一点要特别注意。例如：

What should be noted is that adverbial adjuncts must

precede, not follow, the head words which they modify or restrict.　For example:

他不欢迎我们。
（不能说成"他欢迎不我们"）
(One can not say 他欢迎不我们.)
任务很明确。
（不能说成"任务明确很"）
(It is ungrammatical to say 任务明确很.)
我对他说："别去了。"
（不能说成"我说对他…"）
(There is no such form as 我说对他…)
他明天要接待外国贵宾。
（不能说成"他要接待外国贵宾明天"）
(It is wrong to say 他要接待外国贵宾明天.)
他始终不满足已经取得的成果。
（不能说成"他不满足已经取得的成果始终"）
(One can not say他不满足已经取得的成果始终.)

（二）状语和结构助词"地"。

Adverbial adjuncts and the structural particle 地.

有些状语后边需要用助词"地"，有的不能用"地"，有的用不用"地"都可以。状语后边用不用"地"，一般规律可归纳如下：

Some adverbial adjuncts must be followed by 地, others must not and with still others 地 is optional. The general rules guiding the use of 地 are summed up as follows:

1.下列情况都需要用"地"：

地 must be used under the following circumstances;

状　语 Adverbial Adjuncts	例　句 Examples
动词： Verbs:	大家注意地听着。
形容词兼属动词的双音词 Dissyllabic adjectives including their verb conversions	他高兴地笑了。
表示情态的双音词 　　Dissyllabic adjectives of emotion	他惭愧地低下了头。 她轻松地唱了一个歌。
双音词的重叠形式 　　Reduplicated form of adjectives	大家舒舒服服地睡了一觉。 我们要仔仔细细地汇报。
联合词组：动词 Coordinative phrases: Of verbs	他们连说带笑地走过来了。
动宾词组 　　Of verbal phrases	社员们有目的有计划地安排生产。
形容词 　　Of adjectives	双方亲切友好地交换了意见。
主谓词组： Subject-predicate phrases	她心疼地看了孩子一眼。
偏正词组：动词性的 Endocentric phrases: Verbal	他不满意地走了。
形容词性的 　　Adjectival	他十分谦虚地介绍了自己的作品。

数量词组：重叠形式 N-Mw phrase: 　　Their reduplicated forms	你们两个两个地排好队。
固定词组： Set phrases	我们兴高彩烈地谈论着。

2. 下列情况不用"地"：

地 is not used under the following circumstances:

状　语 Adverbial Adjuncts	例　句 Examples
副词：在动词谓语前 Adverbs: 　　Before verb predicates	很多领导人都出席了这个 　宴会。 通知已经发出去了。 这次试验终于成功了。 我多么希望当一个汉语教 　师啊！
在形容词前 Before adjectives	这种花真香。 昨天冷，今天更冷。 这几天他的情绪很正常。
在副词前 Before other adverbs	他也不知道。 他一直十分乐观。
介词结构： Prepositional phrases:	我们在月光下散步。 大家为贵宾们的幸福干杯。 他对我很好。 在一定的条件下，我们同 　意这个设计。

名词：表示时间 Nouns: Of time 　表示处所 　Of locality	星期五我们去大使馆。 我们昨天拿到了护照。 前边来了一个人。
助动词： Auxiliary verbs: 　在助动词前 　Before other auxiliaries	办公的地方应该安静。 我们应该能解决这个难题。
形容词：单音词 Monosyllabic Adjectives	快走啊！ 学习语言一定要多听多说。
代词： Pronouns:	你不该这样说。
偏正词组：名词性的 Nominal endocentric phrases	我这个月病了两天。
数量词组： N-Mw phrases:	这次我们输了两个球。
方位词组： Locality phrases:	我来北京以前没看见过这种动物。 窗户上挂着窗帘。

3. 下列情况用不用"地"都可以：
地 is optional under the following circumstances:

状　语 Adverbial Adjuncts	例　句 Examples
形容词：单音词的重叠形式 Adjectives:　Reduplicated form of monosyllables	学生要好好（地）学习。 你们慢慢（地）走。
双音词修饰双音词 Dissyllabic　adjectives modifying　other dissyllabic　words	我们都努力（地）学习。 他全面（地）解释了这个 问题。

（三）副词连用时的次序。

The order of adverbs used in succession.

有的副词常连在一起作状语。副词连用时要注意先后次序，修饰成分总是在被修饰的成分前边，一定不能弄错，不然就会把意思弄错或者根本不能说明什么意思。例如：

Two or more adverbs are often used in succession as adverbial adjuncts.　When thus used, attention should be paid to their order: the modifying one always precedes the modified one and this order can not be reversed. Otherwise the meaning will be changed or become illogical or ungrammatical.　For example:

很多大学生都常常参加业余演出。

（不能说"常常都"）

(One can not say 常常都.)

十年前的这件事我已经不记得了。

（不能说"不已经"）

(不已经 is ungrammatical.)

（我们都来了。）他们也都来了。

（我不是技术员。）她也不是技术员。

"也" 总是在 "都" 或 "不" 的前边，不能说 "都也" 或 "不也"。

The adverb 也 always precedes 都 or 不, therefore there is no such forms as 都也 or 不也.

（四）表示时段的数量词组或名词性偏正词组也可以作状语，表示在某段时间里发生了什么情况。例如：

N-Mw phrases and nominal endocentric phrases of duration can also be used as adverbial adjuncts expressing sth. happens during the period indicated by such a phrase. For example:

> 他三夜没睡觉了。
>
> 这几位青年七个月完成了一年的任务。

（五）"很少" 作状语。

很少 as adverbial.

表示强调极少的程度时可以用 "很少" 作状语。例如：

很少 is used as an adverbial adjunct to express the idea of "seldom" or "rarely". For example:

> 这个地区很少下雨。　　我很少跳舞。
>
> 他平常很少说话。

"很多" 不能作状语，不能说 "很多下雨" 等。

Note that 很多, the opposite of 很少, can not be used adverbially, therefore there is no such form as 很多下雨, etc.

（六）复杂的状语。

Complicated adverbial adjuncts.

一个句子里，状语有时包括好几类词或词组，表示好几种修饰关系。例如：

In a sentence, there may be several adverbial adjuncts which are made of words or phrases of different classes to express different relationships. For example:

> 他们也都不喜欢这种游戏。

朋友们都关心地对我说："你一定要安心休养。"

我十分遗憾地跟他一起离开了那里。

一般来说，这些并用的词和词组按下列次序排列。

Generally speaking, these adverbial adjuncts are arranged in the following order:

表示时间——地点——范围——程度——情态或方式——对象、工具、方向等——（中心语：动词或形容词谓语）

Time + Place + Scope + Degree + Emotion (or Manner) + Target, Instrument, Direction, etc. + (Head word: a verb or adjective predicate)

昨天——在家里——都——很——兴奋地——跟他——（说）

上星期日——在公园里——只（是）——十分——简单地——（谈了谈）

（七）状语和定语。

A comparison of adverbial adjuncts and attributives.

状语和定语都是前加修饰成分，它们的不同点可简单列表如下：

The difference between adverbial adjuncts and attributives, both being premodifying elements, are summed up briefly in the following table:

状　语 Adverbial Adjuncts	定　语 Attributives
1．在谓语前边 Before the predicate	在主语或宾语前边 Before the subject or object
2．多在动词、形容词前边 Mostly before verbs or adjectives	多在名词前边 Mostly before nouns
3．有的状语后边带结构助词"地"	有的定语后边带结构助词"的"

Some adverbial adjuncts are followed by the structural particle 地	Some attributives are followed by the structural particle 的.
4. 多由副词、助动词、介词结构充当	多由名词、代词、形容词充当
Most adverbial adjuncts are adverbs, auxiliary verbs or prepositions.	Most attributives are nouns, pronouns or adjectives.

练 习 26
Exercise 26

用横线标出下列句子的状语，并指出每个状语是由哪类词或词组充当的。

Underline the adverbial adjuncts in the following sentences and state what kinds of word or phrase they are.

例: 我们的想法完全不同。（形容词）

Model: (Adjective)

1. 我们暂时在这儿休息一下。
2. 昨天我朋友突然发生不幸。
3. 大家热烈地祝贺他的成功。
4. 观众常为电影里（的）人物的命运担心。
5. 他对这种雕刻艺术非常有兴趣。
6. 这些问题任何时候都应该重视。
7. 他们都非常珍惜自己的青春。
8. 他原来比较乐观。
9. 最近他们几个人实在太辛苦了。
10. 这几句话他们应该能翻译。

11. 你明天一定要早来。

12. 我们顺利地到达了这个港口。

13. 他往热水瓶里灌开水。

14. 你们不要那样弄。

15. 他上星期四对我说了这件事。

16. 到底你们明天下午去不去?

17. 他今天能回到北京。

18. 他从很远的地方给我们带来了不少好东西。

第六节 补 语
Section VI　Complements

一、什么叫补语 Definition

在动词或形容词谓语后面补充说明谓语的词和词组叫补语,被补充的词叫中心语。补语是补充说明动作经历的时间、数量、程度、结果、趋向或可能以及事物性状的程度等的后加成分。例如:

A word or phrase attached to a verb or adjective predicate to complete the meaning is called a complement and the word to which the complement is attached is the head word. In other words, complements are postmodifying elements to show the duration, quantity, degree, result, direction or possibility of an action and the extent of the quality of a thing. For example:

在动词谓语后边的补语:中心语(动词谓语)——补语

Complements following verb predicates: Modified word (verb predicate) + complement

他写了一上午。　　　　他下来了。

他写了两遍。 　　　　　他跑下来了。

他写得很好。 　　　　　他上午写得完。

他写完了。

在形容词谓语后边的补语：中心语（形容词谓语）——补语

Complements following adjective predicates: Modified
word (adjective predicate) + complement

他高一米七。 　　　　　她的优点多得很。

我比他大一点儿。 　　　　这儿的交通方便极了。

二、补语的语法特点　Grammatical features

（一）补语一定在中心语后边。

The complement always comes after the head word.

（二）补语主要由形容词、动词和数量、补充词组等充当。

Mainly adjectives, verbs, numeral-measure word phrases,
complementary phrases, etc. can act as complements.

（三）补语和中心语之间常带结构助词"得 (de)"。

The structural particle 得 (de) often occurs between the
head word and the complement.

（四）带补语的动词谓语后边一般可带宾语。

Usually a verb predicate with a complement can take an
object.

三、补语的种类　Classification of complements

从表示的意义和结构特点两方面看，补语一般可以分为以下
五种：

In terms of both meaning and structure, complements can
be classified into five kinds:

（一）结果补语

The complement of result (Resultant complement)

（二）程度补语

The complement of degree (Degree complement)

（三）数量补语

The complement of quantity (Quantitative complement)

（四）趋向补语

The complement of direction (Directional complement)

（五）可能补语

The complement of potentiality (Potential complement)

现分别介绍如下。

These complements will be introduced respectively in the rest of this section.

四、结果补语 The complement of result

（一）什么叫结果补语。 Definition.

在动词谓语后边表示动作结果的补充成分叫结果补语。例如：

The complement of result is a complementary element following a verb predicate, indicating the result of an action. For example:

中心语（动词谓语）——结果补语（动词、形容词或介词结构）

Head word (verb predicate) + complement of result (a verb, an adjective or a prepositional phrase)

我能听懂他的话。

（"听"是动词、谓语、中心语；"懂"是动词、结果补语）

(听 is a verb, the predicate of the sentence and the head word of the complement. 懂 is also a verb and it is the complement of result of the verb 听.)

我看见他了。

衣服都洗干净了。

（"洗"是动词、谓语、中心语； "干净"是形容词、结果补语）

(洗 is a verb, the predicate of the sentence and the head word of the complement. 干净

288

is an adjective and it is the complement of result of the verb 洗.)

这个标点我用错了。

这路公共汽车开往北京火车站。

（"开"是动词、谓语、中心语；"往北京火车站"是介词结构、结果补语）

(开 is a verb, the predicate of the sentence and the head word of the complement. 往北京火车站 is a prepositional phrase and the complement of result of the verb 开.)

（二）结果补语的语法特点。Grammatical features.

1． 结果补语和中心语结合得很紧。

The complement of result and its head word are very closely linked to each other.

2． 结果补语主要由动词、形容词充当。

Mainly verbs and adjectives can be used as complements of result.

3． 带结果补语的动补词组后边可以带宾语。

The verb in a verb-complement of result phrase can take an object.

4． 带结果补语的动补词组的否定式一般是在动词谓语前边用否定副词"没（有）"。

没（有）is used before the verb predicate to negate a verb-complement of result phrase.

5． 带结果补语的动补词组后边一般可以带动态助词"了"、"过"。

The aspectual particles 了 and 过 can be attached to a verb-complement of result phrase.

（三）能作结果补语的词和词组。

Words and phrases which can serve as complements

of result.

1. 动词。

Verbs.

他改完那篇稿子了。　　　　我一定寄给你。

我找着他的地址了。　　　　大家已经记住了。

他碰倒了一个花瓶。

2. 形容词。

Adjectives.

我们要准备好明天的考试。　　我来晚了。

这次招待会用的钱都算清楚了。　这些练习都做对了。

他过惯了这种生活。

3. 介词结构。

Prepositional phrases.

这架飞机飞往广州。

春天燕子飞向北方。

毕业的同学已经愉快地走向社会。

（四）使用结果补语时需要注意的问题。

Points that merit special attention.

1. 动词谓语和带结果补语的动补词组在意义上的区别是，前者只说明进行某个动作或行为，后者还说明动作或行为的结果。例如"我听了一个报告"只说明进行了"听"这个动作；而"我听懂了那个报告"还能说明"听"的结果是"懂"了。因此当我们要表示一个动作及其结果时，常在动词谓语后边用结果补语。例如：

The difference in meaning between a verb predicate and a verb-complement of result phrase lies in the fact that the former states only the proceeding of an action while the latter shows the result as well as the proceeding of the action, for instance, in 我听了一个报告, the verb 听 indicates only the action, whereas in 我听懂了那个报告, the phrase 听懂 shows both the action 听 and its result 懂. Therefore when we want to express an action with its result, the complement of result is often used after the verb predicate. For example:

她染了一块布。	我听汉语广播呢。
她染完了。	声音太小，我没听清楚。
他昨天洗了一条床单。	她在厨房烧菜。
他没洗干净。	菜烧烂了。
他要写一篇广播稿。	
今天他写好了。	

2．当我们要说明动作的结果达到某处所时，必须用结果补语表示。例如：

The complement of result must be used when we express that sth. reaches a certain place as the result of an action. For example:

那些杂志别放在椅子上。

这些黄油和蔬菜下午送到宾馆。

一定不能说"别在椅子上放"，"下午到宾馆送"。

We can never say 别在椅子上放，下午到宾馆送。

3．动词和结果补语的搭配。

Collocations of verbs and complements of result.

只有在意义上能补充说明动作结果的动词或形容词才能作结果补语。常用作结果补语的动词有：会、完、见、懂、开、着(zháo)、住、在、到、给、倒、掉、死、通……。常用作结果补语的形容词有：对、错、好、坏、大、早、晚、快、慢、烂、惯、清楚、干净、整齐……。

Only those verbs and adjectives that, in terms of meaning, can indicate the results of actions can be used as complements of result. The following verbs are often used as complement of result: 会，完，见，懂，开，着(zháo)，住，在，到，给，倒，掉，死，通 .... And adjectives such as 对，错，好，

坏，大，早，晚，快，慢，烂，惯，清楚，干净，整齐 …are commonly used as complement of result.

请看下列常见的动词和结果补语的搭配简表。

Here is a table showing the commonest collocations of verbs and complements of result.

（1）由动词充当结果补语的动补词组。

Verb- 'complement of result' phrases in which the complements are verbs.

谓语（动词） The predicate (verbs)				结果补语 （动词） Complements of result (verbs)	动补词组 Verb- 'complement of result' phrases			
作	写	改	抄		作完	写完	改完	抄完
画	看	听	念		画完	看完	听完	念完
读	谈	说	学习	完	读完	谈完	说完	学习完
吃	喝	买	准备		吃完	喝完	买完	准备完
卖	用	洗	翻译		卖完	用完	洗完	翻译完
听	看	遇	碰		听见	看见	遇见	碰见
望	闻			见	望见	闻见		
开	打	睁	拿		开开	打开	睁开	拿开
切	翻	解	推	开	切开	翻开	解开	推开
搬	敲				搬开	敲开		
抓	拿	握	拉		抓住	拿住	握住	拉住
捆	接	关	站	住	捆住	接住	关住	站住
停	记	扶	绑		停住	记住	扶住	绑住

学	念		会	学会	念会		
听	看		懂	听懂	看懂		
买	借	找	睡	着 (zháo)	买着	借着	找着	睡着

坐	站	躺	住		坐在	站在	躺在	住在
放	挂	写	记	在	放在	挂在	写在	记在
抄	画	忘	贴		抄在	画在	忘在	贴在

看	来	走	跑		看到	来到	走到	跑到
开	运	讲	说	到	开到	运到	讲到	说到
骑	追	找	买		骑到	追到	找到	买到
遇	碰	请	学习		遇到	碰到	请到	学习到

送	交	留	传		送给	交给	留给	传给
递	还	寄	献	给	递给	还给	寄给	献给
借	卖	输	租		借给	卖给	输给	租给

（2）由形容词充当结果补语的动补词组。

Verb- 'complement of result' phrases in which the complements are adjectives.

谓语（动词） The predicate (verbs)	结果补语（形容词） Complements of result (adjectives)	动补词组 Verb- 'complement of result' phrases
说　写　念　算 分析　翻译　回答 做	对	说对　写对　念对　算对 分析对　翻译对　回答对 做对

	错	说错　写错　念错　算错 分析错　翻译错　回答错 做错
写　算　做　翻译 放　拿　坐　准备 收　安排　计划	好	写好　算好　做好　翻译好 放好　拿好　坐好　准备好 收好　安排好　计划好
说　看　写　念 讲　问	清楚	说清楚　看清楚　写清楚 念清楚　讲清楚　问清楚
洗　擦　收拾 打扫　扫	干净	洗干净　擦干净　收拾干净 打扫干净　扫干净
住　过　吃	惯	住惯　过惯　吃惯
睁　张	大	睁大　张大

4．结果补语要紧接在动词谓语后边，两者之间不能插入任何成分。例如：

The complement of result immediately follows the verb predicate and no element can be inserted between them. For example:

（1）中间不能加动态助词"了"。

"听懂"、"学会"、"看见"等不能说成"听了懂"、"学了会"、"看了见"等。

The aspectual particle 了 can not be inserted.

One can not insert 了 into the verb-complement phrases 听懂，学会，看见 etc., so there are no such forms as 听了懂，学了会，看了见， etc.

（2）中间不能加宾语。

"学好汉语"、"听完音乐"等不能说成"学汉语好"、

"听音乐完"等。

No object is allowed between verb and its complement of result.

One can not place objects in the phrases 学好汉语，听完音乐 etc., between the verbs and thei complements, therefore its wrong to say 学汉语好，听音乐完, etc.

（3）中间不能加结构助词"得"，否则结构和意思就变了。"写完"是动词和结果补语，如果加上"得"说成"写得完"，就成了动词和可能补语，表示"能写完"的意思。

No insertion of the structural particle 得 is allowed between the verb and its complement of result. But 得 can be used between a verb and its potential complement which is different from the verb-complement of result phrase in structure and meaning, e.g. 写完 is a verb-complement of result phrase. If 得 is inserted, the phrase becomes a verb-complement of potentiality, meaning 能写完 (can finish writing).

5．宾语的位置。Position of the object.

带结果补语的动补词组后边可以带宾语。宾语一定要放在动词谓语和补语后边，而不能放在动词谓语和补语之间。例如：

The verb-complement of result phrase can take an object which comes after the whole phrase, not between the verb and its resultant complement. For example:

> 他们已经开完会了。

> 我看懂这篇文章了。

不能说成"开会完"或"看这篇文章懂"。

There are no such forms as 开会完 or 看这篇文章懂。

6．谓语后边一般只能带一个结果补语。例如：

Usually the predicate can only take one complement of result. For example:

> 我听见他的声音了。　　　　你的话记在脑子里了。

这条铁路建成了。

一定不能说"听见清楚"、"建成完"、"记住在"等。

One can never say 听见清楚，建成完，记住在，etc.

7. 带结果补语的动补词组的否定式一般是在动词谓语前边用副词"没（有）"。例如：

The verb-complement of result phrase is usually negated by the adverb 没（有）which precedes the verb predicate. For example:

我没问清楚。　　　　这本书没寄走。

他没坐在沙发上。

只有在表示假设或强调否定的意愿时，可以用副词"不"。例如：

The adverb 不 can only be used to express supposition or an emphatic negative desire. For example:

你不说清楚，我们就不能帮助你。

（意思是：如果你不说清楚，就…；你一定要说清楚，我们才能帮助你。）

(The sentence means 如果你不说清楚，就…；你一定要说清楚，我们才能帮助你。)

我就不说清楚。

（意思是：我一定不照你的希望说清楚。）

(The sentence means 我一定不照你的希望说清楚。)

8. 带结果补语的动补词组后边可以带动态助词"了"和"过"。例如：

The verb-complement of result phrase can be followed by the aspectual particles 了 or 过. For example:

他画完了那张风景画了。

那几个基本观点他都讲透了。

我们请到了一位地理专家。

他们从外边抬进了两张桌子。

上个月他在火车上遇见过老马。

我以前看见过这种植物。

但不能带动态助词"着"，绝不能说"他画完着"、"他看见着"等。

But 着 can not be used with such a phrase, though it is also an aspectual particle, e.g. one can not say 他画完着，他看见着, etc.

9. 有的动词有时能作别的动词的结果补语，但本身不能带结果补语。例如：

There are verbs that can serve as complement of result but can not take one themselves. For example:

<blockquote>
看懂　骑到　　放在　　送给　　借着　　吃完
</blockquote>

有的动词能带结果补语，但本身不能作结果补语。例如：

On the other hand, there are verbs which can take complements of result but can not serve as complement of result themselves. For example:

<blockquote>
看见　听到　睁开　　张大　　含在　　拿走
</blockquote>

10. 几个常见的结果补语。

Some verbs commonly used as complement of result.

（1）动词"见"。

The verb 见.

"见"常作动词的结果补语，表示通过动作看到或听到某人或事物。但能带结果补语"见"的动词不多。例如：

As a complement of result, 见 means "to see or hear sb. or sth. through the action", but it can only match a few verbs. For example:

<blockquote>
看见　望见　　　　（人、事物）

　　　　　　　　　（Person or thing）

遇见　碰见　　　　（人、事）

　　　　　　　　　（Person or thing）
</blockquote>

听见	（声音）
	(Sound)
闻见	（味道）
	(Smell)

（2）动词"在"。

The verb 在.

"在"常作动词的结果补语，表示人或事物通过某种动作达到或停留在某处，动补词组后边常带表示方位、处所的宾语。例如：

As a complement of result, 在 means "(a person or thing) to reach or remain at a certain place through the action". The V + 在 phrase is often followed by an object of location or place. For example:

他躺在草地上。　　　作报告的人站在大家前面。

我们坐在礼堂里。　　　通知公布在大门口了。

（3）动词"到"。

The verb 到.

"到"作动词的结果补语，表示人或事物通过某种动作到达某处，达到某种目的、或者动作持续到某时。动补词组后边常带表示处所、时间的宾语。例如：

As a complement of result, 到 expresses that a person or thing reaches a certain place, achieves a goal or an action continues till a certain time. The V + 到 phrase is often followed by an object of place or time. For example:

他已经回到家了。

这本书我今天一定要看到三十五页。

我找到他的房间了。

每天晚上他都学习到十一点。

（4）动词"给"。

The verb 给.

"给"作动词的结果补语，表示施事者通过某种动作形式把人、物给某人或单位。动补词组后边要带指人或单位、集体的宾语，有时带两个宾语。例如：

As a complement of result, 给 expresses the idea that the doer sends a person or thing to somebody or some organization through the action. The V + 给 phrase often takes an object of personal reference or one of unit or collective. Sometimes it may take two objects. For example:

> 他交给经理一封介绍信。
>
> 母亲留给我一件珍贵的礼物——金戒指。
>
> 哥哥寄给我两张照片。
>
> 那本外文杂志他还给图书馆了。

（5）动词"开"。

The verb 开.

"开"作动词的结果补语，表示通过某种动作使某人或事物分开或离开原来的地方，使关闭的东西打开。例如：

As a complement of result, 开 means "to cause sb. or sth. to fall apart or move away from his/its original place or sth. closed to open through the action. For example:

> 他开开窗户了。　　　　他拿开了旁边的锅。
>
> 你能打开这个盒子吗？　　他解开了捆书的绳子。

另如：

Here are some other examples:

> 睁开（眼睛）　　　　张开（嘴）
>
> 切开（西瓜）　　　　打开（书）
>
> 敲开（门）　　　　　推开（门、手、人）

（6）动词"住"。

The verb 住.

"住"作动词的结果补语，表示通过某种动作，使某人或事物牢固地停留在某处。例如：

As a complement of result, 住 means "to cause sb. or sth. to stay fast at a certain place". For example:

他握住了我的手。　　（握着不放）
　　　　　　　　　　（to hold firmly）

这两件事我都记住了。　（记在脑子里不忘）
　　　　　　　　　　　（to commit to memory）

快抓住他!　　　　　　（不要让他跑掉）
　　　　　　　　　　　（to seize him so that he
　　　　　　　　　　　can not escape）

他站住了。　　　　　　（停下不继续走了）
　　　　　　　　　　　（to stop walking）

汽车停住了。　　　　　（停下不继续开了）
　　　　　　　　　　　（to stop running）

练 习 27
Exercise 27

（一）填上适当的结果补语，并指出词类。

Fill in the blanks with proper complements of result and state whether they are verbs or adjectives.

供选择的词表：

Choose from this list:

　　到、懂、错、完、着、开、给、住、好、坏、干净、
　　整齐、在、见

1. 你记＿＿他的地址吗?

2. 劳驾，递＿＿我那把刷子，可以吗?

3. 你们下午先回＿＿这儿。

4. 他已经擦＿＿那几块玻璃了。

5. 我这个星期应该写＿＿那篇文章。

6. 对不起，我没听＿＿你的问题。

7. 你们走＿＿了，应该往南走。

8. 屋子里太热了，开＿＿窗户吧。

9. 我没听＿＿你的意思。

10. 拿着 (zhe) 这盆花，别摔＿＿了。

（二）改正病句（一定要有结果补语）。

Correct the mistakes in the following sentences (The complement of result must be used.).

1. 我打电话通了。

2. 昨天晚上不找到小高。

3. 我们决心学汉语好。

4. 大家都打了开书。

5. 我不看清楚布告上的字。

6. 病人睁开着眼睛。

7. 这个笑话真笑了死人了。

8. 孩子们都睡了着了。

9. 他能翻译这些句子对。

10. 老师已经讲了到第八课。

五、程度补语 The complement of degree

（一）什么叫程度补语。Definition.

在谓语（动词或形容词）后边补充说明动作进行的程度、情态的词和词组叫程度补语。例如：

A word or phrase which follows the predicate (verb or adjective) to illustrate the degree or manner of an action is called the complement of degree.   For example:

他念得熟。

（"念"是动词、谓语、中心语；"熟"是形容词、程度补语）

301

(念, a verb, is the predicate and the head word;

熟, an adjective, is the complement of degree.)

他说得很流利。

他写得不好。

他累得很。

（"累"是形容词、谓语、中心语；"很"是副
词、程度补语）

(累, an adjective, is the predicate and head word;

很, an adverb, is the complement of degrée.)

今天太阳晒极了。

她写汉字写得很整齐。

他哭得眼睛都红了。

（"哭"是动词、谓语、中心语；"眼睛都红
了"是主谓词组、程度补语，是说"哭"的程度
很厉害，以至于眼睛都红了。）

(哭, a verb, is the predicate and head word; 眼
睛都红了 is an S-P phrase used as complement
of degree, meaning someone cried so bitterly
that his eyes became red.)

（二）程度补语的语法特点。Grammatical features.

1．程度补语和中心语之间必须用结构助词"得 (de)"。

The complement of degree and the head word must be joined
by the structural particle 得 (de).

2．程度补语可由形容词和形容词性偏正词组等充当。

Adjectives and adjectival endocentric phrases can act as
complements of degree.

3．程度补语的否定形式是在助词"得"和形容词补语之间
加副词"不"。

The negative form is made by placing 不 between 得 and
the adjective complement.

4． 带程度补语的动词谓语后边一般可带宾语。

The verb predicate can take an object as well as a complement of degree.

5． 带程度补语的动词谓语后边不能带动态助词"了、着、过"。

The aspectual particles 了,着 and 过 can not be attached to the verb predicate with a complement of degree.

6． 重音一般在程度补语上。

The complement of degree is stressed in a sentence.

（三）能作程度补语的词和词组。

Words and phrases which can serve as complement of degree.

1． 形容词。

Adjectives.

> 他跑得快。 他睡得早，起得晚。
> 他挂得正。 那棵树比这棵树高得多。
> 她长得难看。

2． 代词。

Pronouns.

> 他翻译得怎么样？ 你家院子里的树栽得怎么样了？
> 你玩得怎么样？

3． 副词。

Adverbs.

> 刚才我渴得很。 屋子里暖和极了。
> 这个词的用法难得很。 最近学习紧张极了。
> 他们快乐得很。

4． 偏正词组。

Endocentric phrases.

> 你的表走得太慢了。 他们布置得真漂亮。
> 队伍排得非常整齐。 树上的苹果红得多么可爱。
> 他调查得很深入。

5．联合词组。

Coordinative phrases.

　　　　他写得又快又好。　　　　她穿得朴素而大方。

　　　　弟弟长得又高又胖。

6．补充词组。

Complementary phrases.

　　　　他唱得响亮得很。

　　　　他比我们做得多得多。

　　　　那个演员演一个小姑娘演得象极了。

　　　　这种绸子比那种织得好多了。

7．动宾词组。

Verb-object phrases.

　　　　他讲得有道理。　　　　这间屋子大得能住二十个人。

　　　　我急得冒汗。　　　　他笑得直流眼泪。

8．主谓词组。

Subject-predicate phrases.

　　　　太阳晒得我们不能睁眼。　　我们说得她很不好意思。

　　　　他讲得大家都笑了。　　　　我热得头晕。

（四）使用程度补语时需要注意的问题。

Points that merit special attention.

1．程度补语和结构助词"得 (de)"。

Complements of degree and the structural particle 得 (de).

（1）程度补语和谓语之间一定要用助词"得"，不能遗漏。

例如：

得 must be used between the complement of degree and the predicate and it can in no way be left out. For example:

　　　　他长得很高。　　　　　弟弟爬山爬得很快。

　　　　这件衣服长得多。

绝不能说成"他长很高"、"这件衣服长多"或"弟弟爬山爬很快"等。

304

One can never say 他长很高，这件衣服长多,弟弟爬山爬很快, etc.

（2）程度补语的否定形式也必须用助词"得"。否定副词"不"要放在"得"后边，补语前边。例如：

The particle 得 must also be used in the negative form of the degree complement and the negative adverb 不 is between 得 and the complement. For example:

> 这种点心做得不好吃。

> 这化验报告写得不符合要求。

否定副词"不"不能放在动词谓语前边，不能说成"不做得好吃"或"不写得符合要求"等。

The negative adverb 不 can not be placed before the verb predicate, so one can not say 不做得好吃,不写得符合要求, etc.

（3）主谓词组作程度补语时，要特别注意助词"得"的位置，"得"一定要紧跟在中心语后边，不能弄错。例如：

When the complement of degree is a S-P phrase, it should be noted, 得 must follow the head word (verb). For example:

> 这个菜辣得他直咳嗽。

> 大炮的声音吓得敌人不敢出来。

一定不能说"这个菜辣他得直咳嗽"、"大炮的声音吓敌人得不敢出来"等。

One can never say 这个菜辣他得直咳嗽,大炮的声音吓敌人得不敢出来, etc.

2．宾语的位置。

Position of the object.

（1）要是动词谓语后面同时 带宾语和程度补语，一定要重复动词，程度补语要放在重复的动词后边，助词"得"则要放在重复的动词和程度补语之间。例如。

The verb should be repeated when it takes both an object and a complement of degree. The degree complement comes after the repeated verb and 得 is placed between the repeated verb and the complement. The order is as follows:

动词谓语——宾语——重复的动词谓语——"得"（助词）——程度补语

Verb predicate + Object + Repeated verb predicate + 得 (Particle) + Complement of degree

回答——问题——回答——得——很完整

打——行李——打——得——很结实

种——树——种——得——不多

绝不能说"回答问题得很完整"，"打行李得很结实"、"种树得不多"等。

One can never say 回答问题得很完整，打行李得很结实，种树得不多, etc.

也不能把助词"得"放在动词谓语和宾语之间。不能说"回答得问题很完整"等。

And 得 can not be placed between the verb predicate and the object, e.g. it is wrong to say 他回答得问题很完整, etc.

（2）如果不重复动词，就要把宾语放在动词谓语或者主语前边。例如：

When the object comes before the verb predicate or before the subject, the verb is not repeated. For example:

她汉语说得不错。

生词我们记得很快。

3．形容词充当程度补语时，补语前常带一个表示程度的副词"很、太、真、非常、特别、多（么）"等。例如：

A degree adverb such as 很，太，真，非常，特别，多（么），etc. is often used before an adjective degree complement. For example:

她唱得很好听。　　　　　你的脸晒得真红。

他批评得非常正确。

形容词单独作程度补语一般带有比较的意味。例如：

The adjective used in isolation as complement of degree implies a comparison. For example:

> 他跑得快，你跑得慢。

> 他写得整齐，我写得乱。

4. 副词作程度补语。Adverbs as complement of degree.

副词中只有"很"可以作程度补语，表示程度高，"很"前边一定要用助词"得"。例如：

很、which expresses a high degree, is the only adverb that can be used as a complement of degree and it must be preceded by 得. For example:

> 这间屋子干净得很。

> 我最近忙得很。

副词"极"和助词"了"构成的"极了"可以作程度补语，表示达到极高的程度。"极了"是一个特殊的、不带助词"得"的程度补语。例如：

极了, the combination of the adverb 极 and 了, can serve as degree complements to express the meaning of "extremely" and what is special about it is that it is not preceded by the structural particle 得. For example:

> 开水烫极了。

> 商店里的人多极了。

"（得）很"和"极了"只能在形容词或表示心理活动、感情的动词后边作补语。例如：

（得）很 and 极了 can only be used as degree complements after adjectives or verbs expressing mental activities or emotions. For example:

> 他怕得很。

> 大家对张教授佩服极了。

5. 带程度补语的句子里，要是有状语（表示程度的副词除外），一般放在动词谓语前边。例如：

In a sentence with a complement of degree, the adverbial adjunct, except for a degree adverb, is usually placed in front of the verb predicate. For example:

> 他们一定安排得很周到。
>
> 他常常来得很早。
>
> 工业、农业和商业都发展得很迅速。
>
> 他的字比我写得好看。

如果又有宾语，状语要放在重复的动词谓语前。例如：

If the verb has an object, the adverbial adjunct comes before the repeated verb predicate. For example:

> 他们朗诵诗都朗诵得非常好。
>
> 他讲这个问题已经讲得很清楚了。

要特别注意的是，一定不能把状语放在第一个动词谓语前边。不能说成"他们都朗诵诗朗诵得很好"、"他已经讲这个问题讲得很清楚了"等。

Not that adverbs can never precede the first verb predicate, therefore one can not say 他们都朗诵诗诵朗得很好，他已经讲这个问题讲得很清楚了，etc.

6. 程度补语和状语的区别。

Differences between degree complements and adverbial adjuncts.

汉语里动词谓语后面可带形容词充当的程度补语，前面可以带形容词充当的状语。它们用的结构助词虽然不同，但要区别二者的不同还是不容易的，外国人学起来常遇到困难，要特别注意。例如：

In Chinese, a verb predicate can take an adjectival degree complement as well as an adjectival adverbial adjunct. It is not easy to distinguish the two, though they need different structural particles. This constitutes a major difficulty to foreign learners of Chinese. For example:

　　　　他写信写得很快。　　　　　（程度补语）

　　　　　　　　　　　　　　　　　(Degree complement)

　　　　他很快地写了一封信。　　　（状语）

　　　　　　　　　　　　　　　　　(Adverbial adjunct)

　　形容词充当的程度补语是补充说明中心语动作进行的程度的，是描写性的；而形容词状语是修饰动作进行的状态、方式的，是叙述性的。程度补语前的中心语表示的动作一般是已完成或是经常发生的。下面举例说明。

　　The adjectival degree complement is descriptive in nature and it tells the degree or extent of the action indicated by the head word (verb), whereas the adjectival adverbial adjunct tells the "attitude" or manner of an action and it is facttelling. The head word of the degree complement usually indicates a completed or habitual action. Here are some examples:

快跑! ——意思是跑的时候要用较快的速度。

　　　　It means "to run at a great speed or quickly".

他跑得快。——意思是根据他过去或现在跑的情况，说明

　　　　　　　　他跑的速度快。

　　　　It means that we know it by our experience that he runs fast.

你们要仔细检查，免得发生错误。

　　　　——意思是：检查时要仔细，要弄对。

　　　　It means "be careful when examine it and to get everything right."

我们仔细地检查了，没发现错误。

　　　　——意思是：用仔细的态度检查过了，都对。

　　　　It means "to have examined carefully, everything is all right".

他们检查得很仔细，不会有错误了。

309

——意思是：他们已经检查了，而且很仔细，错的
地方也改正了。

It means "they have already examined it,
and have done it carefully, and have corrected
all mistakes".

有的形容词只能作状语，而不能作程度补语。例如：

Some adjectives can only function as adverbial adjuncts,
not as complements of degree. For example:

我们一定努力工作。

（不说"学习得努力"、"工作得努力"；可以说
"学习努力"，"工作努力"，但这些是主谓词
组）

(Here one does not use such forms as 学习得
努力，工作得努力; but it is possible to say
学习努力 and 工作努力 which are S-P phrases.)

练 习 28
Exercise 28

（一）用程度补语完成下列句子。

Complete the following sentences with complements of
degree.

1. 他开汽车开得＿＿＿＿＿。
2. 昨天晚上他睡得＿＿＿＿＿，现在还没起床。
3. 那天晚会上的节目表演得＿＿＿＿＿。
4. 小张他们的房间布置得＿＿＿＿＿。
5. 我朋友汉语说得＿＿＿＿＿，日语说得＿＿＿＿＿。
6. 我家门前的果树长得＿＿＿＿＿。
7. 我游泳游得＿＿＿＿＿，滑冰滑得＿＿＿＿＿。

8. 这条裤子做得_____。

9. 我午饭吃得_____，现在不饿。

10. 他做中国饭做得_____。

（二）改正病句（一定要有程度补语）。

Correct the mistakes in the following sentences (Complements of degree must be used in the correct sentences.)

1. 我们每天都起很早。

2. 他念课文念流利。

3. 他穿太多了。

4. 他对我关心很。

5. 他搜集资料得很完全。

6. 她考虑问题得十分全面。

7. 这个电影有意思得极了。

8. 我们都说汉语说得不太好。

9. 这间屋子不打扫得干净。

10. 他们俩都打乒乓球打得很好。

六、数量补语　The complement of quantity

（一）什么叫数量补语。Definition.

在谓语（动词或形容词）后边，补充说明动作行为经历、延续的时间、动作进行的次数或人和事物的长度、高度等数量的词和词组，叫数量补语。数量补语一般可分为以下三种：

A complement of quantity is a word or phrase attached to the predicate (a verb or an adjective) to specify the duration an action covers, the frequency at which an action happens or the length, height of a person or thing. There are three kinds:

1. 表示动作次数的数量补语，又叫动量补语。

Those specifying the frequency of an action, or the complement of frequency.

中心语（动词谓语）——动量补语（数词—动量词）

Modified word (verbal predicate) + complement of frequency (numeral — verbal Mw)

去——一次　　　　　敲——两下儿

看——三遍

2．表示时段的数量补语，又叫时量补语。

Those specifying the duration of an action, or the complement of duration.

中心语（动词谓语）——时量补语（数词—名量词—名词）

Modified word (verbal predicate) + complement of duration (numeral + nominal Mw + noun)

谈——十分钟　　　讨论——一天

写——两小时

3．表示长度、高度等的数量补语，又叫名量补语。

Those specifying length or height, or the complement of nominal measure.

中心语（形容词谓语）——名量补语（数词——名量词）

Modified word (adjective predicate) + complement of nominal measure (numeral + nominal Mw)

高——三公尺　　　　远——一公里

长——七十公分　　　大——三岁

宽——一米　　　　　短——一点儿

多——三公斤

（二）数量补语的语法特点。Grammatical features.

1．数量补语和中心语要紧紧相连。

The complement of quantity follows the head word immediately.

2．数量补语多由数量词组充当。

Most complements of quantity are numeral-measure word phrases.

312

3．带数量补语的谓语后边一般可以带宾语。

A predicate with a complement of quantity can take an object.

4．带数量补语的动词或形容词 谓语 后一般可带动态助词"了"。

The aspectual particle 了 can be used after a verb/adjective predicate with a complement of quantity.

（三）能作数量补语的词组。

Phrases that can act as complement of quantity.

1．数量词组。

Numeral-measure word phrases.

这本小说他看了两遍。　　　这张桌子长一米。

弟弟打了他一下儿。　　　　他比我高一点儿。

他刚才去了一回了。　　　　这包白糖重两公斤。

你等一会儿。　　　　　　　他们学哲学学了三年。

他找你找了一天。

2．偏正词组。

Endocentric phrases.

他打电话打了三分钟。　　　他比你小两个月。

我们打太极拳打了一个早晨。

（四）使用数量补语时需要注意的问题。

Points that merit special attention.

1．关于动量补语。

The complement of frequency.

由动量词构成的数量词组常用在动词谓语后边作补语，表示动作的次数。例如：

Numeral-verbal measure word phrases are often used after a verbal predicate as a complement to specify the frequency at which an action happens. For example:

这个电影我想看两遍。　　　我明天去一趟书店。

他去过一次长城。

动量补语一定不能放在动词谓语前边，不能说成"这个电影我想两遍看"等。

The complement of frequency can not be placed in front of the verb predicate, so it is wrong to say 这个电影我想两遍看, etc.

2. 关于时量补语。

The complement of duration.

由数量词组和名词构成的偏正词组常用在动词谓语后边作补语，表示动作行为经历和持续的时间。例如：

The endocentric phrase made up of a N-Mw phrase and a noun is often used after a verbal predicate as a complement specifying how long an action lasts. For example:

我看电视看了两个钟头。

我只锻炼三十分钟。

他每天听汉语广播听三刻钟。

由数词和带量词性的名词构成的数量词组也可以作时量补语。例如：

An N-Mw phrase consisting of a numeral and a measure noun can also behave as a complement of duration. For example:

我们要玩一天。

我在中国住了两年。

3. 关于名量补语。

The complement of nominal measure.

由名量词构成的数量词组常用在形容词谓语后边作补语，补充说明人或事物的长度、高度、宽度、深度等。例如：

An N-Mw phrase including a nominal measure word is often used after an adjective predicate as a complement to specify length, height, width, depth, etc. For example:

314

他高一米七六。　　　　　这条马路宽八米。

他比你瘦一点儿。

4.数量补语和宾语的位置。

Positions of the complement of quantity and the object.

（1）带动量补语的动词谓语后边如果有宾语，名词宾语要放在动量补语后边。例如：

A noun object comes after the complement of frequency of the verb predicate. For example:

我们明天要演两场话剧。　 你去一趟商店吧。

他来过两次我们学校。

代词宾语要放在动量补语前边。例如：

A pronoun object comes before the complement of frequency. For example:

我找了他两回。

她叫了我们一声。

指人的名词宾语也常放在动量补语前边。例如：

A noun object of personal reference is also placed before the complement of frequency. For example:

姐姐拍了张明一下儿。

我看了小高一眼。

（2）带时量补语的动词谓语后边有宾语时，一般要重复动词，时间补语要放在重复的动词谓语后边。例如：

In the case of a verbal predicate with an object and a complement of duration the verb is usually repeated, and the complement follows the repeated verb predicate. For example:

他买书买了半天。

我们听音乐听了一个钟头。

每年冬天我们放假放三个星期。

也可以不重复动词，而把宾语放在时间补语后边。例如：

However, we may also place the object after the complement of duration without repeating the verb. For example:

> 他买了半天书。
>
> 我们听了一个钟头音乐。
>
> 每年冬天我们放三个星期假。

（3）有一类动作一般不能持续，时间补语要放在宾语后边，表示从动作发生到某时的一段时间。例如：

The verb may indicate an action which can not happen continuously and the complement of duration used after it specifies the period from the time the action happens to a certain time. For example:

> 他离开家一年了。　（从离开家到现在有一年时间）
>
> 我毕业两年了。　　（从毕业到现在有两年时间）
>
> 他起床已经一刻钟了。
>
> （从起床到现在有一刻钟时间；一刻钟以前起床的）

比较："他起床起了一刻钟"，是说他起床用了一刻钟时间。

Compare: 他起床起了一刻钟 which means it took him a quarter of an hour to get up.

5．带有数量补语的谓语动词不能重叠。例如：

The predicate verb with a complement of quantity can not be repeated. For example:

> 我们休息一会儿。
>
> 我只写一遍。

一定不能说"我们休息休息一会儿"，"我只写写一遍"。

One can never say 我们休息休息一会儿 and 我只写写一遍．

6．数量补语和副词状语的位置。

Positions of the complement of quantity and adverb adverbial adjunct.

（1）副词状语要在动词谓语之前，不能放在动词谓语后边数量补语前边。例如：

The adverb adverbial adjunct should precedes the verbal predicate, not between the verbal predicate and the complement of quantity.   For example:

今天的晚会他只参加了一个小时。

那个城市我已经去过几次了。

我们大概要走十分钟。

一定不能说成"…他参加了只一个小时"，"…我去过已经几次了"或"我们要走大概十分钟"。

One can never say … 他参加了只一个小时, … 我去过已经几次了 or 我们要走大概十分钟。

（2）如果有宾语，副词状语要放在重复的动词谓语前边，而不能放在带宾语的动词前边。例如：

When an object is present, the adverb adverbial adjunct comes before the repeated verbal predicate rather than before the verb-object phrase.   For example:

他学历史专业刚学半年。

不能说"他学历史专业学刚半年"，也不能说"他刚学历史专业学半年"。

Neither of the following forms are correct: 他学历史专业学刚半年，他刚学历史专业学半年.

7. 数量补语和表示数量的状语。

The complement of quantity and the adverbial adjunct of quantity.

表示动作行为延续的时间或进行次数时，一定要在动词谓语后面用数量补语。例如：

The complement of quantity must be used after the verb predicate when the duration or frequency of an action is referred to.   For example:

他学习了三年汉语。

那篇广播稿他念了三遍。

不能说成"他三年学习了汉语"，"…他三遍念了"。

One can not say 他三年学习了汉语 and ... 他三遍念了。

如果要说明在某段时间或若干遍数内发生或存在的情况时，常在动词谓语前边用表示数量的状语。例如：

The adverbial adjunct of quantity premodifying a verbal predicate indicates the time during which an action happens or exists. For example:

这位劳动模范一年干了一年半的活儿。

我三个月翻译了一本小说。

他两天没回家。

昨天晚上我们一夜没睡觉。

那篇散文他三遍才看懂。

练 习 29
Exercise 29

（一）填上适当的数量补语，并指出是哪种数量补语。

Fill in the blanks with appropriate complements of quantity and state which kind each of them belongs to.

例： 我只说三遍。 （动量补语）

Model: (Complement of frequency)

1. 这件大衣不太合适，长_____。

2. 您的话我没听清楚，再讲_____，可以吗？

3. 那个地方的风景真美，他去过_____。

4. 你们等_____，张大夫马上来。

5. 我学法语只学了_____。

6. 每天早晨他都打_____太极拳。

7. 这课课文的录音我已经听了_____了。

318

8．今天他在家休息了_____。

9．这条河宽_____。

10．我哥哥已经工作_____了。

（二）把下列各组词连成带数量补语的词组。

Combine each group of words into a phrase with a complement of quantity.

1．跳　　舞　　一个晚上

2．作家　　访问　　两次

3．碰到　　一次　　他

4．订婚　　三年　　已经

5．旅行　　一个半月　　在南方

6．打　　网球　　一下午

7．电视　　看　　一个晚上

8．打　　电话　　一次

9．翻译　　小说　　半年

10．一场　　踢　　足球

七、趋向补语　The complement of direction

（一）什么叫趋向补语。　Definition.

在谓语动词后面补充说明动作趋向的词和词组，叫趋向补语。趋向补语可以分为两种。

The complement of direction is a word or phrase attached to a predicate verb to indicate the direction towards which an action proceeds.　There are two kinds:

1．简单趋向补语：来、去

The simple complements of direction: 来 and 去

中心语（谓语动词）——简单趋向补语(动词"来"、"去")

Modified word (predicate verb) + simple complement of direction (verb 来/去)

319

回来　　进去　　拿来　　送去

2. 复合趋向补语：

The compound complements of direction:

上来　　上去　　下来　　下去　　进来　　进去
出来　　出去　　回来　　回去　　过来　　过去
起来

中心语（谓语动词）——复合趋向补语（动补词组）

Modified word (predicate verb) + compound complement of direction (V-C phrase)

跑来回　　走进去　　拿出来　　挂上去

（二）趋向补语的语法特点。Grammatical features.

1. 趋向补语"来"和"去"表示的方向是对说话人讲的，读轻声。

The complements of direction 来 and 去, which are in the neutral tone, indicate the directions related to the speaker.

2. 趋向补语和中心语之间不用结构助词"得 (de)"。

The structural particle 得 (de) does not occur between the head word and the complement of direction.

3. 带趋向补语的动词谓语后边可以带宾语。

The verb predicate with a complement of direction can take an object.

4. 带趋向补语的谓语动词后边可以带动态助词"了 (le)"。

The aspectual particle 了 (le) can be suffixed to the predicate verb with a complement of direction.

（三）能作趋向补语的词和词组。

Words and phrases that can act as complement of direction.

1. 动词。
Verbs.

我上去。　　　　　　　　　这本书借来了。

他下来了。　　　　　　东西已经寄去了。

2．补充词组。

Complementary phrases.

树上的叶子落下来了。　　我们搬进去吧。

我们的国旗升起来了。　　你快拿出去。

（四）使用趋向补语时需要注意的问题。

Points that merit special attention.

1．关于简单趋向补语。

The simple complement of direction.

（1）只有动词"来"和"去"可以在其他动词后边作简单趋向补语。例如：

来 and 去 are the only two verbs that can serve as simple complements of direction.　For example:

上来	上去	下来	下去	
进来	进去	出来	出去	
回来	回去	过来	过去	起来
买来	骑去	借来	送去	

（2）动词"来"和"去"作谓语动词的补语，不是表示动作的实际趋向，而是表示动作与说话人的方向关系；换句话说，"来、去"表示的方向是根据说话人所处的位置决定的。这一点非常重要，外国人要特别注意。例如：

As a complement of direction to the predicate verb, 来 or 去 does not indicate any particular direction in which an action proceeds but the direction in relation to the speaker. In other words, the directions indicated by 来 and 去 are related to the speaker's position. This is a very important point which should be especially noted by foreigners.　For example:

他上来了。　（说话人在上边，"他"从下面朝着说话人的方向"上"）

	(The speaker is already up there and 他 is coming up towards the speaker.)
他出去了。	（说话人在里边；"他"从里边背着说话人的方向往外走）
	(The speaker is inside; 他 is going out from inside or away from where the speaker is.)
他回来了。	（"他"从别处回到说话人那儿，动作朝着说话人进行）
	(他 has returned from another place to where the speaker is.)
他带去了。	（"他"离开了说话人，动作背着说话人进行）
	(他 has gone away from the speaker.)
我们拿来了。	（从别处拿到"我们"这儿了，动作向着说话人进行）
	(Sth. has been taken to 我们.)

① 如果动作朝着说话人进行，一定要用"来"而不能用"去"作趋向补语。例如：

If the motion proceeds towards the speaker, 来 rather than 去, is used. For example:

他向我这儿跑来了。

他给我寄来了一张照片。

绝不能说"他向我这儿跑去了"、"他给我寄去了一张照片"。

One can never say 他向我这儿跑去了 and 他给我寄去了一张照片。

② 如果动作朝着说话人以外的方向进行，一定要用"去"而不能用"来"作趋向补语。例如：

On the other hand, if the motion is away from the

322

speaker, 去, rather than 来, must be used. For example:

（他在楼下）我们（从楼上）下去吧。

（他不在家）他买菜去了。

绝不能说成"他在楼下，我们（从楼上）下来吧"，"他不在家，他买东西来了。"

来 is misused in 他在楼下，我们（从楼上）下来吧 and 他不在家，他买东西来了。

（3）"来"和"去"作趋向补语时，它们和中心语之间不能加助词"得"，否则结构和意思就都变了。例如：

The structural particle 得 can not be used between the head word and 来/去 as complements of direction or the structure and meaning will change. Compare the following two examples:

我们上去。（"去"是动词谓语"上"的趋向补语，"上去"的意思是：到上边去。）

(去 is the complement of direction to the verb predicate 上; 上去 means 到上边去.)

我们上得去。（"去"是动词谓语"上"的可能补语，"上得去"的意思是：能上去。）

(去 is the complement of potentiality to the verb predicate 上；上得去 means 能上去.)

（4）简单趋向补语和宾语的位置。

Positions of the simple complement of direction and the object.

①　如果动词谓语带宾语，表示处所方位的宾语要放在简单趋向补语和中心语之间，不能放在"来"、"去"的后边。例如：

The object of place or locality is placed between the head word and the simple complement of direction 来/去, not after the simple complement of direction. For example:

他上楼来了。 （说话人在楼上）

(The speaker is upstairs.)

他出门去了。 （说话人在家里）

(The speaker is at home.)

他回家来了。 （说话人在家里）

(The speaker is at home.)

他回学校去了。（说话人在学校外边）

(The speaker is outside the school.)

绝不能说成"上来楼"、"出去门"、"回来家"、"回去学校"。

The following forms are wrong: 上来楼，出去门，回来家，回去学校。

② 如果宾语表示人或事物，放在补语"来"或"去"的前边、后边都可以。例如：

The object referring to a person or thing is placed either before or after 来/去. For example:

我要给姐姐寄一套明信片去。

他想从外边搬一把椅子来。

我给姐姐寄去了一套明信片。

他从外边搬来了一把椅子。

（5）简单趋向补语和动态助词"了"的位置。

Positions of the simple complement of direction and the aspectual particle 了.

助词"了"可以放在动词谓语和补语之间或者补语"来、去"后边。例如：

The aspectual particle 了 can be placed between the verb predicate and the simple complement of direction 来/去 or after 来/去.

他买了三公斤梨来。

他带来了一些朋友。

他拿去了一个本子。

但助词"着 (zhe)"不能用在带"来、去"的补充词组后边或者谓语动词后边。绝不能说"他买着来三公斤梨"或者"他买来着三公斤梨"等。

N.B. However, 着, also an aspectual particle, can not be used after a complementary phrase using 来/去 or after the predicate verb, so one can not say 他买着来三斤梨 or 他买来着三公斤梨, etc.

2. 关于复合趋向补语。

The compound complement of direction.

（1）复合趋向补语的构成。

Formation of the compound complement of direction.

复合趋向补语可由下列七个动词和简单趋向补语"来、去"构成的十三个动补词组充当。

The following 13 complementary phrases, which are the combinations of seven verbs and 来/去, act as compound complements of direction.

	上	下	进	出	回	过	起
来	上来	下来	进来	出来	回来	过来	起来
去	上去	下去	进去	出去	回去	过去	

例如：

Examples:

他们爬上山去了。　　　他带回宿舍去了。

山上的大石头滚下来了。　这个月的工资领回来了。

客人走进客厅来了。　　游行队伍走过去了。

代表们陆续走出会场来了。汽车开过来了。

大家都拿出本子来。　　他站起来了。

（2）复合趋向补语作动词谓语的补语时，表示双重的趋向。

例如：

The compound complement of direction afte a verb predicate indicates a dual direction. For example:

他走进去了。

（说话人在外边，动作背着说话人进行，而且是从外往里"走"）

(The motion proceeds from outside to inside and away from the speaker who is outside.)

他从山坡上跑下来了。

（说话人在下边，动作向着说

话人进行，而且是从上边往下边"跑"）

(The motion proceeds from an upper position to a lower position and towards the speaker who is in a low position.)

我们拉回来了。

他们运回去了。

① 复合趋向补语中的"来"和"去"表示的方向和简单趋向补语一样。动作朝着说话人的方向进行时，补语不能用"去"而要用"来"。例如：

来 and 去 in the compound directional complement have the same meaning as the simple directional complement, i.e. when the motion proceeds towards the speaker, 来 is used. For example:

他朝马路这边走过来了。

（说话人在马路这边）

(The speaker is on this side.)

大家拿出票来。

不能说成"他朝马路这边跑过去了"，"大家拿出票去"。

One can not say 他朝马路这边跑过去了 or 大家拿出票去.

动作朝着说话人以外的方向进行时，补语不能用"来"而要用"去"。例如：

And when the action is away from the speaker, 去 is the right complement to be used. For example:

他朝马路那边跑过去了。

（说话人在马路这边）

(The speaker is on this side.)

我们搬进两张桌子去。

（说话人在外边）

(The speaker is outside.)

第一句绝不能说成"他朝马路那边跑过来了"。第二句如果说成"我们搬进两张桌子来"，说话人一定要在里边。

In the first case, one can not say 他朝马路那边跑过来了 and in the second case, the speaker must be inside if he says 我们搬进两张桌子来.

② 动词"上、下、进、出、回、过、起"作其他动词谓语的补语时，表示动作的实际趋向。例如：

The verbs 上，下，进，出，回，过 and 起 as complement indicate the actual directions of a motion in relation to a place. For example:

他走进了客厅。

（"进"是动词谓语"走"的补语；"他"从外边"走"到客厅里边了）

(进 is the complement of the verb predicate 走；他 walked into the sitting room from outside.)

他进客厅去了。

（"进"是谓语，"去"是补语，说话人在外边，"他"从外边到客厅里边了）

(进 is the predicate and 去 its complement; 他 walked into the sitting room from outside

327

where the speaker is.)

他走进客厅去了。

（"走"是谓语，"进去"是补语；说话人在外边，"他"从外边"走"到客厅里边了）

(走 is the predicate and 进去 its complement; 他 walked into the sitting room from outside where the speaker is.)

孩子跑下楼了。

（孩子从楼上往楼下"跑"）

(The child ran downstairs from upstairs.)

她下楼来了。

（说话人在楼下）

(The speaker is downstairs.)

孩子跑下楼来了。

（说话人在楼下，孩子从楼上朝说话人的方向往下"跑"）

(The child ran downstairs where the speaker is from upstairs.)

（3）复合趋向补语和中心语之间如果加上结构助词"得(de)"结构和意思就全变了。例如：

When 得 (de) is inserted between the head word and its compound complement of direction, both the structure and meaning will change. Compare the following:

他跑下来了。

（"下来"是复合趋向补语，"跑下来"指从上边"跑"到下边，说话人在下边）

(下来 is the compound complement of direction and 跑下来 means running from upstairs to downstairs where the speaker is.)

他跑得下来。

（"下来"是可能补语，"跑得下来"指"能跑
下来"）

(下来 is the potential complement and 跑得
下来 means 能跑下来.)

（4）复合趋向补语和宾语的位置。

Positions of the compound complement of direction and
the object.

① 带复合趋向补语的动词谓语也可以有宾语，处所宾语一
定要放在复合趋向补语中间（"来"或"去"之前），不能放在
"来"或"去"后边。例如：

The verb predicate with a compound complement of
direction can take an object. If it is one of locality or place,
it is inserted into the compound complement of direction or
before, not after 来 or 去. For example:

他走进礼堂来了。　　　　　他走过马路来了。

他搬出宿舍楼去了。　　　　他跑回家去了。

绝不能说成"走进来礼堂"、"搬出去宿舍楼"、"走过来
马路"、"跑回去家"

One can never say 走进来礼堂，搬出去宿舍楼，走过来马
路，跑回去家.

② 如果宾语表示人或事物，放在复合趋向补语中间，"来、
去"的前边或后边都可以。例如：

When the object refers to a person or thing, it can be
placed either before or after 来 or 去 or, between the two
constituents of the compound complement of direction. For
example:

同学们举起手来。

他递过一瓶汽水来。

他从地上拣起来一支钢笔。

他们从汽车上卸下来很多粮食。

（5）复合趋向补语和动态助词 "了 (le)" 的位置。

Positions of the compound complement of direction and the aspectual particle 了 (le).

助词 "了" 可以放在复合趋向补语和中心语之间，也可以放在复合趋向补语后边。例如：

The particle 了 can be placed between the compound complement of direction and its head word or after the complement. For example:

狗从狗洞爬了进去。

他给我们送过来了几个苹果。

但助词 "着 (zhe)" 不能用在复合趋向补语后边，绝不能说 "爬进去着"，"送过来着"。如果把助词 "着" 放在复合趋向补语和中心语之间，结构和意思就都变了。例如：

Though it is also an aspectual particle, 着 (zhe), on the other hand, can not be used after a compound complement of direction, so there are no such forms as 爬进去着 and 送过来着. When 着 occurs between the compound complement of direction and head word, the phrase changes its structure and meaning. For example:

狗爬着进去。

（"爬着" 是 "进去" 的状语，表示方式）

(爬着 is the adverbial adjunct of manner of 进去.)

他跑着回来了。

（"跑着" 是 "回来" 的状语，表示方式）

(跑着 is the adverbial adjunct of manner of 回来.)

3．复合趋向补语的引申用法。

The extended meanings of the compound complement of direction.

有的复合趋向补语还可以表示别的意义。下面介绍几种常见

330

的引申用法。

Some of the compound complements of direction have extended meanings among which the following are more commonly seen:

（1）起来

①　可以表示动作开始并继续。例如：

Indicating the start and continuation of an action. For example:

> 听了他的话，大家都笑起来了。
>
> 他到教室的时候，同学们已经练习起来了。

要是有宾语，一定要放在"起"和"来"之间。例如：

The object, when there is one, is placed between 起 and 来. For example:

> 他刚唱完，大家就鼓起掌来了。
>
> 快来吧，他们布置起会场来了。

②　可以表示人或事物从分散到集中。例如：

Expressing the idea that dispersed people or things come together. For example:

> 我们应该团结起来。
>
> 晒干的衣服都收起来了。

③　可以表示动作的实际进行，在句中表示"（做）…的时候"。例如：

Expressing the meaning "when sth. is done, (you will find ...)". For example:

> 他走起来快得很。　　这种东西用起来很方便。
>
> 说起来容易，做起来难。　他批评起人来特别尖锐。

（2）下去

可以表示动作继续进行。例如：

Indicating the continuation of an action. For example:

> 我明年还要在中国学习下去。

我们谈下去吧。

注意，带这种意义的补语时，动词谓语后边不能带宾语。如果有宾语，要放在动词谓语或主语前边，有时要借助其他虚词，如介词"把"。例如：

Note that in this sense, the verb predicate never takes an object after it, but it is possible to have a fronted object, i.e. one brought to the front position or before the verb predicate and sometimes a function word (like the preposition 把) is employed to so place the object. For example:

他汉语法语都要学下去。

这些问题我们还要讨论下去。

他们要把那个话剧排演下去。

一定不能说"我们讨论这些问题下去"或"我们讨论下去这些问题"。

There are no such forms as 我们讨论这些问题下去 or 我们讨论下去这些问题。

（3）出来

① 可以表示事物通过动作而出现或产生了结果，从无到有。例如：

Expressing sth. coming into being as a result of an action. For example:

那张画他画出来了。（画好了一张画）

他的意见都说出来了。（说了他的意见）

这个月的计划他已经订出来了。（订了这个月的计划）

他能叫出我们的名字来。

② 可以表示通过动作识别、分辨人或事物，由隐蔽到暴露。例如：

Expressing the identification of a person or thing or sth. concealed being exposed through the action. For example:

我认出来了，她是张力。

这个机器的毛病我检查出来了。

我听出你的声音来了。

（4）下来

① 可以表示动作或状态由动到静，由明到暗，加深程度等逐步变化的过程。例如：

Expressing the gradual change from an active state to a static state or from brightness into darkness. For example:

天黑下来了。

火车慢慢停下来了。

② 可以表示通过动作使人或事物固定或停留在某处，以免消失、离去或被遗忘。例如：

Indicating sth. being fixed to or remaining at a certain place so that it will not disappear, leave or be forgotten. For example:

张教授讲的内容我们都记下来了。

你能把这儿的风景画下来吗？

这儿有纸，大家都把名字写下来。

练 习 30
Exercise 30

（一）按照说话人的位置，填上趋向补语"来"或"去"。

Fill in the blanks with 来/去 as the speaker's positions suggest.

1. 他进房间_____了。　　　　（说话人在外边）

2. 下午张明方要到科学院_____。（说话人不在科学院）

3. 刘英，你出____一下，可以吗？（说话人在外边）

4. 你准备什么时候回家_____? 　（说话人不在家里）

5. 他们跑上山____了。　　　　　（说话人在山上）

6. 汽车刚开过_____。　　　　（说话人在汽车后边）

7. 我爱人带回_____一束鲜花。　（说话人在家里）

8. 你们搬进几把椅子_____吧。　（说话人在屋里）

9. 晒的衣服从楼上掉下____了。　（说话人在楼下）

10. 他从中国带回____不少著名的小说。（说话人在中国）

（二）填上适当的复合趋向补语。

Fill in the blanks with appropriate compound complements of direction.

1. 春天到了，天气暖和_____了。

2. 经过锻炼，他的身体健康_____了。

3. 最近我们又忙_____了。

4. 这个故事很有意思，您讲_____。

5. 他喜欢这个专业，他要学_____。

6. 他说____话____快极了。

7. 她们高兴得跳____舞____。

8. 您的建议很好，请继续说_____。

9. 布告上的字你看_____了吗？

10. 他跑的速度慢_____了。

11. 那篇文章已经写_____了。

12. 快用照相机照_____。

13. 大家搜集的资料应该集中_____。

14. 我们的业余演出队已经组织_____了。

15. 外边下____雨____了。

（三）把下列各组词连成带趋向补语的动宾词组。

Combine each group of words into a V-O phrase with a
complement of direction.

1. 回来　　宿舍

2. 进去　　剧场

3. 带来　　一瓶醋

4. 走进来　　俱乐部
5. 买回来　　一件红毛衣
6. 抬出去　　一个书架
7. 唱起来　　歌
8. 走起来　　路
9. 寄回去　　一包衣服
10. 走上去　　楼

八、可能补语　The potential complement

（一）什么叫可能补语。　Definition.

在谓语动词后面，补充说明动作能否达到某种结果或情况的词或词组叫可能补语。例如：

A word or phrase following a predicate verb to indicate whether the action will possibly achieve a result or reach a state is called a potential complement. For example:

中心语（谓语动词）——结构助词"得"或"不"——可能补语（动词、形容词或动补词组）

Modified word (predicate verb) + structural particle 得 or 不 + potential complement (V., Adj. or V-C phrase)

做得完　　　埋得好
出不去　　　跳得过去

（二）可能补语的语法特点。　Grammatical features.

1. 可能补语只能由动词、形容词或动补词组充当。

Only verbs, adjectives or verb-complement phrases can act as potential complement.

2. 可能补语和中心语之间必须用结构助词"得 (de)"。

得 (de) must be used between the head word and its potential complement.

3. 否定式是把助词"得"换成"不"。

335

The negative form is made by replacing 得 with 不.

4．带可能补语的动词谓语后可带宾语。

The verb-potential complement phrase can be followed by an object.

5．带可能补语的谓语动词后不能带动态助词"了、着、过"。

The aspectual particles 了，着 and 过 never occur after the predicate verb with a potential complement.

6．带肯定式可能补语的谓语动词前边一般可加用表示可能的助动词。

Generally auxiliary verbs of possibility can be used before a predicate verb with an affirmative potential complement.

7．重音一般在可能补语前边的动词谓语上。

The sentence stress falls on the verb predicate preceding the potential complement.

（三）能作可能补语的词和词组。

Words and phrases that can act as potential complement.

1．动词。

Verbs.

那张桌子他们搬得动。　　这些东西他吃不下。

我解得开这根绳子。

2．形容词。

Adjectives.

这面墙刷得白。　　我记不全。

这个问题他讲得深刻。

3．补充词组。

Complementary phrases.

那张画挂得上去。　　今天他们赶不回来了。

这个大衣柜搬得进去。

（四）使用可能补语时需要注意的问题。

336

Points that merit special attention.

1. 结果补语或趋向补语和中心语之间一般都可以加结构助词"得"构成可能补语。可能补语也可以叫作结果补语或趋向补语的可能式。例如：

A complement of result or direction can be considered as a potential complement when the structural particle 得 is placed before it, therefore the potential complement is also known as the potential form of the complement of result or direction. For example:

结果补语 Complement of result	趋向补语 Complement of direction	可能补语 Potential complement
吃完 看清楚		吃得完 看得清楚
	上去 走过来	上得去 走得过来

2. 可能补语的肯定式一定要用结构助词"得"，否则就变成结果补语或趋向补语了，意思也不同了。例如：

The structural particle 得 must be used with the affirmative form of the potential complement. When 得 is absent, the complement becomes one of result or direction which has different implications. For example:

我们听得懂你说的话。

（"懂"是可能补语）

(懂 is a potential complement.)

我听懂你说的话了。

（"懂"是结果补语）

(懂 is a complement of result.)

这座山我爬得上去。

（"上去"是可能补语）

(上去 is the potential complement.)

这座山我昨天爬上去了。

（"上去"是趋向补语）

(上去 is the complement of direction.)

否定式不用"得"而要换用"不"。例如：

In the negative form, 得 is subsituted by 不. For example:

我们听不懂你说的话。

这座山我爬不上去。

绝不能说"听得不懂"、"爬得不上去"。

One never say 听得不懂, 爬得不上去.

可能补语是形容词时更要注意，如果否定式里也用"得"，就变成程度补语了，例如"听得不清楚"。

Learners should be more cautious of this point when the potential complement is an adjective, because if 得 is used in the negative form, the complement will become one of degree, as in 听得不清楚.

3．可能补语和宾语的位置

Positions of the potential complement and the object

（1）宾语可以直接放在可能补语后边。例如：

The object follows the potential complement immediately. For example:

我听得懂这个广播。　我看得清楚黑板上的字。

他吃不下东西了。　　我们都修理不好这架收音机。

我拿不了这么多书。

（2）宾语也可以放到动词谓语或主语前边。

The object can also be placed before the verb predicate or the subject.

他们中国话都听得懂。

同学们这些生词都记得住。

这本书我一个星期看得完。

前边的小河我们过得去。

这个电影的情节我说得出来。

4．可能补语和助动词

The potential complement and auxiliary verbs

表示可能的助动词"能、可以"等，可以用在带肯定式可能补语的动词前边，意思基本不变。例如：

Auxiliary verbs of possibility (like 能，可以，etc.) can be placed before the verb with an affirmative potential complement and the meaning of the phrase remains the same. For example:

他能写得清楚。

我可以抄得完。

但否定式可能补语前不能用助动词。一定不能说"他能写不清楚"，"我可以抄不完"；也不能说"他不能写得清楚"，"我不可抄得完"。

But no auxiliary verb can be used in the negative form of the verb-potential complement phrase, so one never says 他能写不清楚，我可以抄不完; nor can one say 他不能写得清楚，我不可抄得完

5．只有由"上、下、进、出、回、过、起"和"来、去"构成的动补词组可以作可能补语，其他补充词组一般不能充当可能补语。例如：

Complementary phrases, except for those made up of combinations of 上，下，进，出，回，过，起 and 来/去，are usually not used as potential complements. For example:

他背得出来。

我挤不过去。

6．可能补语和程度补语的区别

Differences between the potential complement and the

degree complement.

可能补语和程度补语都可以由形容词担任；它们和中心语之间都必须用结构助词"得"，所以要学会区别这两种补语。

The necessity of differentiating the potential complement from the degree complement lies in the fact that both of them can be made up of adjectives and in both cases the structural particle 得 is used.

（1）充当可能补语的形容词前不能带任何修饰成分，而充当程度补语的形容词前可以带副词状语。例如：

The adjective potential complement can not be premodified, whereas the adjective degree complement can be premodified by adverb adverbial adjuncts. For example:

他注释得快。（让他注释吧）　　　（可能补语）
(Potential complement)

他注释得快。——他注释得很快。（程度补语）
(Degree complement)

他分配得合理。　　　　　　　（可能补语）
(Potential complement)

他分配得合理——他分配得非常合理。（程度补语）
(Degree complement)

（2）充当可能补语的形容词后不能带其他补充成分，而充当程度补语的形容词后可以带补充成分。例如：

The adjective potential complement can not be postmodified, whereas the adjective degree complement can be postmodified by other complementary elements. For example:

他们配合得好。　　　　　　　（可能补语）
(Potential complement)

他们配合得好——他们配合得好极了。（程度补语）
(Degree complement)

340

$$\begin{cases} 他洗得干净。 & （可能补语） \\ & \text{(Potential complement)} \\ 他洗得干净。——他洗得干净得很。 & （程度补语） \\ & \text{(Degree complement)} \end{cases}$$

（3）否定形式不同。

They have different negative forms.

可能补语的否定式是把助词"得"换成"不"，而程度补语的否定式则是在助词"得"后边、形容词补语前边加"不"。例如：

The negative form of the potential complement is made by replacing 得 by 不, whereas that of the degree complement by inserting 不 between 得 and the adjective.   For example:

$$\begin{cases} 他写不好。（别让他写了） & （可能补语） \\ & \text{(Potential complement)} \\ 他写得不好。（不能参加比赛） & （程度补语） \\ & \text{(Degree complement)} \end{cases}$$

$$\begin{cases} 我算不对。（你算吧） & （可能补语） \\ & \text{(Potential complement)} \\ 我算得不对。（要重新算一下） & （程度补语） \\ & \text{(Degree complement)} \end{cases}$$

（4）构成正反疑问句的形式不同。

They have different affirmative-negative question forms.

带可能补语的句子要并列动补词组的肯定和否定形式；而带程度补语的句子要并列补语的肯定和否定形式。例如：

The affirmative-negative question with a potential complement is made by parallelling the affirmative and negative forms of the verb-complement phrase and that with a degree complement is made by parallelling the affirmative and negative forms of the complement itself.   For example:

他说得全说不全？　　　　（可能补语）
（Potential complement）

他说得全不全？　　　　　（程度补语）
（Degree complement）

他剪得齐剪不齐？　　　　（可能补语）
(Potential complement)

他剪得齐不齐？　　　　　（程度补语）
（Degree complement）

（5）宾语的位置不同。

The object is positioned differently.

带可能补语的动词谓语如带宾语，宾语可直接放在动补词组后边；而带程度补语的动词谓语如带宾语，一般要在宾语后重复一次动词，程度补语在重复的动词后边。例如：

In a sentence with a potential complement, the object is immediately preceded by the verb-complement phrase. In a sentence with a degree complement, the verb must be repeated after the object while the complement of degree follows the repeated verb.　For example:

我们分析得对这些句子。　　　　（可能补语）
(Potential complement)

我们分析这些句子分析得对。　　（程度补语）
(Degree complement)

他布置得好联欢晚会的会场。　　（可能补语）
(Potential complement)

他布置联欢晚会的会场布置得很好。（程度补语）
(Degree complement)

他说不全讨论的内容。　　　　　（可能补语）
(Potential complement)

他说讨论的内容说得不全。　　　（程度补语）
(Degree complement)

现将可能补语和程度补语的区别列表如下。

The following table shows the differences between the potential complement and the degree complement:

	可能补语 Potential complement	程度补语 Degree complement
肯定式 Affirmative form	看得清楚	看得清楚 （或者：看得很清楚） （or 看得很清楚）
否定式 Negative form	看不清楚	看得不清楚
正反问 Affirmative-negative questionform	看得清楚看不清楚	看得清楚不清楚
带宾语 With an object	看得清楚那些字	看那些字看得清楚
前带状语 With a pre-modifying adverbial adjuncts		看得特别清楚
后带补语 With a postmodifying complement		看得清楚极了

　　7．几个常见的可能补语。

Commonly used potential complements.

　　（1）动词"动"。

The verb 动.

　　"动"常作可能补语，表示人或事物有力量通过某动作使自己或使宾语所指的人或事物移动位置。例如：

As a potential complement, 动 means that a person or

thing has the strength to cause himself/itself or the person or thing indicated by the object to move. For example:

（他身体很好，）他担得动。 我们抬得动这张床。

他（累极了，）走不动了。 他扛不动这个箱子。

（2）动词"下"。

The verb 下.

"下"常作可能补语，表示某处有足够的空间容纳一定数量的人或事物。例如：

As a potential complement, 下 means a place has enough space to contain a certain number of people or amount of things. For example:

我们宿舍楼住得下六百人。

那个书柜放得下四百本书。

那个剧场坐不下两千人。

我们两个人吃不下这么多东西。

（3）动词"了 (liǎo)"。

The verb 了 (liǎo).

"了"常作可能补语，表示有可能有能力进行某种动作。例如：

As a potential complement, 了 means there is the possibility or ability to do sth. For example:

明天上午我来得了。

他（明天上午有事，）看不了你们的网球比赛了。

"了 (liǎo)"还可以作形容词的可能补语，表示能达到某种程度或情况。例如：

As the potential complement of an adjective, 了 (liǎo) means it is possible to reach a certain degree or extent. For example:

他一定胖得了。

这张纸大不了了。 （已经裁小了）

(Because it has been cut too small)

练　习　31

Exercise　31

（一）把下列动补词组改成带可能补语的词组。

Turn the following into phrases with potential complements.

　　1.　能上去＿＿＿＿＿＿＿

　　2.　不能数完＿＿＿＿＿＿

　　3.　不能找到＿＿＿＿＿＿

　　4.　能称对＿＿＿＿＿＿＿

　　5.　能推出去＿＿＿＿＿＿

　　6.　不能挂上去＿＿＿＿＿＿

　　7.　能说清楚＿＿＿＿＿＿

　　8.　不能听懂＿＿＿＿＿＿

　　9.　能挡住＿＿＿＿＿＿＿

　10.　能看见＿＿＿＿＿＿

（二）填上适当的可能补语〔动词"动、下、了 (liǎo)"〕。

Fill in the blanks with appropriate potential complements 〔动，下 or 了 (liǎo)〕.

　　1.　我今天累得走不＿＿＿＿＿了。

　　2.　这个房间很大，住得＿＿＿＿＿五个人。

　　3.　我已经吃得很饱了，吃不＿＿＿＿＿了。

　　4.　很抱歉，今天晚上我去不＿＿＿＿＿了。

　　5.　这只箱子太小，放不＿＿＿＿＿这些东西。

　　6.　这件行李不太重，他一个人拿得＿＿＿＿＿。

　　7.　你最近吃得＿＿＿＿＿东西吗？

　　8.　他长得越来越胖，瘦不＿＿＿＿＿了。

　　9.　这间屋子坐不＿＿＿＿＿二十人。

　10.　他们两个人大概抬不＿＿＿＿＿这个衣柜。

附表三： 词类、词组和各种补语的关系

Table 3: Relationships of Different Parts of Speech and Phrases with Complements of Different Kinds

词类、词组 Parts of speech and phrases	结果补语 Result compl.	程度补语 Degree compl.	数量补语 Compl. of quantity 动量 Fre-quency	数量补语 Compl. of quantity 时间 Dura-tion	数量补语 Compl. of quantity 名量 Nominal Measure	趋向补语 Direction compl. 简单 Simple	趋向补语 Direction compl. 复合 Com-pound	可能补语 Potential compl.
动词 Verb	✓					✓		✓
形容词 Adjective	✓	✓						✓
代词 Pronoun		✓						
副词 Adverb		✓						
联合词组 Coordinative phrase		✓						
主谓词组 S-P phrase		✓						

346

	名词性\nNominal	动词,形容词性\nVerbal/adjectival	动量\nVerbal	名量\nNominal	动补\nV-compl.	形补\nAdj.-compl.	介词结构\nPrepositional phrase
动宾词组 V-O phrase					✓		
偏正词组 Endocentric phrase: 名词性 Nominal	✓						
动词,形容词性 Verbal/adjectival				✓			
数量词组 N-Mw phrase: 动量 Verbal		✓	✓	✓			
名量 Nominal							
补充词组 Complementary phrase: 动补 V-compl.		✓					
形补 Adj.-compl.		✓					
介词结构 Prepositional phrase	✓						

"√" 表示该词类或词组可以充当某种补语。

The tick √ indicates the word/phrase which can serve as a particular complement.

347

练　习　32
Exercise 32

（一）用横线标出下列句中的补语，并指出是哪种补语。

Underline the complements in the following sentences and state which kind each of them is.

例：　　　玻璃弄破了他的手。（结果补语）

Model:　　　　　　　　　　（Complement of result）

　　1．你可以躲在这棵大树后边。

　　2．他们对这次旅行的安排满意极了。

　　3．昨天的晚会结束得很早。

　　4．他今天高兴得又唱又跳。

　　5．我已经阅读了三遍。

　　6．那只小鸟飞走了。

　　7．她们两个人搬不动这只大箱子。

　　8．这种乐器一定买得到。

　　9．他的汉语水平比我们高得多。

　　10．今年我们工厂生产出来许多种新产品。

（二）用横线标出下列句中的宾语和补语，并指出它们属哪类词或词组。

Underline the objects and complements in the following sentences and state which kind of a word/phrase each of them is.

例：　　　我看见一头小黄牛。

Model:

　　　　　（见：补语，动词；黄牛：宾语，名词）

　　　　　（见：Complement, verb; 黄牛: Object, noun）

　　1．他骑马骑得很快。

2．他从树上摘下来几个苹果。

3．大人和孩子下了一个钟头象棋。

4．那只蚊子咬了他一下儿。

5．那批货已经装进火车去了。

6．上午他就改完了那篇作文。

7．他们恐怕实现不了那个修建计划。

8．他的胳臂流出血来了。

9．上月他请病假请了两天。

10．我们应该征求一下儿他的意见。

第五章 单 句

Chapter Five   The Simple Sentence

一、什么是句子   Definition

句子是由词或词组按照一定语法规则组成的，能表达一个比较完整的意思，表现一定的语气，有一定的语调；在连续谈话的过程中，句子和句子之间有一个较大的停顿，这种停顿在书面上用句号 "。" 表示。

A sentence is composed of words or phrases arranged according to certain grammatical rules to express a comparatively complete meaning and a certain tone with certain intonation. In connected discourse, there is a stop between each two sentences which is indicated by a "。" (the full stop) in writing.

句子可以分成单句和复句两大类。本章介绍单句的基本结构和用途。

Sentences can be divided into two categories: the simple sentence and the complex sentence. The basic structure and function of the simple sentence are introduced in this chapter.

二、单句的基本结构

The basic structure of the simple sentence

一个单句一般是由主语和谓语两个部分组成的，主语部分在前，谓语部分在后。一个单句可以包含一个或几个词或词组。

A simple sentence usually consists of two sections: the subject section and the predicate section, with the former preceding the latter.   It may contain one or several words or phrases.

从句子是否具备主语和谓语两个部分来看，句子可以分成主谓句和非主谓句两类。

Sentences can be classified, in terms of whether they contain one or two sections, into the subject-predicate (S-P) sentences and the non-subject-predicate (Non-S-P) sentences.

（一）主谓句。   The S-P sentence.

1．什么是主谓句。   Definition.

包括主语和谓语两个部分的句子叫主谓句。也叫双部句。例如：

A sentence containing the subject section and the predicate section is called a S-P sentence or a two-member sentence. For example:

主语部分——谓语部分

The subject section + the predicate section

　　　他们——研究中国历史。　　　明天——新年。

　　　我们——是中文系的学生。　　　桂林——山水太美了。

　　　这里——真安静。

2．主谓句的种类。   Variety of S-P sentences.

按谓语部分的结构特点，主谓句一般可以分动词谓语句、形容词谓语句、名词谓语句和主谓谓语句四种。

According to the different structures of the predicate, the S-P sentences can be classified into four kinds: a) those with verbal predicate; b) those with adjectival predicate; c) those with nominal predicate and d) those with S-P phrase as predicate.

（二）非主谓句。   Non-S-P sentences.

1．什么叫非主谓句。   Definition.

不同时包括主语和谓语两个部分，或分不出主语或谓语部分的句子叫非主谓句。也叫单部句。例如：

A sentence is called a Non-S-P sentence or a one-member sentence if it does not contain or cannot be divided into the subject and the predicate sections. For example:

下霜了。 请坐！

开演了。 看！

多（么）危险哪！ 火车！

禁止吸烟！ 他呢？

（谁参加这次座谈会？）我（参加这次座谈会）。

（你写什么？）（我）写日记。

2．非主谓句的种类。 Variety of Non-S-P sentences.

非主谓句可以分成无主句、独语句和简略句三种。

Non-S-P sentences can be classified into three kinds: a) the subjectless sentence; b) the one-word sentence and c) the elliptical sentence.

三、单句的用途 Functions of the simple sentence

单句可以表达陈述、疑问等不同的意思和语气。从不同的用途和语气来看，句子可以分成陈述句、疑问句、祈使句和感叹句四类。

The simple sentence expresses different meanings and tones such as a declaration, an interrogation, etc. Sentences can be classified, in terms of function and tone, into four kinds: a) the declarative sentence; b) the interrogative sentence; c) the imperative sentence and d) the exclamatory sentence.

四、现将句子的类别列表如下

The classification of sentences is shown in the following diagram:

句子的种类
Types of Sentences

单句
Simple sentences

复句
Complex sentences

按结构分
Classified in terms of structure

按用途分
Classified in terms of function

主谓句
（双部句）
S-P sentences
(Two-member
sentences)

非主谓句
（单部句）
Non-S-P sen-
tences (One-
member sen-
tences)

动词谓语句
S-P sentence with
a V-predicate

形容词谓语句
S-P sentence with
an Adj.-predicate

名词谓语句
S-P sentence with
a N-predicate

主谓谓语句
S-P sentence with
a S-P phrase as
predicate

无主句
Subjectless sen-
tence

独语句
One-word sen-
tence

简略句
Elliptical sentence

陈述句
Declarative sentence

疑问句
Interrogative sentence

祈使句
Imperative sentence

感叹句
Exclamatory sentence

353

下面分两部分介绍主谓句、非主谓句和按用途分的各种单句。

The next two parts will deal respectively with the S-P sentence, the non-S-P sentence and the simple sentences classified in terms of function.

第一部分　按结构分类

Part One　Classification of Sentences in Terms of Structure

第一节　动词谓语句

Section I　Sentences with Verbal Predicates

一、什么叫动词谓语句　Definition

以动词为谓语、叙述主语"做什么"的句子叫动词谓语句。

A sentence with a verb as the predicate to state what the person or thing indicated by the subject does is called a sentence with a verbal predicate.

汉语里，动词谓语句是大量的，在各类句子中占绝对优势，谓语部分的结构方式也最多，这里先介绍一般的比较简单的结构。一般动词谓语句的基本格式有三种：

In Chinese, sentences with a verbal predicate are numerous and occupy the overwhelming majority of sentences and there are more ways of constructing the predicate of this type of sentence than other types. Here we shall introduce the simplest and most common ones. Sentences with a verbal predicate normally have three basic structures:

1. 主语——谓语（动词）

Subject + predicate (a verb)

　　　大家——唱。

　　　我们——劳动。

2. 主语——谓语（及物动词）——宾语

Subject + predicate (a transitive verb) + object

　　　他们——买——乐器。

　　　张老师——教——我们。

3. 主语——谓语（及物动词）——间接宾语——直接宾语

Subject + predicate (a transitive verb) + indirect object + direct object

　　　我——送——他——一支笔。

　　　他——教——新学生——汉语。

二、动词谓语句的语法特点　Grammatical features

　　一般动词都可以充当谓语。其特点见第二章第二节"二、动词的语法特点"。

Generally speaking, any verb can serve as predicate. For the grammatical features, please refer to Section II, Chapter Two.

三、使用动词谓语句需要注意的问题

Points that merit special attention

　　（一）谓语动词。

The predicate verbs.

1. 充当谓语的动词没有形态变化（见第二章"动词"一节）。

The verb used as a predicate has no morphological changes. (See the section of Verbs in Chapter Two.)

2. 谓语说明主语"是什么"时，一定要用动词"是"。例如：

The verb 是 is to be used when the predicate states "what the subject is." For example:

北京是中国的首都。

那是博物馆。

不能说成"北京中国的首都"、"那博物馆"。

There are no such forms as 北京中国的首都 or 那博物馆.

（二）动词谓语和宾语。

The verbal predicate and the object.

1. 由及物动词充当的谓语后面可以带宾语（见第四章 第三节"宾语"）。

The verb can take an object if it is a transitive one. (See Section III The Object, Chapter Four.)

动词谓语后边带一个宾语的句子叫单宾语动词谓语句。例如：

The sentence is called a sentence with a transitive verb predicate if the verb predicate is followed by one object. For example:

他还书。　　　　　　他妈妈是教师。

她送我们。　　　　　　他有一张今天晚上的杂技票。

2. 动词谓语后边带两个宾语的句子叫双宾语动词谓语句。第一个宾语指人或集体、单位，是间接宾语；第二个宾语指事物，是直接宾语。例如：

The sentence is called a sentence with a ditransitive verb predicate if the verb predicate is followed by two objects with the first one referring to a person, collective or unit and the second to a thing. For example:

他借图书馆一本小说。　　哥哥给我一束花。

她送我一套教材。　　　　售货员找我一块三毛钱。

可以带双宾语的动词不多（见第二章"动词"一节）。

In Chinese, only a limited number of verbs are ditransitive. (See the section of verbs in Chapter Two.)

这两个宾语的次序是固定的，不能调换。不能说"他借一本

356

小说图书馆"、"哥哥给一束花我"等。

The order of the two objects is fixed and is not reversable, so one can not say 他借一本小说图书馆，哥哥给一束花我, etc.

3．宾语的位置一般在动词谓语后面，但有时为了强调和对比，宾语也可以放到动词谓语前面或主语前面，成为前置宾语。（见第四章第三节"宾语"）

The object usually follows the verb predicate, but sometimes it can be placed before it or even before the subject for emphasis or contrast. Such is known as the fronted object. (See Section III The Object, Chapter Four.) For example:

4．谓语由不及物动词充当时，一定不能带宾语。例如：

No object is used if the predicate is an intransitive verb. For example:

最近他常咳嗽。

我们八点出发。

不能说成"他常咳嗽几口"、"我们八点出发学校"。

One can not say 他常咳嗽几口 or 我们八点出发学校.

5．有些由动宾关系构成的动词作谓语时，后边不能再带宾语。例如：

No other object can be used when the predicate is a verb formed by a V-O construction. For example:

我明年毕业。　　　　我们要分手了。

我们每天见面。

一定不能说"我明年毕业大学"、"我每天见面他"、"他要分手我们了。

One can never say 我明年毕业大学，我每天见面他，他要分手我们了.

如果要说明对象或处所等，常用介词结构作状语。例如：

To specify the receiver or target of an action or the place, an adverbial adjunct made of a prepositional phrase is used.

For example:

我明年（从）大学毕业。　他要和我们分手了。

我每天跟他见面。

（三）动词谓语句的否定形式。

The negative form of a sentence with a verb predicate.

1. 在谓语动词前边加否定副词"不"，表示"不愿意"、"不准备"、"经常不"、"将不"等意思。例如：

不 is used before the predicate verb to express "unwillingness", "unreadiness", "always not", "will not", etc. For example:

我不学习法语。　　　他不是我们企业的职员。

老马不在家。

否定副词"不"一定要放在谓语动词前边，而不能放在谓语动词后边表示否定。一定不能说"老马在不家"等。

The negative adverb 不 must precede but not follow the predicate verb. One can never say 老马在不家, etc.

2. 谓语是动词"有"时，否定式永远是"没有"。例如：

The negative form of the verb 有 as predicate is 没有. For example:

我们都没有这种词典。　　这些牛肉没有十公斤。

二月没有三十天。　　　这把锁没有钥匙。

那个商店没有我要的那种帽子。

一定不能说"我们都不有这种词典"或"二月有没三十天"等。

It is impossible to say 我们都不有这种词典，二月有没三十天, etc.

3. 否定动作未发生或未完成时，在谓语动词前边用否定副词"没（有）"。例如：

With an action that did not or has not taken place or been completed, the negative adverb 没（有）is used before the predicate verb. For example:

他没找我。

他没放弃这次学习的机会。

4．关于动词谓语后边带各类补语时的否定形式，见第四章第六节。

For the negative forms of the verb predicate followed by vaious complements, please refer to Section VI, Chapter Four.

5．关于谓语动词后边带动态助词时的否定形式，将在第六章介绍。

The negative forms of predicate verbs with aspectual particles will be introduced in Chapter Six.

练　习　33
Exercise 33

（一）用横线标出下列动词谓语句中的动词谓语和宾语。

Draw a line under the predicate and a double line under the object in each sentence.

例：

Model: 我开汽车。

1．我们喝牛奶。

2．妈妈倒茶。

3．我要开窗户。

4．她有一对漂亮的花瓶。

5．他买了三公斤鱼。

6．我们经常在图书馆看杂志。

7．他很爱他的姑姑。

8．大家都很信任你。

9．他们筷子和叉子都会用。

10．她们想打羽毛球。

11. 你可以介绍介绍这个情况。

12. 1949年中国人民获得了解放。

13. 我们准备深入地钻研一下这个问题。

14. 教授非常赞成学生们提出来的建议。

15. 今年暑假我们打算去风景优美的南方。

（二）用横线标出下列动词谓语句中动词谓语的状语。

Underline the adverbial adjuncts of the verbal predicates in the following sentences:

例：　他每天早上六点起床。

Model:

1. 他向窗户外边看了看。

2. 今天有一点儿冷。

3. 他最近更喜欢唱歌了。

4. 明天他们要重新做一次试验。

5. 他替我捆好了行李。

6. 我和朋友们一连去了三次颐和园。

7. 每一个公民都必须遵守国家的法律。

8. 这几个工厂都提前完成了生产任务。

9. 关于那次战争的情况，我们了解得也很不够。

10. 我们对这些奇怪的现象一定要进行彻底的调查。

（三）用横线标出下列动词谓语句中动词谓语的补语，并指出是哪种补语。

Underline the complements of the verbal predicates in the following sentences and state what kinds of complement they are.

例：　他们归纳出了几条规律。（结果补语）

Model:　　　　　　　　　　　（Complement of result）

1. 这件事办得很顺利。

2. 我们约好明天去劳动人民文化宫。

3. 这两个词的用法要区别开。

4. 我们已经学完第五章了。

5. 这间屋子坐得下二十个人。

6. 他说汉语说得很不错。

7. 东西都装进箱子里去了。

8. 他喊得楼上的人都听见了。

9. 今天讲不完这篇文章了。

10. 他昨天去了一趟友谊商店。

第二节 形容词谓语句

Section II　Sentences with Adjectival Predicates

一、什么叫形容词谓语句　Definition

　　以形容词为谓语、描写主语"怎么样"的句子叫形容词谓语句。

The sentence with an adjectival predicate is one in which the predicate is an adjective telling "how" the subject is.

　　形容词谓语句的基本格式是：

The basic patterns of such a sentence are:

　　（一）肯定式：主语——谓语（形容词）

The affirmative form: Subject + predicate (adjective)

　　　　　　他——高，我——矮。

　　　　　　我们——大，他们——小。

　　（二）否定式：主语——状语（副词"不"）——谓语（形容词）

The negative form: Subject + adverbial adjunct (the adverb 不) + predicate (adjective)

　　　　　　这张桌子——不——旧。

　　　　　　今天——不——冷。

二、形容词谓语句的语法特点　Grammatical features

形容词可以直接充当谓语。其特点见第二章第四节"二、形容词的语法特点"。

Adjectives can be used independently as the predicate. For the grammatical features of adjectives, please refer to Section IV, Chapter Two.

三、使用形容词谓语句需要注意的问题

Points that merit special attention

（一）谓语形容词的否定形式前边一般不用动词"是"，如用"是"，则表示强调、肯定的意思，"是"要重读。例如：

In the negative form, the verb 是 is normally not used (When so used, it signifies emphasis and affirmation and 是 should be stressed.) For example:

这条围巾不厚。

（一般不说"这条围巾是不厚"）

(Usually one does not say 这条围巾是不厚.)

这儿不好玩。

（一般不说"这儿是不好玩"）

(Usually one does not say 这儿是不好玩.)

形容词谓语句的否定形式是在谓语形容词前加否定副词"不"，而不能在主语和谓语形容词之间用"不是"。不能说"这条围巾不是厚"、"这儿不是好玩"。

The negative form of a sentence with an adjectival predicate is made by placing the negative adverb 不 before the predicate adjective. It is wrong to put 不是 between the subject and the predicate adjective, therefore, one can never say 这条围巾不是厚 and 这儿不是好玩.

（二）谓语形容词和"很"。

The predicate adjective and the adverb 很.

1. 肯定形式的谓语形容词前边常用副词"很"，一般不表示明显的程度，"很"要轻读，重音在谓语形容词上。不用"很"

时，常有对比的意思。例如：

The adverb 很 often precedes the affirmative form of a predicate adjective. Here 很 does not express an obvious degree and the sentence stress falls on the adjective rather than 很. The sentence implies a contrast if 很 is absent. For example:

> 这间房子很亮。
>
> 这间房子亮。（那间暗。）

如果要表示"很"的程度，"很"就要重读。例如：

When a high degree is expressed, 很 should be stressed. For example:

> 这本书很有意思。
>
> 这双袜子很长。

常见的表示程度的副词还有："非常、特别、相当、十分、比较、更、最、太、真"；这些副词都可以放在谓语形容词前边作状语。例如：

Other degree adverbs are: 非常，特别，相当，十分，比较，更，最，太，真，etc.; All these adverbs are used as adverbial adjuncts before predicate adjectives. For example:

> 他的发言真精彩。　　　　我特别着急。
>
> 那个剧场相当不错。

2. 否定形式的谓语形容词前边如用"很"，表示程度高。例如：

很 expresses a high degree when used before the negative form of the predicate adjective. For example:

> 这张桌子很不好。　　（非常"不好"）
>
> 那把椅子很不结实。　　（非常"不结实"）

如果"很"在否定副词"不"的后边，表示程度不高，例如：

If it follows a negative adverb 不, 很 expresses a low degree.

For example:

> 今天天气不很冷。（不太冷）
>
> 我哥哥不很胖。（不太胖。）

（三）形容词谓语后边只能带程度补语和数量补语。例如：

Only complement of degree and complement of quantity can occur after an adjectival predicate. For example:

> 他的心慌得很。　　　　反动派凶恶极了。
>
> 他累得走不动了。　　　　他高多了。
>
> 他睏得直闭眼。　　　　他比以前胖一点儿。
>
> 他瘦得老同学都认不出来了。这个小朋友高一米五。

练 习 34
Exercise 34

（一）把下列形容词谓语句改为否定形式。

Turn the following sentences negative:

1. 今天天气很凉快。
2. 今天的客人很多。
3. 他们俩很亲密。
4. 这个客厅很干净。
5. 那个孩子很诚实。
6. 他刚买的那件衬衫很贵。
7. 这里的交通很方便。
8. 这儿的空气很新鲜。
9. 这个号码很对。
10. 这课的语法很难。

（二）选词填空。

Choose one from the words given in bracket to fill in each blank.

1. 这条裙子的样子＿＿＿＿＿好看。（非常，都）
2. 河边的小草＿＿＿＿＿嫩。（一起，特别）
3. 我们最近＿＿＿＿＿忙。（还不算太忙）（比较，不）
4. 刚才小王＿＿＿＿＿不安。（很，常常）
5. 我（能参加这样盛大的庆祝大会）感到＿＿＿＿＿兴奋。

    （经常，十分）

6. 这个公园＿＿＿＿＿美。（相当，再）
7. 这个错误＿＿＿＿＿明显了。（只，太）
8. 北京的秋天＿＿＿＿＿凉快。（特别，太）
9. 我的座位＿＿＿＿＿舒服。（又，最）
10. 他住的房间＿＿＿＿＿大了。（太，真）

（三）用横线标出下列形容词谓语句中形容词谓语的补语，并指出是哪种补语。

Underline and name the complements of the adjectival predicates in the following sentences.

例：

Model: 目前形势有利得很，（程度补语）(Complement of degree)

1. 他画的那条线斜极了。
2. 这条裤子长一米。
3. 这种布的质量差得很。
4. 这种自行车便宜多了。
5. 那个教室小多了。
6. 这根绳子粗一点儿。
7. 那个箱子重得一个人提不动。
8. 解放以前，他爷爷奶奶的生活苦极了。
9. 这儿安静得多。
10. （这本书一百页，那本书九十页）这本书厚一点儿。

第三节　名词谓语句

Section III　Sentences with Nominal Precicates

一、什么叫名词谓语句 Definition

以名词、名词性偏正词组等作谓语，表示藉贯、年龄、日期、节气、职业、节日、钱数等的句子，叫名词谓语句。

A sentence with a noun predicate is one in which the predicate is a noun or a nominal endocentric phrase etc. indicating native place, age, day or date, solar terms, occupation, festival, amount of money, ect.

名词谓语句的基本格式是：

The basic pattern for this kind of sentence is:

主语——谓语（名词、数词、数量词组或名词性偏正词组）

Subject + predicate (a noun, a numeral, a N-Mw phrase or nominal endocentric phrase)

> 他——研究生。（名词）
>> (Noun)

> 昨天——阴天。
> 明天——元旦。
> 今天——三十（号）。（数词）
>> (Numeral)

> 他——十九岁。（数量词组）
>> (N-Mw phrase)

> 他——中国人。（名词性偏正词组）
>> (Nominal endocentric phrase)

> 这辆自行车——一百八十六块钱。

二、名词谓语句的语法特点 Grammatical features

（一）名词谓语句的谓语可由少数名词、数词、数量词组或名词性偏正词组直接充当。例如：

Only a limited number of nouns, numerals, N-Mw phrases or nominal endocentric phrases can serve as the predicate of such a sentence. For example:

> 她医生。　　　　　　　明天十月四号。
>
> 今天晴天。　　　　　　这块肥皂六毛六。
>
> 他二十一（岁）。　　　他哪里人？
>
> 现在五点半。

（二）某些名词谓语句中的谓语前边可以有状语。例如：

Some of the predicates of such sentences can be premodified by adverbial adjuncts. For example:

> 今天已经星期五了。　　他今年二十多岁了。
>
> 现在才六点。　　　　　这些一共八块九毛三。

三、使用名词谓语句需要注意的问题

Points that merit special attention

（一）汉语里名词谓语句比较少。主语和谓语之间不用动词"是"连接。例如：

There are not very many sentences with noun predicates in Chinese. The verb 是 does not occur between the subject and the predicate. For example:

> 下星期一春节。　　　　这块手绢五毛。
>
> 我二十。　　　　　　　他外国人。

如果在名词谓语句的谓语前边用上动词"是"，就变成了动词谓语句。

When the verb 是 is inserted between the subject and the predicate, the sentence turns into one with a verbal predicate.

（二）否定名词谓语时要在原句谓语前边用"不是"，而不能只用"不"。例如：

The negative form is made by putting 不是, rather than

367

不, before the predicate.   For example:

主语 ——	状语 ——	谓语 ——	宾语
Subject +	adverbial adjunct +	predicate +	object
	（副词"不"）	（动词"是"）	（名词）
	(The adverb 不)	(The verb 是)	(Noun)
			（数词）
			(Numeral)
			（数量词组）
			(N-Mw phrase)
			（名词性偏正词组）
			(Nominal endo- centric phrase)

下星期一不是春节。　　这块手绢不是五毛。

我不是二十。　　　　　他不是外国人。

不能说成"下星期一不春节"、"我不二十"、"这块手绢不五毛"、"他不外国人"。

One can not say 下星期一不春节，我不二十，这块手绢不五毛，他不外国人， etc.

（三）时间词和表示时间的副词可放在表示数量或时间的名词性谓语前作状语；时间词也可以放在主语前边。例如：

In such a sentence, if the predicate expresses quantity or time, an adverbial adjunct of time (a noun or adverb of time) can be used before the predicate.   Nouns of time can also precede the subject.   For example:

他今年十八（岁）。

（时间词在谓语数词前）

(The time noun precedes the predicate.)

去年他十七。

（时间词在主语前）

(The time noun precedes the subject.)

今天已经二十九号了。

（副词"已经"表示时间）

(The adverb 已经 expresses a time reference.)

后天才春节呢。

（副词"才"表示时间）

(The adverb 才 expresses a time reference.)

（四）名词谓语句一般都比较短，结构比较简单，多用于口语。

Usually a sentence with a noun predicate is short, simple in structure and is used more often in spoken Chinese.

练 习 35
Exercise 35

（一）在下列名词谓语句前边划上"√"。

Put a √ before sentences with nominal predicates.

1. 今天星期五。

2. 他们都是阿拉伯人。

3. 这件大衣二百五十块钱。

4. 后天是开斋节。

5. 现在夏天了。

6. 今年他五十五岁。

7. 今天复活节。

8. 今年是一九八一年。

9. 这是一千块钱。

10. 他炊事员，我服务员。

（二）把练习（一）中的句子改成否定式。

Turn the sentences in Exercise 1 negative.

例：

Model: 明天圣诞节。——→明天不是圣诞节。

第四节 主谓谓语句

Section IV The sentence with an S-P Phrase as the Predicate

一、什么叫主谓谓语句 Definition

以主谓词组为谓语的句子，叫主谓谓语句。

A sentence with a S-P phrase as the predicate is one in which the predicate is a S-P phrase.

主谓谓语句的基本格式是：

The basic patterns are:

（一）主语——谓语〔主谓词组："主" ——"谓"〕

Subject + predicate 〔S-P phrase: subject-predicate〕

他——身体　好。

兔子——尾巴　短。

这个士兵——胸部　受伤了。

（二）主语——谓语〔主谓词组："主" ——"谓"（及物动词）——"宾"（数量词组）〕

Subject+predicate 〔S-P phrase: subject-predicate (transitive verb)-object (N-Mw phrase)〕

《汉英词典》——我　有　一本。

这种上衣——小王　做了　一件。

二、主谓谓语句的语法特点 Grammatical features

（一）谓语由主谓词组直接充当。例如：

The S-P phrase serves as the predicate by itself. For example:

那个工程师水平很高。

那个司机态度好。

他们公司这个规定不合理。

　　　　　这种颜色的裙子我还有一条。

　　　　　沙发那几个商店都有不少。

　　　　　这种网子我只要一个。

　　（二）主谓谓语句的主语和谓语里的"主"或"宾"所指的人或事物有一定的所属关系。（见第三章第二节四、1—2）

The person or thing denoted by the subject or object in the predicate S-P phrase is a part of or belongs to the subject of the sentence. (See Section II, 4, 1--2, Chapter Three)

　　（三）主谓谓语句的否定形式是在谓语里的"谓"前边加否定副词"不"或"没（有）"。例如：

The negative form is made by putting the negative adverb 不 or 没（有）before the predicate of the S-P phrase. For example:

　　　　　那位小姐钢琴弹得不太熟练。

　　　　　这架收音机声音不清楚。

　　　　　我们单位年轻人不少。

　　　　　那种袜子他没买两双。

　　　　　学习心得他没写三篇。

　　　　　这种词典我没有两本，只有一本。

　　（四）主谓谓语句中谓语前可带状语。例如：

The predicate of the sentence can be premodified by adverbial adjuncts. For example:

　　　　　他这几天心情不太好。

　　　　　这个地区以前地多人少。

　　　　　那个售货员始终态度很好。

　　　　　这种梳子我刚丢了一把。

三、使用主谓谓语句需要注意的问题

Points that merit special attention

　　（一）主谓谓语句中主语和谓语之间不用动词"是"或代词来连接。例如：

The subject and predicate of the sentence are not connected by the verb 是 or any pronoun.   For example:

我胃有点儿不舒服。

这种明信片我买了一套。

一般不能说成"我是胃有点儿不舒服"、"这种明信片是我买了一套"。也不能说成"我是那个胃有点儿不舒服"、"这种明信片是那个我买了一套"。如果用"是",意思就变了。

Usually one does not say 我是胃有点儿不舒服,这种明信片是我买了一套;   nor can one say 我是那个胃有点不舒服,这种明信片是那个我买了一套。 If 是 is used, there will be a change in meaning in the sentence.

（二）主谓谓语句的谓语部分——主谓谓语。

The predicate section of such a sentence — the S-P phrase predicate.

1. "主谓词组"作谓语时,其中的"主"常属于全句主语,而"谓"常由形容词充当,描写性比较强。例如:

The subject in the S-P phrase belongs to the subject of the sentence, and the predicate in the S-P phrase is often an adjective which is descriptive in nature.   For example:

那个姑娘眼睛很大。

（主谓谓语中"眼睛"是"主",是属于全句主语"那个姑娘"的;"大"是"谓",是形容词,"眼睛很大"是描写全句主语的。）

(In the S-P phrase, the subject 眼睛 belongs to the sentence subject 那个姑娘;大 is an adjective which is the predicate of the S-P phrase and 眼睛很大 describes the sentence subject.)

这个窗帘颜色很好。

2. 主谓谓语中的"主"属于全句主语,而"谓"是由动词充当时,这个动词一般是表示被动意思的。例如:

372

When the subject in the S-P phrase belongs to the sentence subject and the predicate of the S-P phrase is a verb, the verb is notionally in the passive. For example:

那个战士腿断了。

（"腿"是属于"那个战士"的，"腿"是被弄"断"的）

(腿 belongs to 那个战士 and is broken as the result of the action 弄.)

这件衣服扣子掉了。

3．主谓谓语中的"谓"是由及物动词充当时，它的宾语常由数量词组充当，而且是属于全句主语的一部分。例如：

When the predicate of the S-P phrase is a transitive verb, the object of the verb is usually a N-Mw phrase and is a part of the sentence subject. For example:

这种花我栽了两盆。

那本寓言我已经看了三十多页了。

如果不带数量宾语，那么句子的结构和意思就都变。例如：

If the transitive verb goes without the object (N-Mw phrase), both the structure and meaning of the sentence will change. For example:

这种颜色的窗帘我买了。

（"窗帘"是前置宾语）

(窗帘 is the fronted object.)

那本书我已经看了。

（"书"是前置宾语）

(书 is the fronted object.)

（三）时间词作状语，也可以放在主谓谓语句句首。例如：

The time nouns used as adverbial adjuncts can also be placed at the beginning of the sentence. For example:

昨天我牙疼。

现在他膝盖不疼了。

以前那个地区树多极了。

（四）主谓谓语的"主"是由动词充当时，"谓"常由形容词充当，表示程度的副词只能放在"谓"前边作状语，而不能放在主谓谓语前边。例如：

When the subject of the S-P phrase is a verb, its predicate is usually an adjective. The degree adverb used as an adverbial adjunct can only precede the predicate of the S-P phrase rather than that of the sentence.　For example:

这些工人劳动特别积极。

（"劳动积极"是主谓谓语）

(劳动积极 is the S-P phrase predicate.)

他工作非常认真。

（"工作认真"是主谓谓语）

(工作认真 is the S-P phrase predicate.)

她学习很努力。

（"学习努力"是主谓谓语）

(学习努力 is the S-P phrase predicate.)

不能说成"工人特别劳动积极"、"他非常工作认真"、"她很学习努力"。

There are no such forms as 工人特别劳动积极，他非常工作认真，她很学习努力，etc.

练　习　36
Exercise 36

（一）用横线标出下列主谓谓语句中谓语部分的主语。

Underline the subjects of the predicate S-P phrases in the following sentences.

例：

Model: 昨天我<u>腰</u>酸。

1. 那朵花颜色真好看。

2. 这种皮帽子他有一顶。

3. 这把锁钥匙丢了。

4. 那种厚毛衣哥哥买了一件。

5. 这些古代修建的塔结构很不一般。

6. 那个工程师技术水平不断提高。

7. 这几个词用法比较特别。

8. 你要的参考资料我借回来了两本。

9. 奶奶胳臂摔了。

10. 她服务态度非常好。

（二）改正病句。

Correct the mistakes in the following sentences.

1. 他背昨天受伤了。

2. 代表资格他取消了。

3. 我是那个头有一点儿晕。

4. 这个青年非常工作吃苦。

5. 这个地方很气候不错。

附表四： 四种主谓句的简要情况表

Table 4, The Four Types of Subject-Predicate Sentences

主 谓 句 S-P sentences	例 句 Examples	表 示 的 意 义 Meaning and usage
动词谓语句 Sentence with a verbal predicate	大家唱。 —— 他们买乐器。 —— 我送他一本书。	谓语叙述主语"做什么" The predicate states what the subject does.
形容词谓语句 Sentence with an adjectival predicate	他高，我矮。	谓语描写主语"怎么样" The predicate states "how" the subject is.
名词谓语句 Sentence with a nominal predicate	明天星期天。	谓语只限于表示籍贯、年龄、日期、节气、职业、钱数等 The predicate is limited to indicating native place, age, day or date, solar terms, occupation, amount of money.
主谓谓语句 Sentence with a S-P phrase predicate	他身体好。 —— 《汉英词典》我有一本。	谓语表明与主语的所属关系 The predicate indicates a certain relation to the subject.

基 本 格 式 Basic patterns	结 构 特 点 Structural features	否定形式 Negative forms
主—谓（动词）S-PV 主—谓—宾 S-P-O 主—谓—间接宾语 —直接宾语 S-P-O (ind.)-O(dir.)	谓语动词前可带各类状语 The predicate verb can take all types of adv. adjuncts 谓语动词后可带各类补语 The predicate verb can take all types of complements. 谓语动词后可带动态助词 The predicate verb can take aspectual particles.	"不"—谓（动词） 不＋P V "没（有）"—谓（动词） 没（有）＋P V
主—谓（形容词） S-P (adj.)	谓语形容词前可带状语 The predicate adjective can be premodified by all types of adv. adjuncts. 谓语形容词后可带程度补语或数量补语 The predicate adjective can take a complement of degree or quantity.	"不"—谓（形容词） 不＋P (adj.)
主—谓（名词、数词、数量词组或名词性偏正词组） S-P (noun, numeral, N-Mw phrase or nominal endocentric phrase）	谓语前可用时间状语 The predicate can be premodified by an adverbial adjunct of time.	
主——谓〔主谓词组："主"—"谓"（形容词）〕 S-P [S-P phrase: S-P (adj.)]	谓语前可用时间状语 The predicate can be premodified by an adverbial adjunct of time.	主谓词组："主"—"不"—"谓" S-P phrase: S- 不 -P
主—谓〔主谓词组："主"—"谓"（及物动词）—"宾"（数量词组）〕 S-P [S-P phrase: S-P (TV)-O (N-Mw phrase)]		主谓词组："主"—"没（有）"—"谓" S-P phrase: S-没（有）-P

练 习 37
Exercise 37

指出下列句子是哪类主谓句。

Indicate which kind of S-P sentence each of the following is.

例：　　　这件事实在太突然了。

Model:　　　（形容词谓语句）

(Sentence with an adjectival predicate)

1. 我的房间号码是三〇二。

2. 我北京人。

3. 一公里等于两（华）里。

4. 那匹马跑得真快。

5. 现在三点三刻。

6. 这个湖水不深。

7. 这本书内容很丰富。

8. 他对人很和气。

9. 外边冷极了。

10. 这行字印得不太清楚。

11. 这个消息很重要。

12. 他给我的印象很深刻。

13. 我已经实现了第一个愿望。

14. 他眉毛比较长。

15. 外祖父今年七十五岁。

16. 这本儿童读物编得很好。

17. 这份卷子八十五分。

18. 这课练习每个学生要填二十个词。

19. 这位老师脾气非常好。

20. 他最近离婚了。

378

第五节 无主句

Section V   The Subjectless Sentence

一、什么叫无主句 Definition

没有主语部分的句子叫无主句。例如：

The subjectless sentence is a sentence without the subject section.   For example:

下雾了。

散会了。

要学好一门专业，一定要刻苦。

欢迎参观。

保持清洁。

二、无主句的类别 Kinds of the subjectless sentence

（一）说明自然现象的。例如：

Those indicating weather conditions.   For example:

刮风了。   下雪了。

打雷了。

（二）表明事实情况的。例如：

Those making general statements.   For example:

现在下课。   该打针了。

吃饭了。

（三）表示泛指的。例如：

Those of general reference.   For example:

要学好一种语言，应该多听多说。

应该早睡早起。

没有调查就没有发言权。

（四）表示祈使的。例如：

Those expressing a command.   For example:

　　　爱护花木！　　　　　　　不要乱扔果皮！

　　　小心火车！　　　　　　　不要与司机谈话！

（五）成语、格言、口号等。例如：

Idioms, maxims, slogans, etc. For example:

　　　知彼知己

　　　　（意思是：对对方和自己的情况都很了解）

　　　　(Know both your rival and yourself.)

　　　种瓜得瓜，种豆得豆

　　　　（意思是：种什么就能得到什么）

　　　　(Plant melons and you get melons, sow beans
　　　　and you get beans — you'll reap whatever you
　　　　sow.)

　　　向英雄学习！

　　　锻炼身体，保卫祖国！

三、无主句的语法特点　Grammatical features

（一）这种句子的结构可以是动宾词组等。

Structurally the subjectless sentence may be a V-O phrase.

（二）主语是补不出或不必说出的。

This kind of sentence is used when the doer of the
action is unclear or unnecessary to tell.

四、使用无主句需要注意的问题

Points that merit special attention

（一）汉语里有一些说明自然现象的句子，一般是不用主语
的，而且连形式主语也不需要。例如：

In Chinese, no subject, not even a formal subject is used
with sentences indicating weather conditions.   For example:

　　　刮风了。

　　　　（不说"天刮风了"，更不能说"它刮风了"）

　　　　(One does not say 天刮风了, nor does one say

它刮风了·)

出太阳了。

（不能说"天出 太阳了"，更 不能说"它出太阳了"）

(One does not say 天出太阳了， nor does one say 它出太阳了·)

（二）有些句子无法说出主语是谁或是什么。例如：

In some sentences, it is difficult to tell who or what the subject is. For example:

开始了。

（意思是：到开始的时候了。不能说成"它到开始的时候了"或"它开始了"）

(It means 到开始的时候了. One can not say 它到开始的时候了 or 它开始了.)

上课了。

（意思是：到上课的时间了。不能说成"它是到上课的时间了"或"它上课了"）

(It means 到上课的时间了. One can not say 它是到上课的时间了 or 它上课了.)

（三）表示泛指或祈使时，一般不必明确指出主语，意思也很清楚。例如：

In sentences expressing a general reference or a command, as the meaning is clear, no subject is necessary. For example:

注意安全!

（指"有关的人"要注意安全）

(The subject might be "people concerned".)

应该努力学习一门专业。

（泛指"一般人"都应该）

(The subject might be "people at large".)

第六节 独语句

Section VI The One-Word/Phrase Sentence

一、什么叫独语句 Definition

只包含一个词或偏正词组的句子叫独语句。例如：

This is a sentence containing only one word or one endocentric phrase. For example:

一九八一年十月一日秋。　　　怎么？

多（么）伟大啊！　　　　　　好的。

烟！　　　　　　　　　　　　他呢？

安静！

二、独语句的类别 Kinds of the one-word/phrase sentence

（一）表示时间地点。例如：

Those indicating time or place. For example:

一九八〇年　春　留学生宿舍。　八楼二〇四号。

六月一日星期五。

（二）表示赞叹。例如：

Those expressing admiration. For example:

好球！　　　　　　　　　　　　跳得太好了！

多（么）精彩的表演啊！

（三）表示突然发现。例如：

Those expressing a sudden discovery or realization. For example:

蛇！　　　　　　　　　　　　汽车！

火！

（四）表示提醒。例如：

Those expressing a warning. For example:

（五）表示称呼。例如：

Those indicating a form of address. For example:

老马，你现在有工夫吗？　　　小华，快来一下。

钱老师，您早！

（六）表示同意、反对或疑问。例如：

Those expressing agreement, objection or doubt. For example:

好吧！（我知道了。）

得了！（你不能去，我去。）

什么？（你说的我不相信。）

三、独语句的语法特点　Grammatical features

（一）独语句只包含一个词或偏正词组，根本分不出主语和谓语。

As this kind of sentence contains only one word/endocentric phrase, it is impossible to divide it into the two sections of subject and object.

（二）独语句常由名词、动词、形容词、代词或偏正词组构成。例如：

The one-word/phrase sentence is usually made of a noun, a verb, an adjective or an endocentric phrase. For example:

北京！　　　　　看！

危险！　　　　　怎么样？

四月的早晨。　　字典呢？

真麻烦！

四、使用独语句需要注意的问题

Points that merit special attention

（一）表示时间地点的独语句用于说明情况，特别是常用于日记、剧本中。例如：

The one-word/phrase sentence expressing time or place is used to tell the state of things, especially in a diary, and stage directions in dramatic pieces. For example:

一九八一年十一月五日上午。

老师的办公室。

（二）独语句中表示赞叹、突然发现或提醒时，常带惊叹语调和语气，书面上常用惊叹号"！"。例如：

The one-word / phrase sentence expressing admiration, sudden discoveries or warning often has a tone of surprise. In writing, an exclamation mark(!) is often used. For example:

好！　　　　　　　　加油！

地震！

（三）独语句可以事物为说明的对象，也可不以事物为说明的对象。例如：

This kind of sentence may or may not refer to a material object. For example:

飞机！　　　　　　　（名词）
　　　　　　　　　　　(Noun)

多热烈的晚会！　　　（名词性偏正词组）
　　　　　　　　　　　(Nominal endocentric phrase)

怎么，你不想去了？（疑问代词）
　　　　　　　　　　　(Interrogative pronoun)

谢力，咱们走吧！　　（名词——称呼）
　　　　　　　　　　　(Personal noun, a vocative)

第一种情况是由名词或名词性偏正词组构成的。第二种情况是由表示称谓的名词或动词、形容词、代词等构成的。

The first two examples are sentences composed of a noun and a nominal endocentric phrase respectively and the other two are of personal nouns (vocatives), verbs, adjectives, pronouns, etc.

（四.）指人或事物的名词、代词或名词性偏正词组常和语气助词"呢"连用，表示疑问。意思是"在哪儿"、"到哪儿去了"或"怎么样"。例如：

The modal particle 呢 often follows a noun, a pronoun or nominal endocentric phrase of personal or non-personal reference to express interrogation, meaning 在哪儿 (where), 到哪儿去了 (where is ...) or 怎么样 (how about ...). For example:

> 弟弟呢？
>> （意思是：弟弟在哪儿呢？）
>> (It means 弟弟在哪儿呢？)
> 她呢？
>> （意思是：她去哪儿了？她怎么不在这儿？）
>> (It means 她去哪儿了？她怎么不在这儿？)
> 我的手套呢？
>> （意思是：我的手套在哪儿呢？）
>> (It means 我的手套在哪儿呢？)
> 我看这本小说，你呢？
>> （意思是：你看哪本小说？）
>> (It means 你看哪本小说？)

第七节 简略句

Section VII The Elliptical Sentence

一、什么叫简略句 Definition

由于语言环境清楚或加上手势、表情等辅助动作也能明确地表达意思时，常不说出全句，或者去主语部分或省去谓语部分，或省去句中任何一部分的句子叫简略句。例如：

It is not always necessary to say complete sentences when the context is clear or when the meaning can be readily understood with the assistance of non-linguistic features such as gestures, facial expressions, etc. Thus we can omit the subject, the predicate or any other element of a sentence. This is known as the elliptical sentence. For example:

（你去城里吗？）——（我）不去（城里）。

（省去主语、宾语）

(The subject and object are omitted.)

（你现在去哪儿？）——（我现在去）商店。

（省去主语、谓语和状语）

(The subject and predicate are omitted.)

（谁去公园？）——我（去公园）。

（省去谓语、宾语）

(The predicate and object are omitted.)

二、简略句的语法特点　Grammatical features

（一）简略句的结构可以是一个词或词组。

Structurally the elliptical sentence can be made of a word or a phrase.

（二）简略句都不能离开上下文。

The elliptical sentence can not be used out of context.

（三）对话时常用简略句。

The elliptical sentence is commonly used in conversation.

三、使用简略句需要注意的问题

Points that merit special attention

（一）简略句只能在一定的语言环境中使用，也就是说不能脱离当时环境和上下文。例如：

The elliptical sentence is only used in a certain context, in other words, one can not use the elliptical sentence without such a context. For example:

你看电影吗？——看。　不看。

你上午有课吗？——有。　没有。

谁（敲门）？——我。

（你）去哪儿？——邮局。

（二）在不影响语意的表达、不会产生误会的前提下，句子要尽量简洁，常只说一个词或词组。例如：

One can make the sentence as simple as possible, so long as it can bring forth the meaning fully, or, it does not result in misunderstanding.　For example:

现在几点了？——九点。

　　　（不一定说"现在九点了"）

　　（It is not necessary to say　现在九点了.）

老马在这儿住了一个星期，是吗？——是（的）。

　　　（不必重复全句）

　　（It is not necessary to repeat the sentence all over again.）

附表五：　三种非主谓句的简要情况表
Table 5:　The Three Kinds of Non-S-P Sentence

非主谓句 Non-S-P sentences	例　句 Examples	表示的意义和类别 Meanings and types	特　点 Features
无主句 Subject-less sen-tences	开演了。	1. 说明自然现象的 Indicating weather conditions 2. 说明事实情况的 Making general statements 3. 表示泛指的 Making general reference 4. 表示祈使的 Expressing a command	1. 可单独表示完整的意思 Expressing a complete meaning independently. 2. 一般由动词或动宾词组构成 Usually made of a verb or a verbal phrase 3. 不需要或根本不能补出主语 Unnecessary or impossible to tell the subject

387

		5 成语、格言、口号等 Idioms, maxims, slogans, etc.	
独语句 One-word /phrase sentences	真美啊!	1.表示时间地点 Indicating time or place 2.表示赞叹 Expressing admiration 3.表示突然发现 Expressing a sudden discovery 4.表示提醒 Expressing a warning 5.表示称呼 Indicating a form of address 6.表示同意、反对或疑问 Expressing agreement, objection or doubt	1.一般可单独表示完整的意思 Generally expressing a complete meaning independently 2.一般由一个词或偏正词组构成 Normally made of a word or an endocen- tric phrase 3.不需要或不能补出省略成分 Unnecessary or im- possible to give the omitted elements
简略句 Elliptical sentences	（你看中文杂志吗？） （我）看（中文杂志）。	多用于对话中 Chiefly used in conversations	1.不能离开上下文 Unable to be independ- ent of a context 2.可由一个词或词组构成 Made of a word or a phrase 3.能补出省略的成分 The omitted elements can be given

练 习 38
Exercise 38

（一）用 "√" 标出下列句子中的非主谓句，并指出是哪类非主谓句。

Mark the Non-S-P sentences in the following and state what kinds they are.

例：　　电线！　　　（√独语句）
Model:　　　　　（√ One word sentence)

　1．下雪了。
　2．前进！
　3．我们几个人经常互相帮助。
　4．多大的西瓜啊！
　5．他来了。
　6．我们请来了几位专家。
　7．别客气！
　8．来客人了。
　9．我的世界地图呢？
　10．厕所！

（二）补出下列各句中省略的部分。

Give the omitted elements in the following elliptical sentences.

　1．＿＿＿＿＿应该经常锻炼身体。
　2．＿＿＿＿＿保持清洁。
　3．哪件衣服是你的？这件＿＿＿＿＿。
　4．今天星期几？＿＿＿＿＿星期二。
　5．你好！最近学习忙不忙？＿＿＿＿＿＿不太忙。
　6．他怎么了？＿＿＿＿累了。

第二部分 按用途分类
Part Two Classification of Sentences in Terms of Function

第八节 陈 述 句
Section VIII The Declarative Sentence

一、什么叫陈述句 Definition

叙述一件事或说明看法的句子叫陈述句。全句是陈述语调，句末用句号"。"。例如：

The declarative sentence or statement is one used to state a thing or a view. The sentence is uttered in the declarative tone and a full stop(。) is written at the end. For example:

他们种树。　　　　　今天宰牲节。

月亮真圆。　　　　　他这个人仔细。

二、陈述句的语法特点 Grammatical features

（一）陈述句可有各类句子结构的形式。例如：

The declarative sentence can take all the forms of sentences as classified in terms of structure. For example:

这是玛丽的男朋友。　　他分析得很深刻。

桌子上的钟是刚买的。　我们在沙滩上晒了一会儿

锁在这儿。　　　　　　太阳。

暖水瓶里有开水。　　　他的发音很准确。

飞机起飞了。　　　　　他写的文章很通俗。

主席讲话了。　　　　　这套山水画三十块钱。

大家都很关心这件事。　他日本人，她朝鲜人。

爸爸送我一件生日礼物。这位主任工作能力很强。

您这儿坐。

（二）否定形式跟各类句子的否定形式一样。例如：

The negative forms of the declarative sentence are the same as those of the sentences classified in terms of structure. For example:

那不是红墨水。　　　　今天不是星期六。

这种筷子不是竹子做的。这匹马驮不了那么多东西。

钥匙不在我这儿。　　　我英语说得不太好。

他不喜欢这种式样。　　我今天实在没有工夫。

这样做不合适。　　　　报纸还没到。

他不能否认自己过去犯　他没抄完那部分资料。

　　罪的事实。　　　　　我没看过京剧。

三、使用陈述句需要注意的问题

Points that merit special attention

（一）陈述句的语调一般是降调。汉语的句调和字调是两回事，字调的升降不受句调升降的影响。例如：

The declarative sentence is usually uttered in the falling tone. What should be noted is that in Chinese, such a intonation is different from the four tones whose contours are not affected by the intonation. For example:

这儿有火柴 (chái)。

他喜欢踢足球 (qiú)。

上两句句末的"柴"字和"球"字都是第二声，是升调，但全句是降调，不能把升调字也说成降调。

In the above two examples 柴 and 球 are both in the second tone which is rising, but the sentences end with the falling tone. Therefore, a character in the rising (or second) tone should not be turned into the falling (or fourth) tone when the sentence as a whole is in the falling tone.

（二）陈述句可以是主谓句，也可以是非主谓句。例如：

The declarative sentence may be one in the S-P structure or in the Non-S-P structure.   For example:

工人们提了许多合理化建议。（动词谓语句）

(With a verbal predicate)

他的病严重得很。　　　　　（形容词谓语句）

(With an adjectival predicate)

这顶帽子十五块（钱）。　　（名词谓语句）

(With a noun predicate)

这个工人技术熟练。　　　　（主谓谓语句）

(With a S-P phrase predicate)

响铃了。　　　　　　　　　（无主句）

(Subjectless)

星期日。　　　　　　　　　（独语句）

(One word)

（你出席招待会吗？）出席。（简略句）

(Elliptical)

第九节　疑　问　句

Section IX　　The Interrogative Sentence

一、什么叫疑问句　Definition

提出问题、有表示疑问的语调、句末用问号 "?" 的句子，叫疑问句。例如：

An interrogative sentence is one used to ask a question

which is uttered in the interrogative tone and a question mark(?)
is written at the end.   For example：

　　　　　　那位是美国人吗？

　　　　　　谁喊你？

　　　　　　你们去哪儿？

　　　　　　这是什么树？

　　　　　　您的电话号码是多少？

　　　　　　你喝不喝咖啡？

　　　　　　他有没有战胜困难的勇气？

　　　　　　中医和西医能不能很好地结合？

　　　　　　您二位吃中餐还是吃西餐？

　　　　　　是不是他父亲不允许他这样做？

　　　　　　他要参加绿化城市的工作，你呢？

　　　　　　你汉语学了多长时间？

二、疑问句的种类　常见的疑问句有下面七种：

Types of interrogative sentence: there are 7 types of commonly used interrogative sentences:

　　（一）　用语气助词"吗"构成的疑问句。

Those in which the modal particle 吗 is used.

　　（二）用疑问代词构成的疑问句。

Those in which the interrogative pronouns are used.

　　（三）正反疑问句。

The affirmative-negative question.

　　（四）用连词"还是"的选择式疑问句。

The alternative question using the conjunction 还是.

　　（五）用"是不是"提问的疑问句。

Those in which 是不是 is used.

　　（六）用语气助词"呢"构成的疑问句。

Those in which the modal particle 呢 is used.

　　（七）用副词"多"构成的疑问句。

393

Those in which the adverb 多 is used.

现分别介绍如下：

The above seven kinds of interrogative sentences are introduced respectively as follows:

三、用"吗"的疑问句

The interrogative sentence in which 吗 is used

（一）什么是用"吗"的疑问句。 Definition.

在陈述句（肯定或否定形式）句尾加上表示疑问的语气助词"吗"，表示问话人希望得到肯定或否定的答复的疑问句就叫用"吗"的疑问句。它的基本格式是：

陈述句——"吗"？

An interrogative sentence (or a question) using 吗 is a question formed by adding the interrogative particle 吗 at the end of a declarative sentence (affirmative or negative) to express that the questioner is expecting an affirmative or negative answer. The basic pattern is:

Declarative sentence + 吗？

例如：

Examples:

　　　　您是张书记——吗？
　　　　常吃这种药有坏处——吗？
　　　　高原气候你能适应——吗？
　　　　该休息了——吗？

（二）用"吗"的疑问句的特点。 Grammatical features.

1. 用"吗"的疑问句的词序跟陈述句完全一样。例如：

The word order follows exactly that of the declarative sentence. For example:

　　　　｛他去工地。　　　　　（陈述句）
　　　　　　　　　　　　　　　　（Declarative sentence)
　　　　｛他去工地吗？

394

$$\left\{\begin{array}{l}\text{她是护士。} \qquad \text{（陈述句）}\\ \qquad\qquad\qquad\qquad \text{(Declarative sentence)}\\ \\ \text{她是护士吗？}\end{array}\right.$$

$$\left\{\begin{array}{l}\text{他们不看电影。} \quad \text{（陈述句）}\\ \qquad\qquad\qquad\qquad \text{(Declarative sentence)}\\ \\ \text{他们不看电影吗？}\end{array}\right.$$

2． 这种疑问句一般是升调。例如：

It is generally uttered in the rising tone. For example:

　　　　你们进城吗？ ⌒

　　　　这是新买的手套吗？ ⌒

　　　　外边冷吗？ ⌒

3． 这种疑问句也可以不用"吗"，而用表示疑问的语调——升调；书写时句尾一定要用问号"？"，含有不清楚或不相信的意思。例如：

It can be expressed by the rising tone with 吗 absent. In writing, the question mark(?) must be used. Such a question implies non-understanding or doubt. For example:

　　　　他是一个体操运动员？ ⌒

　　　　他们近来都好？ ⌒

4． 回答时用肯定式或否定式都可以。例如：

Either an affirmative or negative answer is possible. For example:

　　　　他是你们学院的院长吗？

　　　　　　是。（他是我们学院的院长。）

　　　　　　不是。（他不是我们学院的院长。）

　　　　讲座开始了吗？

　　　　　　开始了。

　　　　　　没开始。

　　　　你喜欢熊猫吗？

　　　　　　喜欢。

不喜欢。

下雨了吗？

下了。

没下。

（三）使用带"吗"的疑问句需要注意的问题

Points that merit special attention

1. 汉语里只要在陈述句句尾用上"吗"就可以构成用"吗"的疑问句，而"吗"前面的陈述句词序完全不变，不能把谓语动词放在这种疑问句句首。例如：

A declarative sentence becomes interrogative when 吗 is placed at the end without any change in the word order. The predicate verb can in no way be fronted to the beginning of the sentence. For example:

这是竹子吗？　（不能说成"是这竹子吗？"）
　　　　　　　（One can not say 是这竹子吗？）
这根竹子直吗？（不能说成"是这根竹子直吗？"）
　　　　　　　（One can not say 是这根竹子直吗？）
你能谅解他吗？（不能说成"能你谅解他吗？"）
　　　　　　　（One can not say 能你谅解他吗？）
他们有奖金吗？（不能说成"有他们奖金吗？"）
　　　　　　　（One can not say 有他们奖金吗？）

如果说成"是这竹子吗"和"有他们奖金吗"，意思和结构就都变了。

The meaning and structure will change completely if one says 是这竹子吗 and 有他们奖金吗.

2. 这种疑问句的句重音一般都在谓语上，"吗"是轻声字，它的音高随着前一个字的声调而变化。

The sentence stress of this kind of question falls on the predicate. 吗 is in the neutral tone and its pitch changes with the tone of the preceding syllable.

四、用疑问代词的疑问句

The interrogative sentence in which the interrogative pronouns are used

（一）什么是用疑问代词的疑问句。　Definition

在陈述句中要着重询问的部分用疑问代词所构成的疑问句，是用疑问代词的疑问句。它的基本格式是：

This kind of interrogative sentence is formed by replacing the element in a statement that is asked about with an interrogative pronoun. The basic patterns are:

1．主语（疑问代词）——谓语？

Subject (interrogative pronoun) + predicate?

例如：

Examples:

> 谁——回答？
>
> 什么——倒了？

2．主语——谓语——宾语（疑问代词）？

Subject + predicate + object (interrogative pronoun)?

例如：

Examples:

> 你——买——什么？
>
> 他们——在——哪儿？

3．主语——谓语（疑问代语）？

Subject + predicate (interrogative pronoun)?

例如：

Examples:

> 我的发言提纲——怎么样？
>
> 你——怎么了？

（二）用疑问代词的疑问句的特点。Grammatical features

1．这种疑问句和陈述句的词序完全一样。例如：

It follows exactly the word order of the declarative sentence.

For example:

他在这儿。　　　　　（陈述句）
　　　　　　　　　　　（Declarative sentence）

谁在这儿？　　　　　（"谁"在主语位置上）
　　　　　　　　　　　（谁 in the subject position）

他在哪儿？　　　　　（"哪儿"在宾语位置上）
　　　　　　　　　　　（哪儿 in the object position）

我的自行车坏了。　　（陈述句）
　　　　　　　　　　　（Declarative sentence）

谁的自行车坏了？　　（"谁"在定语位置上）
　　　　　　　　　　　（谁 in the attributive position）

什么坏了？　　　　　（"什么"在主语位置上）
　　　　　　　　　　　（什么 in the subject position）

哪辆车坏了？　　　　（"哪"在定语位置上）
　　　　　　　　　　　（哪 in the attributive position）

你的自行车怎么了？　（"怎么"在谓语位置上）
　　　　　　　　　　　（怎么 in the predicate position）

2. 疑问代词放在要求答案的位置上。例如：

The interrogative pronoun is positioned where the answer is expected.　For example:

谁熟悉这里的情况？
　　　　（要求回答主语"谁"）
　　　　（Asking about the subject 谁）

他们贴什么？
　　　　（要求回答宾语"什么"）
　　　　（Asking about the object 什么）

他怎么了？
　　　　（要求回答谓语"怎么"）
　　　　（Asking about the predicate 怎么）

你怎么来的？

（要求回答状语"怎么"）

(Asking about the adverbial adjunct 怎么)

哪个研究生是他推荐的？

（要求回答定语"哪"）

(Asking about the attributive 哪)

你们省汉语普通话推广得怎么样？

（要求回答补语"怎么样"）

(Asking about the complement 怎么样)

3． 这种疑问句一般是降调。重音在疑问代词上。例如：

It is usually pronounced in the falling tone. The sentence stress is on the interrogative pronoun. For example:

这是谁的大衣？　　　你们的学制是几年？

你喜欢什么专业？　　　这批体育用品怎么样？

（三）使用有疑问代词的疑问句需要注意的问题。

Points that merit special attention.

1． 汉语里这种疑问句的词序和陈述句完全一样，只要把疑问代词放在要求答案的位置上即可，而不是把疑问代词一律放在句首。这一点要特别注意。例如：

What should be specially noted is that the word order of such a question is exactly the same as that of the declarative sentence, i.e. the question is formed by putting the interrogative pronoun in the position where the answer is located, not at the beginning. For example:

谁躲在门后边了？

——小弟弟（躲在门后边了）。

那是谁的袜子？

（不能说"谁的袜子是那"）

(There is no such form as 谁的袜子是那.)

——（那是）小王的（袜子）。

这是什么花？

399

（不能说"什么花是这"）

(One can not say 什么花是这。)

——（这是）玫瑰花。

你的飞机票在哪儿？

（不能说"哪儿是你的飞机票"）

(哪儿是你的飞机票 means sth. different.)

——（我的飞机票）在他那儿。

三加七是多少？

（不能说"多少是三加七"）

(It is wrong to say 多少是三加七.)

——（三加七是）十。

你是哪国留学生？

（不能说"哪国留学生是你"）

(There is no such form as 哪国留学生是你.)

——（我是）英国（留学生）。

那个司机开车开得怎么样？

（不能说"怎么样那个司机开车开得"）

(One can not say 怎么样那个司机开车开得.)

——（那个司机开车开得）很稳。

这个字怎么念？

（不能说"怎么这个字念"）

(One can not say 怎么这个字念.)

——（这个字）念 guāng（光）。

2. 这种用疑问代词的疑问句一般都不能在句尾加"吗"。例如：

吗 can not usually be used in this kind of question. For example:

谁是这儿的负责人？

这套家具怎么样？

不能说成"谁是这儿的负责人吗"、"这套家具怎么样吗"。

400

There are no such forms as 谁是这儿的负责人吗 and 这套家具怎么样吗.

3. 疑问代词 "谁" 不论用在哪个位置上，形式都不变。例如：

The interrogative pronoun 谁 undergoes no change in form whatsoever, no matter how it functions. For example:

谁有今天晚上的京剧票？（"谁" 在主语位置上）

(谁 in the subject position)

喂，你是谁啊？ （"谁" 在宾语位置上）

(谁 in the object position)

这是谁的皮包？ （"谁" 在定语位置上）

(谁 in the attributive position)

4. 一般来说，问什么就回答什么，怎么问就怎么回答。例如：

Generally speaking the answer should follow the same pattern as the question. For example:

你是哪国人？

我是美国人。

一般不这样回答："我从美国来" 或 "我住在美国"。

One generally does not answer this question by saying 我从美国来 or 我住在美国.

5. 这种疑问句句尾常用语气助词 "呢" 或 "啊"。语气比较婉转。例如：

The modal particles 呢 or 啊 can be used at the end of such questions to make their tone more tactful. For example:

网球拍子在哪儿呢？（网球拍子在哪儿啊？）

他们商量什么呢？

谁发言呢？

这包东西怎么寄呢？

五、正反疑问句 The affirmative-negative question

（一）什么是正反疑问句。 Definition.

并列谓语的肯定与否定形式表示疑问，要求作出肯定或否定的答复的疑问句是正反疑问句。它的基本格式是：

This is a question formed by putting the affirmative and negative forms of the predicate together and the answer expected is either affirmative or negative. The basic patterns are:

1．主语——谓语——"不（没）"——谓语——（宾语）？

Subject + predicate + 不 (or 没) + predicate + (object)?

例如：

Examples:

　　　　方向——对——不——对？

　　　　效果——好——不——好？

　　　　他　——是——不——是——内科大夫？

　　　　你　——换——不——换——房间？

　　　　天上——有——没——有——星星？

　　　　他　——参加——没——参加——联欢会？

2．主语——谓语——宾语——"不（没）"——谓语？

Subject + predicate + object + 不 (or 没) + predicate?

例如：

Examples:

　　　　他——是——内科大夫——不——是？

　　　　你——换——房间——不——换？

　　　　天上——有——星星——没——有？

（二）正反疑问句的特点。　Grammatical features.

1．肯定形式在前，否定形式在后。例如：

The affirmative form of the predicate precedes the negative form. For example:

　　　　你　来　不来？

　　　　地上　湿　不湿？

　　　　你们的看法　一致　不一致？

　　　　他　看　没看？

2. 动词谓语后如有宾语，宾语一般在肯定和否定形式的动词谓语之后。例如：

The object, if there is one, generally comes after the affirmative and negative forms of the verbal predicate. For example:

> 那张报　是　不是　今天的？
> 你今天参观　不参观　美术展览？
> 你看　不看　这本杂志？
> 楼上有　没有　阅览室？
> 他　写　没写　信？

也可以把宾语放在肯定和否定形式的动词谓语之间，也就是把否定形式的动词谓语放在句尾。例如：

It is also possible to place the object between the affirmative and negative forms of the verbal predicate. In other words, the negative form can also come at the end of the question. For example:

> 你参观　展览　不参观？
> 你看　这本杂志　不看？
> 楼上有　阅览室　没有？
> 他写　信　没写？

3. 回答时用肯定式或否定式都可以。例如：

Either the affirmative or negative answer is possible. For example:

> 你打不打羽毛球？　　明天上午你有时间没有？
> 打。　　　　　　　　有。
> 不打。　　　　　　　没有。

4. 这种疑问句一般是升调。

Generally this kind of question is in the rising tone.

（三）使用正反疑问句需要注意的问题。

Points that merit special attention.

1. 正反疑问句中谓语的肯定、否定形式的先后次序不能颠倒，肯定形式一定要放在否定形式前边。例如：

The affirmative form of the predicate must precede the negative form and this order can not be reversed. For example:

他是不是牙科医生？　　这儿的空气干燥不干燥？

您喝不喝凉开水？

绝不能说成"你不是是牙科医生"、"您不喝喝凉开水"，"这儿的空气不干燥干燥"。

One can in no way say 你不是是牙科医生，您不喝喝凉开水 and 这儿的空气不干燥干燥.

2. 用正反形式提问时，谓语前边一般不能带表示程度的副词状语。例如：

Usually the predicate in such a question can not be modified by degree adverb. For example:

你们的工作条件好不好？

那儿的名胜古迹多不多？

不能说成"你们的工作条件非常好不好"、"那儿的名胜古迹很多不多"。

One can never say 你们的工作条件非常好不好，那儿的名胜古迹很多不多.

你喜欢不喜欢听古典音乐？

不能说成"你十分喜欢不喜欢听古典音乐"。

One can not say 你十分喜欢不喜欢听古典音乐.

3. 在正反疑问句里，如果谓语前边有助动词，就要并列助动词的肯定和否定形式，一定不能并列谓语的肯定、否定形式。这一点非常重要。例如：

When the predicate is preceded by an auxiliary verb, it is the affirmative and negative forms of the auxiliary verb, rather than the predicate verb, that are to be placed together. This is a very important point to be noted. For example:

你能不能来？

你们想不想爬山？

我们大家应该不应该冷静一点儿？

一定不能说"你能来不来"、"你们想爬不爬山"、"我们大家应该冷静不冷静"。

One can never say 你能来不来, 你们想爬不爬山 and 我们大家应该冷静不冷静.

4．正反疑问句句尾不能加"吗"。例如：

吗 never occurs at the end of an affirmative-negative question. For example:

他是不是经理？　　学校周围有没有旅馆？

雨大不大？

一定不能说"他是不是经理吗"、"雨大不大吗"、"学校周围有没有旅馆吗"。

One can not say 他是不是经理吗, 雨大不大吗 and 学校周围有没有旅馆吗.

5．这种疑问句句尾可以用语气助词"呢"或"啊"，表示缓和语气。例如：

To moderate the tone, 呢 or 啊 can be used at the end of such a question. For example:

他们划不划船呢？　　他有没有女朋友呢？

他是不是大会主席呢？　　那个城市美不美呢？

六、用"还是"的选择式疑问句

The alternative question using 还是

（一）什么是选择式疑问句。Definition.

用连词"还是"并列几种情况，要求答话人选择一项回答的疑问句，叫选择式疑问句。它的基本格式是：

This is a question in which several alternatives are paralleled by the conjunction 还是 for the answerer to choose. The basic patterns are:

405

1. 主语——谓语₁——(宾语₁)——"还是"——谓语₂——（主语₂）？

Subject + predicate₁ + (object₁) + 还是 + predicate₂ + (object₂)?

例如：

Examples:

那儿 远 还是 近？

你 休息 还是 工作？

你 住 这儿 还是（住） 那儿？

他 是 美国人 还是 英国人？

2. 主语₁——谓语₁——(宾语)——"还是"——主语₂——谓语₂——（宾语）？

Subject₁ + predicate₁ + (object) + 还是 + sudject₂ + predicate₂ + (object)?

例如：

Examples:

张老师 讲 还是 王老师 讲？

你们 买 水果 还是 我们 买？

他 高 还是 你 高？

3. 主语——状语₁——谓语₁——(宾语)——"还是"——状语₂——谓语₂？

Subject + adverbial adjunct₁ + predicate₁ + (object) + 还是 + adverbial adjunct₂ + predicate₂?

例如：

Examples:

你们 明天 去 还是 后天 去？

你 在食堂 吃 饭 还是 在家 吃？

（二）选择式疑问句的特点。Grammatical features.

1. "还是"用在所问的两种或两种以上的情况之间。例如：

还是 is used between every two alternatives. For example:

你去图书馆还是（去）体育馆？

406

（"还是"连接的是"图书馆"和"体育馆"两个地方。）

(还是 connects the two place nouns 图书馆 and 体育馆.)

那座楼是电化教学楼还是图书馆楼？

（"还是"连接的是"电化教学楼"和"图书馆楼"两个地方。）

(还是 connects 电化教学楼 and 图书馆楼.)

你上午来还是下午来还是晚上来？

（"还是"连接的是"上午来"、"下午来"和"晚上来"三种情况）

(还是 connects 上午来，下午来 and 晚上来.)

2．"还是"连接的可以是词或词组。例如：

The alternatives connected by 还是 may either be words or phrases. For example:

你听还是看？　　　　　　（动词）

(Verb)

你们来这儿还是去那儿？（动宾词组）

(V-O phrase)

你去还是他去？　　　　（主谓词组）

(S-P phrase)

3．要求对方任选一种回答。例如：

The answerer is required to choose one from the alternatives. For example:

那位新来的会计是男的还是女的？

是女的。

是男的。

明天你去公园还是去大使馆？

去公园。

去大使馆。

4．这种疑问句的语调，一般是并列的每一项末尾都用升调，但只在句尾用一个问号"?"。

There is a rise in tone of voice after each alternative, but only one question mark(?) is used at the end of the whole question.

（三）使用选择式疑问句需要注意的问题。

Points that merit special attention.

1．使用第 3 种基本格式时，如果状语不是询问所在，状语一般只在前边出现一次，后边不再重复。例如：

In the 3rd pattern, the adverbial adjunct, except one asking about location, occurs only once, i.e. there is no need to repeat it later.　For example:

你在宿舍复习还是预习？

这个句子问的是"做什么"，而不是问地点，一般不需要重复状语"在宿舍"，不说"你在宿舍复习还是在宿舍预习"。如要问地点，可以说：

This sentence asks "what is done" rather than "where it is done", so there is no need to repeat the adverbial adjunct 在宿舍 and one does not say 你在宿舍复习还是在宿舍预习. To ask "where", one may say:

你在教室复习还是在宿舍复习？

再如：

Another example:

你下个月回国还是去别的国家？

这个句子问的是"去哪儿"，而不是问时间，因此状语"下个月"只在前边出现一次。如要问时间，可以说：

This sentence asks "where to go", not "when", therefore the time adverbial adjunct 下个月 occurs only once. To ask "when", one uses this form:

你下个月回国还是这个月回国？

又如：

A third example:

他们从汽车上抬下来的还是背下来的？

这个句子问的不是从哪儿拿下来的，因此不说"他们从汽车上抬下来的还是从汽车上背下来的"。

This sentence is not asking "from where they have carried sth.", so one does not say 他们从汽车上抬下来的还是从汽车上背下来的.

2. 用连词"还是"连接动词"是"时，为使句子简洁，只用一个"是"字。例如：

To make the sentence terse, when 还是 occurs before the second verb 是 only one 是 remains, for example:

他是你哥哥还是你弟弟？

不能说成"他是你哥哥还是是你弟弟"。

There is no such form as 他是你哥哥还是是你弟弟.

如果连接其他动词，问的是宾语时，"还是"后边可不再重复动词。例如：

When connecting verbs other than 是 and where the object is asked about, the verb after 还是 is optional, for example:

你去公园还是（去）博物馆？

你喝热茶还是（喝）凉开水？

3. 回答这种疑问句时，也可以不加以选择，而是全部肯定或全部否定。例如：

The answer to this kind of question, instead of being chosen from the laternatives, may be one of total affirmation or negation, for example:

你买这本书还是那本书？　　你去还是他去？

都买。　　　　　　　　　都去。

都不买。　　　　　　　　都不去。

4．这种疑问句句尾不能加"吗"。例如：

吗 is not used at the end of such a question.　For example:

你爷爷是记者还是作家？

你买的是《汉英词典》还是《英汉词典》？

一定不能说成"你爷爷是记者还是作家吗"，"你买的是《汉英词典》还是《英汉词典》"吗。

One can never say 你爷爷是记者还是作家吗 and　你买的是《汉英词典》还是《英汉词典》吗.

5．这种疑问句句尾可以用语气助词"呢"或"啊"，表示缓和语气。例如：

呢 or 啊 may be used at the end of such a question to moderate the tone.　For example:

你们想看芭蕾舞还是（看）话剧呢？

你买中文版的《红楼梦》还是英文版的啊？

6．连词"还是"有时用于陈述句里表示不确定。也就是说，用疑问的形式表示陈述的语气，句尾要用句号"。"。例如：

Sometimes 还是 is used in a statement to express uncertainty.　In other words, it is a statement in the interrogative form.　At the end of such a question, a full stop(。) rather than a question mark(?) is used.　For example:

我不知道他今天还是明天到达北京。

我还没考虑好买这种还是买那种。

七、用"是不是提问的疑问句　The 是不是 question

（一）什么是用"是不是"的疑问句。　Definition.

要对某情况得到进一步证实，可以用"是不是"表示疑问，就成了用"是不是"的疑问句。它的基本格式是：

This is a question used to get sth. confirmed.　Its basic patterns are:

1．主语——"是不是"——谓语——（宾语）？

Subject + 是不是 + predicate + (object)?

410

例如：

Examples:

他是不是转达了我们对专家的慰问？

那两个国家是不是建交了？

昨天的晚会是不是特别热闹？

2．"是不是"——主语——谓语——（宾语）？

是不是 + Subject + predicate + (object)?

例如：

Examples:

是不是他转达了我们对专家的慰问？

是不是那两个国家建交了？

是不是昨天的晚会特别热闹？

3．主语——谓语——（宾语）——"是不是"？

Subject + predicate + (object) + 是不是?

例如：

Examples:

他转达了我们对专家的慰问是不是？

那两个国家建交了是不是？

昨天的晚会特别热闹是不是？

（二）用"是不是"的疑问句的特点。Grammatical features.

1．"是不是"一般放在谓语前边。例如：

Generally 是不是 precedes the predicate. For example:

他是不是住三〇九号？

她是不是病了？

"是不是"还可以放在句首或句尾。例如：

是不是 can also be placed at the beginning o˙ the end
of the question.   For example:

是不是竞赛计划已经改变了？

是不是你丢了一块手表？

他误会了我的意思是不是？

他很不满意是不是？

2．"是不是"可用于各类句子中。例如：

是不是 can be used with any kind of statement．For example:

你是不是是写完毕业论文了？

这种毛衣是不是太薄？

这张照片是不是人太小了？

你是不是有这种成语词典？

是不是该出发了？

3．这种疑问句一般是升调。

This kind of question is usually in the rising tone.

4．回答时用肯定式或否定式都可以。例如：

The answer may be either an affirmative or a negative one．For example:

您找张老师是不是？　　　是不是下雪了？

是。　　　　　　　　　　是。

不（是），我找王老师。　没有。

（三）使用带"是不是"的疑问句需要注意的问题。

Points that merit special attention.

1．动词"是"作谓语的句子，一般用正反疑问句，很少用"是不是"疑问句。例如：

This form is seldom used with a 是-sentence, where the affirmative-negative question is generally used．For example:

这是不是您的？

他是不是北京大学的学生？

不能说成"这是不是是您的"、"他是不是是北京大学的学生"。

One can not say 这是不是是您的 and 他是不是是北京大学的学生 and one rarely says 是不是这是您的 or 他是北京大学的学生是不是.

2．"是不是"有时用在谓语前，表示建议、征求对方同意。

例如：

Sometimes 是不是 precedes the predicate to express a suggestion or to ask for the hearer's consent. For example:

　　　　我们是不是在这儿坐一会儿？

　　　　你是不是可以问问他？

　　　　您是不是多写几篇报道？

　　"是不是"也可以放在句首，但不能用在句尾。不说"我们在这儿坐一会儿是不是"，"你可以问问他是不是"等；而常在句尾用"好不好"或"怎么样"，可以说"我们在这儿坐一会儿好不好"或"你可以问问他，怎么样"。

In this case, 是不是 can also be used at the beginning of the question, not at the end. Instead of 我们在这儿坐一会儿是不是 or 你可以问问他是不是, etc. one uses 好不好 or 怎么样 at the end, e.g. 我们在这儿坐一会儿好不好 or 你可以问问他，怎么样, etc.

　　3．这种疑问句句尾不能加"吗"，但可以加"呢"或"啊"，语气比较缓和。例如：

吗 never occurs at the end of such a question. But 呢 or 啊 can be added to give a moderate tone. For example:

　　　　他们是不是配合得很密切呢？

　　　　你是不是有很多朋友啊？

不能说"他们是不是配合得很密切吗"。

One can not say 他们是不是配合得很密切吗.

八、用"呢"的疑问句 Questions using the particle 呢

　　（一）什么是用"呢"的疑问句。Definition.

　　在独语句句尾加上助词"呢"表示疑问，询问人或事物在哪儿、怎么样的句子，是用"呢"的疑问句。它的基本格式是：

The question using 呢 is one in which the particle 呢 is added to the end of a one-word/phrase sentence to express interrogation of where or how the person or thing concerned is.

The basic patterns are:

1. 词——"呢"？

Word ＋ 呢？

例如：

Examples:

老马——呢？　　　　（我想看话剧，）你——呢？

钢笔——呢？

2. 偏正词组——"呢"？

Endocentric phrase ＋ 呢？

例如：

Examples:

你的请示报告——呢？

（这位作家很年轻，）那位——呢？

（二）用"呢"的疑问句的特点。Grammatical features.

1. 这种疑问句是由词或偏正词组和语气助词"呢"构成的。例如：

This kind of question is composed of a word or endocentric phrase and the modal particle 呢. For example:

照片呢？

我的照片呢？

2. 这种疑问句一般是升调。

This kind of question is spoken in the rising tone.

3. 要求回答人或事物所在的地方或情况。例如：

The answer expected is one telling where or how the person or thing in question is. For example:

我的自行车呢？　　在楼下。

你参加这个会，他呢？　　他也可能参加。

（三）使用带"呢"的疑问句需要注意的问题。

Points that merit special attention.

1. 这种疑问句句尾不能加"吗"。例如：

414

吗 can not be used at the end of such a question. For example:

　　　　我的头巾呢?

　　　　姐姐呢?

不能说"我的头巾呢吗"等。

One can not say 我的头巾呢吗, etc.

2. 这种疑问句的特点是句尾用"呢",跟其他疑问句后边可以加"呢"的情况不同。除了用"吗"的疑问句后边不能再加"呢"以外,其他疑问句一般都能在句尾加"呢",表示缓和语气或进一步追问。例如:

This kind of question is characterized by the use of the particle 呢 at the end, but is different from other types of questions with 呢 at the end. Other than those questions using 吗, where 呢 does not occur, most other questions generally use 呢 to express a moderate tone or a detailed inquiry. For example:

　　　　哪个答案对呢?

　　　　这条紫颜色的围巾好不好呢?

　　　　他会不会明天来呢?

　　　　你喜欢音乐还是体育呢?

　　　　将来你是不是要研究化学呢?

但不能说"这条路对吗呢"。

But one never says 这条路对吗呢.

九、用副词"多"的疑问句 Questions using the adverb 多

　　(一)什么是用"多"的疑问句。Definition.

　　用副词"多"询问程度、数量的句子是用"多"的疑问句。它的基本格式是:

This is a question in which the adverb 多 is used to inquire about degree or quantity. Its basic patterns are:

1. 主语——"多"——谓语(形容词)?

415

Subject + 多 + predicate (adjective)?

例如：

Examples:

这座纪念碑——多——高？

这条大街——多——宽？

你弟弟——多——大？

2．主语——谓语（动词"有"）——宾语（"多"——形容词）？

Subject + predicate (the verb 有) + object (多 + adjective)?

例如：

Examples:

这块肉——有——多重？

那条公路——有——多长？

（二）用"多"的疑问句的特点。 Grammatical features．

1．副词"多"多用在单音形容词前边。例如：

The adverb 多 usually precedes a monosyllabic adjective. For example:

这口井多深？

那棵大树有多粗？

2．"多"多用在表示积极意义的形容词前边。例如在"高、长、远、宽、深、重、厚、粗、大"等形容词前。

The adjectives following 多 are "good" in meaning, e.g. 高，长，远，宽，深，重，厚，粗，大， etc.

3．这种疑问句一般是升调。

This kind of question is spoken in the rising tone.

4．回答时一般要用数量词组说明程度。例如：

In the answer, a numeral-measure word phrase is generally used to tell the degree. For example:

这座纪念塔多高？ 三十一米（高）。

这条鱼有多重？　　　　有两公斤（重）。

他多大了？　　　　　　二十八（岁）了。

那条铁路有多长？　　　大约有两千公里（长）。

（三）使用带"多"的疑问句需要注意的问题。

Points that merit special attention.

1."多"后边只能是一个词，不能是词组。

Only words, not phrases, can follow 多.

2.这种疑问句句尾可以带语气助词"呢"或"啊"，但不能带"吗"。例如：

呢 or 啊 can be used at the end of such a question, but not 吗. For example:

这件大衣多长呢？

那儿离我们学校有多远啊？

不能说"这本字典多厚吗"。

One can not say 这本字典多厚吗.

附表六: 七种疑问句的简要情况表
Table 6: The Seven Types of Questions

疑问句 Questions	例句 Examples	表示的意义 Meanings and Usages	基本格式 Basic patterns	结构特点 Structural features	回答方式 Manner of Reply	语调类型 Intonation types
(一)用"吗"的疑问句 Questions using 吗	他是中国人吗?	询问情况的肯定或否定 The hearer is expected to confirm or deny what is asked.	陈述句——吗? [主——谓——(宾)] Statement [S—P—(O)] to + 吗? is Statement	词序跟陈述句完全一样;句尾有"吗" The word order of a follows that of a statement. 吗 is used at end of sentence.	或答肯定,或答否定 The answer is either an affirmative or a negative one.	升调 Rising
(二)用疑问代词的疑问句 Questions using interrogative pronouns	谁敲门?	着重询问某人、某事物或某种情况 Asking about a person, a thing or a state of affairs	1.(主)(疑问词)? —谓—(宾)? (S) (Interrog. PN)? —P—(O)? 2.主—谓—(宾)? 疑问代词 S—P—(O) (Interrog. PN)? 3.主—(谓) where S—(P)— (Interrog. PN)?	词序跟陈述句完全一样;疑问代词在要求答案的位置上 The word order follows that of a statement. The interrogative pronoun is positioned where the answer is expected.	回答所询问的人、事物或情况 Answered by giving the information required	降调 Falling
(三)正反疑问句 Affirmative-negative questions	你去不去北京?	询问某情况的肯定或否定 The hearer is expected to confirm or deny what is asked.	1.主—谓—(宾)—"不(没)"? S—P—不—(O)? P—(O)? 2.主—谓?—宾—"不(没)"? S—P—O—不? (没)—P?	并列谓语的肯定形式和否定形式;肯定式在否定式前边 The affirmative and negative forms are put together with or the former preceding the latter.	或答肯定,或答否定 The answer is either an affirmative or a negative one.	升调 Rising

类别	例句	作用 Function	格式 Structure	说明 Description	语调
(四)用"还是"的疑问句 Questions using 还是	他是教师还是干部?	询问人或事物在哪几种情况中哪一种 Requesting one of two or more possible answers about a person or thing	1. 主—谓—(宾$_1$)—还是—谓$_2$—(宾$_2$)? S—P$_1$—(O$_1$)—还是—P$_2$—(O$_2$)? 2. 主$_1$—谓—(宾)—还是—主$_2$—谓—(宾)? S$_1$—P$_1$—P$_2$—(O)? 3. 主—状$_1$—谓$_1$—(宾)—还是—状$_2$—谓$_2$—(O)? S—adv.$_1$—P$_1$—adv.$_2$—P$_2$?	"还是"连接两个或两个以上的词或词组提同所问几项中一项回答 Two or more words/phrases are connected. Choose one answer from two or more alternatives.	升调 Rising
(五)用"是不是"的疑问句 Questions using 是不是	他是不是住三〇九号?	进一步求证发种情况或征求同意 Used to get sth. confirmed	1. 主—是不是—谓—P—(宾)? S—是不是—P—(O)? 2. 是不是—主—谓—S—P—(O)? 是不是—S—P—(O)? 3. 主—谓—(宾)—是不是? S—P—(O)—是不是?	"是不是"可放在各类句子中提问 是不是 can be used with any kind of a statement to form a question.	升调 Rising
(六)用"呢"的疑问句 Questions using 呢	画家呢?	询问人或事物在哪儿或怎么样 Asking where or how a person or thing is	1. 词—"呢"? Word + 呢? 2. 偏正词组—"呢"? Endocentric phrase + 呢?	多用于独语句中 Used mostly in one-word/phrase sentence.	升调 Rising
(七)用副词"多"的疑问句 Questions using 多	这座楼多高?	询问程度、数量 Asking about degree or quantity	1. 主—"多"—谓(单音形答词)? S—多—P (monosyllabic adj.)? 2. 主—"有"—宾("多")—O(多—形答词)? S—P(有)—O(多—adj.)?	"多"多用在表示积极意义的单音形容答词前边 多 is used with monosyllabic adjectives in "good" sense. 一般要用数量词组回答具体程度 Give the degree which is indicated by a N-Mw phrase.	升调 Rising

练 习 39
Exercise 39

用横线标出下列疑问句的主要特点，并回答。

Underline the characteristics of the following questions and answer them.

例：

Model: 信筒在哪儿？

答：

Answer: 信筒在学校门口。

1. 他在电视台工作吗？
2. 你坐"地铁"不坐？
3. 这艘轮船大不大？
4. 你喜欢哪种方式呢？
5. 外边的雾是不是很大？
6. 他们今天会来吗？
7. 这是不是新闻广播？
8. 你有没有那篇论文？他呢？
9. 这个游泳池有多长？
10. 他的脾气好不好呢？
11. 你吃米饭还是馒头？
12. 您多大年纪了？
13. 他是不是已经给你买了火车票？
14. 那位是新来的校长吗？
15. 船票容易买还是飞机票容易买？
16. 那座城市建设得漂亮不漂亮？
17. 谁告诉了你这个消息？
18. 这次的考题（考试题目）很难是不是？
19. 我明天休息，你呢？
20. 你在家准备还是去图书馆？

第十节 祈 使 句

Section X   The Imperative Sentence

一、什么叫祈使句   Definition

表示命令、请求、催促、劝告或商量，有表示祈使语气的语调的句子叫祈使句。句尾常用句号"。"或感叹号"！"。它的基本格式是：

The imperative sentence is one expressing command, request, urging, advice, warning or consultation and having an imperative tone.   At the end of such a sentence, a full stop (。) or an exclamation mark(!) is used.   Its basic pattern is:

（主语）——谓语

(Subject) + predicate

例如：

Examples:

（你）——出去！

（你们）——快修改吧！

（您）——请在这儿等候！

（你们）——别走了！

（咱们）——走吧！

二、祈使句的语法特点   Grammatical features

（一）祈使句常不用主语。例如：

The subject is often absent in an imperative sentence.   For example:

进来！

请坐！

快跑！

慢慢吃！

好好休养！

（二）祈使句的谓语一般由动词充当。

The predicate of an imperative sentence is usually a verb.

（三）祈使句常在句首用动词"请"。例如：

The verb 请 is often used at the beginning of an imperative sentence. For example:

请进！

请发表意见。

请转告他。

（四）否定形式的祈使句中常在句首或谓语前用副词"别、不要、不必"等，表示劝阻或制止。例如：

In a negative imperative sentence, the adverbs 别, 不要, 不必, etc. are used at the beginning or before the predicate to express dissuasion or prevention. For example:

别大声说话！

我们不要这样做。

不用送了！

如果用"请"，"请"要放在"别"的前边。例如：

When 请 is used, it must be put before the negative adverb. For example:

请别客气！

请不要忘记。

（五）祈使句一般是降调，句尾用句号"。"或感叹号"！"。

Usually an imperative sentence is spoken in a falling tone and a full stop(。) or exclamation mark(!) is used at the end.

三、使用祈使句需要注意的问题

Points that merit special attention

（一）汉语里，凡用动词"请"表示祈使的句子，"请"一定要放在句首，"请"后边可以是动词或动词性词组。例如：

In Chinese, when the verb 请 is used in an imperative

sentence, it must be placed at the beginning and is followed by a verb or verbal phrase.　For example:

> 请进!
>
> 请喝茶!
>
> 请站起来!
>
> 请开门!
>
> 请打开书。

一定不能把"请"放在句尾，不能说成"进来请"、"喝茶请"等。

请 never occurs at the end of the sentence, hence 进来请，喝茶请，etc. are wrong.

（二）用"请"的祈使句中，主语"我"或"你"常略去不说。

When 请 is used, the subject (我 or 你) is often omitted.

第十一节　感　叹　句

Section XI　The Exclamatory Sentence

一、什么叫感叹句　Definition

表示赞美、喜爱、惊讶、厌恶等各种感情，有表示感叹的语调的句子叫感叹句。句尾用感叹号"!"。它的基本格式是：

The exclamatory sentence is a sentence expressing praise, fondness, surprise, detestation, etc. and having an exclamatory tone.　The exclamation mark(!) is used at the end.　Its basic pattern is:

（主语）——谓语

(Subject)+predicate

例如：

Examples:

今天的球赛精彩得很！

这些汉字写得漂亮极了！

这两只熊猫多可爱啊！

你买的盆景真好！

太暗了！

二、感叹句的语法特点　Grammatical features

（一）感叹句里常用表示程度很高的副词作状语，最常见的有"多（么）、真、太"等。例如：

Adverbs expressing high degree such as 多（么），真，太, etc. are often used in an exclamatory sentence as adverbial adjuncts. For example:

这座山真高！

这个消息多（么）鼓舞人！

联欢会的内容太丰富了。

（二）感叹句里常用表示程度很高的副词等作补语。例如：

Words such as adverbs of high degree are often used as complements in an exclamatory sentence. For example:

外边凉快极了！

今晚的月亮圆得很！

我困死了！

（三）感叹句句尾常用语气助词"啊"或"了"。例如：

The modal particles 啊 or 了 are often used at the end of an exclamatory sentence. For example:

这个城市多（么）整洁啊！

他遇到的困难太多了！

（四）感叹句一般是降调。书面上句尾要用感叹号"！"。

An exclamatory sentence is usually spoken in the falling tone. In writing an exclamation mark(!) is used at the end.

三、使用感叹句需要注意的问题

Points that merit special attention

（一）感叹句里常用"多（么）…啊"或"太…了"表示赞美、惊叹。例如：

多（么）…啊 or 太…了 are often used to express praise and surprise in an exclamatory sentence.　For example:

这里多（么）安静啊！

他对我们太好了！

（二）有的感叹句可以由一个词或词组构成，但一定要加上表达情感的语调。例如：

Sometimes an exclamatory sentence has but one word/phrase.　In this case, it can be fully expressed only when it is spoken with a tone of emotion.　For example:

好！

两条小金鱼！

（三）表示程度的副词"很"、"非常"等一般只能用在陈述句里作状语，而不用在感叹句里作状语。例如：

Degree adverbs like 很，非常，etc. can only be used as adverbial adjuncts in statements, but not in exclamatory sentences.　For example:

外边非常凉快。　　　　　　　（陈述句）
　　　　　　　　　　　　　　　(Statement)
外边多（么）凉快啊！　　　　（感叹句）
　　　　　　　　　　　　　　　(Exclamatory sentence)

这种车跑得很快。　　　　　　（陈述句）
　　　　　　　　　　　　　　　(Statement)
这种车跑得多（么）快啊！　　（感叹句）
　　　　　　　　　　　　　　　(Exclamatory sentence)

不能说"外边非常凉快啊"或"这种车跑得很快啊"。

It is not right to say 外边非常凉快啊 or 这种车跑得很快啊.

附表七： 按用途分类的四种句子的简要情况表

Table 7: The Four Kinds of Sentence Classified in Terms of Function

四种句子 The four kinds of sentences	例句 Examples	表示的意义 Meanings	结构特点 Structural features	语调 Intonations	书面标记 Punctuations
陈述句 Declarative	他去工厂。他很细心。他北京人。他工作认真。下雨了。	叙述一件事。To make a statement	有各类句子的结构形式。Take all sentence forms classified in terms of structure	一般是降调 Normally in the falling tone	句末用句号"。" Full-stop(。)
疑问句 Interrogative	他去工厂吗？他去哪儿？他去不去？他去还是你去？他是不是语法书呢？我的语法书呢？他多高？	提出问题。To ask a question	有各类句子的结构形式。All sentence forms classified in terms of structure can be turned interrogative.	一般是升调 Normally in the rising tone	句末用问号"？" Question mark(?)
祈使句 Imperative	请坐下！你别去！	提出要求。To put forward a command	可以没有主语；可以只有一个词或词组。It can go without the subject; It may have only one word/phrase.	一般是降调 Normally in the falling tone	句末用句号"。"或感叹号"！" Full-stop(。) or exclamation mark(!)
感叹句 Exclamatory	好极了！多快啊！	表示感情 To express some emotion	可以没有主语；可以只有一个词或词组。It can go without the subject; It may have only one word/phrase.	一般是降调 Normally in the falling tone	句末用感叹号"！" Exclamation mark(!)

练　习　40
Exercise 40

（一）按各类句子的基本格式改正下列病句。

Correct the mistakes in the following sentences according to the basic patterns of the different kinds of sentences.

1. 他不上海人。
2. 他听音乐在自己的房间。
3. 他是很高。
4. 大家都有没这样的信封。
5. 他进去食堂了。
6. 都我们不去机场。
7. 下星期日同学们都来我。
8. 他每天睡觉得很早。
9. 他搬到学生宿舍从家里去。
10. 我们的作业本都在老师。
11. 明年八月我们快要回国了。
12. 这是他写书。
13. 什么地图是这？
14. 他是不政府官员。
15. 朋友们从别的城市来了都。
16. 他今天起很早。
17. 他能听那个报告懂。
18. 哪儿在你妹妹？
19. 他送一块手绢我。
20. 它下雪了。
21. 你去不去植物园吗？
22. 这句话应该什么说？

23. 是这只公鸡你家的吗？

24. 我们都不有那样的车。

25. 他已经回来宿舍了。

26. 北京冬天是不是很冷吗？

27. 哪儿是玛丽？

28. 哪国人是你？

29. 坐下请！

（二）造句。Make sentences.

1. 写出十个动词谓语句（肯定句、否定句各五个），并标出谓语动词。

Make ten sentences with verbal predicates (five in the affirmative and five in the negative) and underline the predicate verbs of your sentences.

2. 写出六个形容词谓语句（肯定句、否定句各三个），并标出谓语形容词。

Make six sentences with adjectival predicates (three in the affirmative and three in the negative) and underline the predicate adjectives of your sentences.

3. 写出两个名词谓语句（肯定句、否定句各一个）。

Make two sentences with noun predicates (one in the affirmative and one in the negative).

4. 写出两个主谓谓语句。

Make two sentences with S-P phrase predicates.

5. 写出各类疑问句十个，并回答。

Make ten questions of different types and answer them.

6. 写出各种非主谓句十个。

Make ten non-S-P sentences.

7. 写出两个祈使句。

Make two imperative sentences.

8. 写出两个感叹句。

Make two exclamatory sentences.

第六章　动作的状态
Chapter Six　Aspects of an Action

一、什么是动作的状态　Definition

　　一个动作可以处在进行、持续或者完成等不同的情况中，这就是动作的状态。

An action may be in the stage of progression, continuation or completion, and these different stages of an action are known as aspects.

　　汉语里动作的状态和动作发生的时间，不完全表现在同一个语法形式里。动作的状态和时间有关，但不表示时间。汉语里经常用副词和动态助词来表示动作所处的状态；而时间则主要由时间词、表示时间的副词或词组来表示。这一点是外国人要特别注意区别的。

In Chinese, the aspect and the time of an action are not entirely expressed in one grammatical form. The state of an action has something to do with the time, but does not indicate the time. Thus adverbs and aspectual particles are often used to denote the different states of an action while the time of an action is mainly expressed by nouns, adverbs or phrases denoting time. Special attention should be called to this point by foreign learners.

　　举例来说，汉语里用动态助词"了 (le)"表示动作的完成，但动作并不一定都是在过去时间里发生的。例如："他来了"只能表示"来"的动作已完成；而在"昨天他来了"和"你看，他来了"里才表示动作实现和完成的时间是"昨天"和说话的时候（现在）。如果要表示将来完成，还要有其他条件。

For instance, in Chinese the aspectual particle 了 (le) is used to indicate the completion of an action, but it does not necessarily show that the action took place in the past, e.g. 他来了 only shows the action of 来 is completed, whereas in sentences 昨天他来了 and 你看，他来了 the time of the realization and completion of the action 昨天 and the time of speaking（现在）are all expressed. If we want to express the future completion of an action, other conditions are needed.

无论动作处于哪种状态以及发生在什么时间，谓语动词的形式都不改变，比如上面的"来"。

The form of the predicate verb (like 来 in the above examples) remains unchanged no matter what state the action is in and no matter when it takes place.

二、常见的几种动作状态的表示方法分节介绍如下。

The common ways of indicating aspects of an action shall be dealt with in the following sections.

第一节 动作的进行

Section I The Progressive Aspect of an Action

一、表示动作正在进行的形式

Forms indicating the progressive aspect of an action

汉语里，要表示一个动作正在进行，可以在谓语动词前边加副词"正"、"在"或"正在"，句尾加上语气助词"呢(ne)"。基本格式是：

The adverbs 正, 在 or 正在 may be added prior to the predicate verb and the modal particle 呢 (ne) at the end of a sentence to indicate that an action is in progress. The basic patterns are as follows:

1. 主语 ——— 状语 ———谓语—(宾语)—(呢)
　　　　　　 （副词"正"、"在"或"正在"） （动词）

Subject +· adverbial adjunct + predicate + (object) + (呢)
　　　　　 (adverbs正,在or正在)　　(verb)

例如：

Examples:

　　　他们正开会（呢）。

　　　　（"开会"的动作正在进行）

　　　　(The action of 开会 is going on)

　　　他们在休息（呢）。

　　　　（"休息"正在进行）

　　　　(休息 is going on)

　　　她们正在晒衣服（呢）。

　　　　（"晒衣服"的动作正在进行）

　　　　(The action of 晒衣服 is going on)

　　　他们正在调查（呢）。

　　　　（"调查"正在进行）

　　　　(调查 is going on)

2. 主语 ——— （状语） ———谓语—(宾语)—"呢"
　　　　　　 （副词"正"、"在"或"正在"） （动词）

Subject + (adverbial adjunct) + predicate + (object) + 呢
　　　　　 (adverbs正,在or正在)　　(verb)

例如：

Examples:

　　　他们（正）开会呢。

　　　他们（在）休息呢。

他们（正在）调查呢。

她们（正在）晒衣服呢。

二、用"正在…呢"表示动作正在进行的特点

Grammatical features

（一）副词"正"、"在"、"正在"和语气助词"呢"可以单独使用，或同时用在一个句子里，形成"正在…呢"格式。例如：

The adverbs 正, 在, 正在 and the modal particle 呢 can either be used by themselves or be used in combination in the same sentence forming the construction 正在…呢. For example:

他正演出。　　　　　工人们正搞技术革新呢。

她在唱歌。　　　　　农民们正在种麦子呢。

他们正在表演节目。　战士们在练习投弹呢。

她们跳舞呢。

（二）"正在…呢"中间的成分可以是动词、动宾词组或动词性偏正词组。例如：

The elements between 正在…呢 may be a verb, a V-O phrase or a verbal endocentric phrase. For example:

他们在挑选呢。　　　　（动词）
　　　　　　　　　　　　（Verb）

他们正在挑选优良品种呢。（动宾词组）
　　　　　　　　　　　　（V-O phrase）

我们正一块儿座谈呢。　（偏正词组）
　　　　　　　　　　　　（Endocentric phrase）

（三）用"正"、"在"、"正在"、"…呢"或"正在…呢"表示一个动作正在进行时，动作进行的时间可以是现在、过去或将来。动作进行的时间要用时间词或数量、方位等词组来表示。例如：

When 正, 在, 正在, …呢 or 正在…呢 are used to indicate an action in progress, the action may take place either in the present, the past or the future. The time of the action is expressed by time nouns, or by N-Mw and locality phrases, etc. For example:

他倒茶呢。

我在贴邮票。

今天上午九点我在上课。

下午三点以前我在交待工作。

昨天我们去他家的时候，他正在弹钢琴。

明天你到这儿的时候，他会在等你。

（四）动作进行的否定形式是在谓语动词前边加否定副词"没"。

The negative form of the progressive aspect of an action is made by placing the negative adverb 没 before the predicate verb.

"没" —— （ "在" ） —— 谓语动词

没 + （在） + the predicate verb

例如：

For example:

他没（在）看书，他在写信呢。

我们没（在）聊天，我们讨论学习方法问题呢。

昨天我写信的时候，他没（在）听收音机。

回答时的否定式可以只说 "没有"。例如：

To give a negative answer to a question, one may simply say 没有. For example:

你在洗衣服吗？

没有。（我在收拾东西。）

他正在搞设计吗？

没有，他正在画图。

三、使用"正在…呢"表示动作的进行时需要注意的问题
Points that merit special attention

（一）副词"正"、"在"和"正在"表示的意思基本相同。"正"着重表示某时间，"在"着重表示处于进行状态，"正在"既指时间又指状态。

The meaning of the adverbs 正，在 and 正在 is essentially the same, only, 正 emphasizes a certain period of time, 在 emphasizes being in the state of progression, while 正在 refers to both time and state.

（二）有些动词不能用于"正在…呢"中间。最常见的有以下几种：

Some verbs can not be used between 正在…呢. Following are the most common ones:

1．表示判断、领有、存在等动词，如："是、在、具有、存在、叫、姓、叫作、属于、等于…"

Verbs indicating judgment, possession, existence, etc., such as 是，在，具有，存在，叫，姓，叫作，属于，等于…

2．表示感知的动词，如："知道、认识、感到、感觉、明白、清楚、懂…"

Verbs indicating sensation, e.g. 知道，认识，感到，感觉，明白，清楚，懂…

3．表示心理活动的一些动词，如："怕、愿意、喜欢、羡慕、可惜…"

Verbs indicating psychological activities, such as 怕，愿意，喜欢，羡慕，可惜…

4．表示出现、消失的动词，如："开始、停止、生、死、忘、去、掉…"

Verbs indicating emergence, disappearance, such as 开始，停止，生，死，忘，去，掉…

5．表示趋向的一些动词，如："来、去、进、出、过…"

Some of the verbs indicating direction, such as 来，去，进，出，过…

（三）表示动作正在进行的副词"正在"前边不能用动词"是"。例如：

The verb 是 can not be used before the adverb 正在 indicating an action in progress. For example:

他正在作报告呢。

不能说成"他是正在作报告呢"。

One can not say 他是正在作报告呢.

如果在"正在"前边加"是"，表示的意思就变成了证实后边的情况，"是"要重读。

When used before 正在, 是 confirms what follows and 是 should be stressed.

（四）动作正在进行和时间。

An action in progress and the time.

动作正在进行的状态可以发生在过去、现在或将来。"正在…呢"只表示动作处于进行状态，如果没有特别指明时间或无明确的语言环境，一般可指说话时的"现在"发生的。但如果要明确表示发生的时间，就要用时间词或表示时间的词组。这一点要特别注意。例如：

The progressive aspect of an action may take place either in the past, the present or the future. 正在…呢 only shows that an action is in progress. We may generally think the action takes place in the present if the time is not clearly indicated or shown by the context. What should be specially noted is that time nouns or phrases indicating time should be used if we want definitely to show the time when the action takes place. For example:

他正在做实验。

一般来说，这句话指的是说话时的"现在"。而下面的句子由于有表示具体时间的词或词组，可以分别指明动作的进行发生在过去或者将来：

Generally speaking, the above sentence refers to "the

present" i.e. the time of speaking, but when the time is clearly referred to by a time noun or phrase, as in the following sentences, the action may be proceeding in the past or in the future, as the case may be.

昨天下午三点他正在做实验。（过去）

(Past)

上星期五我找他的时候，他正在做实验。（过去）

(Past)

下星期五你找他的时候，可能他正在做实验。(将来)

(Future)

无论动作的进行发生在过去、现在还是将来，谓语动词的形式都不变，例如上面的"做（实验）"。

No matter when the action in progress may take place (in the present, past or future), the form of the predicate verb remains unchanged, like 做（实验） in the above sentences.

（五）表示动作进行的否定式的句子里，谓语动词前用了副词"没（有）"，表示动作进行的副词"正"和助词"呢"都不能再保留，而副词"在"是可以保留的，特别是在主动说明正在进行的否定状态时一般要保留"在"。例如：

In the negative form of the progressive aspect, if the adverb 没（有） is used before the predicate verb, the adverb 正 and the particle 呢 indicating an action in progress can no longer remain in the sentence. However, the adverb 在 may be kept, and this is, especially true when a negative statement is made to explain that an action is not in progress. For example:

他没在看电视。（他可能去朋友那儿了。）

(He may have gone to his friend.)

我们没在讨论，你进来吧。

如果用否定式回答别人的问题，常不用副词"在"。例如：

The adverb 在 is often omitted when giving a negative

answer. For example:

> 他在看电视吗?
>
> > 没有。
> >
> > 他没（在）看电视，他出去了。
>
> 你们在讨论吗?
>
> > 没有。
> >
> > 我们没（在）讨论，我们聊天呢。

（六）对动作进行的提问和回答。

Asking about an action in progress and the ways to answer.

1． 如要询问某动作是否正在进行时，一般可在句尾加语气助词"吗"。如果回答是肯定的，常只说"对"或"是"；如果回答是否定的，常只说"没有"。例如：

Normally the modal particle 吗 may be placed at the end of a sentence to inquire if an action is in progress. We often say 对 or 是 if the answer is affirmative while 没有 is used if the answer is negative. For example:

> 他们在打球吗?
>
> > 对。（他们在打球。）
> >
> > 没有。（他们没打球，他们打扫球场呢。）
>
> 他们正在理发吗?
>
> > 是。（他们正在理发。）
> >
> > 没有。（他们没在理发。）

2． 如果询问正在进行何种动作时，一般用疑问代词"什么"提问。例如：

The interrogative pronoun 什么 is normally used to inquire what action is going on. For example:

> 你做什么呢?
>
> > 我看报呢。
>
> 他们在做什么?
>
> > 他们在修改那篇报道。

她在抄写什么?

她在抄写一篇文章。

回答用"做什么"提问的问句时,只说进行的动作,不再重复动词"做"。不能说"我做看报呢"等。

When answering questions with 做什么, one only needs to say the action going on without repeating the verb 做. One can not say 我做看报呢 etc.

(七)表示动作进行的句子里,如有介词结构"在…"作的状语,可在句尾用助词"呢";或在介词"在"前边用副词"正",而不能加"正在"。例如:

If there is an adverbial adjunct formed by the prepositional structure 在… in a sentence indicating an action in progress, we may either place the particle 呢 at the end of the sentence or use the adverb 正 rather than 正在 before the preposition 在. For example:

他在宿舍睡觉呢。

他们正在楼上研究问题。

现在她正在游泳池游泳。

不能说"他正在在宿舍睡觉"等。

One can not say 他正在在宿舍睡觉, etc.

(八)谓语动词前边加上副词"在",可表示动作反复进行或长期持续,而副词"经常、常常、时常、一直"等一定要放在副词"在"的前边。例如:

When the adverb 在 is put before the predicate verb, it may indicate the repetition or long-term continuation of an action while 在 can also be premodified by adverbs like 经常,常常,时常,一直, etc. For example:

我们经常在考虑这个问题。

父亲常常在提醒孩子们。

大家一直在等你。

不能说"我们在经常考虑…"等。

One can not say 我们在经常考虑…, etc.

（九）"正在…（呢）"不能和表示动作完成的动态助词"了"并用。不能说"他正在听音乐了"、"他们正在排练节目了"等。

正…在（呢）can not be used together with the aspectual particle 了 which indicates the completion of an action. One can not say 他正在听音乐了, 他们正在排练节目了, etc.

（十）"正在…呢"中间不能用动补词组。不能说"他正在写完呢"等。

No verb-complement phrase can be used between 正在…呢. One can not say 他正在写完呢, etc.

练 习 41
Exercise 41

（一）用表示动作正在进行的副词"在"改写下列句子。

Rewrite the following sentences using the adverb 在 to indicate an action in progress.

例：

Model: 他听音乐。——→他在听音乐。

1. 我们喝咖啡。
2. 他尝我做的点心。
3. 那个演员唱歌。
4. 我朋友打电话。
5. 他们踢足球。

（二）用表示动作正在进行的副词"正在"改写下列句子。

Rewrite the following sentences using the adverb 正在 to indicate an action in progress.

例:

Model: 大家晒太阳。——>大家正在晒太阳。

   1. 那位老师辅导学生。

   2. 我们商量克服困难的办法。

   3. 他安排课外活动。

   4. 国家领导人检阅军队。

   5. 我们建设自己的国家。

（三）用表示动作正在进行的"正在…呢"改写下列句子。

Rewrite the following sentences using 正在…呢 to indicate the progression of an action.

例:

Model: 他们陪同贵宾。——>他们正在陪同贵宾呢。

   1. 我切菜。

   2. 他在海关联系。

   3. 那位老师傅介绍经验。

   4. 她们在体育馆里比赛。

   5. 他们慰问受伤的战士。

（四）用肯定式回答下列问题。

Answer the following questions in the affirmative.

例:

Model: 你在刷走廊吗？——>对。（我在刷走廊。）

   1. 他正在打字吗？

   2. 你在画画儿吗？

   3. 他们正在听录音吗？

   4. 孩子们在游泳吗？

   5. 记者正在写访问报道吗？

（五）用否定式回答下列问题。

Answer the following questions in the negative.

例:

Model: 他在录音吗？——>没有。（他没在录音。）

1. 他们在搬家吗?
2. 老师正在讲语法吗?
3. 你在预习新课吗?
4. 工人们在砍树吗?
5. 运动员正在练基本动作吗?

（六）改正病句。

Correct the following sentences.

1. 他不在吃饭，他在休息。
2. 他们正在写完总结。
3. 我们正在在实验室做实验。
4. 他正在去操场了。
5. 我们都在喜欢这种山水画呢。
6. 大家在常常思考您提出的问题。
7. 刚才我不在对照这两本外文书。
8. 那个售货员没正在包点心。
9. 我正在做翻译这篇稿子呢。
10. 他正在有一个收音机。

第二节　动作的持续

Section II　The Continuous Aspect of an Action

一、表示动作在持续的形式

Forms indicating the continuous aspect of an action

　　汉语里要表示一个动作或动作结果的状态在持续，可在谓语动词后边加动态助词"着 (zhe)"。基本格式是：

　　The aspectual particle 着 (zhe) when occurring after the predicate verb indicates the continuation either of an action or of a state as the result of an action. The basic pattern is as follows:

主语——谓语（动词）——"着"——（宾语）

Subject + predicate (verb) + 着 + (object)

例如：

Examples:

他眼睛闭着。

（"闭"的动作在持续）

(The continuation of the action 闭.)

那个妇女抱着一个男孩子。

（"抱"的动作在持续）

(The continuation of the action 抱.)

窗户开着，门关着。

（"开"和"关"的动作已经完成，但"开"和"关"的状态仍在持续）

(The actions of 开 and 关 have been completed but the states of 开 and 关 continue.)

她穿着一件黄衬衫。

（"穿"的动作已完成，"穿"的结果的状态仍在持续）

(The action of 穿 has been completed but the state of the result of 穿 continues.)

二、用"着 (zhe)"表示动作持续的特点

Grammatical features

（一）谓语动词和动态助词"着"紧紧相连。例如：

The predicate verb and the aspectual particle 着 go closely together. For example:

在晚会上，年轻人唱着、跳着。

夜深了，他房里的灯还亮着。

（二）动词谓语的宾语要放在助词"着"后边。例如：

The object of the verbal predicate is preceded by the particle 着. For example:

> 他手里拿着一束花。
>
> 他们都带着照相机。
>
> 我们俩抬着一个皮箱。

（三）动作或动作结果的状态持续的时间可以发生在过去、现在或将来，要用时间词或词组来表示。例如：

The continuation of an action or a state as the result of an action may take place in the past, the present or the future. The time is referred to by time nouns or time phrases. For example:

> { 昨天这儿停着很多车。
>
> { 今天这儿又停着很多车。
>
> { 明天这儿还会停着很多车。
>
> { 晚上九点以前，这个阅览室的门开着。
>
> { 晚上九点以后，这个阅览室的门关着。

（四）动作的持续和进行可以同时发生。例如：

The continuation and the progression of an action may take place simultaneously. For example:

> 他正打着电话呢。
>
> 她在织着毛衣呢。
>
> 我们正在谈着话呢。

（五）动作或动作结果状态的持续的否定形式是在谓语动词前边加副词"没"。例如：

The negative form of the continuation of an action or a state as the result of an action is made by placing the adverb 没 before the predicate verb. For example:

"没" —— 谓语动词 —— "着"

没 + predicate verb + 着

> 他没站着。

443

上边的窗户没开着。

今天他没戴着那顶皮帽子。

花瓶里没插着鲜花。

用否定式回答时可只用"没有"。例如：

没有 may be used alone as a negative answer. For example:

床上铺着花床单吗？

没有。（床上铺着白床单。）

三、使用"着 (zhe)"表示动作持续时需要注意的问题

Points that merit special attention

（一）谓语动词和动态助词"着"。

The predicate verb and the aspectual particle 着.

谓语动词和助词"着"粘合得很紧，助词"着"应紧跟在谓语动词后边，它们之间不能插入任何其他成分。

着 must follow the predicate verb immediately and no element can be inserted between them.

1. 动词谓语如带宾语，宾语只能放在动词和"着"后边。例如：

If the verb predicate takes an object, the object can only be placed after the verb and 着. For example:

他们跳着舞呢。

我靠着一张桌子。

不能说成"他们跳舞着呢"等。同样，由"动宾"构成的词作谓语时，"宾"也要放在"着"后边，例如"鼓着掌"、"鞠着躬"不能说成"鼓掌着"、"鞠躬着"。

One can not say 他们跳舞着呢 etc. Similarly, when words of the V-O construction act as predicate, the object should also be placed after 着, e.g. 鼓着掌, 鞠着躬 can not be said as 鼓掌着, 鞠躬着.

2. 动词谓语和助词"着"之间不能插入结果补语。例如：

No complement of result can be inserted between the verb

predicate and the particle 着. For example:

　　　　他正写着一封家信。

　　　　我看着电视呢。

　　不能说成"他正写完着一封家信"、"我看清楚着电视呢"。

One can not say 他正写完着一封家信，我看清楚着电视呢.

　　（二）动作的持续和时间。

The continuation of an action and the time.

　　动作的持续状态可以发生在过去、现在或将来。动态助词"着"只表示动作处于持续状态，如果没有特别指明时间一般指"现在"、"说话时"发生的。但如要明确表示发生的时间，就要用时间词或表示时间的词组。这一点要特别注意。例如：

The state of continuation of an action may take place either in the past, present or future. The aspectual particle 着 only indicates the state of continuation. If the time is not particularly referred to, it normally implies that the continuation takes place in the present or at "the time of speaking". But time nouns or time phrases must be used if the time is to be referred to definitely. Special attention should be called to this point. For example:

　　　　他注意地听着教授的话。

　　一般来说，这句话指的是说话时的"现在"。而下面的句子由于有表示具体时间的词和词组，可以分别指明动作的持续发生在过去或将来：

Generally speaking, the time reference for this sentence is the "present" as it is spoken. But the following sentences state clearly that the continuation of the action takes place in the past and future owing to the presence of words or phrases indicating specific time.

　　　　昨天上课的时候，他注意地听着教授的话。（过去）

　　　　　　　　　　　　　　　　　　　　　　　　(Past)

明天上课的时候，我们一定注意地听着教授的课。

（将来）
(Future)

　　无论动作的持续发生在过去、现在还是将来，谓语动词的形式都不变，比如上面的"听"。

The form of the predicate verb remains unchanged no matter when the continuation of the action takes place (past, present or future), like 听 in the above sentence.

　　（三）能带动态助词"着"的动词有一定的局限性。见第二章第十一节四、（三）"动态助词和动词"1。

There are certain restrictions on the use of the aspectual particle 着 with certain verbs. (See Point 1 of "The aspectual particles and verbs", 4 (3), Section XI, Chapter II.)

　　（四）表示动作结果的状态仍持续存在的"着"不能和表示动作进行的"在"、"正在"用在一起。例如：

着 when indicating the continuation of the result of an action can not be used together with 在, 正在 when they indicate the progression of an action. For example:

　　　　墙上挂着一张世界地图。

　　　　窗台上摆着两盆花。

　　　　校园里种着很多果树。

不能说"墙上正在挂着一张世界地图"等。

One can not say 墙上正在挂着一张世界地图, etc.

　　（五）表示动作持续的句子里不能用表示动作完成的动态助词"了"。例如"门开着"、"他醒着"，不能说成"门开着(zhe)了"、"他醒着了"。

The aspectual particle 了, indicating the completion of an action, can not be used in a sentence showing the continuation of an action, e.g., one can say 门开着，他醒着， but not 门开着 (zhe) 了，他醒着了.

（六）否定式里，谓语动词后边的助词"着"必须保留。例如：

In the negative form, the particle 着 after the predicate verb must remain where it is. .For example:

> 墙上没挂着世界地图。
>
> 我没带着伞。

如果说成"我没带伞"，只是否定"带伞"这个动作，而不能说明是持续动作的否定。

If one says 我没带伞, it is only the negation of the action 带伞 rather than the negation of the continuation of the action.

如果不是特别强调数量，否定式里宾语前一般不用数量词组。例如：

Generally speaking, N-Mw phrases do not occur before the object of the negative form if the quantity is not particularly emphasized. For example:

> 桌子上摆着两只花瓶吗？
>
> 没有，只摆着一只花瓶。

如果强调数量才用数量词组，而且是重音所在。例如：

N-Mw phrases are only used when the quantity is emphasized and they are always stressed in this case. For example:

> 我没带着十块钱，只带着六块钱。

（七）动作持续的提问和回答。

Asking about a continuous action and the ways to answer.

如要询问某动作或动作结果的状态是否持续，常用的提问方式是：

If one wants to inquire whether an action or the state of the result of an action still continues, the following question forms are most commonly used:

1. 在用助词"着(zhe)"的陈述句句尾加上"没有"。不论回答是肯定的还是否定的，助词"着"一般都要保留。例如：

没有 is placed at the end of a declarative sentence with the particle 着 (zhe) kept in. 着 is normally kept in the sentence no matter whether the answer is affirmative or negative. For example:

他躺着没有？——躺着呢。

——没有，他没躺着。

你带着汉语词典没有？——带着呢。

——没有，没带着。

2. 在用助词"着"的陈述句句尾加上语气助词"吗"。例如：
The modal particle 吗 is added at the end of a declarative sentence using the particle 着. For example:

录音机开着吗？——开着呢。

——没有，没开着。

外边下着雨吗？——下着呢。

——没有，没下（着）（雨）。

但一般属自然现象的，否定式中可不用"着"。
However, 着 is optional in the negative answer to a question concerning weather conditions.

3. 如果问句中有状语，一般要先回答"对"或"是"，再用主谓句回答。例如：
If there is an adverbial adjunct in the interrogative sentence, normally the short answer 对 or 是 precedes a full answer formed of an S-P sentence. For example:

书架上整整齐齐地摆着许多外文书吗？

对，书架上整整齐齐地摆着许多外文书。

你家屋前屋后都种着花吗？

是，我家屋前屋后都种着花。

（八）动词后边加助词"着"可用在动词谓语前作状语，表示后一动作进行的方式。例如：
Verbs with the aspectual particle 着 can be used adverbially

to modify a verb predicate, expressing the manner of the action indicated by the predicate verb. For example:

> 我坐着看书。
>
> 演员站着唱歌。
>
> 他笑着说："欢迎，欢迎！"
>
> 他低着头走路。
>
> 他握着我的手说："太谢谢你了！"

（九）如要指出动作持续的处所，一定要把表示处所的介词结构"在…"放在动词谓语前边作状语，而不能放在"着"后边。例如：

The prepositional phrase 在… as an adverbial adjunct indicating locality must be placed before the verb predicate rather than after 着 if we want to point out the place where the continuous action is carried out. For example:

> 他在后边站着。
>
> 我们都在草地上坐着。
>
> 地图在墙上挂着。

一定不能说"他站着在后边"、"我们都坐着在草地上"或"地图挂着在墙上"等。

One can never say 他站着在后边，我们都坐着在草地上，地图挂着在墙上，etc.

（十）说明某处有某种现象在持续的句子里，表示处所的词或词组常用在句首，但前边不用介词"在"。例如：

Nouns or phrases of place often occur at the beginning of a sentence indicating that a certain phenomenon continues in a certain place. But the preposition 在 is not used before the place nouns or phrases. For example:

> 外边下着小雪。
>
> 那儿围着不少人。
>
> 台上坐着各单位的代表。

床上铺着一条漂亮的床单。

桌子上放着一个钟。

不能说成"在外边下着雨"、"在床上铺着漂亮的床单"等。

One can not say 在外边下着雨，在床上铺着漂亮的床单, etc.

练　习　42
Exercise　42

（一）用动态助词"着 (zhe)"改写下列句子。

Rewrite the following sentences using the aspectual particle 着 (zhe).

例：　　他们和工人们高兴地谈话。

Model:　　　——他们和工人们高兴地谈着话。

1. 屋子里开电扇。
2. 院子里种了两棵树。
3. 她们挑选合适的礼物。
4. 他和朋友快乐地唱歌。
5. 公路旁边停了三辆小汽车。
6. 他肩上扛了一个箱子。
7. 下雨的时候我们都打伞。
8. 那个翻译同志穿了一套灰衣服。
9. 我叫他的时候，他正在抄写一篇散文。
10. 我进屋的时候，妹妹正念一首诗。

（二）用（　　）里的动词和助词"着"改写下列句子。

Rewrite the following sentences using the verbs in brackets and the particle 着.

例：　　桌子上有一瓶蓝墨水。（放）

Model:　　　　一　桌子上放着一瓶蓝墨水。
　　　1．书架上有很多书和词典。　　（摆）
　　　2．箱子里有他的一件新雨衣。　（收）
　　　3．他嘴里有一块糖。　　　　　（含）
　　　4．他手里有一盒火柴。　　　　（拿）
　　　5．床上有一对绣花枕头。　　　（放）
　　　6．墙上有一张气象纪录表。　　（挂）
　　　7．碗里有米饭。　　　　　　　（盛）
　　　8．旅馆门口有许多汽车。　　　（停）
　　　9．桥上有许多人。　　　　　　（站）
　　10．他有一副黑边眼镜。　　　　（戴）

（三）填入适当的动词和助词"着"。
Fill in the blanks with proper verbs and the particle 着.
例：
Model: 他站着作报告。
　　　1．我们都＿＿＿茶下棋。
　　　2．他＿＿＿我的肩膀说："明天一定来啊！"
　　　3．她＿＿＿水果去朋友家。
　　　4．他们＿＿＿音乐休息。
　　　5．大家＿＿＿掌欢迎客人。

第三节　动作的完成

Section III　The Perfect Aspect of an Action

一、表示动作完成状态的形式

Forms indicating the perfect aspect of an action

汉语里，要表示一个动作的实现或完成，可在谓语动词后边加上动态助词"了(le)"。基本格式是：

In Chinese, the aspectual particle 了 (le) may occur after

the predicate verb to indicate the completion of an action. The basic pattern is as follows:

主语——谓语（动词）——"了"——（宾语）

Subject + predicate (verb) + 了 + (object)

例如：

Examples:

他成功了。

他答应了。

他答应了这个要求。

他进了北京语言学院。

二、用动态助词"了 (le)"表示动作完成的特点

Grammatical features

（一）动词谓语和动态助词"了"之间不能插入宾语，宾语要放在动态助词"了"后边。例如：

The object occurs after the aspectual particle 了 instead of being put between it and the verb predicate. For example:

我写了两封信。

他买了一盒巧克力。

（二）汉语里动作的完成状态可以发生在过去、现在或将来时间。动作完成的时间要用时间词或词组来表示。例如：

A completed action may take place either in the past, present or future. The time of a completed action is denoted by time nouns or phrases. For example:

上星期他看了一场球赛。

昨天他获得了博士学位。

新闻记者都进去了。

代表们都走出来了。

下午我们发了言再去。

下星期三我们一定离开了那个城市。

（三）动作完成的否定形式是在谓语动词前边加上否定副词

"没"。

The negative form of the perfect aspect of an action is made by placing the negative adverb 没 before the predicate verb.

"没"——谓语动词

没 + predicate verb

例如：

Examples:

> 他没买录音机。
>
> 领导没批准这个设计。
>
> 他没拒绝这个邀请。

三、使用"了 (le)"表示动作完成时需要注意的问题

Points that merit special attention

（一）动态助词"了"和宾语。

The aspectual particle 了 and the object.

1. 带助词"了"的动词谓词后边如果有名词宾语，宾语前边常带数量词组或其他定语。例如：

If a noun object occurs after the verb predicate with the particle 了, N-Mw phrases or other attributives are often used before the object. For example:

> 他拿了三支粉笔。
>
> 客人们访问了汽车厂的两个工人家庭。
>
> 我们了解了不少情况。

2. 如果动词谓语的宾语简单，只有一个词，一般要具备下面的某一个条件。

A verb predicate with a single word object usually has one of the following features.

（1）在句尾加语气助词"了 (le)"，动词后边的动态助词"了"常常省去不用。而句尾的"了"既表示动作的完成，又表示动作实现的语气。例如：

When the modal particle 了 (le) is used at the end of a sentence, the aspectual particle 了 after the verb is often omitted. The 了 at the end of the sentence indicates the completion of the action, also expressing a tone of the action being realized. For example:

他洗（了）脸了。

我看（了）报了。

（2）在动词谓语前或主语前用上状语。例如：

An adverbial adjunct is used either before the verb predicate or before the subject. For example:

我已经告诉了他。

昨天我们跟张先生一起照了相。

（3）"动词谓语——'了'——简单宾语"后边必须另有谓语动词或分句，表示后一个动作是在前一个动作完成之后进行的。例如：

The "verb predicate + 了 + single word object" construction must be followed by another verb or clause, expressing the idea that the second action takes place only after the completion of the first one. For example:

他买了东西再来。

扫了地他就出去了。

他换了衣服就去办公室了。

（二）有一些动词不能表示动作或变化，后边不能加表示动作完成的动态助词"了"。见第二章第十一节四"（三）动态助词和动词"2。

The aspectual particle 了 can not be suffixed to verbs that do not indicate action or change. For details of this, refer to point 2 of "The aspectual particles and the verb", 4 (3), Section XI, Chapter II.

（三）动作的完成和时间。

The perfect aspect of an action and the time.

动作的完成状态可以发生在过去、现在或将来。动态助词
"了"只表示动作处于完成状态，如果没有特别指明时间，一般
指"现在""说话时"发生的。但如要明确表示时间，就要用时
间词或表示时间的词组。这一点要特别注意。例如：

The completion of an action may either take place in the
past, present or future. The aspectual particle 了 only shows
that an action is in the state of completion. If the time is not
specifically pointed out, it normally refers to "the present",
"the time of speaking". What should be specially noted is that
a time noun or phrase must be used to give a clear time reference.
For example:

　　　　他们参观了一个美术馆。

一般来说，这句话指的是"说话时"的"现在"以前完成
的。而下面的句子由于有具体的时间词或词组，可以分别指明动
作的完成发生在过去、现在或将来。

Normally this sentence shows that the action is completed
before "the present" i.e. the time of speaking. But when the
time is clearly referred to by a time noun or phrase, as in the
following sentences, the completion of the action may take
place in the past, present or future, as the case may be.

　　　　昨天上午他们参观了一个美术馆。　　（过去）
　　　　　　　　　　　　　　　　　　　　　　　(Past)

　　　　他们刚参观了一个美术馆。　　　　　（现在）
　　　　　　　　　　　　　　　　　　　　　　　(Present)

　　　　明天上午他们参观了美术馆就去教育部。（将来）
　　　　　　　　　　　　　　　　　　　　　　　(Future)

无论动作的完成发生在过去、现在还是将来，谓语动词的形
式都不变，比如上面的"参观"。

The form of the predicate verb remains unchanged no matter
when the action is completed (past, present or future) like 参观

in the above sentences.

（四）动词谓语带结果补语时，"了"一定要放在动补词组后边，而不能插入动补之间。例如：

了 must be placed after the V-C phrase rather than inserted in it when the verb predicate takes a complement of result. For example:

他讲完了两个问题。

我们听懂了他的讲演。

不能说"他讲了完两个问题"、"我们听了懂他的讲演"。

One cannot say 他讲了完两个问题，我们听了懂他的讲演.

（五）否定式里，谓语动词后的动态助词"了"不能保留。这点要特别注意。例如：

Note that the aspectual particle 了 after the predicate verb should be dropped in the negative sentence. For example:

他没买录音机。

昨天我们没参观那个展览。

我没看懂这篇论文。

一定不能说"他没买了录音机"、"昨天我们没参观了那个展览"、"我没看懂了这篇论文"。

One can never say 他没买了录音机，昨天我们没参观了那个展览，我没看懂了这篇论文.

（六）表动作完成的提问和回答。

Asking about a completed action and the ways to answer.

如要询问某动作是否完成时，常用下面几种提问方法。

The following ways of forming interrogative sentences are commonly used to inquire whether an action has been completed.

1.　在有"了"的陈述句句尾加上"没有"。

没有 is added to the end of a declarative sentence with 了.

主语——谓语（动词）——（宾语）——"了"——"没有"？

Subject + predicate (verb) + (object) + 了 + 没有？

例如：

Examples:

你们研究了没有？

研究了。

没有。（没研究。）

你订《旅游》杂志了没有？

订了。

没有。（没订。）

问句和肯定的答句中一定要用"了"。如果回答是否定的，可以只用"没有"，或用"'没'——谓语（动词）"，而谓语动词后边一定不能再用"了"。

了 must be used both in the question and the affirmative answer. If the answer is in the negative, one can only use 没有, or "没 + predicate (verb)" and 了 should not be used after the predicate verb.

2. 在带"了"的陈述句句尾加"吗"。例如：

吗 is added to the end of a declarative sentence with 了 For example:

你考虑了吗？

考虑了。

没有。（没考虑。）

3. 用"是不是"提问。肯定的回答可以只用"是"或"对"，否定的回答常用"没有"。例如：

是不是 is used to form an interrogative sentence. To give a definite answer only 是 or 对 need be used whereas 没有 is often used to form a negative answer. For example：

他病了是不是？

是。（他病了。）

对。（他病了。）

没有。（他没病。）

（七）说明一个经常或有规律地发生的动作的谓语动词后边，不能再用动态助词"了"。例如：

The aspectual particle 了 can not be used after the predicate verb indicating a habitual or regular a ction. For example:

> 每天他都打网球。
>
> 冬天我常常滑冰。
>
> 每到节日他们都举行晚会。

不能说"每天他都打（了）网球了"、"冬天我常常滑（了）冰了"或"每到节日他们都举行（了）晚会了。"

One can not say 每到节日他们都举行（了）晚会了，冬天我常常滑（了）冰了 or 每天他都打（了）网球了。

（八）主谓谓语句中谓语部分的"主"如由动词充当，后边一律不能用动态助词"了"。例如：

In a sentence with a S-P phrase as the predicate if the subject in the predicate part is a verb, the aspectual particle 了 can never be used after it. For example:

> 他们学习很好。
>
> 大家工作特别认真。
>
> 我们收获不小。

不能说"他们学习了很好"、"大家工作了特别认真"或"我们收获了不小"。

One can not say 他们学习了很好，大家工作了特别认真 or 我们收获了不小.

（九）动态助词"了"只能放在重叠动词之间表示动作的完成而不能放在重叠动词之后。例如：

The aspectual particle 了 can only be placed between reduplicated verbs, but not after them, when indicating the completion of an action. For example:

> 昨天我们在一起聊了聊（天）。

星期天我看了看朋友就回来了。

不能说"昨天我们在一起聊聊了（天）"或"星期天我看看了朋友就回来了"。

One can never say 昨天我们在一起聊聊了（天）or 星期天我看看了朋友就回来了。

练 习 43
Exercise 43

（一）用动态助词"了 (le)"改写下列句子。

Rewrite the following sentences using the aspectual particle 了 (le).

例：　　我看电影。　──　我看了一个电影。

Model:　　　　　　──　我看（了）电影了。

  1. 他听广播。
  2. 我预先通知他。
  3. 运动员们上场。
  4. 他丢一副手套。
  5. 他给我们介绍沙漠地区的情况。
  6. 她在五年里掌握三种外语。
  7. 明天他下课以后去你那儿。
  8. 我上月在上海认识一位老知识分子。
  9. 他跟爱人一起写出一本三十万字的小说。
  10. 那个研究所为国家培养一批年青的研究工作人员。

（二）把下列句子改成疑问句，并用否定式回答。

Turn the following into interrogative sentences and give negative answers.

例：　　我吃了饭了。　──　你吃饭了没有？

Model:　　　　　　没有。（我没吃。）

1. 他出院了。

2. 她脱了厚毛衣了。

3. 我敲了门了。

4. 他在银行存了一些钱。

5. 那个偷东西的人逃走了。

6. 昨天他画了一张山水画。

7. 他向我道歉了。

8. 我们交换了对这件事的看法。

9. 他们座谈了学习方法的问题。

10. 他们搜集了许多有关森林的资料。

（三）改正下列病句。

Correct the following sentences.

1. 他去了医院。

2. 他们下了课。

3. 他在我宿舍坐坐了。

4. 去年夏天我们常游泳了。

5. 上次美国留学生没看了足球比赛。

6. 我们没买了那种瓷器。

7. 昨天我们在友谊宾馆不看节目。

8. 他们俩已经翻译了完那篇文章。

9. 明天下午他看朋友再买东西。

10. 明天我们去公园了。

第四节　动 作 将 要 发 生

Section IV　An Action That is Going to Take Place

一、表示动作将要发生的形式

Forms expressing an action that is going to take place soon

汉语里要表示一个动作将要发生时，可以用副词"要"和语气助词"了"形成的"要…了"。基本格式是：

The pattern 要…了 formed by the adverb 要 and the modal particle 了 may be used to indicate that an action is going to take place relatively soon. The basic pattern is:

（主语）——状语（副词"要"）——谓语（动词）——（宾语）——"了"

(Subject) + adverbial adjunct (the adverb 要) + predicate (verb) + (object) + 了

例如：
Examples:

　　　我们要毕业了。
　　　他要出院了。
　　　要开学了。

二、用"要…了"表示动作将要发生的特点
　　Grammatical features

（一）表示将要发生动作的动词或动宾、动补词组放在"要…了"中间，"了"在句尾。例如：

Verbs or V-O, V-C phrases indicating that an action is going to take place should be inserted into 要…了 in which 了 is at the end of the sentence. For example:

　　　春天要来了。
　　　飞机要起飞了。
　　　运动员要入场了。

（二）"要…了"前边可以加副词"就、快、马上、眼看、将"等作状语，表示动作很快要发生。例如：

要…了 may be premodified by adverbs such as 就，快，马上，眼看，将， etc., indicating that an action is going to take place very soon. For example:

461

客人就要来了。　　火车马上要开了。

冬天快要到了。　　眼看要到时间了。

西瓜快要熟了。　　夜幕将要降临了。

（三）主要表示将来时间发生，但也表示过去时间的"将要发生"。例如：

要…了 mainly indicates that an action is going to take place in the future, but it also indicates that an action was going to take place sometime in the past. For example:

昨天飞机要起飞的时候，忽然下雨了。（过去）

(Past)

（四）动作将要发生的否定形式常用"还没…（呢）"这个格式。例如：

The pattern 还没…（呢）is used to indicate that an action has not yet taken place.　For example:

他还没离开学校（呢）。

他还没叠完衣服（呢）。

学校还没放假（呢）。

三、使用"要…了"表示动作将要发生时需要注意的问题

Points that merit special attention

（一）如要表示动作立刻要发生，常在"要…了"前加副词"就"，而且可以在"就要"前边或主语前边用上表示时间的词或词组。例如：

To indicate that an action is about to take place, we often use the adverb 就 in front of 要…了, furthermore we may use time nouns or phrases before 就要 or before the subject. For example:

我们一月十五号就要考试了。

明天我就要回国了。

（二）如要表示动作很快要发生，常在"要…了"前边加副词"快"，也可以只说"快…了"。例如：

To indicate that an action is going to take place immediately, we often place the adverb 快 in front of 要…了, or one can simply say 快…了 only. For example:

风快（要）停了。

衣服快（要）干了。

她快（要）当大夫了。

他姑姑快（要）成为地理专家了。

在用"快（要）…了"表示动作将要发生的句子里，前边不能用表示具体时间的词或词组。不能说"明年我们快毕业了"或"他三点快来了"等。

In a 快（要）…了 sentence indicating that an action is going to take place, no words or phrases denoting concrete time can be used in front of it, therefore, one can not say 明年我们快毕业了, 他三点快来了, etc.

（三）表示过去时间里的动作将要发生时，动词后边不能用语气助词"了"。例如：

The modal particle 了 can not be used when an action in the past was going to take place. For example:

昨天客人要到的时候，我父亲刚从外边回来。

去年他要访华（访问中国）的时候，我正在北京。

（四）提问形式和回答方法。

Asking about an action that is going to take place and ways to answer.

如要询问一个动作是否将要发生时，一般在用"要…了"的陈述句句尾加上语气助词"吗"或"吧"。肯定式的回答可以只用"对"或"是"；否定式的回答常用"还没（有）呢"。例如：

Normally the modal particle 吗 or 吧 is added to the end of a declarative sentence using 要…了 to inquire whether an action is going to take place. The affirmative answer may be made by using 对 or 是 only, while 还没（有）呢 is often used for the negative. For example.

> 报告会就要开始了吗?

> 对。（就要开始了。）

> 还没（有）呢。

> 你们七月就要放暑假了吧？

> 是。

> 还没定呢。还不一定。

（五）"将要…了"一般用于书面语。例如：

将要…了 is generally used in written Chinese. For example：

> 我们将要分别了。

> 她将要出席本届联合国大会了。

练 习 44
Exercise 44

（一）用表示动作将要发生的 "要…了" 改写下列句子。

Rewrite the following sentences using 要…了 indicating that an action is going to take place.

例： 他们下个月进行毕业实习。

Model： ──他们下个月要进行毕业实习了。

1. 他发言。
2. 我们迟到。
3. 他们学校七月放假。
4. 他们回来。
5. 码头工人卸货。
6. 音乐会结束。
7. 队伍马上出发。
8. 明天上午中央民族歌舞团到北京。
9. 五分钟以后我们登上山顶。

10．欢迎新同学的晚会开始。

（二）给下列句子填上"就"或"快"。

Insert 就 or 快 in the following sentences.

例：　　北京一点三刻要到了。

Model：　　——北京一点三刻就要到了。

1．我们今天下午要离开中国了。

2．他们俩要结婚了。

3．他马上要起床了。

4．演出五分钟以后要开始了。

5．船三点要开了。

6．联合组织要成立了。

7．学校要放暑假了。

8．商店要关门了。

9．天要黑了。

10．先进工作者大会下午两点要开始了。

（三）改正下列病句。

Correct the following sentences.

1．下星期一她快要来北京了。

2．他明年九月快要当中学教师了。

3．报名日期月底快要截止了。

4．这条重要新闻七点快要广播了。

5．那座办公大楼下星期快要盖好了。

6．那两个国家今年十二月快要正式建交（建立外交关系）了。

7．全市人民代表大会五月六号快要召开了。

8．他父亲写的那本书下半年快要出版了。

9．参加这次国际会议的代表们明天快要到了。

10．那个国家的驻华（中国）大使馆三天以后快要正式办公了。

第五节　动作的过去经历

Section V　Actions as Past Experience

一、表示动作过去经历的形式

Forms expressing an action as past experience

汉语里要表示过去曾经有过某种经历时，可以在谓语动词后边加上动态助词"过 (guo)"。基本格式是：

To express a certain experience in the past, one can place the aspectual particle 过 (guo) after the predicate verb. The basic pattern is:

主语——谓语（动词）——"过"——（宾语）

Subject + predicate (verb) + 过 + (object)

例如：

Examples:

他来过。　　　　　　　他学过中医。

我吃过这种药。　　　　他没有灰过心。

我尝过她做的菜。

二、用动态助词"过"表示动作过去经历的特点

Grammatical features

（一）宾语要放在动词谓语和动态助词"过"后边。例如：

The object should be placed after the "predicate verb +过" phrase. For example:

我看过这个电影。

他去过那儿。

（二）谓语动词前边可以同时用副词"曾经"。例如：

Besides 过, the adverb 曾经 can be used before the predicate verb. For example:

466

我曾经学过法文。

他曾经去过非洲。

她曾经表演过芭蕾舞。

（三）动作过去经历的否定形式是在谓语动词前边加副词"没"。例如：

The negative form for an action as past experience is made by placing the adverb 没 before the predicate verb. For example:

"没" ——谓语动词—— "过"

没 + predicate verb + 过

我没看过这个电影。

他没学过西班牙文。

她没去过北京图书馆。

回答时的否定式可以只用"没有"。例如：

The negative answer can be made by using 没有 only. For example:

你见过这种珍奇的动物吗？

没有。（我没见过。）

三、使用动态助词"过"表示动作过去经历时需要注意的问题

Points that merit special attention

（一）谓语动词和动态助词"过"。

The predicate verb and the aspectual particle 过.

1. 动词谓语如带宾语，宾语只能放在助词"过"后边，而不能插在谓语动词和"过"中间。例如：

If the verb predicate takes an object, the object should only occur after the particle 过 rather than between the predicate verb and 过. For example:

我看过京剧。

他去过日本。

一定不能说成"我看京剧过"或"他去日本过"。

One can never say 我看京剧过 or 他去日本过.

2．动词谓语如带结果补语，结果补语要紧跟在动词谓语后边，放在谓语动词和助词"过"中间，而不能放在"过"之后。例如：

If it takes a complement of result, the predicate verb is immediately followed by the complement of result, i.e. between the predicate verb and the particle 过 rather than after 过. For example:

> 他看见过我哥哥。
> 那个医生治好过我的病。

一定不能说成"他看过见我哥哥"或"那个医生治过好我的病"。

One can never say 他看过见我哥哥 or 那个医生治过好我的病".

（二）不能用于表示动作完成状态的动词，一般也不能用于表示动作的过去经历。见第二章第十一节四"（三）动态助词和动词"2。

As actions that have no perfect aspect usually can not take place as past experience, verbs expressing such actions can not be used with 了 or 过 either. See Point 2 of "The aspectual particles and the verb", 4 (3), Section XI, Chapter Two.

（三）否定式里，谓语动词后边的动态助词"过"必须保留。例如：

In the negative form, the aspectual particle 过 after the predicate verb must be kept. For example:

> 他没听过这个歌。
> 我们没谈过这件事。

如果不保留"过"，意思就变了。

The meaning will be changed without 过.

（四）提问形式和回答方法。

Asking about an action as past experience and ways to

answer.

如要询问是否有过某种经历时，常用下面三种形式。

The following three forms are often used to inquire whether an action has taken place as past experience.

1. 在用动态助词"过"的陈述句句尾加上"没有"。例如：

没有 is added to the end of a declarative sentence with the aspectual particle 过. For example:

主语——谓语（动词）——"过"——（宾语）——"没有"？

Subject + predicate (verb) + 过 + (object) + 没有？

你洗过海水澡没有？

洗过。

没洗过。

他们来过这里没有？

来过。

没来过。

2. 在用动态助词"过"的陈述句句尾加上"吗"。例如：

吗 is added to the end of a declarative sentence with the aspectual particle 过. For example:

她演过话剧吗？

演过。

没演过。

你爬过这座山吗？

爬过。

没爬过。

3. 并列"谓语动词——'过'"的肯定、否定形式。例如：

Parallel the affirmative and the negative forms of the "predicate verb + 过" phase For example:

你们去（过）没去过桂林？

去过。

没去过。

他搞（过）没搞过这样的设计？

搞过。

没搞过。

问句中第一个"过"可以省去不用。

The first 过 in the above questions is optional.

不论用哪种形式提问，肯定式的回答都可以只用"谓语动词——'过'"，否定式的回答都可以只用"没有"或"'没'——谓语动词——'过'"。

All of the above three types of questions can be answered affirmatively by using the "predicate verb + 过" phrase alone and they can be answered negatively simply by a "没有/没 + predicate verb + 过" phrase.

（五）状语在用动态助词"过"的句中的特点。

Features of the adverbial adjunct in a sentence using the aspectual particle 过.

1．状语表示的时间必须是确定的。例如：

The time referred to by the adverbial adjunct must be definite. For example:

昨天我们在海边散过步。

去年他们游览过长城。

不能说成"我们常常在海边散过步"或"有一天他们游览过长城"。

It's wrong to say 我们常常在海边散过步 or 有一天他们游览过长城.

2．否定句中如有介词结构作状语，否定副词"没（有）"一般放在介词结构前边。例如：

The negative adverb 没（有）is normally placed before the prepositional phrase if there is one in a negative sentence used as an adverbial adjunct. For example:

我们没在那儿游过泳。

他没给我们讲过课。

我没跟他一起工作过。

练 习 45
Exercise 45

（一）用表示过去经历的动态助词"过"改写下列句子。

Rewrite the following sentences using the aspectual particle 过 indicating an action as past experience.

例：　　他去中国。

Model：　　──他去过中国。

1. 她一直没有失望。
2. 两年以前他姐姐在中国工作。
3. 那个工厂去年生产这种药。
4. 这位著名的医生给我父亲治病。
5. 那个地区有这种传染病。
6. 他十三岁的时候在这个中学学习。
7. 去年我看了两次国际乒乓球比赛。
8. 他写博士论文的时候参考了这几本书。
9. 我哥哥在小学学英语，在中学学日语，在大学学西班牙语。
10. 他们学校的登山运动员去年受到严格的训练。

（二）把下列句子改成否定式。

Turn the following negative.

例：　　我们学过这个歌。

Model：　　──　我们没学过这个歌。

1. 他在农村劳动过。
2. 别人批评过他。
3. 他拒绝过他朋友的邀请。

4． 他观察过这儿的地理状况。

5． 上星期我请过事假。

6． 他们测量过这条河。

7． 老师给我们讲过这个学校的历史。

8． 我们征求过他对这次试验的意见。

9． 那位教授指导过新来的研究生。

10． 我们学院上星期一举行过一次学术报告会。

（三）把练习（二）的句子改成句尾带"没有"的问句。

Turn the sentences in（二）interrogative ending with 没有.

例： 我们学过这个歌。

Model： ——你们学过这个歌没有？

附表八：五种动作状态的简要情况表
Table 8: The Five Aspects of an Action

动作状态 Aspects	例 句 Examples	表示的意义 Functions	基本格式 Basic patterns	结构特点 Structural features	动作状态的时间 Time	否定形式 Negative forms	正反式提问形式和回答 Affirmative-negative questions and short answers
动作的进行 Progressive	他们正在开会呢。	表示动作正在进行。 Indicating an action is going on	主—状（正、在或正在）—谓（动词）—（宾）+呢。 S + adv. adjunct 正、在 or 正在 + PV + (O) + 呢.	谓语动词前常用副词"正、在、正在"；语气助词"呢"只能放在句尾。 The adverbs 正, 在, 正在 are often used before the predicate verb; the modal particle 呢 can only be put at the end of a sentence.	可指过去、现在或将来，用时间词或词组表示。 Used in past, present or future with time nouns or phrases.	"没—谓（动词）—（宾）"。 没+PV+(O).	

| 动作的持续
Continuous | 他抱着一个孩子。 | 表示动作或动作结果在持续。Continuation of an action or the result of an action. | 主—谓（动词）—"着"—（宾）。S + PV + 着 + (O) | 宾语要放在动态动词"着"后边；可和"正在…呢"并用。The object is placed after the aspectual pariticle 着; 着 can be used together with 正在…呢 | 同上。Ditto. | "没"—谓（动词）—"着"—（宾）。没 + PV + 着 + (O). | 谓（动词）—"着"—"没"—"有"？PV + 着 + 没 + 有？
谓（动词）—"着"—"没"—谓（动词）—"着"？PV + 着 + 没 · + PV + 着？
谓（动词）—"着"—"呢"。"着"—"着"呢？PV+着+呢·
"没"—谓（动词）—"着"。没 + PV + 着。 |

动作的完成 Perfect	他答应了。	表示动作的实现或完成。 Realiza-tion or comple-tion of an action	主—谓（动词）—"了"—（宾）。 S + PV + 了 + (O).	宾语要放在动态助词"了"后边；"谓（动词）—了"—宾（一个词）"不能独立成句。 The object is placed after the aspectual particle 了. "PV + 了 + O (one word)" can not be used by itself.	同上。 Ditto.	"没"—谓（动词）—（宾）。 没 + PV + (O).	谓（动词）"了"—"没有"? PV + 了 + 没有? 谓（动词）—"没"—谓（动词）? PV + 没 + PV? 谓（动词）"了"—没有。 PV + 了 + 没. "没有"—谓（动词）。 没有 - PV.
动作将要发生 Action about to happen	我们要毕业了。	表示动作将要发生。 An action that is going to take place	（主）—状要—谓（动词）—（宾）—"了"。 (S) + adv. adjunct 要 + PV + (O) + 了。	"要"前边可用副词"就"、"快"等。 Adverbs 就, 快 etc. may be used before 要.	一般用于将来。 Normally used in the future.	"还没"—谓（动词）—（宾）—"呢"。 还没 + PV + (O) + 呢。	

475

| 动作的过去经历 Past experience | 他治过这种病。 | 表示过去有过某种经历。 An action as past experience | 主—谓(动词)—"过"—(宾)。 S + PV + 过 + (O). | 宾语要放在动态助词"过"后边；谓语动词前常用副词"曾经"。 The object should be placed after the aspectual particle 过; the adv. 曾经 is often used before the predicate verb. | 一般用于过去。 Normally used in the past. | "没"—谓(动词)—"过"—(宾)。 没 + PV + 过 + (O). | 谓(动词)—"过"—"没有"? PV + 过 + 没有? 谓(动词)—"过"—"没"—谓(动词)—"过"? PV+过+没+PV+过? 谓(动词)—"过"。 PV + 过. 没有。 没有. "没"—谓(动词)—"过"。 没+PV+过. |

第七章　特殊的动词谓语句

Chapter Seven　Sentences with Special Verbal Predicates

第五章已介绍过单句的种类，其中动词谓语句的一般句式是"主语──谓语动词──（宾语）"。还有几种谓语部分结构比较特殊的动词谓语句，常见的有：

In Charpter Five we discussed different types of simple sentences. Among them is the sentence with a verb predicate whose basic pattern is: "Subject + predicate verb + (object)". Apart from this, there are several types of sentences with verb predicates whose structures are quite special. Here are those that are commonly used:

"是"字句

The 是-sentence

"有"字句

The 有-sentence

"把"字句

The 把-sentence

"被"字句

The 被-sentence

连动句

Sentences with verbal constructions in series

兼语句

Pivotal sentences

存现句

Existential sentences

本章将分节进行介绍。

They will be dicussed separately in the following sections.

第一节 "是" 字句

Section I   The 是-sentence

一、什么叫 "是" 字句 Definition

以动词 "是" 作谓语的句子，叫 "是" 字句。"是" 字句的基本格式是：

Sentences with 是 as the predicate are known as 是-sentences. The basic pattern is:

主语—— "是" ——宾语

Subject + 是 + object

例如：

Examples:

你是我们的好朋友。　　三加五是八。

房子后边是块草地。　　我工作的单位是新华书店。

我是电影公司的。

"是" 字句的 "是" 可以表示不同的意思。（见第二章第二节第四项中动词 "是"）

是 in a 是-sentence may indicate various meanings. (Refer to Verb 是 in 4, Section II, Chapter II)

二、"是" 字句的特点 Grammatical features

（一）主语和宾语的构成成分。

Constituents of the subject and the object.

1．"是" 字句的主语可以是名词、代词、动词、形容词、数量词组、联合词组、"的"字结构、动宾词组、补充词组、偏正词组、主谓词组、方位词组、同位词组。例如：

The subject of the 是 -sentence may be a noun, a pronoun, a verb, an adjective, a N-Mw phrase, a coordinative phrase, a 的-phrase, a V-O phrase, a complementary phrase, an endocentric phrase, an S-P phrase, a locality phrase, or an appositive phrase. Here are some examples:

主人是小高的姑姑。 （名词）
(Noun)

您是我们的朋友。 （代词）
(Pronoun)

参观也是一种学习。 （动词）
(Verb)

热心是他的特点。 （形容词）
(Adjective)

十四点是下午两点。 （数量词组）
(N-Mw phrase)

主观和客观是一个问题的两个方面。
（联合词组）
(Coordinative phrase)

不幸的是他摔伤了。 （"的"字结构）
(的-phrase)

听音乐是我的一种爱好。 （动宾词组）
(V-O phrase)

休息得好是很重要的条件。 （补充词组）
(Complementary phrase)

太骄傲是他的缺点。 （偏正词组）
(Endocentric phrase)

他们来是交流经验的。 （主谓词组）
(S-P phrase)

电影院西边是俱乐部。　　　（方位词组）
　　　　　　　　　　　　　（Locality phrase）
我们俩都是演员。　　　　　（同位词组）
　　　　　　　　　　　　　（Appositive phrase）
　　2．动词谓语"是"后边的宾语可以是名词、代词、动词、形容词、数量词组、联合词组、"的"字结构、动宾词组、主谓词组、补充词组、偏正词组、同位词组。例如：

The object following the predicate verb 是 may be: a noun, a pronoun, a verb, an adjective, a N-Mw phrase, a co-ordinative phrase, a 的-phrase, a V-O phrase, an S-P phrase, a complementary phrase, an endocentric phrase, or an appositive phrase. Following are some examples:

他是知识分子。　　　　　　（名词）
　　　　　　　　　　　　　（Noun）
他说的那位同志是你。　　　（代词）
　　　　　　　　　　　　　（Pronoun）
这也是休息。　　　　　　　（动词）
　　　　　　　　　　　　　（Verb）
他的特点是谦虚。　　　　　（形容词）
　　　　　　　　　　　　　（Adjective）
这是三百克。　　　　　　　（数量词组）
　　　　　　　　　　　　　（N-M phrase）
这些东西是书、本子和笔。（联合词组）
　　　　　　　　　　　　　（Coordinative phrase）
这个杯子是红的。　　　　　（"的"字结构）
　　　　　　　　　　　　　（的-phrase）
他最喜欢的是唱歌。　　　　（动宾词组）
　　　　　　　　　　　　　（V-O phrase）
这次的旅行计划是大家一起走。　（主谓词组）
　　　　　　　　　　　　　（Subject-Predicate phrase）

我们的任务是捆好。　　　（补充词组）
(Complementary phrase)

我的意见是明天去。　　　（偏正词组）
(Endocentric phrase)

跳舞的是她们姐妹三个。（同位词组）
(Appositive phrase)

（二）动词谓语"是"后边不能带补语或动态助词"了"、
"着"、"过"。〔见第二章第二节第四项中（三）〕

The verb predicate 是 can not take complements or any of the aspectual particles 了，着，过. (Refer to 4 (3), Section II, Chapter Two)

（三）动词谓语"是"前边可以加副词状语。例如：

Adverb-adverbial adjuncts can occur before the verb predicate 是. For example:

明天又是星期六了。

他已经是国家干部了。

这位可能是新请来的专家。

（四）"是"字句的否定式是在谓语动词"是"前边加否定
副词"不"。否定的"是"字句的基本格式是：

The negative form of the 是-sentence is formed by placing the negative adverb 不 before 是. The basic pattern of the negative 是 -sentence is:

主语——"不是"——宾语

Subject + 不是 + object

例如：

Examples:

她不是大夫。

那儿不是研究所。

他不是司机。

三、使用"是"字句需要注意的问题

Point that merit special attention

（一）动词"是"在任何情况下形式都不变，可以表示任何时间、任何地点、任何人或事物，没有时间、状态、人称、性别或单复数的区别。例如：

The verb 是 remains unchanged in form under all circumstances. It can denote any time, place, person or thing and undergoes no morphological changes of time, aspect, person, gender or number. For example:

她是我姑妈。	他们是作家。
我是他弟弟。	这是摩托车。
去年他是学生。	现在是下午四点。
今年他是教师。	

（二）"是"字句的否定式

The negative form of the 是-sentence

1. 动词"是"的否定式一定要用"不是"，否定副词"不"要放在"是"前边，汉语里一定不能说成"是不"，这一点要特别注意。例如：

The negative form of the verb 是 must be 不是 with the negative adverb 不 placed before 是. What should be particularly noted is that the form 是不 does not exist in Chinese. Study the following examples:

他不是中国人。

这不是你的眼镜。

前面那座楼不是电视大楼。

一定不能说"他是不中国人"、"这是不你的眼镜"、"前面那座楼是不电视大楼"等。

It's ungrammatical to say 他是不中国人，这是不你的眼镜，前面那座楼是不电视大楼， etc.

2. 除了少数表示范围的副词可以放在"不"和"是"的中

间以外，其他副词一般都不能插入。例如：

Except for a few adverbs of range, generally speaking, other adverbs cannot be inserted between 不 and 是, for example:

> 他们不都是学生。
>
> 他不只是一个作家。
>
> 这些原料不全是他们工厂的。

（三）"的"字结构作"是"的宾语时，"的"前边可以是名词、代词、动词、形容词、数量词组、联合词组、动宾词组、主谓词组、补充词组、偏正词组，这样的宾语常常是表示主语的类别的。例如：

When a 的-phrase serves as the object of 是，的 can be preceded by a noun, a pronoun, a verb, an adjective, a N-Mw phrase, a coordinative phrase, a V-O phrase, an S-P phrase, a complementary phrase or an endocentric phrase. A 的-phrase as the object of 是 is often used to categorize the subject. For example:

这支笔是老师的。	（名词）
	（Noun）
那块手绢是他的。	（代词）
	（Pronoun）
这只鸡是吃的。	（动词）
	（Verb）
他的头发是黄的。	（形容词）
	（Adjective）
这种罐头是一斤的。	（数量词组）
	（N-Mw phrase）
这些信是他和他妹妹的。	（联合词组）
	（Coordinative phrase）
他是送信的。	（动宾词组）
	（V-O phrase）

他是我们请来的。　　　　（主谓词组）
　　　　　　　　　　　　（S-P phrase）

这些碗是洗干净的。　　　（补充词组）
　　　　　　　　　　　　(Complementary phrase)

这间卧室是他哥哥的。　　（偏正词组）
　　　　　　　　　　　　(Endocentric phrase)

（四）表示存在的"是"和"在"。

是 and 在 indicating existence.

1. 要说明某处存在的物体是某物时，可以用下列格式表示：

The following pattern may be used to show what the object existing in a certain place is:

表示方位的词或词组（主语）——动词"是"（谓语）——表示所处、人或事物的词或词组（宾语）

Locality noun or phrase (subject) + the verb 是 (predicate) + noun or phrase of place, person or thing (object)

例如：

Examples:

旁边是一片草地。　　　操场中间是足球场。
前边是一条小河。　　　他后边是一个衣柜。
食堂西边是学生宿舍区。　桌子上是一些书和报。
学校对面是一个研究院。　我和他中间是老马。

表示方位的词或词组前边不用介词"在"，不说"在旁边是一片草地"、"在前边是一条小河"等。这些"是"也不能换用"在"，不能说"食堂西边在学生宿舍区"、"他后边在一个衣柜"等。

The preposition 在 can not occur before a locality noun or phrase. One can not say 在旁边是一片草地, 在前边是一条小

484

河．etc. 是 in the above sentences can not be replaced by 在,
so one can not say 食堂西边在学生宿舍区, 他后边在一个衣柜,
etc.

表示存在的"是"字句里，主语和宾语不能颠倒过来，不能
说"一片草地是旁边"或"足球场是操场中间"等。

The positions of the subject and the object in the 是-
sentence indicating existence are not commutable, so one
can not say 一片草地是旁边 or 足球场是操场中间, etc.

2．如要表示某人、某事物存在于某处时，谓语要用动词"在"，
格式如下：

If one wants to express "somebody or something exists
in a certain place", the verb 在 should be used as the predicate.
Here is the pattern:

表示人或事物的词或词组（主语）——动词"在"（谓语）
——表示方位的词或词组（宾语）

Noun or phrase of personal or non-personal reference
(subject) + the verb 在 (predicate) + Noun or phrase of place
(object)

例如：

Examples:

研究院在学校对面。　　花园在后边。

老马在我和他中间。　　停车场在前边。

（五）"是"表示等同时，"是"前后的主语和宾语可以互
换，意思没什么变化。例如：

When 是 indicates equality, the subject preceding 是 and
the object following it are commutable without affecting the
meaning. For example:

中华人民共和国的首都是北京。

——北京是中华人民共和国的首都。

《一件小事》的作者是鲁迅。

　　　　　　　　——→鲁迅是《一件小事》的作者。

　　　　　桂林是我的家乡

　　　　　　　　——→我的家乡是桂林。

　　（六）谓语动词"是"表示判断、存在、等同、类别时不能
省略。例如：

When the predicate verb 是 indicates judgment, existence,
equality or category, it can not be left out. For example:

　　　　　　这是眉毛。　　　　　　九减三是六。

　　　　图书馆旁边是实验室。　　那种药是治感冒的。

不能说"这眉毛"或"图书馆旁边实验室"等。

One does not say 这眉毛 or 图书馆旁边实验室，etc.

练　习　46
Exercise 46

（一）把下列"是"字句改成否定式。

Turn the following sentences negative.

例：

Model: 那是黑板。——→那不是黑板。

　1．那是广播站。

　2．这个消息是我们听到的。

　3．这辆电车是去北海的。

　4．这是一个秘密。

　5．这两张船票是那位先生的。

　6．排球队的队员都是南方人。

　7．他是外科大夫。

　8．跳远比赛的冠军是他。

　9．那个录音机是他刚买的。

　10．广场南边是历史博物馆。

11. 我后边是张明。

12. 这个主意是他出的。

13. 今天是星期二。

14. 高方是我妹妹。

15. 滑雪是他的爱好。

（二）把练习（一）中的"是"字句改成正反疑问句。

Turn the 是-sentences in （一） into affirmative-negative questions.

例：

Model:　　那是黑板。——→那是不是黑板？

（三）改正病句。

Correct the following sentences.

1. 这是不豆子。

2. 这句话是不他说的。

3. 他是我旁边。

4. 俱乐部是体育馆西边。

5. 球场北边是不游泳池。

6. 今天是不星期天。

7. 电影院是旅馆东边。

8. 那件事情是不关于他的。

9. 那几位旅客日本人。

10. 这那位老人的皮帽子。

第二节　"有"字句

Section II　The 有-sentences

一、什么叫"有"字句　Definition

以动词"有"作谓语的句子，叫"有"字句。"有"字句的基本格式是：

Sentences with the verb 有 as the predicate are known as 有-sentences. The basic pattern of a 有-sentence is:

主语——"有"——宾语

Subject + 有 + object

例如：

Examples:

她有很多钱。	明天他们有约会。
我有一些体会。	一天有二十四小时。
他有经验。	我们都有《汉语课本》。
现在我有事。	

"有"字句的"有"可以表示不同的意思。（见第二章第二节第四项中动词"有"）

有 in the 有-sentence may have various meanings. (Refer to Verb 有, in 四, Section II, Chapter Two)

二、"有"字句的特点 Grammatical features

（一）主语和宾语的构成成分。

Constituents of the subject and object.

1．"有"字句的主语可以是名词、代词、动词、数量词组、联合词组、"的"字结构、方位词组、同位词组等。例如：

The subject in the 有-sentence may be a noun, a pronoun, a verb, a N-Mw phrase, a coordinative phrase, a 的-phrase, a locality phrase or an appositive phrase. For example:

飞机场有很多架飞机。	（名词）
	(Noun)
他有照片。	（代词）
	(Pronoun)
休息有很多方式。	（动词）
	(Verb)
一斤有十两。	（数量词组）

488

                                        (N-M phrase)

他和我有一个学习计划。   （联合词组）
                                        (Coordinative phrase)

申请奖学金的有十几个人。   （"的"字结构）
                                        (的-phrase)

公园里有很多人。   （方位词组）
                                        (Locality phrase)

他们几个人都有飞机票了。   （同位词组）
                                        (Appositive phrase)

2．动词谓语"有"后边的宾语可以是名词、代词、联合词组、"的"字结构、同位词组等。例如：

The object following the verb predicate 有 may be a noun, a pronoun, a coordinative phrase, a 的-phrase or an appositive phrase. For example:

我有地图。   （名词）
                                        (Noun)

参加舞会的有她。   （代词）
                                        (Pronoun)

他有一台录音机和一台电视机。   （联合词组）
                                        (Coordinative phrase)

我有蓝的。   （"的"字结构）
                                        (的-phrase)

家里只有她们母女俩。   （同位词组）
                                        (Appositive phrase)

（二）动词谓语"有"前边可以加副词状语。例如：

The verb predicate 有 may be premodified by adverb adverbial adjuncts. For example:

明天我也许有时间。

他们下星期六还有活动。

他经常有约会。

489

我们都有今天的电影票。

（三）谓语动词"有"后边可以带动态助词"了"、"过"，但不能带补语。例如：

The predicate verb 有 can take the aspectual particles 了，过 after it, but it can not take a complement. For example:

我的家乡有了很大的变化。

现在他们都有了幸福的家庭。

这位老人有过那样的想法。

图书馆有过这种刊物。

（四）"有"字句的否定式是在谓语动词"有"前边加否定副词"没"，基本格式是：

The negative form of the 有-sentence is made by placing the negative adverb 没 before the predicate verb 有. The basic pattern of the negative form of 有-sentence is:

主语——"没有"——宾语

Subject + 没有 + Object

例如：

Examples:

他们没有矛盾。　　　今天没有风。

我没有蓝的。　　　　我没有这种圆珠笔。

三、使用"有"字句需要注意的问题

Points that merit special attention

（一）在表示不同时间、人称、性别或单复数的"有"字句里，"有"的形式都不变。例如：

The form of 有 remains unchanged in the 有-sentence despite any change of time, person, gender or number. For example:

一年有十二个月。　　你们有地图吗？

她有一个哥哥。　　　前边有一座桥。

后天学校里有舞会。

（二）"有"字句的否定式。

The negative form of the 有-sentence.

1．"有"的否定形式是"没有"。否定副词"没"要放在"有"前边，汉语里一定不能说成"有没"或"不有"。这一点要特别注意。例如：

The negative form of 有 is always 没有，with the negative adverb 没 preceding 有．The learner should especially note that 有没 or 不有 never occur in Chinese. Study the following examples:

> 我没有中国地图。　　他今天没有时间。
>
> 客厅里没有他。　　　这个月没有三十一天。

一定不能说"我有没中国地图"、"他今天有没时间"或"客厅里不有他"、"这个月不有三十一天"等。

One can never say 我有没中国地图，他今天有没时间 or 客厅里不有他，这个月不有三十一天，etc.

2．一般情况下，"没有"后边不用数词"一"和量词构成的数量词组，不说"他没有一支钢笔"，而说"他没有钢笔"。如要说明数量不多，不够满足要求，可在"没有"后边用"很多、许多、好些"或其他数量词组作宾语或宾语的定语。例如：

Generally speaking, a "一 + measure word" phrase does not occur after 没有，one does not say 他没有一支钢笔，instead one say 他没有钢笔．If one wants to express the idea "the quantity is not big enough to meet the needs", then 很多，许多，好些 or other N-Mw phrases may be placed after 没有 as the object or an attributive of the object. For example;

> 他没有很多钱，只有五块钱。
>
> 他没有两支钢笔，只有一支。

3．"没有"后边有宾语时，可以省略为"没"。例如：

When 没有 is followed by an object, the short form 没 can be used. For example:

他没（有）收音机。

但单独回答问题或在句尾时要用"没有"。例如：

But 没有 must be used when answering questions by itself, or when it occurs at the end of a sentence. For example:

你有没有录音机？　　　　没有。

他有字典没有？　　　　　没有。

练 习 47

Exercise 47

（一）把下列"有"字句改成否定式。

Turn the following sentences negative.

例：

Model:　　他有汉英词典。—→他没有汉英词典。

1. 明天有雨。
2. 小李现在有一点儿事。
3. 他们有证明。
4. 我家有这种花。
5. 她有一本日记。
6. 他叔叔有一个儿子。
7. 他们都有这种鞋。
8. 这个学校有游泳池。
9. 那个运动员有二十几岁。
10. 他们组有十二个人。

（二）把练习（一）中的"有"字句改成正反疑问句。

Turn the above sentences into affirmative - negative questions.

例：　　他有汉英词典。　—→他有没有汉英词典？

Model:　　　　　　　　（或：他有汉英词典没有？）

（三）把下列"有"字句改成用"是不是"的疑问句：

Turn the following sentences into questions with 是不是：

例：　　我有一个姨。——→你是不是有一个姨？

Model：　　　　　　　　　（或：你有一个姨是不是？）

　　　　　　　　　　　　（或：是不是你有一个姨？）

1．他外祖父有一些珍贵的资料。

2．他有一个美好的理想。

3．一公斤这样的西红柿有五个。

4．那位老大爷有两个孙女。

5．学校旁边有一个商店。

6．那个俱乐部有二十个工作人员。

7．电影院对面有个邮局。

8．我的老师有很多外国学生。

9．前边那条小河上没有桥。

10．明天上午没有四节课。

（四）改正病句。Correct the following sentences.

1．我有没世界地图。

2．明天有没体育课。

3．他不有小汽车。

4．桌子上不有铅笔和尺。

5．他爸爸有没六十岁。

6．这些苹果不有十公斤。

7．在一个学年里有两个学期。

8．弟弟没有一个照相机。

9．墙上有画儿没？　没。

10．外边有树没？　有两棵。

第三节 "把"字句

Section III The 把-sentence

一、什么叫"把"字句 Definition

由介词"把"及其宾语作状语的动词谓语句叫"把"字句，表示对某人、某事物施加某种动作并强调使某人、某事物产生某种结果或影响。"把"字句的基本格式是：

A sentence with a verb predicate modified by the preposition 把 and its object is called the 把 -sentence. The 把-sentence indicates that an action is applied to somebody or something with the emphasis that the action will bring about a result or influence. The basic pattern is:

施事者——介词"把"——受事者——动词——其他成分
（主语）　　　（状语）　　　（谓语）

Doer of the action + the preposition 把 + receiver of the action + verb + (subject) (adverbial adjunct) (predicate)

other elements

例如：

Examples:

> 他把鸡蛋吃了。
>
> 你们把照相机带着。
>
> 弟弟把伞弄坏了。
>
> 我把设计图带来了。
>
> 你把地扫扫。
>
> 队长把队员召集起来了。
>
> 大家把会场布置得漂亮极了。

我把您的电话号码记一下。

我们把东西放在他那儿。

老张把这本小说翻译成英文了。

她把论文交给马教授了。

司机同志把老大娘送到火车站了。

二、"把"字句的特点 Grammatical features

（一）"把"字句的主语一定是施事者，是动词谓语表示的动作的发出者。例如：

The subject of a 把-sentence must be the doer of the action, denoted by the verb predicate. For example:

他把那个剧本看完了。

（剧本是"他"看的，而且"看完"了。

用一般的句式表示是：他看完那个剧本了。 ）

(The play is read by他, and he has finished the action of reading.

The normal form is: 他看完那个剧本了.)

她把那篇散文拿走了。

（散文是"她"拿的，而且"拿走"了。

用一般句式表示是：她拿走了那篇散文。 ）

(The prose is taken by她 and she took it away.

The normal form is: 她拿走了那篇散文.)

（二）"把"字句里介词"把"的宾语在意义上是动词谓语代表的动作的接受对象，即受事者。例如：

Notionally the object of 把 in a 把-sentence is the recipient or receiver of the action indicated by the verb predicate. For example:

我们把那只公鸡吃了。

（"吃"的就是"公鸡"。

用一般句式表示是：我们吃了那只公鸡了。 ）

(What we have eaten is the 公鸡.

The normal form is: 我们吃了那只公鸡了.）

他把收音机关上了。

（"关"的就是"收音机"。

用一般句式表示是：他关上收音机了。）

(What he has turned off is the 收音机.

The normal form is: 他关上收音机了.）

（三）"把"字句的谓语一定是及物动词，而且一般是能支配或影响介词"把"的宾语的。例如：

The predicate in a 把-sentence must be a transitive verb and normally a verb that can govern or influence the object of 把. For example:

她把头发剪短了。	（可以说"剪头发"）
	(We may say 剪头发)
他把地理教材借去了。	（可以说"借教材"）
	(We may say 借教材)
我们把奖学金领来了。	（可以说"领奖学金"）
	(One may say 领奖学金)

（四）"把"字句的动词谓语后边一般都要带其他成分，说明动作的结果或影响。谓语动词后边的"其他成分"可以是动态助词"了"或"着"、重叠的动词、各种补语等。例如：

The verb predicate of the 把-sentence is usually followed by some other element (like the aspectual particles 了 or 着, the repetition of the verb or a complement of any kind) to indicate the result or effect of the action. For example:

你把瓶里的桔子水喝了。	（助词"了"）
	(The particle 了)
你把那个包提着。	（助词"着"）
	(The particle 着)
我把邮票贴上了。	（结果补语）
	(Complement of result)

他把那张纸踩脏了。　　　（结果补语）
　　　　　　　　　　　　　（Complement of result）

他把客人送出去了。　　　（趋向补语）
　　　　　　　　　　　　　（Directional complement）

他们把树根埋得很深。　　（程度补语）
　　　　　　　　　　　　　（Complement of degree）

我们把衣服收拾一下吧。　（数量补语）
　　　　　　　　　　　　　（Complement of quantity）

我把这双鞋刷刷。　　　　（重叠的动词）
　　　　　　　　　　　　　（Reduplicated verb）

（五）少数动词如"在、到、成、给"等充当动词谓语的补语时，用"把"字句。例如：

When the few verbs like 在，到，成，给， etc. act as the complement of predicate verb, a 把-sentence is used. For example：

他把桌子上的粉笔放在盒子里了。

她把那个小女孩儿抱到我面前。

我把这些句子翻译成汉语了。

（六）介词"把"前边可以带状语。例如：

The preposition 把 can have an adverbial adjunct before it. For example：

你快把雨衣穿上。

她下星期四把研究计划送来。

你应该把那句多余的话改掉。

他也把这件事忘了。

（七）"把"字句的否定式一般是在介词"把"前边用否定副词"没（有）"。例如：

The negative form of the 把-sentence is normally made bv using the negative adverb 没（有）before the preposition 把. For example：

大会主席没把话讲完。

工作人员还没把大会决议印出来。

他没把回信带来。

那个作家还没把他的新小说写好。

三、使用"把"字句需要注意的问题

Points that merit special attention

（一）没有支配或影响人或事物的作用的动词一般不能充当"把"字句的谓语。例如：

Generally speaking, verbs that can not be applied to govern or influence people or things are not used as the predicate of the 把-sentence. These verbs include:

1. 不表示动作变化的动词，如：

Those that do not indicate change, such as:

是　有　在　象　姓　等于……

2. 表示感知的一些动词，如：

Those that denote senses, such as:

知道　认识　觉得　同意　听　听见　懂……

3. 表示心理活动的一些动词，如：

Those that express mental activity, such as:

怕　喜欢　愿意　希望……

4. 表示始终的动词，如：

Those that indicate commencement, continuation or conclusion, such as:

开始　继续　出发　完……

5. 表示趋向的动词，如：

Those that indicate direction, such as:

进　出　上　下　起　过　回　来　去……

6. 表示躯体本身动作的动词，如：

Those that indicate physical movement, such as:

坐　站　立　躺　蹲　睡……

不能说"他们把礼堂进了"、"我把他的主张同意了"或
"他把椅子坐了"等。

One cannot say 他们把礼堂进了，我把他的主张同意了 or
他把椅子坐了， etc.

（二）介词"把"的宾语一般是确指的，前边常有指示代词
或其他定语，或者是指对话双方都明确的人或事物。例如：

The object of the preposition 把, which is usually premodified by an attributive (such as a demonstrative pronoun, etc.),
is normally definite or refers to a person or thing known to
both the speaker and the hearer. For example:

他把盘子里的那条鱼吃了。

（他吃的是"盘子里的那条鱼"）

(What he has eaten is 盘子里的那条鱼)

他把蚊子打死了。

（他打的是刚才叮人的"蚊子"）

(What he hit is the 蚊子 that bit him just now)

（三）"把"字句的谓语动词后边要有"其他成分"。

In a 把-sentence, the predicate verb must be followed by
some other element.

1． 不能只用一个单音动词。例如：

A monosyllabic verb can not be used by itself. For
example:

我们把录音机打开。

他把字典买来了。

他把那杯茶喝了。

不能说"我们把录音机打"、"他把字典买"或"他把那杯
茶喝"等。

One can not say 我们把录音机打, 他把字典买 or 他把那
杯茶喝， etc.

2． 除少数带结果意义的双音动词外，一般双音动词也不能

用作"把"字句的谓语。例如，我们可以说：

In general, dissyllabic verbs can not act as the predicate of a 把-sentence, but the resultative dissyllabic verbs of result are exceptions, e.g. one can say:

　　　　他们已经把这个问题解决了。

　　　　我们一定把这个任务完成。

不能说"我们把礼堂布置"、"他把事情的经过叙述"等。

One can not say 我们把礼堂布置，他把事情的经过叙述，etc.

　　3. 可能补语不能用在"把"字句动词谓语后边，不能说"我把作业做得完"。"把"字句里要用助动词"能"或"可以"等表示可能的意思，如"我能把作业做完"。

A potential complement does not occur after the verb predicate in a 把-sentence, so one can not say 我把作业做得完. Instead, the auxiliary verb 能 or 可以 that expresses possibility should be used, e.g. 我能把作业做完。

　　4. 动态助词"过"不能用于"把"字句的谓语动词后边，不能说"他把这种点心吃过"等。

The aspectual particle 过 does not occur after the predicate verb in a 把-sentence. One can not say 他把这种点心吃过, etc.

　　（四）有些谓语动词后边的结构比较复杂，必须用介词"把"将谓语后边的动作对象移到谓语动词的前边。常见的有下面几种。

Some predicate verbs are followed by fairly complicated constructions, thus the object of the action after the predicate should be brought forward to before the predicate verb. These constructions include the following:

　　1. 动词"在"作动词谓语的结果补语，后边带表示处所的宾语，说明人或事物通过动作的影响而处于某地时，必须用"把"字句。例如：

The verb 在 taking an object of locality, acts as the complement of result for the verb predicate, showing where the person or thing is as the result of the action.   For example:

　　　　他把省下来的钱存在银行里。

　　　　他把别人送的画报都摆在书架上了。

　　　　我把那张彩色照片挂在墙上。

　　　　他把邮票贴在信封上了。

　　　　她把洗干净的衣服放在床上了。

不能说"他存省下来的钱在银行里"、"我挂那张彩色照片在墙上"等。

One can not say 他存省下来的钱在银行里, 我挂那张彩色照片在墙上, etc.

2　动词"到"作动词谓语的结果补语，后边带表示处所的宾语，说明人或事物受到动作的影响而达到某处时，必须用"把"字句。例如：

The verb 到 taking an object of place, acts as the complement of result for the verb predicate, showing where the person or thing has arrived as the result of the action. For example:

　　　　他把汽车开到大门口了。

　　　　姑娘把那匹马牵到草原上去了。

　　　　社员们把种子撒到地里了。

　　　　他们把受伤的战士送到医院了。

　　　　裁判把那两个运动员叫出球场去了。

3.　动词"给"作动词谓语的结果补语，后边带表示对象的宾语，说明人或事物通过动作的媒介达到了某对象处，这时必须用"把"字句。例如：

The verb 给 with an object indicating the recipient of the action acts as the complement of result for the verb predicate, showing that the person or thing reaches where another person or thing is through the action. For example:

　　　　他把火车票交给了我。

售货员把一个绿色的杯子递给他。

代表团团长把团员们介绍给大家。

我把那本汉语词典送给朋友了。

一般不说"他交火车票给了我"、"团长介绍团员们给大家"等。

One generally does not say 他交车票给了我，团长介绍团员们给大家， etc.

4．动词"成"作动词谓语的结果补语，后边带表示结果的宾语，说明人或事物通过动作的影响成为某种人或物时，必须用"把"字句。例如：

The verb 成 with an object of result functions as the complement of result for the verb predicate, showing that the person or thing indicated by the object of 把, affected by the action, has become one of another kind. For example:

那个魔术师把纸变成花儿了。

我们把座位摆成圆形了。

我们把这些肯定句改成否定句了。

那个研究生把自己研究的心得写成论文了。

不能说"那个魔术师变纸成花儿了"、"我们改这些肯定句成否定句了"等。

One can not say 那个魔术师变纸成花儿了，我们改这些肯定句成否定句了，etc.

5．动词谓语后边带复合趋向补语和表示处所的宾语时，必须用"把"字句。例如：

The 把-sentence must be used when the verbal predicate takes a compound directional complement and an object of place. For example:

老师把新同学带进教室来了。

大夫把那个病人送回家去了。

我们把这几件东西搬上楼去吧。

（五）表示假设或不准备对某人某事物施加某动作时，"把"字句也可以用否定副词"不"表示否定。例如：

The negative adverb 不 may be placed before 把 to indicate negation if we want to express a supposition or unwillingness to carry out a certain action towards a certain person or thing. For example:

> 我不想把这件事告诉他。
>
> 他不愿意把时间浪费掉。
>
> 你为什么不把你的意见说出来？
>
> 你不把病养好，就不能参加下个月的活动。

练 习 48
Exercise 48

（一）把下列句子改成"把"字句。

Turn the following into 把-sentences.

例：

Model:　　他喝完汤了。——→他把汤喝完了。

1. 我做完今天的家庭作业了。

2. 他写完毕业论文了。

3. 鸡吃光了地上的米。

4. 弟弟撕破了爸爸看的报。

5. 大家都戴上了耳机。

6. 他已经穿好了大衣。

7. 妈妈拿出来了刀子和叉子。

8. 他领来了奖学金。

9. 工人们修好了那条公路。

10. 那只猴子拿走了小朋友给的花生。

（二）把练习（一）项改成的"把"字句再改成否定式。

Turn the 把-sentences in Exercise （一）into the negative form.

例：

Model:　　他把汤喝完了。——→他没把汤喝完。

（三）完成下列"把"字句。

Complete the following 把-sentences.

例：

Model:　　他把那本小说看__完__了。

1. 他把桌上的水擦_____了。

2. 那位同志把开会的通知告诉_____了。

3. 我把自行车骑_____了。

4. 他把手表戴_____了。

5. 我们把电扇关_____了。

6. 服务员把饭菜送_____了。

7. 他把眼镜掉到_____了。

8. 老师把那个句子写在_____了。

9. 他把今天晚上芭蕾舞的票给_____了。

10. 昨天我把那几张照片寄给_____了。

11. 我们几个人把乒乓球台子抬到_____了。

12. 风把桌子上的报纸刮到_____了。

13. 他把刚买的水果放在_____了。

14. 我们把他送的花插在_____吧。

15. 那个青年把自己的雨衣挂在_____了。

16. 她把那件毛衣洗_____了。

17. 我的朋友把那篇报道翻译成_____了。

18. 我们把那些句子改_____吧。

19. 那个作家把他最近写的书送给_____了。

20. 明天你们大家都把字典带_____。

（四）改正病句。

Correct the following sentences.

1. 他把面包吃。
2. 我把不懂的地方写。
3. 我朋友把我的信带。
4. 他把存在银行里的钱取。
5. 我把墙上的画儿拿。
6. 他写自己的名字在本子上。
7. 我写"本子"成"木子"了。
8. 同学们把这些资料看得完。
9. 我们放这些点心在盘子里。
10. 我昨天不把那封信寄出去。
11. 他把那块绸缎没送给别人。
12. 他一定能把这个问题解决得了。
13. 弟弟藏他的脏衣服在床底下。
14. 那个技术员改这种机器成新的了。
15. 他把要洗的衣服放在洗衣机了。

第四节 "被" 字 句

Section IV The 被-sentence

一、什么叫 "被" 字句 Definition

由表示被动的介词"被"及其宾语作状语的动词 谓 语 句 叫
"被"字句,说明某人、某事物受到某动作的影响而产生某种结
果。"被"字句所叙述的行为多表示主语不愿发生 或 受 到 损 害
的,其基本格式是:

The sentence with a verb predicate which is modified by
the passive preposition 被 and its object as an adverbial adjunct
is called the 被-sentence. The 被-sentence expresses that a
person or thing (the subject) is subject to a certain result with

the influence of the action, and, more often that not, it describes an action that the subject is not willing to accept or an action from which the subject will suffer. The basic pattern of the 被-sentence is: S + 被 + O₁ + V + ～ : Sは O に V された

受事者——介词 "被"——施事者——动词——其他成分
（主语）   （状　　语）   （谓语）

| Receiver of the action | + | the preposition 被 | + | doer of the action | + verb + |
| (subject) | | (adverbial adjunct) | | (predicate) | |

other elements

例如：

Examples:

铁路被大水冲坏了。

那些运动员被观众围住了。

那块骨头被狗吃了。

那块布被他们弄湿了。

他的母亲被敌人杀死了。

那棵树被大风刮倒了。

这件事被他们知道了。

刚才说的话被她听见了。

我被老师批评了。

我们都被录取了。

二、"被"字句的特点　Grammatical features

（一）"被"字句的主语一定是受事者，是接受谓语所表示的动作的对象，可以指人或事物。例如：

The subject, either of personal or non-personal reference, of the 被-sentence must be the receiver or recipient of the action indicated by the predicate. For example:

那位科学家被我们请来了。

（"请"的对象是"那位科学家"。

506

用一般句式表示是：我们请来了那位科学家。）

(The object of 请 is 那位科学家.

The normal form is: 我们请来了那位科学家.)

那个特务的阴谋被公安人员粉碎了。

（"粉碎"的对象是"那个特务的阴谋"。

用一般的句式表示是：公安人员粉碎了那个特务的阴谋。）

(The object of 粉碎 is 那个特务的阴谋.

The normal form is: 公安人员粉碎了那个特务的阴谋.)

（二）"被"字句里介词"被"的宾语在意义上是谓语表示的动作的发出者，即施事者，有时可以省略。例如：

The object of the preposition 被 is the agent or doer of the action indicated by the predicate in meaning, but it can be omitted sometimes. For example:

那只大象被捉住了。

（一般是指"人"捉住了"那只大象"。

(Normally it implies that some people have caught 那只大象.)

他的病被治好了。

（一般是指"医生"治好了"他的病"。）

(Normally it implies that 医生 has cured 他的病.)

窗户被吹开了。

（一般是指"风"吹开了"窗户"。）

(Normally it implies that 风 has blown open the 窗户.)

（三）"被"字句的谓语一定是及物动词，而且一般是能支配或影响句中主语的。例如：

The predicate in a 被-sentence must be a transitive verb

that normally can govern or affect the subject. For example:

飞机场工人的罢工被政府镇压了。

（可以说"镇压罢工"。）

(One may say 镇压罢工.)

那个破瓶子被我扔了。

（可以说"扔瓶子"。）

(One may say 扔瓶子.)

我的网球拍子被小王借走了。

（可以说"借拍子"。）

(One may say 借拍子.)

（四）"被"字句的动词谓语后边一般都要带"其他成分"，说明动作的结果或影响。谓语动词后边的"其他成分"可以是动态助词"了"或"过"、补语、宾语等。例如：

The verb predicate in a 被-sentence is normally followed by some other element indicating the result or influence of the action. The "other element" may be the aspectual particle 了 or 过, a complement, an object, etc. For example:

她被大家说服了。　　（助词"了"）

　　　　　　　　　　（Particle 了）

他们被老师表扬过。　　（助词"过"）

　　　　　　　　　　（Particle 过）

浴室被他俩弄脏了。　　（结果补语）

　　　　　　　　　　（Complement of result）

礼堂被大家布置得很漂亮。（程度补语）

　　　　　　　　　　（Complement of degree）

哥哥被他朋友叫出去了。（趋向补语）

　　　　　　　　　　（Directional complement）

那套纪念邮票被他送给朋友了。

　　　　　　　　　　（结果补语和宾语）

　　　　　　　　　　（Complement of result and object）

那张小方桌被他们搬到那个房间去了。

（结果补语和宾语）

(Complement of result and object)

他被人推了一下。　　　（数量补语）

(Complement of quantity)

（五）介词"被"前边可以带状语。例如：

An adverbial adjunct may occur before the preposition
被. For example:

那个男孩子昨天被狗咬了。

我的自行车刚被人骑走。

我也被朋友拉去了。

（六）"被"字句的否定式一般都是在介词"被"前边加否
定副词"没（有）"。例如：

The negative form of the 被-sentence is generally made
by placing the negative adverb 没（有）before the preposition
被. For example：

那只小羊没被老虎咬伤。

这支队伍从来没被敌人打败过。

我的手没被开水烫伤。

桌子上的东西没被人动过。

那个村子没被占领。

（七）口语里常用介词"叫"或"让"表示"被动"，后边
一定要带宾语。例如：

In spoken Chinese, the preposition 叫 or 让 is often applied
to indicate the passive, though they must be followed by an
object. For example:

他让汽车撞伤了。

那对花瓶叫人拿走了。

她的帽子叫风刮掉了。

我的毛巾让水冲走了。

三、使用"被"字句需要注意的问题

Points that merit special attention

（一）没有支配或影响作用的动词一般不能充当"被"字句的谓语。〔参看本章第三节第三项中（一）〕

Verbs that can not govern or influence normally can not act as the predicate in a 被-sentence. (See （一）in 三, Section III, Chapter Seven)

（二）如不必或不能说出具体的主动者时，介词"被"或"叫、让"的宾语可以用表示泛指的"人"。例如：

When it is not necessary or impossible to tell the actual doer of the action, the word 人 of generic reference can be used as the object of the preposition 被，叫 or 让. For example:

> 张大夫被人请去了。
>
> 录音机被人搬到别的教室去了。
>
> 我们让人锁在房间里了。
>
> 院子里的花儿叫人摘了。

但介词"被"与"叫、让"的用法不完全相同。介词"被"可以不带宾语（主动者），直接用在动词谓语前边，只表示主语是被动的。这是其他介词所没有的一种特殊用法，可以算是一种省略。例如：

But the usage of the prepositions 被 and 叫，让 is not always the same. 被 may be placed directly before the verb predicate without taking an object (the doer of the action), showing only that the subject is passive. This is a unique usage that other prepositions do not have. It may be considered a kind of elliptical construction. Study the following examples:

> 那个姑娘被欺骗了。
>
> 这位师傅被选作工人代表了。
>
> 帝国主义被赶出中国了。
>
> 图书馆的新书都被借出去了。

而介词"叫、让"后边一定要带宾语（主动者），这一点要特别注意。例如：

Notice that the prepositions 叫, 让 must have objects (doers of the action). For example:

> 作报告的同志让我们请来了。
>
> 我的秘密叫他知道了。
>
> 图书馆的新书都让人借走了。

不能说"作报告的同志让请来了"或"图书馆的新书都叫借走了"等。

One can not say 作报告的同志让请来了 or 图书馆的新书都叫借走了, etc.

（三）"被"字句的谓语动词后边一定要有其他成分。

The predicate verbs must be followed by some other element in a 被-sentence.

1．不能只用一个单音动词。例如：

A monosyllabic verb can not be used by itself. For example:

> 他被朋友请去了。
>
> 桌上的报被我弄湿了。

不能说"他被朋友请"、"桌上的报被我弄"等。

One can not say 他被朋友请, 桌上的报被我弄, etc.

2．可能补语不能用在"被"字句的动词谓语后边。不能说"屋子被他收拾得干净"等。

A potential complement can not be placed after the verb predicate in a 被-sentence. One can never say 屋子被他收拾得干净, etc.

3．动态助词"着"不能用于"被"字句中谓语动词后边，不能说"那本书被他拿着"等。

The aspectual particle 着 can not be used after the predicate verb in a 被-sentence. One can not say 那本书被他拿着, etc.

（四）有些不能发出动作的事物作主语时，后边的动词谓语本身就带有被动的意思，汉语里如不需要特别指明主动者（或施事者），一般不用介词"被"。这种句子可以叫作意义上表示被动的句子。例如：

In Chinese, when the subject of a sentence is something that can not do any action, the verb predicate itself can express the passive, therefore, if it is not especially necessary to specify the doer of the action, the preposition 被 is not used. These can be called notionally passive sentences. Here are some examples:

> 字写了。
> 墨水送来了。
> 身体检查了。

不说"字被写了"、"墨水被送来了"或"身体被检查了"等。

One does not say 字被写了，墨水被送来了 or 身体被检查了，etc.

练 习 49
Exercise 49

（一）把下列"把"字句改成"被"字句。

Turn the following 把-sentences into 被-sentences.

例：

Model:　他把那瓶汽水喝了。——→那瓶汽水被他喝了。

1. 我们把敌人打败了。
2. 他把电视机弄坏了。
3. 虫子把这几棵菜咬坏了。
4. 她把暖水瓶打碎了。
5. 大风把广告刮破了。

512

6．我把这张画儿的颜色涂坏了。

7．他把屋子里的东西都弄乱了。

8．我们把院子里的雪扫到一边去了。

9．战士们把那些枪运走了。

10．孩子们把那些小椅子搬到院子里去了。

（二）把下列"被"字句改成否定式。

Turn the following 被-sentences into the negative form：

例：　　　那辆摩托车被人骑坏了。

Model：　　　──→那辆摩托车没被人骑坏。

1．排球被人拿走了。

2．那只狼被人捉住了。

3．那条黑狗被人打死了。

4．树上的叶子被风刮下来了。

5．那条路已经被那些工人铺好了。

6．那个村子被占领了。

7．我们的申请被批准了。

8．那个售货员被商店经理叫去了。

9．那个沙漠地区被征服了。

10．我的脖子被蚊子咬了。

第五节　连 动 句

Section V　Sentences with Verbal
Constructions in Series

一、什么叫连动句　Definition

两个（或两个以上）动词或动词性词组用在同一个句子里，担任同一个主语的谓语，这样的动词谓语句叫连动句。连动句的基本格式是：

A sentence in which two or more verbs or verbal constructions are used as the predicate of the same subject is called a sentence with verbal constructions in series. The basic pattern is:

主语——谓语1——（宾语1）——谓语2——（宾语2）

Subject + predicate₁ + (object₁) + predicate₂ + (object₂)

例如：

Examples:

我去看。　　　　　我有时间看报。

我去看杂技。　　　她买酸牛奶喝。

他骑自行车去。　　他骑自行车去公园玩。

他骑自行车去公园。

二、连动句中前后两个谓语动词的关系

Relations between the two predicate verbs in a sentence with verbal constructions in series

（一）后一动词表示前一动词的目的。例如：

The second verb indicates the purpose of the first. For example:

我去寄信。

他去南京旅行。

两个谓语动词都可以带宾语。例如：

Both predicate verbs can take objects. For example:

同学们进城看杂技了。

我们找他谈重要的事情。

（二）前一动词及其宾语表示后一动词的手段、方式。例如：

The first V-O construction indicates the means or manner of the second. For example:

他用左手写。

我坐飞机去。

她们坐飞机去广州。

我们用汉语谈话。

（三）后一动词表示前一动词的目的，而前一动词的宾语在意义上也是后一动词的动作对象。前一动词要带宾语，后一动词一般不带宾语。例如：

The second verb indicates the purpose of the first whose object is notionally also that of the second, so generally the second verb does not have an object of its own. For example:

我倒水喝。

他买衣服穿。

我们自己做饭吃。

他要你的设计图看看。

（四）前一动词是"有"，后一动词常是补充说明"有"的宾语的用途的；"有"的宾语在意义上也是后一动词的动作对象。前一动词要带宾语，后一动语带不带宾语都可以。例如：

When the first verb is 有, the second is usually one giving information on the way to use the thing indicated by the object of 有. Notionally, the object of 有 is also that of the second verb which can go with or without an object of its own. For example:

我有笔用。

他们都有报纸看。

我们有新项目要研究。

我有几个问题问老师。

我每天都有时间锻炼身体。

今天老师没有参考材料发给大家。

三、连动句的特点 Grammatical features

（一）连动句的谓语可以是两个动词。例如：

The predicate of a sentence with verbal constructions in series may be only two verbs. For example:

我去找。

他们来参观。

（二）连动句的谓语动词可以都带宾语，也可以是其中任何一个动词带宾语。例如：

The predicate verbs of a sentence with verbal constructions in series may both take objects or only one of them may take an object. For example:

> 我去找他。
>
> 我去图书馆找。
>
> 我去宿舍找他。

（三）状语一般放在第一个谓语动词前边。例如：

An adverbial adjunct, if there is any, is normally placed before the first predicate verb. For example:

> 你快去告诉他。
>
> 他想乘车去。
>
> 我们也坐船去旅行。
>
> 小张要买一份说明书看。
>
> 他们现在有机会学习技术。

（四）否定式一般在第一个谓语动词前用否定副词"不"或"没有"。例如：

The negative form is generally made by placing the negative adverb 不 or 没有 before the first predicate verb. For example:

> 他们不去旅游了。
>
> 我们不来这儿看电视了。
>
> 我没挨他坐。
>
> 今天咱们没工夫谈下去了。

四、使用连动句需要注意的问题

Points that merit special attention

（一）连动句里两个谓语动词的前后次序是不能改变的，否则意思就变了，或者就不成话了。例如：

The order of the two predicate verbs can not be changed, otherwise, the meaning of the sentence will be changed, or the

516

sentence will not make any sense. For example:

1. 我去宿舍叫他。

（"去宿舍"的目的是"叫他"。）

(The purpose of 去宿舍 is 叫他.)

我叫他去宿舍。

（"叫他"的目的是"去宿舍"。）

(The purpose of 叫他 is 去宿舍.)

2. 我倒凉开水喝。

（把凉开水倒在杯子里，再喝凉开水。）

(First I poured cold water into the glass, then drank it.)

如果倒过来说"我喝倒凉开水"，就不成话了。

If the order is reversed and the sentence will become 我喝倒凉开水 which does not make any sense at all.

尤其需要注意的是：表示方式、手段的动词及其宾语一定要放在前边。例如：

It must be specially noted that verbs indicating means and manner together with their objects should be placed before other verbs. For example:

他用英语讲课。

我用钢笔写信。

她骑自行车去朋友家。

不能说成"他讲课用英语"、"我写信用钢笔"或"她去朋友家骑自行车"。

It will be another structure if one says 他讲课用英语, 我写信用钢笔 or 她去朋友家骑自行车.

（二）连动句中如果要强调动作已完成，一般是在句尾用助词"了"，或者把助词"了"放在第二个谓语动词后边。例如：

In a sentence with verbal constructions in series, if one wants to emphasize the completion of an action, one normally puts the aspectual particle 了 at the end of the sentence, or after the second predicate verb. Study the following examples:

> 他们都去礼堂听报告了。
>
> 他们去礼堂听了一个报告。
>
> 我们去阅览室看了一会儿画报。

不能说"他们去了礼堂听报告"等。

One can not say 他们去了礼堂听报告, etc.

（三）连动句中如有表示时间的状语可以放在句首。例如：

An adverbial adjunct indicating time in a sentence with verbal predicates in series occurs at the beginning. For example:

> 下午你到办公室找我一下。
>
> 三年以前她来中国访问过。

但不能把状语放在第二个谓语动词前边。不能说"他们去都看电影了""他来中国三年以前访问过"等。

But one can never put the adverbial adjunct before the second predicate verb. One can not say 他们去都看电影了 or 他来中国三年以前访问过， etc.

（四）连动句的否定式。

The negative forms of a sentence with verbal constructions in series.

1. 连动句的否定形式是把否定副词"不"或"没（有）"放在第一个谓语动词前边，否定的是整个谓语部分，不能把否定副词放在第二个谓语动词前边。例如：

The negative form of a sentence with verbal constructions in series is made by putting the negative adverb 不 or 没（有） before the first predicate verb. As what one negates is the whole predicate part, the negative adverb can never be put before the second predicate verb. For example:

> 我不出去买东西。
>
> 他不坐汽车进城。

一般不说"我出去不买东西"、"他坐汽车不进城"。

Generally speaking, one does not say 我出去不买东西,
他坐汽车不进城。

2. 第一个谓语动词为"有"的否定式是"没有"。例如:

When the first predicate verb is 有, the negative form is
没有. For example:

　　　　他没有时间去公园。

　　　　我没有本子用了。

一定不能说"他不有时间去公园"、"我不有本子用了"。

One can never say 他不有时间去公园,我不有本子用了。

(五)动词性联合词组作谓语,不属于连动句。例如:

A sentence with a coordinative phrase as predicate (as in
the following) is not considered a sentence with verbal constructions in series. For example:

　　　　她们在写诗画画儿。

　　　　天天早上他都打太极拳、散步。

　　　　他每星期天上午写信、会客。

这些联合词组中的动词次序可以颠倒,意思没什么变化。也
可以说成:

The verbs in these coordinative phrases can be reversed
without affecting the meaning.　One can well say:

　　　　她们在画画儿、写诗。

　　　　天天早上他都散步、打太极拳。

　　　　他每星期天上午会客、写信。

(六)连动句和动词性联合词组作谓语的区别。

Differences between a sentence with verbal constructions in
series and one with coordinative verbal phrases as the predicate.

这两者在形式上有些相似,需要注意区分。请看下表:

They are similar in form in some ways, so attention should
be called to their differences.　See the following table:

连动句 Sentences with verbal constructions in series	动词性联合词组作谓语的句子 Sentences with coordinative verbal phrases as the predicate
例句： 他上街买东西。 Example:	例句： 她们跳舞、唱歌。 Example:
1.两个动词或动词性词组的次序固定，不能颠倒 The order of the two verbs or verbal phrases is fixed, and it can not be reversed.	两个动词或动词性词组的次序可以颠倒 The order of the two verbs or verbal phrases can be reversed
2.两个动词或动词性词组不是并列的关系，而是说明和被说明的关系 The two verbs or verbal phrases are not in coordination, but in a modification relation	两个动词或动词性词组是并列的关系 The two verbs or verbal phrases are in coordination
3.不能加关联词语，不能说：他又上街又买东西。 Correlatives can not be used. One can never say 他又上街又买东西	能加关联词语 Correlatives can be used: 他们又跳舞又唱歌。
4.前后意义连贯，中间没有语音停顿 The two verbal constructions make complete sense and no pause is allowed in speaking.	前后意义联系不大，中间可有语音停顿 The two verbal phrases are not so closely related to each other in meaning and there may be a pause in speaking.

练　习　50

Exercise 50

（一）完成下列连动句。

Complete the following sentences with verbal constructions in series.

例：

Model：　他坐出租汽车去大使馆

1．我们一起去上海＿＿＿＿＿＿＿＿＿。

2．同学们都进城＿＿＿＿＿＿＿＿＿。

3．我要找老师＿＿＿＿＿＿＿＿＿。

4．大家走路＿＿＿＿＿＿＿＿＿。

5．晚上我们去电影院＿＿＿＿＿＿＿。

6．昨天他去邮局＿＿＿＿＿＿＿＿。

7．我们常用英语＿＿＿＿＿＿＿＿。

8．他借书＿＿＿＿＿＿＿＿＿＿。

9．我烧开水＿＿＿＿＿＿＿＿＿。

10．我们用钢笔＿＿＿＿＿＿＿＿。

11．他们有可能＿＿＿＿＿＿＿。

12．最近我没有空＿＿＿＿＿＿＿。

（二）把下列连动句改成否定式。

Turn the following sentences into the negative form.

例：

Model：　他刚才骑车回家了。—→他刚才没骑车回家。

1．他们去公园玩儿了。

2．我们去游泳池游泳。

3．老师去他们班讲课。

4．我去图书馆还书。

5. 我找他们下棋。

6. 咱们买几瓶汽水喝吧。

7. 我们有地方踢球。

8. 他有时间打网球。

9. 我有兴趣滑冰。

10. 他打电话通知我了。

11. 这儿有椅子坐。

12. 他每天用盐水漱口。

13. 我屋里有箱子放衣服。

14. 现在他有工作做了。

15. 他跟中国朋友用汉语聊天。

16. 我母亲去大使馆参加宴会了。

17. 我朋友常用圆珠笔写信。

18. 我开汽车去北京（飞）机场。

第六节 兼语句

Section VI Pivotal Sentences

一、什么叫兼语句 Definition

一个句子里有两个谓语，前一个谓语（动词）的宾语兼作后一谓语的主语，这个成分叫兼语，这样的动词谓语句叫兼语句。兼语句的基本格式是：

Of the two predicates in a sentence the object of the first predicate (verb) is at the same time the subject of the second one. This element is called the pivot and sentences with verb predicates of this kind are known as pivotal sentences. The basic pattern of pivotal sentences is as follows:

主语——谓语（动词）——兼语——兼语的谓语

Subject + predicate (verb) + pivot + predicate of the pivot

例如：

Examples:

他请我去。

（"请"的宾语和"去"的主语都是"我"，

"我"是兼语）

（我 is the object of 请 and the subject of 去, i.e.

the pivot.）

我们让他来我们这儿。

（"让"的宾语和"来"的主语都是"他"，

"他"是兼语）

（他 is the object of 让 and the subject of 来,

i.e. the pivot.）

老师叫我们念课文。	（"我们"是兼语）
	(我们 is the pivot)
我有一个哥哥很勇敢。	（"哥哥"是兼语）
	(哥哥 is the pivot)
外边有人敲门。	（"人"是兼语）
	(人 is the pivot)
是校长请您。	（"校长"是兼语）
	(校长 is the pivot)
这个好消息使人兴奋得很。	（"人"是兼语）
	(人 is the pivot)

二、兼语句中两个谓语动词的关系

Relations between the two predicate verbs in a pivotal sentence

（一）兼语的谓语表明前一个动作要达到的目的、产生的结果。例如：

The pivotal predicate indicates the purpose and result of the action indicated by the first verb in the sentence. For example:

我们请你唱一支歌。

我求姐姐去一趟。

虚心使人进步，骄傲使人落后。

（二）前一个谓语是动词"有"，兼语的谓语（动词或形容词等）说明前一个谓语的宾语（兼语）"做什么"或"怎么样"例如：

When the first predicate is the verb 有, the pivotal predicate (a verb, an adjective, etc.) clarifies the pivot or the object of the first predicate 做什么 or 怎么样. For example:

我有几个朋友来北京了。

屋子里有人说话。

他有一把伞很好看。

（三）前一个谓语是动词"是"，兼语的谓语动词起解释说明的作用。例如：

When the first predicate is the verb 是, the pivotal predicate is an explanatory verb. For example:

是老马帮助他。

是外语系组织这次活动。

三、兼语句的特点 Grammatical features

（一）谓语的构成成分。

The constituents of the predicate.

1. 兼语句有两个谓语。第一个谓语由动词充当，而且带宾语，这宾语又是第二个谓语的主语，即兼语。

A pivotal sentence has two predicates of which the first one is performed by a verb that takes an object and the object, i.e. the pivot, is at the same time the subject of the second predicate.

2. 前一谓语一般由表示请求、使令等意义的动词充当。如："请、让、叫、使、命令、禁止"等。

In general, verbs indicating request, command, etc. act

as the first predicate, e.g. 请，让，叫，使，命令，禁止，etc.

3. 兼语的谓语可以是动词或形容词等。例如：

The pivotal predicate may either be a verb or an adjectives.
For example:

大家想请您谈谈感想。	（动词）
	(Verb)
我们一定选老张当代表。	（动词）
	(Verb)
这件事使我很难过。	（形容词）
	(Adjective)
他们有一个小女孩很活泼。	（形容词）
	(Adjective)

（二）兼语的谓语（动词）后边可以带宾语。例如：

The pivotal predicate (verb) can take an object. For example:

他请我们去他家。

我们班有三个男同学参加比赛。

是他们要出租汽车。

（三）两个谓语前都可以带状语。例如：

Both predicates can be modified by adverbial adjuncts. For
example:

他昨天请我们吃饭。

老师常常让我们互相学习。

我留他多住几天。

这件事的确使我们非常高兴。

（四）兼语的谓语（动词或形容词）后边可以带补语。例如：

The pivotal predicate (verb or adjective) can take a complement after it. For example:

他有一个姐姐跳舞跳得很好。

大家让你准备得好一点儿。

这个城市有一个公园安静极了。

（五）有些兼语句没有主语，称为无主语兼语句；第一个谓语常用动词"请"、"有"或"是"。例如：

Some pivotal sentences have no subject and they are called subjectless pivotal sentences. In such sentences verb 请, 有 or 是 often serves as the first predicate. For example:

> 请你不要大声说话。
> 有一件衬衫从楼上掉下来了。
> 外边有人找你。
> 上星期六是我给你打电话。

（六）兼语句的否定式一般是在第一个谓语前用否定副词"没（有）"或"不"。例如：

The negative form if the pivotal sentence is generally made by placing the negative adverb 没（有）or 不 before the first predicate. For example:

> 他没请我们看京戏。
> 大夫没让我吃这种药。
> 敌人的严密控制并没使我们屈服。
> 我们这儿没有人叫山本。
> 父亲不让我们这样做。
> 不是我要租这套房子。

四、使用兼语句需要注意的问题

Points that merit special attention

（一）第一个谓语（动词）和兼语之间不能插入其他成分。例如：

No element can be inserted between the first predicate (verb) and the pivot. For example:

> 他请我们去他家。
> 他请我们明天去他家。
> 明天他请我们去他家。
> 他明天请我们去他家。

不能说"他请明天我们去他家"。

One can not say 他请明天我们去他家。

（二）谓语（动词）"有"的宾语一般是不定指的人或事物，常带数量定语。例如：

The object of the predicate (verb) 有 is normally indefinite and often has N-Mw attributive before it. For example:

刚才有一位同志来看你。

我有好几本新书很有意思。

（三）兼语句的第一个谓语还可以由表示鼓动、选派、赞扬、怨恨等动词充当。例如：

Verbs indicating agitation, selection, praise, resentment, etc. may also act as the first predicate in a pivotal sentence. These verbs in clude:

1．求、要、需要……

例如：　　　我求你去办一件事，可以吗？

Examples:　老张，现在要小王马上来吧。

2．祝、鼓励、号召、动员……

例如：　　　祝你身体健康。

Examples:　上级命令他们立刻出发。

3．留、接、带、教育、帮、帮忙……

例如：　　　他经常帮那位老大爷做事。

Examples:

4．夸、夸奖、称赞……

例如：　　　人人夸他是个好青年。

Examples:

5．嫌、怨、恨、讨厌……

例如：　　　大家都嫌他态度不够好。

Examples:

（四）兼语句的否定式。

The negative forms of the pivotal sentence.

1. 表示请求、使令一类的动词作第一个谓语时，兼语句的否定式一般是在第一个谓语前边加否定副词"没（有）"或"不"。

When verbs indicating request or command serve as the first predicate, the negative form of the pivotal sentence is normally made by placing the negative adverb 没（有）or 不 before the first predicate.

（1）用"没（有）"否定动作达到的目的、产生的结果。例如：

没（有）is used to express that a goal is not attained or a result not produced through the action. For example:

这次我们没选他当组长。

我没让他麻烦您。

我们没请她系统地介绍戏剧发展史。

（2）用"不"否定意愿。例如：

不 is used to negate a desiderative verb. For example:

他们几个人不让我来。

这个月我不请他作客。

2. 第一个谓语是动词"有"时，否定式可以有三种情况：

When the verb 有 acts as the first predicate, there are three possible negative forms:

（1）"有"的否定式是"没（有）"。例如：

没（有）is used to negate the verb 有. For example:

他没（有）东西放在我这儿。

我没（有）朋友住在那个旅馆。

（2）在兼语的动词谓语前用"不"或"没（有）"否定。例如：

Either 不 or 没（有）is possible for negating the predicate verb of the pivot. For example:

他有一个叔叔不在北京工作。

我有一个本子没用过。

（3）在兼语的形容词谓语前用"不"否定。例如：

不 is used to negate the adjectival predicate of the pivot. For example:

> 这儿有一间空房子不大。
>
> 她有两个汉字不对。

3．无主语兼语句的否定形式。

The negative form of a subjectless pivotal sentence.

（1）第一个谓语是动词"有"的，用"没"否定。例如：

When the verb 有 acts as the first predicate, 没 is used to negate it. For example:

> 上午没（有）人找你。
>
> 我们这儿没有同学是日本人。

（2）第一个谓语是动词"是"的，用"不"否定。例如：

When the verb 是 acts as the first predicate, 不 is used to negate it. For example:

> 不是我去过那儿。

4．在否定形式的兼语句中，否定副词"没(有)"或"不"一般都要放在第一个谓语动词前面，而不放在兼语的谓语前边。例如：

In the negative form of a pivotal sentence, the negative, adverb（没有）or 不 is generally placed before the first predicate rather than before the predicate of the pivot. For example:

> 他们没让我出院。
>
> 队长不叫我去他那儿。
>
> 刚才不是我们叫你。

不能说"他们让我没出院"、"队长叫我不去他那儿"等。

One can not say 他们让我没出院，队长叫我不去他那儿, etc.

如表示制止、劝阻，常在兼语的谓语前边用"别"、"不要"等否定副词。例如：

However, the negative adverbs 别, 不要, etc. are often used before the predicate of the pivot to indicate prevention, dissuasion. For example:

　　　　他们让我别出院。

　　　　队长叫我不要去他那儿。

　（五）关于无主语兼语句。

About subjectless pivotal sentences.

　1．第一个谓语是动词"有"或"是"时，"有"或"是"前边可以带表示时间、处所的状语。例如：

When the verb 有 or 是 acts as the first predicate, adverbs of time or locale may occur before 有 or 是. For example:

　　　　明天有一个朋友来我家。

　　　　操场中间有几个同学在打太极拳。

　　　　教学楼南边有两个大屋子是电影厅。

　　　　今天是我值班。

　　　　刚才是他在弹钢琴。

　　　　外边是弟弟他们在打球。

　2．前一个谓语是"请"、"禁止"等动词时，兼语常省略不用。例如：

When verbs like 请，禁止, etc. act as the first predicate, the pivot is often omitted. For example:

　　　　请进！

　　　　请喝茶！

　　　　禁止通行。

　　　　禁止停车。

　（六）关于兼语和连动的结合使用。

Pivotal constructions and verbal constructions in series used in combination.

　1．兼语句中兼语后边可以带连动结构。例如：

The pivot in a pivotal sentence may take a verbal construction in series after it. For example:

　　　　他请我们来这儿商量怎么合作的问题。

530

领导派他去管理那个水库。

2 连动句中第二个谓语（动词）后边可以带兼语。例如：

The second predicate (verb) in a sentence with verbal constructions in series may take a pivot. For example:

我们来北京请您给我们介绍经验。

昨天有一位青年祝我们成功。

（七）兼语句和主谓词组作宾语的句子。

Pivotal sentences and sentences with S-P phrases as the object.

兼语句和主谓词组作宾语的句子在形式上有些相似，需要注意区别。请看下表：

It should be noted that pivotal sentences and sentences with S-P phrases as the object are similar in form in some ways, therefore we should distinguish them from each other. See the following table:

	兼语句 Pivotal Sentences	主谓词组作宾语的句子 Sentences with S-P phrases as the object
例句 Example	他请我吃饭。	我们知道你帮助他。
1.	第一个谓语动词常是带有请求、使令、引导等意义的，如：请、叫、让、使…… The first predicate verb often has the meaning of request, command, guidance, etc., e.g. 使，请，叫，让…	谓语动词常是表示感觉或心理活动的，如：知道、希望、听见、认为…… The predicate verbs often indicate senses, or mental activities, e.g. 知道，希望，听见，认为…

2.	谓语动词所涉及的对象只限于人或事物。 The object of the predicate verb is limited to persons or things.	谓语动词所涉及的对象是人、事物及其动作或状况。 The object of the predicate verb is a person, a thing or other action or state.
3.	第一个动词谓语和兼语之间不能停顿或插入状语。 不能说"他请，我吃饭"或"他请下午我吃饭"。 Neither a pause nor an adverbial adjunct may occur between the first verb predicate and the pivot, e.g. one can not say 他请，我吃饭 or 他请下午我吃饭.	动词谓语和宾语（由主谓词组充当的）之间可以停顿或插入状语。例如： 我们知道，你帮助他。 我们知道这些天你帮助他。 Both pauses and adverbial adjuncts may occur between the verb predicate and the object (performed by S-P phrases),e.g. 我们知道，你帮助他. 我们知道这些天你帮助他.

练 习 51
Exercise 51

（一）把下列各组句子连成兼语句，并用横线标出兼语。

Combine the following groups of sentences together so that they can become pivotal sentences and underline the pivots.

例： 他请朋友们。
Model: 朋友们看杂技。
　　　　──→他请<u>朋友们</u>看杂技。

1. 老师叫你们两个人。

   你们两个人快走。

2. 我们国家的大使请我们留学生。

   我们留学生去大使馆看电影。

3. 我请那几位同志。

   那几位同志告诉我去天安门的路。

4. 他们在外边叫我。

   我跟他们一起打乒乓球。

5. 我有一个好朋友。

   那个好朋友是医生。

6. 他有三支钢笔。

   他的三支钢笔都是黑色的。

7. 宿舍楼前面有好几个中国学生。

   那几个中国学生在托排球。

8. 医院南边有一个小商店。

   那个小商店晚上开门。

9. 我从前有个同学。

   他唱歌唱得特别好。

10. 我们有一位外国老师。

    她教我们阿拉伯语。

（二）用横线标出下列句子中的兼语和主谓词组充当的宾语。

Underline the pivots and the S-P phrases as the object in the following sentences.

例： 他让<u>我</u>今天去他那儿。 （兼语）

Model: (Pivot)

他希望<u>我今天去他那儿</u>。（主谓词组作宾语）

(S-P phrase used as an object)

1. A 张老师叫我们听音乐。

   B 张老师知道我们爱听音乐。

533

2. A 我请朋友看电影。

   B 我听说他很喜欢看电影。

3. A 他说他哥哥是（一个）医生。

   B 他有一个哥哥是医生。

4. A 他盼望我们在这儿比赛。

   B 他让我们在这儿比赛。

5. A 小伙子很害怕他们的爱情被破坏。

   B 小伙子努力使他们的爱情不被破坏。

第七节　存　现　句

Section VII　Existential Sentences

一、什么叫存现句 Definition

　　句首用表示处所、时间的词或词组，说明某处、某时存在、出现或消失某人某事物，这样的无主句叫存现句。存现句的基本格式是：

　　A sentence at the beginning of which words or phrases denoting place, time are used to indicate the existence, appearance or disappearance of a thing or a person and which is without subject is known as an existential sentence. The basic pattern is:

　　表示处所、时间的词或词组（状语）——表示存在、出现或消失的动词（谓语）——动态助词——表示存在、出现或消失的名词（人或事物）（宾语）

　　Noun or phrase of place or time (adverbial adjunct) + verb indicating existence, appearance or disappearance (predicate) +

aspectual particle + person or thing that exists, appears or disappears (object)

例如：

Examples:

客厅里坐着两位客人。

桌子上放着不少西红柿。

前天我们那里搬进了几家人家。

医院里抬来了一个摔伤的病人。

他们班走了两个学生。

他们房间丢过东西。

二、存现句的特点 Grammatical features.

（一）句首状语的构成成分。

The constituents of the beginning adverbial

句首状语多由方位词，方位词组或时间词组充当。例如：

Locality nouns phrases or time phrases often act as the adverbial adjunct at the beginning of such a sentence, e.g.

东边跑来一匹马。

门口站着几个人。

早上走了三位旅客。

晚上八点半来过两个干部。

我们单位来了一位专家。

学校旁边又盖了一座大楼。

（二）谓语的构成成分。

The constituents of the predicate.

存现句的谓语一般由表示存在、出现或消失的动词充当，谓语动词后边常带动态助词"着"、"了"或"过"。例如：

Verbs indicating existence, appearance or disappearance normally act as the predicate of an existential sentence. The aspectual particle. 着，了 or 过, is often attached to the predicate verb. For example:

画儿上画着一对小猫。

村子里死了一个人。

昨天出过一会儿太阳。

（三）宾语的构成成分。

The constituents of the object.

存现句的宾语是指人、事物的名词，宾语前边常带表示数量的词。例如：

Nouns of personal or non-personal reference can serve as the object of an existential sentence and the object is often premodified by a numeral-measure phrase. For example:

广场上停着不少小汽车。

天空出现了一朵朵白云。

隔壁搬走了两户人家。

（四）动词谓语前边还可以带副词状语。例如：

The verb predicate may be premodified by an adverb adverbial adjunct. For example:

两边墙上都挂着山水画。

游泳池旁边还放着很多长椅子。

他房前又种了一些菜。

早上五点多已经走了几位旅客。

（五）动词谓语后可以带补语。例如：

The verb predicate may take a complement after it. For example:

他家花园里又种上了一种花。

上个月考进来一名打字员。

（六）存现句的否定式是在谓语动词前边用否定副词"没（有）"。例如：

The negative form of an existential sentence is made by adding the negative adverb 没（有） to the predicate verb. For example:

最近我家没来客人。

这个本子上没写着名字。

这半年生产队里没伤过一个人。

（七）存现句没有主语。

An existential sentence does not have a subject.

三、使用存现句需要注意的问题

Points that merit special attention

（一）关于充当谓语的动词。

On the predicate verbs.

1. 能作存现句谓语的动词有一定的限制，意义上大都与事物的位置或位置的移动有关。常见的有：

Verbs that can act as the predicate of existential sentences are limited to those that deal with the position or the change of position of something. Common verbs of this kind include:

（1）常用来表示存在的动词。

Verbs often used to indicate existence, such as:

A．指人、事物等静止时的姿势、状态。例如：

Those referring to postures or states of persons or things when they are in a state of rest, e.g.

坐、站、睡、贴、躺、住、停……

床上躺着一个人。

昨天他家住着一位客人。

B．指安放物品的动作。例如：

Those referring to actions of placing things. For example：

放、挂、摆、种、写、画、绣……

那儿挂着两件上衣。

牌子上写着："请不要吸烟！"

（2）常用来表示出现的动词。

Verbs often used to indicate appearance.

A．来、出、起、出现……。例如：

来、出、起、出现… as in these examples:

脸上起了一个小包。

城里出了一件新闻。

B．带简单趋向补语的一些动词：上（来）、下（来）、进（来）、出（来）、起（来）、过（来）。例如：

Some verbs that take simple directional complements:
上（来），下（来），进（来），出（来），起（来），过（来）， as in the following:

剧场里出来了很多观众。

刚才过来几个少先队员。

C．带复合趋向补语"…来"的动词：走（出来）、开（过来）、露（出来）……

Verbs that take compound directional complements…来：走（出来），开（过来），露（出来）…，as in the following examples:

西边开过来一列火车。

对面山上跑下来一群羊。

（3）常用来表示消失的动词：死、消失、丢、掉……

Verbs often used to indicate disappearance: 死，消失，丢，掉….

生产队里丢了一只羊。

（4）有的动词既可表示出现，也可表示消失：走、开、跑、搬

The following verbs can indicate either appearance or disappearance: 走，开，跑，搬

A、单独用时表示消失。例如：

When used individually, they denote disappearance. For example:

他家跑了一只鸡。

队里走了一个裁判。

B．与趋向补语合用时表示出现或消失。例如：

When used with a directional complement, they indicate appearance or disappearance. For example:

后边跑来一个小伙子。

刚才开过去一辆汽车。

2．一般说来，凡与人或物的位置或位置移动的关系不大的动词不能作存现句的谓语，如：

Generally speaking, verbs that have little to do with positions or changes of positions of persons or things cannot serve as predicate in an existential sentence, such as the following:

吃、喝、洗、扫、谈、看、想、懂、听、爱、喜欢、怕、恨、哭、笑、知道、明白、送、还、借……。

（二）句首的状语。

Adverbial adjuncts at the beginning of an existential sentence.

1．汉语里，存现句中指处所或时间的状语要放在句首——动词谓语前边，而不能放在动词谓语后边。例如：

In Chinese, the adverbial adjunct of place or time in an existential sentence should be placed at the beginning of a sentence i.e. before the verb predicate rather than after it. For example:

桌子上摆着很多好看的盘子。

下午五点运来了一批家具。

不能说"很多好看的盘子摆着桌子上"、"一批家具运来了下午五点"。

One cannot say 很多好看的盘子摆着桌子上, 一批家具运来了下午五点.

2．存现句中表示处所或时间的状语前一般不用介词"在"或"从"。例如：

The preposition 在 or 从 does not generally occur before the adverbial adjunct of place or time. For example:

车上装着许多机床。

前边来了一些参观的人。

早上六点就走了一批旅游者。

一般不说"在车上装着许多机床"、"在早上六点就走了一批旅游者"或"从前边来了一些参观的人"。

One does not normally say 在车上装着许多农具，在早上六点就走了一批旅游者，or 从前边来了一些参观的人。

3. 表示处所或时间的词或词组可以并用。例如：

Place and time nouns or phrases can be used together. For example:

我们机关上个月来了一位新领导。

明年这个地方要搬走几个工厂。

（三）谓语动词和动态助词。

The predicate verb and the aspectual particles.

1. 表示存在的谓语动词后边可以加动态助词"着"，表示人或事物处于静止状态。例如：

The aspectual particle 着 may be used after the predicate verb indicating existence, showing that a person or thing is in a state of rest. For example:

隔壁住着一位大夫。

墙上挂着一张世界地图。

桌子上摆着电视机。

屋后种着一棵果树。

谓语前边不能再加表示动作正在进行的副词"正"或"在"，不能说"墙上在挂着一张世界地图"、"桌子上正摆着电视机"等。

When 着 is used, the predicate cannot be modified by the adverb 正 or 在, the progressive indicators, e.g. one cannot say 墙上在挂着一张世界地图，桌子上正摆着电视机， etc.

2. 表示出现和消失的谓语动词后边可以加动态助词"了"。例如：

The aspectual particle 了 may be added to the predicate verbs indicating appearance or disappearance. For example:

那个旅馆来了不少旅游者。

昨天上午走了好些旅客。

3. 表示存在或出现的谓语动词后边可以加动态助词"过"。例如：

The aspectual particle 过 may be used after predicate verbs indicating existence or appearance. For example:

我们家乡种过这种豆子。

我的手上出过一些红点儿。

（四）谓语动词和补语。

The predicate verbs and complements.

存现句的动词谓语后边只能带趋向补语或结果补语。例如：

Only complements of direction and result can occur after the verb predicate in an existential sentence. For example:

上个月搬来几个大学生。

（简单趋向补语）

(Simple directional complement)

楼上掉下来一朵花。

（复合趋向补语）

(Compound directional complement)

十点半开过去一列火车。

（复合趋向补语）

(Compound directional complement)

我们班转走一个同学。

（结果补语）

(Complement of result)

其他补语都不能用于存现句中。

No other complements can be used in existential sentences.

（五）否定句中，指人或事物的名词（宾语）前不需要加数

541

量词或指示词。例如：

In the negative form of an existential sentence, the nominal object of personal or non-personal reference is usually not modified by a numeral-measure word phrase or a demonstrative modifier. For example:

公园门口没停着车。

后边没开来汽车。

不说"公园门口没停着一辆车"或"后边没开来那辆车"

One does not say 公园门口没停着一辆车 or 后边没开来那辆车。

练　习　52
Exercise 52

把下列句子改成存现句。

Rewrite the following and turn them into existential sentences.

例：　　　有一个孩子从前边跑来了。

Model:　　　──→前边跑来了一个孩子。

1．有几辆卡车从后边开来了。
2．有几个同学从教室里走出来。
3．有一堆黄瓜在地上放着。
4．有两个石狮子蹲在公园门口。
5．有很多人站在俱乐部门前。
6．有一个病人从病房里推出来了。
7．有一对青年夫妇从我们楼里搬走了。
8．刚才有只鸭子死了。
9．有几个军官从飞机上下来。
10．有十几个工人从车间里出来。

附表九：几种特殊动词谓语句的简要情况表

Table 9 : Sentences with Special Verb Predicates

特殊的动词谓语句 Sentences with special verb predicates	例句 Examples	表示的意义 Meanings	基本格式 Basic patterns	特点 Grammatical features	否定形式 Negative forms	反正式提问和简略回答 Affirmative-negative questions & short answers
"是"字句 "是"—Sentence	他是我的朋友。房后边是块菜地。他的衬衫是白的。	表示判断、存在、等同、类别等。Indicating judgment, existence, equality, category, etc.	主—谓—宾（动词"是"）S — PV — O（是）	"是"后边不能带补语或动态助词。是 can take neither a complemen nor an aspectual particle.	"不"—"是"	是不是……？ —是。—不是。

543

句型	例句	意义	结构	说明	否定	疑问
"有"字句 有—sentence	我有事。明天他们有约会。	表示领有、存在、包含、列举或达到（某个数量）等。Indicating possession, existence, inclusion, enumeration or attainment of certain quantity.	主—谓—宾。（动词"有"）S—PV—O. (有)	"有"后边不能带补语。有 cannot take a complement after it.	"没"—"有"	有没有……？有。没有。
"把"字句 把—sentence	你把地扫扫。你把鸡蛋吃了。我把那个字写走了。他把行李放在我这儿了。	表示对某人某事物施加某种动作，使其产生某种结果或影响。Indicating that an action is applied to sb. or sth. with the emphasis that the action will bring about a result or influence.	主（施事者）—状（介词"把"及宾）—谓（及物动词）—其他成分。S (doer)—adv. adjunct (把 and its O)—P (TV)—other elements.	谓语一定是及物动词；状语一般是在"把"前边。The predicates must be transitive verbs; the adverbial adjunct normally occurs before 把.	"没"—"把" 没把？	……（了）？一对（或"是"）。没有。

544

"被"字句 被—sen- tence	那棵树被大 风刮倒了。 我们的话被 她听见了。 我们都被录 取了。 他被人叫去 了。	表示某人某事物 受到某种动作的 影响，产生某种 结果。 Expressing that a person or thing achieves a certain result under the in- fluence of an action.	主（受事者）—状（介词"被"）— 及宾（及物动词）—谓 其他成分。 S (receiver) — adv. adjunct (被 and its O) — P (TV) — other elements.	谓语一般是表 示积极动作的 及物动词；状 语一般在"被" 字前边；"被" 的宾语可省 略。 The pre- dicates are normally transitive verbs denot- ing active actions; The adverbial adjunct is before 被； object of 被 can be omitted.	"没"— "被"	……（了） 没有? 一对（或 "是"）。 一没有。

连动句 Sentence with verbal constructions in series	我去看杂技。他骑自行车去颐和园。我倒杯水喝。我有时间看报。The second verb indicates the purpose of the first verb or indicates the use of the object of the first verb. Sometimes the first verb indicates the manner in which the	主—谓（动词₁）—（宾）—谓（动词₂）—（宾）。S—P(V₁)—(O)—P(V₂)—(O).	状语一般在第一个动词前边，动态动词"了"多放在第二个动词后边。The adverbial adjunct is normally in front of the first verb; the aspectual particle 了 is often placed after the second verb.	"没"—谓（动词）......；"不"—谓（动词）没—P V₁...；不—P V₁...	谓（动词₁）—"不"—谓动词₁）......—不。P(V₁)—不—P(V₁)...? PV₁. —不.

| 兼语句
Pivotal sentence | 他请我去。
我们让他来这儿。
有人敲门。
是校长请您。 | 兼语的谓语表示前一动作要达到的目的，产生到结果，或说明前一动作的宾语的情况，或起解释说明的作用。
The pivotal predicate indicates the purpose or result of the first verb; or action of the second verb is executed. Occasionally the two verbs share the same object. | 主—谓（动词）—兼语—兼语的谓语（动词/形容词）—（宾）。
S — PV — pivot — P of (V or adj.) pivot — O. | 兼语前的谓语由表示请求、使令、引导等意义的动词充当；兼语的谓语后边可带补语；兼语的谓语动词后可带宾语，一般是不定指的人或事物。
Verbs denoting request, | "没"或"不"—谓（动词）…
没(or 不)—PV
… | 谓（动词）—"没"（或"不"）—谓（动词）……（了）……？没有？
一谓（动词）—"了"，—没—谓有。
PV—没(or 不)—P.V—？—（了）没有？ |

	— PV — 了. —没有。
command, guidance act as the first predicate; the predicate of the pivot can take a comple-ment; the predicate verbs of the pivot can take object which are normally indefinite persons or things.	
describes or explains the object of the first verb.	

存现句 Existential sentence	桌子上放着不少西红柿。北边走来十几个人。医院里死了一个病人。	表示在某处或某时存在、出现或消失某人某事物。Indicating the existence, appearance or disappearance of a person or thing at a certain place or time.	状(表示处所或时间的词或词组)—谓(表示存在或消失的动词)—宾。(表示存在、出现或消失的名词(人或事物) Adv. adjunct (place or time noun/phrase) — P (verbs of existence, appearance or disappearance) — O (noun denoting a person or thing that exists, appears or disappears.)	没有主语;谓语动词后一般都带动态助词;谓语动词多为"坐、放、来、出、死……"。 No subject; aspectual particles occur after the predicate dicate verbs normally; very often the predicate dicate verbs are 坐、放、来、出、死…	……(了)没有? —谓(动词) —动态助词。 —没有。 …了没有? — PV — aspectual particles. —没有。

第八章 表示比较的方法

Chapter Eight　Ways of
Expressing Comparison

汉语里表示比较的方法很多，常见的有下面几种：

In Chinese, there are many ways to express comparison
and the common ones are as follows:

一、用介词"比"

　　By using the preposition 比

二、用介词"跟"

　　By using the preposition 跟

三、用动词"有"

　　By using the verb 有

四、用动词"象"

　　By using the verb 象

五、用"不如"

　　By using 不如

六、用"越来越"

　　By using 越来越

下面分节介绍。

They will be introduced in the following sections in turn.

第一节　用"比"表示比较

Section I　Using 比 to Express Comparison

一、用介词"比"表示比较的意义

The meanings of 比 in expressing comparison

如要表示两个人或两种事物在性状或程度上的差别，可以用介词"比"引出比较的对象，再用谓语表示比较的结果。用"比"表示比较的句子的基本格式是：

If one wants to indicate the difference in property or degree of two persons or two things, the preposition 比 may be used to introduce the one as the standard of comparison, and the predicate of a 比-sentence indicates the result of comparison. The basic pattern of a sentence using 比 to indicate comparison is:

被比较的人或事物——介词"比"——比较的人或事物——

（主语）　　　　　　　　　（状语）

比较的结果——（具体差别）

（谓语）　　　　（补语）

The person or thing to be compared +

(subject)

the preposition 比 +　the standard of comparison
　　　　　　　　　　(person or thing)　　　　　+

(adverbial adjunct)

the result of comparison + concrete differences.

(predicate)　　　　　　　(complement)

例如：

Examples:

牛肉比猪肉便宜。

今天比昨天冷。

他比我高。

这儿比那儿安静。

他比我有经验。

你去比他去合适。

他比我们了解那里的情况。

他说汉语说得比我流利。

他比我们会唱歌。

巧克力比牛奶糖贵一块钱。

这种毛衣比那种（毛衣）漂亮得多。

那本杂志比这本（杂志）多十页。

您比过去瘦多了。

这个月的产量比上个月（产量）增加了百分之五。

天气一天比一天暖和了。

二、用"比"表示比较的特点

Grammatical features

（一）介词"比"和比较对象构成的介词结构主要是在谓语前作状语。例如：

The 比-phrase, i.e. the preposition 比 and its object (the person/thing against which the comparison is made mainly occurs before the predicate as the adverbial adjunct. For example:

她比我大。

这种肥皂比那种（肥皂）好。

这个标志比那个明显。

（二）介词结构"比…"后边的谓语由形容词或某些动词充当。例如：

Adjectives or certain verbs can function as the predicate

after the 比-phrase. For example:

> 他比我保守。　　　　　　　（形容词）
> (Adjective)
>
> 哥哥比姐姐了解情况。　　　（动词）
> (Verb)

（三）介词"比"前边和后边的词或词组一般是同类的。例如：

Words or phrases both before and after the preposition 比 are generally of the same type. For example:

> 汽车比自行车快。
>
> （"汽车"和"自行车"都是名词）
> (Both 汽车 and 自行车 are nouns)
>
> 他比我大一点儿。
>
> （"他"和"我"都是代词）
> (Both 他 and 我 are pronouns)
>
> 这条路比那条（路）宽。
>
> （名词性偏正词组）
> (Nominal endocentric phrases)
>
> 坐火车比坐飞机慢。　　　（动宾词组）
> (V-O phrases)
>
> 你讲比他讲更好。　　　　（主谓词组）
> (S-P phrases)

（四）介词结构"比…"后边、谓语前边可以用副词"更"、"还"或"还要"作状语，表示程度上更进一层。例如：

The adverb 更, 还 or 还要 as adverbial adjunct can be used after the 比-phrase and before the predicate to denote a further degree. For example:

> 这个公园比那个（公园）更美。
>
> （"那个公园"相当美）
> (那个公园 is rather beautiful)

今天比昨天还热。

（"昨天"相当热）

(昨天 was rather hot)

他用的方法比我的（方法）还要简单。

（"我的方法"相当简单）

(我的方法 is rather simple and convenient)

这个城市比那个城市还要繁华。

（"那个城市"相当繁华）

(那个城市 is rather bustling)

（五）介词结构"比…"后的谓语（形容词或动词）能带补语。例如：

The predicate (adjective or verb) after the 比-phrase can have a complement after it. For example:

马比牛跑得快。

哥哥比她高三厘米。

我的负担比你的重得多。

（六）用"比"表示比较的否定形式是在介词"比"前边上否定副词"不"。例如：

The negative form of a sentence using 比 to indicate comparison is simply made by putting the negative adverb 不 before the preposition 比. For example:

今天不比昨天冷。　　这样做不比那样做好。

他不比你矮。　　　　她起得不比你晚。

三、用"比"表示比较时需要注意的问题

Points that merit special attention

（一）可以在介词结构"比…"后面作谓语的动词（或助动词）有一定的限制，常见的有：

Verbs (or auxiliary verbs) that can act as the predicate after the 比-phrase are limited to the following:

1. 表示愿望、爱好、思维活动的动词或助动词。例如：

Verbs or auxiliary verbs expressing wish, interest, mental activities, as in:

他朋友比他还爱这个地方。

他们俩比我喜欢这个职业。

弟弟比妹妹更懂得这个道理。

你比小王更关心她。

我比他更想去南方旅行。

他比咱们大家还愿意参加这次足球比赛。

2．表示增加或减少的动词。例如：

Verbs that indicate increase or decrease, as in:

这个月蔬菜的产量比上个月增加了。

他现在的生活水平比过去提高了。

今天的气温比昨天降低了三、四度。

这次参加演出的人数比上次减少了几个。

3．表示"善于"的助动词及其后边的动词。例如：

Auxiliary verbs with the meaning of "be good at" and the verbs following them, as in:

他比这个年轻人能说。

（指"口才好"）

(Referring to 口才好)

你比我能团结人。

（指"善于和别人搞好团结"）

(Referring to 善于和别人搞好团结)

她比你会唱会跳。

（指"唱得好，跳得好"）

(Referring to 唱得好，跳得好)

他们两个人比我能写会画。

（指"善于书写和绘画"）

(Referring to 善于书写和绘画)

4．带程度补语的动词。例如：

Verbs that can take complements of degree, as in:

咱们比他们走得快。

老张比老马来得早。

汉字他比我写得漂亮。

句子里有补语时，介词结构"比…"也可以放在补语前边、动词谓语后边。例如：

When there is a complement in the sentence, the 比-phrase can also be put between the verb predicate and the complement, as in:

咱们走得比他们快。

老张来得比老马早。

汉字他写得比我漂亮。

5．表示"多、大"等意思的动词"有"。例如：

The verb 有 expressing the idea of 多 or 大, as in:

他比我们有办法。

（"有办法"表示"办法多"）

（有办法 means 办法多）

这篇学术论文比那篇（学术论文）有水平。

（"有水平"表示"水平高"）

（有水平 means 水平高）

她的发言比别人的有内容。

（"有内容"表示"内容丰富"）

（有内容 means 内容丰富）

谓语动词"有"后边要带宾语，常见的还有"有学问，有知识，有经验，有魄力"等。

The predicate verb 有 should take an object after it, and here are some other common phrases: 有学问，有知识，有经验，有魄力。

6．前边带"早"、"晚"或"多"、"少"等状语的动词。例如：

Verbs modified by 早, 晚 or 多, 少 as adverbial adjuncts, as in:

他比我早来五分钟。　　　他比大家晚去一个月。

我比你多跑四百米。　　　我比她少学了半年。

这样的动词谓语后边还要有数量补语来表示比较结果的具体差别，如上面句子里的"五分钟"、"四百米"等。

Such verb predicates must be followed by complements of quantity to indicate concrete difference of the result of comparison, like 五分钟，四百米 in the above examples:

（二）介词"比"前后的两个成分如是名词性偏正词组，而中心语名词相同时，常省去"比"后边的中心语；但定语不能省去。例如：

When the two elements both before and after the preposition 比 are nominal endocentric phrases, and the modified nouns are identical, the modified word in the nominal endocentric phrase after 比 is often omitted. But the attributive can never be omitted. For example:

这个生产队比那个（生产队）富。

这座山比那座（山）高得多。

这儿的名胜古迹比那儿的（名胜古迹）多。

如果定语是表示领属关系的，省略中心语后一定要用结构助词"的"。例如：

If the attributive indicates the relationship of possession, when the modified word is omitted, the structural particle 的 must be used. For example:

我的洗衣机比你的（洗衣机）小。

我们的学校比他们的（学校）大。

你的儿子比我的（儿子）大两岁。

绝不能省去"的"而说成"我的洗衣机比你小"等。

One can never leave out 的 and say 我的洗衣机比你小, etc.

（三）"比…"后边、谓语前边不能用表示程度的副词"很"、"非常"、"十分"等。不能说"今天比昨天很暖和"，"他比我工作得非常好"等。

Degree adverbs such as 很,非常,十分, etc. never occur before the predicate after the 比-phrase. One can never say 今天比昨天很暖和，他比我工作得非常好, etc.

（四）介词结构"比…"后的形容词谓语常带的补语有下面几种情况。

Complements that often follow the adjectival predicate after the 比-phrase are as the follows：

1. 用数量补语"一点儿"或"一些"，表示比较的双方差别不大。例如：

Using 一点儿 or 一些 as a quantity complement to indicate that the difference between the two objects is not great. For example:

> 这个提包比那个轻一点儿。
>
> 这条裤子的颜色比那条深一些。

2. 用程度补语"多"，表示比较的双方差别很大。例如：

Using the degree complement 多 to indicate that the difference between the objects compared is great. For example:

> 这只鸭子比那只肥得多。
>
> 新盖的宿舍楼比那几座楼漂亮得多。
>
> 这儿的水果比我们那儿的多得多。

3. 用数量词组作补语，表示比较双方的具体差别。例如：

Using a N-Mw phrase as complement, specifying the concrete difference between the two sides of comparison. For example:

> 我比他大一岁，他比我小一岁。
>
> 黄瓜比西红柿便宜一毛（钱）。
>
> 这个单位的男青年比女青年多一倍。

（五）否定形式"不比…"只说明"前者不比后者更…"，而不表示"后者比前者…"。例如"他不比我高"，不能说明"我比他高"，虽然实际上可能是"我比他高"。

The negative form 不比… only shows "the former is not more . . . than the latter", but it does not have the implication of "the latter is more . . . than the former", e.g. 他不比我高 does not mean" 我比他高, though it may actually be the case.

还要注意的是：不能把否定副词"不"放在谓语前边，不能说"他比我不高"等。汉语里还常用反义词表示相反的意思，例如"我比他高"，相反的意思也可以说成"我比他矮"。

Another point to be noted is that the negative adverb 不 does not occur before the predicate. One cannot say 他比我不高, etc. In Chinese, antonyms are often used to indicate contrary meanings, e.g. the opposite of 我比他高 may be 我比他矮。

（六）汉语里比较两个人的年龄时，谓语只能由"大"或"小"充当，一定不能用"多"或"少"表示。例如：

In Chinese, when comparing the ages of two people, only 大 or 小 can serve as the predicate and we can never use 多 or 少 in this case. For example:

我比你大，他比你小。

（我二十一岁，你十九岁，他十八岁）

(I am twenty-one, you are nineteen and he is eighteen.)

哥哥比弟弟大得多，弟弟比哥哥小得多。

（哥哥二十岁，弟弟十三岁）

(For example, the elder brother is twenty while the younger brother is thirteen.)

姐姐比哥哥大一点儿，哥哥比姐姐小一点儿。

（姐姐二十二岁，哥哥二十岁）

(The case may be that the elder sister is 22
while the elder brother is 20.)

一定不能说"我比你多，他比你少"等。

One can never say 我比你多，他比你少，etc.

比较年龄的具体差别时，要用"岁"表示，而不能用"年"。例如：

When specifying the concrete difference of age by comparison, 岁 rather than 年 is used. For example:

> 我比你大两岁，他比你小一岁。
>
> 伯母比伯父小五岁。

一定不能说"我比你大两年"等。

One can never say 我比你大两年，etc.

（七）"多"、"少"或"早"、"晚"作状语，一定要放在谓语动词前边，而不能放在"比"前边。例如：

When 多，少，or 早，晚 are used as adverbial adjuncts, they must occur before the predicate verb, never can they occur before 比. For example:

> { 我比他多买了一本《旅游天地》。
>
> { 他比我少买了一本。

> { 我比他晚到三分钟。
>
> { 他比我早到三分钟。

一定不能说"我多比他买了一本"或"我晚比他到三分钟"等。

One can never say 我多比他买了一本 or 我晚比他到三分钟，etc.

（八）表示程度累进时，可以在"比"的前后同时用"一"和量词（或具有量词性质的名词）构成固定格式"数词'一'——量词——'比'——数词'一'——量词"，作状语。常见的格式有"一天比一天"、"一年比一年"、"一次比一次"等。例如：

When a continuous increase in degree is expressed, one uses this fixed phrase as an adverbial adjunct: — -measure word

560

+ 比 + 一 -measure word. Note that measure word in this phrase may be a noun which can function as a measure word. Here are some common phrases: 一天比一天, 一年比一年, 一次比一次. For example:

> 天气一天比一天凉快了。

> 人民的生活一年比一年富裕。

> 他的考试成绩一次比一次好。

这种格式不能放在主语前边，不能说"一天比一天天气凉快了"等。

This type of phrase cannot occur before the subject. One can never say 一天比一天天气凉快了, etc.

（九）如要比较同一事物在不同时间的变化，就可以在"比"后边用时间词语。例如：

Time nouns may occur after 比 to compare changes of one thing in different periods of time. For example:

> 这孩子的身体比以前好多了。

练　习　53
Exercise 53

把下列句子改成用介词"比"表示比较的句子。

Rewrite the following sentences by using 比 to indicate comparison.

例1.　　　她唱得好，我唱得不太好。

Model 1.　　　——>她唱得比我好。

　　　　　　　或：她比我唱得好。

　　　　　or:

例2.　　　这座楼十层，那座楼十二层。

Model 2.　　　——>这座楼比那座楼低两层。

或：那座楼比这座楼高两层。

or:

例3. 他七点五十分去上课，我七点五十五分去上课。

Model 3. ——他比我早去五分钟。

或：我比他晚去五分钟。

or:

1. 这座山高六千米，那座山高四千米。
2. 这个礼堂有一千个座位，那个礼堂有七百个座位。
3. 这篇短文有两千字，那篇有一千五百字。
4. 他父亲六十岁，他母亲五十八岁。
5. 这条路三十公里，那条路二十四公里。
6. 昨天气温二十五度，今天二十七度。
7. 这间屋子宽五米，那间宽六米半。
8. "大"字三笔，"夫"字四笔。
9. 他日语说得好，你日语说得更好。
10. 我中国画会画一点儿，他中国画画得不错。
11. 我晚上十一点睡觉，我朋友晚上十点半睡觉。
12. 我们九点到会场，他们九点一刻到会场。
13. 这个食堂中午十一点三刻开门，那个食堂十二点开门。
14. 谢力买了三本《汉英小词典》，李华买了一本《汉英小词典》。
15. 张英在大学学了五年，马明在学大学了四年。

第二节 用"跟"表示比较

Section II Using 跟 to Express Comparison

一、用介词"跟"表示比较的意义

Meaning of 跟 to express comparison

如要区别两个人或两种事物的异同，可以用介词"跟"引出比较的对象，再用谓语表示比较的结果。用"跟"表示比较的句子的基本格式是：

To indicate whether two persons or things are the same or different, the preposition 跟 is used to introduce the one as the standard of comparison and the predicate of such a sentence tells the result of comparison. The basic pattern is:

被比较的人或事物——介词"跟"——比较的人或事物——

（主语）　　　　　　　（状语）

比较的结果（异同）

（谓语）

The person or thing to be compared +

(subject)

the preposition 跟 + the standard of comparison +

(person or thing)

(adverbial adjunct)

result of comparison (same or different)

(predicate)

例如：

Examples:

这张画跟那张画一样。

他学的专业跟你学的专业一样。

他的爱好跟我的爱好差不多。

我的想法跟你的想法相同。

去他那儿跟来我这儿一样。

你买跟我买一样。

二、用"跟"表示比较的特点

Grammatical features

（一）介词"跟"和比较对象构成的介词结构主要是在谓语前作状语。例如：

The 跟-phrase (跟 + the object of comparison) is mainly used to premodify the predicate adjunct as an adverbial. For example:

> 她的围巾跟你的围巾一样。
>
> 这件衣服的颜色跟那件衣服的颜色差不多。
>
> 这篇文章的观点跟那篇文章的观点相同。

（二）"跟"和"一样"常用在一起，构成固定格式"跟……一样"，可以作定语、补语，也可以在其他形容词或某些动词谓语前作状语。例如：

The preposition 跟 and the adjective 一样 are often used together to form the construction 跟……一样 behaving as an attributive, complement or adverbial adjunct modifying an adjective or a certain verb. For example:

> 这座桥跟那座桥一样雄伟。
>
> （作状语）
>
> (As an adverbial adjunct)
>
> 我跟他一样喜欢文艺。
>
> （作状语）
>
> (As an adverbial adjunct)
>
> 他写汉字写得跟你一样好看。
>
> （作状语）
>
> (As an adverbial adjunct)
>
> 我要买一本跟他那本一样的词典。
>
> （作定语）
>
> (As an attributive)
>
> 她长得跟她母亲一样。
>
> （作补语）
>
> (As a complement)

564

（三）介词"跟"前边和后边的词或词组一般是同类的。例如：

In general, words or phrases before and after 跟 belong to the same type. For example:

面包跟米饭一样好吃。

（名词）

(Nouns)

我们跟你们一样要全心全意为人民服务。

（代词）

(Pronouns)

这个湖跟那个湖一样深。

（名词性偏正词组）

(Nominal endocentric phrases)

他们俩跟她们俩一样爱唱歌。

（同位词组）

(Appositive phrases)

游泳跟滑冰一样是很有意思的体育活动。

（动宾词组）

(V-O phrases)

你去跟他去一样。

（主谓词组）

(S-P phrases)

（四）"跟…一样"的否定形式是在"一样"前（或"跟"前）用否定副词"不"。例如：

The negative form of 跟……一样 is made by placing the negative adverb 不 before 一样 (or before 跟). For example:

我的意见跟他的意见不一样。

我买的照相机跟你的不一样。

她的裙子不跟你的一样。

三、用"跟"表示比较时需要注意的问题

Points that merit special attention

（一）常用在介词结构"跟…"后的形容词"差不多"有时用在"一样"或"相同"前边作状语。例如：

The adjective 差不多 after the 跟-phrase sometimes occurs before 一样 or 相同 acting as an adverbial adjunct. For example:

这个提包跟那个差不多一样。

他讲的内容跟你讲的差不多相同。

（二）介词"跟"前后的两个成分如果是名词性偏正词组，而中心语名词相同时，常省去"跟"后边的中心语；但定语不能省去。例如：

When the two elements before and after the preposition 跟 are nominal endocentric phrases in which the modified nouns are the same, the one after 跟 is often omitted, but the attributive should be kept. For example:

这件大衣跟那件（大衣）一样。

这种钢笔的价钱跟那种（钢笔的价钱）一样。

他写的汉字跟丁力写的（汉字）一样好看。

如果定语是表示领属关系的，省略中心语时一定要用上结构助词"的"。例如：

With a possessive attributive the structural particle 的 must be used when the modified word is left out. For example:

我的录音机跟你的（录音机）一样。

我的老师跟他的（老师）一样有经验。

他的男孩子跟我的（男孩子）一样大。

（三）"跟…相同"的否定式是"跟…不同"。例如：

The negative form of 跟…相同 is 跟…不同. For example:

我的看法跟他的不同。

这种墨水的颜色跟那种不同。

否定式"跟…不一样"中还可以在"不"前或后用表示程度的副词"很"、"太"或"都"等作状语。例如：

In the negative form 跟…不一样, degree adverbs 很, 太 or 都 etc. may occur either before or after 不 serving as an adverbial adjunct. For example:

　　这个词的意思跟那个词不太一样。

　　这几包东西的重量跟那几包不都一样。

　　我的打算跟他的很不一样。

　　这种产品的质量跟那种太不一样了。

（四）"跟…一样"和结构助词。

跟……一样 and structural particles.

1. "跟…一样"作定语时，后面一定要用结构助词"的"。例如：

When 跟…一样 acts as an attributive, the structural particle 的 must be added. For example:

　　他要买一本跟你那本一样的日记本。

　　我丢了一条跟那条一样的围巾。

2. "跟…一样"作状语时，后边一般不用结构助词"地"。例如：

When 跟…一样 acts as an adverbial adjunct, the structural particle 地 is generally not used. For example:

　　他跟你一样热情。

　　这里的社会秩序跟那里的一样好。

　　这儿的果树跟你们那儿的一样多。

　　爸爸跟妈妈一样爱听京剧。

　　我跟她一样衷心祝愿您试验成功。

3. 如有助动词，一般要放在"跟…一样"后边。例如：

If there is an auxiliary verb in the sentence, it is normally placed after 跟…一样. For example:

　　小王跟你们俩一样能写会画。

　　他跟你们一样想去杭州玩玩。

（五）用"跟"表示比较和用"比"表示比较。

Difference between 跟 and 比 in expressing comparison.

用"跟"只表示两个人或两种事物是否相同；而用"比"还可以进一步表示具体的差别。例如：

跟 shows only whether the two persons or things are the same whereas 比 can further indicate the concrete differences between them. For example:

<blockquote>
这支钢笔跟那支钢笔不一样。

这支钢笔比那支好。

这支钢笔的颜色比那支深。

这支钢笔的样子比那支好看。

你弟弟跟你不一样。

你弟弟比你聪明。

你弟弟比你高。

你弟弟比你长得漂亮。
</blockquote>

要特别注意的是，一定不能把"比"和"一样"用在一起，不能说"这支钢笔比那支一样"等。

It should be noted that 比 and 一样 cannot be used in combination. One cannot say 这支钢笔比那支一样, etc.

练 习 54
Exercise 54

（一）用"跟…一样"改写下列句子。

Rewrite the following sentences using 跟…一样.

例： 这座山高三千米，那座山也高三千米。

Model： ——这座山跟那座一样高。

1. 李华想去旅行，马明也想去旅行。

2. 这条路长三十公里，那条路也长三十公里。

3. 我想学化学，他也想学化学。

4． 他父亲今年六十五岁，我父亲今年也六十五岁。

5． 这块玻璃很厚，那块也很厚。

6． 她买的书是中文的，我买的也是中文的。

7． 他在考虑这个问题，我们也在考虑这个问题。

8． 他们俩来往很密切，我们俩来往也很密切。

9． 这个措施很具体，那个措施也很具体。

10． 这种拖拉机是中国制造的，那种也是中国制造的。

（二）用"跟…不一样"改写下列句子。

Rewrite the following sentences using 跟…不一样.

例： 这块地里的豆子密，那块地里的稀。

Model： ——→这块地里的豆子跟那块地里的不一样。

1． 这是大信封，那是小信封。

2． 这个箱子是黄的，那个箱子是红的。

3． 马明学英语，李华学阿拉伯语。

4． 老张四十八岁，老马四十二岁。

5． 他们在北京学习，我们在上海学习。

6． 他是大夫，你是工程师。

7． 这个公园里树特别多，那个公园里花特别多。

8． 你们用这种方法分析，他们用另一种方法分析。

9． 我早上六点起床，弟弟早上六点半起床。

10． 他有七八本中文杂志，我只有两本。

第三节　用"有"表示比较

Section III　Using 有 to Express Comparison

一、用"有"表示比较的意义

Distinct meanings

如要表示两个人或两种事物在某方面有相似之处，可以用动词"有"引出比较的对象，再用谓语表示比较的方面或达到的标准。用"有"表示比较的句子的基本格式是：

When we want to compare in what respect two persons or things are alike, the verb 有 is used to introduce the one as the standard of comparison. In such a ·sentence, the predicate tells that the person or thing has reached the standard in a certain respect. The basic pattern is:

被比较的人或事物——动词"有"——比较的人或事物——
　　（主语）　　　　　　　　　　（状语）

"这么"（或"那么"）——比较的方面、标准
　　（状语）　　　　　　　　（谓语）

The person or thing to be compared +

(subject)

the verb 有 + the standard of comparison (person or thing)

(adverbial adjunct)

+ 这么 (or 那么) + respect of comparison

(adverbial adjunct)　　（predicate）

例如：

Examples:

他有你画得这么好。　　　这棵古树有楼那么高。

她有你这么爱笑。　　　　这间屋子有那间那么大。

二、用"有"表示比较的特点

Grammatical features

（一）动词"有"和比较对象构成的动宾词组在谓语形容词（或某些动词）前作状语。例如：

The 有-phrase （有 + the object of comparison) premodifies the predicate adjective (or a certain verb) as an adverbial adjunct. For example:

570

这条绳子有那条那么长。

我的头发有你的那么黑。

她有我这么喜欢小动物。

（二）动宾词组"有…"后面的谓语多由"高、大、长、厚、多、深、宽、粗、远"等形容词或某些能表示程度的动词充当。例如：

The adjectives 高，大，长，厚，多，深，宽，粗，远,etc. and some degree verbs can act as the predicate premodified by the 有-phrase. For example:

这个湖有那个那么深。	（形容词） (Adjective)
这种苹果有那种那么甜。	（形容词） (Adjective)
他家的人有我家的这么多。	（形容词） (Adjective)
那只猫有这只这么会捉老鼠。	（动　词） (Verb)

（三）"有"前边和后边的词或词组一般是同类的。例如：

Words or phrases before and after 有 are of the same type. For example:

小王有小马那么聪明。	（名词） (Nouns)
他有你这么爱看小说。	（代词） (Pronouns)
这种点心有那种点心那么好吃。	（名词性偏正词组） (Nominal endocentric phrases)

（四）动宾词组"有…"和谓语之间常用指示代词"这么"或"那么"表示程度。例如：

The demonstrative pronoun 这么 or 那么 often occurs

571

between the 有-phrase and the predicate to denote degree. For example:

> 这个西瓜有糖那么甜。
>
> 我的女儿有我爱人那么高了。
>
> 他说话的声音有她的这么细。

（五）用"有"表示比较的否定式是"没有…"。例如：

The negative form of 有 to indicate comparison is 没有…. For example:

> 弟弟没有妹妹高。
>
> 这种布没有那种结实。
>
> 你没有我努力。

三、用"有"表示比较时需要注意的问题

Points that merit special attention

（一）可以用在"有…"后边的谓语动词和用在"比…"后边的基本相同〔请看本章第一节第三部分第（一）条〕。

Predicate verbs used after 有… and 比… are mainly the same 〔refer to 三（一）Section I of this chapter〕.

（二）"有"前后的两个成分如是名词性偏正词组，而中心语名词相同时，常省去"有"后边的中心语；但定语不能省去。例如：

When the two elements before and after 有 are nominal endocentric phrases and in which the two modified nouns are the same, the one after 有 may be omitted, but the attributive cannot be omitted. For example:

> 这种打字机有那种（打字机）好。
>
> 他的房间没有我的（房间）宽。
>
> 那座山有这座（山）这么高。

如果定语是表示领属关系的，省略中心语后，一定要用结构助词"的"。例如：

With a possessive attributive the structural particle 的 must be used when the modified word is omitted. For example:

我的中文书没有你的（中文书）多。

这次他的考试成绩没有你的（考试成绩）好。

姐姐的帽子没有妹妹的（帽子）漂亮；

一般不能说成"我的中文书没有你多"等。

Generally speaking, one cannot say 我的中文书没有你多, etc.

（三）"有…"有"达到…"的意思，后面的谓语表明达到的程度，谓语后面不能再带具体数量。例如：

"有…" has the meaning of "reaching..." and the predicate after it indicates the degree of an action or a state, so no words of concrete number and measurement can follow the predicate. For example:

这筐水果有十斤重，那筐水果也有十斤重。

这筐水果有那筐重。

他高一米七六，我高一米七八。

他没有我高。

但不能说"这筐水果有那筐重十斤"或"他没有我高一点儿"等。

But one cannot say 这筐水果有那筐重十斤 or 他没有我高一点儿 etc.

（四）"有…"也可以用在补语形容词前面作状语。例如：

"有…" can also occur before the complement adjective acting as the adverbial adjunct. For example:

他说汉语说得有中国人（那么）好。

她说英语说得有英国人那么流利。

他跑得没有你快。

（五）用"没有"表示比较和用"比"表示比较。

Difference between 没有 and 比 in expressing comparison.

用"没有"表示比较的句子一般都可以改成用"比"的句子，

但要把前后两个成分的位置对调一下。例如：

Generally speaking, sentences with 没有 can be turned into sentences using 比, with the positions of the two elements before and after 没有 exchanged. For example:

　　　　我没有他细心。

　　　　──── 他比我细心。

　　　　这个阶段的任务没有上个阶段的重。

　　　　──── 上个阶段的任务比这个阶段的重。

　　　　这种面（粉）没有那种白。

　　　　──── 那种面（粉）比这种白。

练　习　55
Exercise 55

用表示比较的"有…"或"没有…"改写下列句子。

Rewrite the following sentences by using "有…" or "没有…"

例：　　　买这本词典的人比买那本的人多。

Model:　　──── 买那本词典的人没有买这本的多。

　　1．订这种报的人比订那种报的人少。

　　2．我的女儿二十岁，他的女儿也二十岁。

　　3．今年的夏天跟去年的夏天一样热。

　　4．这座桥跟那座桥不一样长。

　　5．这间客厅的光线不比那间的好。

　　6．这个城市的人口比那个城市的多。

　　7．他每天晚上工作三小时，我每天晚上工作两小时。

　　8．这个游泳池深四米，那个游泳池也深四米。

　　9．你写字写得很整齐，他写字写得不太整齐。

　　10．他们俩打网球打得比你们俩好。

574

11. 司机开车比大使开得快。
12. 这本书比那本厚得多。
13. 这本小说比那本有意思。
14. 友谊宾馆离我们学校五公里，颐和园离我们学校九公里。
15. 昨天气温比今天高。

第四节 用"象"表示比较

Section IV Using 象 to express Comparison

一、用动词"象"表示比较的意义

Meaning of 象 to express comparison

如要表示两个人或两种事物相象，可以用动词"象"引出比较对象，或后面再用谓语表示比较的方面或标准。用"象"表示比较的基本格式有两种：

To express that two persons or things are similar, the verb 象 may be used to introduce the one as the standard of comparison. The predicate of such a sentence tells the respect of comparison. There are two basic patterns:

1. 被比较的人或事物——动词"象"——比较的人或事物
    （主语）　　　　　　（谓语）　　　　　（宾语）
    The person or thing to be compared + the verb 象
    　　　　　　　　(subject)　　　　　　　　　　(predicate)
    + the standard of comparison (person or thing)
    　　　　　　　　　　　　(object)

例如：
Examples:

575

他象他爸爸。

他象一个军事专家。

这种东西的形状象火箭。

2. 被比较的人或事物——

（主语）

动词"象"——比较的人或事物——"这么"（或"那么"）

（状语）

——比较的方面、标准

（谓语）

The person or thing to be compared +

(subject)

the verb 象 + the standard of comparison + 这么 (or 那么)

(person or thing)

(adverbial adjunct)

+ respect of comparison

(predicate)

例如：　S 象 O_1 O_2 ⇒ S は O_1 のように O_2 だ.

Examples:　S + 象 + n + 这么 + Adj 或 V

他象他爸爸这么勇敢。

小马象小高这么喜欢体育运动。

这两天象冬天那么冷。

二、用"象"表示比较的特点

Grammatical features

（一）"象"作谓语的比较句，特点跟一般动词谓语句一样。

Features of a sentence with 象 as the predicate to express comparison are the same as that of an ordinary sentence with a verb predicate.

（二）"象"和比较对象构成的动宾词组，常在形容词或动词充当的谓语前作状语。谓语前一般要用指示代词"这么（这样）"或者"那么（那样）"。例如：

The 象-phrase (象 + the object of comparison) often serves as the adverbial adjunct before an adjective or verb predicate. <u>Generally speaking, demonstrative pronoun 这么（这样）or 那么（那样） should be used before the predicate.</u> For example:

> 他象他爸爸那么高。
>
> 这次任务象上次那么紧急。
>
> 她象她姐姐那样了解中国。

（三）"象"前后的两个成分一般是同类词或词组。例如：

The two elements before and after 象 are usually of the same type. For example:

> 鸭肉象鸡肉那么香。　　　　（名词）
> 　　　　　　　　　　　　　(Nouns)
>
> 他象你这样刻苦。　　　　　（代词）
> 　　　　　　　　　　　　　(Pronouns)
>
> 今天象昨天那么凉快。　　　（名词——时间词）
> 　　　　　　　　　　　　　(Nouns — time nouns)
>
> 这些书象那些书那样受读者欢迎。
> 　　　　　　　　　（名词性偏正词组）
> 　　　　　　　　　(Nominal endocentric phrases)
>
> 滑冰象游泳那么有意思。　　（动宾词组）
> 　　　　　　　　　　　　　(V-O phrases)

（四）"象"的否定式是"不象"。例如：

The negative form of 象 is 不象. For example:

> 他不象他哥哥。
>
> 他不象他爸爸那样健康。
>
> 她不象五十岁的人。
>
> 今天不象昨天那么热。

三、用"象"表示比较时需要注意的问题

Points that merit special attention

（一）"象"作谓语时，前边可用表示程度的副词作状语。例如：

When 象 is used as the predicate, adverbs of degree may occur before it as its adverbial adjunct. For example:

> 他很象一个演员。
>
> 小王非常象记者。

但用"象…"作状语表示比较的句子里，"象"前边不能用表示程度的副词。不能说"他很象他爸爸那么高"等。

But in sentences using 象… as adverbial adjuncts to express comparison, adverbs of degree can never occur before 象. One cannot say 他很象他爸爸那么高, etc.

（二）在用"象…"作状语的比较句里，"这么（这样）"或"那么（那样）"只能放在谓语前边，而不能放在"象"前边。例如：

In sentences of comparison using 象… as the adverbial adjunct, 这么（这样） or 那么（那样） can only be placed before the predicate, one can never put it before 象. For example:

> 他的眼睛象你的这么好看。
>
> 我们的家乡象公园那样美。

不能说"他的眼睛那样象你的好看"等。

One cannot say 他的眼睛那样象你的好看, etc.

（三）"象"前后两个成分是名词性偏正词组，而中心语相同时，常省略后一个中心语，但定语不能省去。定语如是表示领属关系的，省略中心语后，一定要用结构助词"的"。例如：

When the two elements before and after 象 are nominal endocentric phrases in which the modified nouns are the same, the one after 象 is often omitted, but the attributive should remain. With a possessive attributive the structural particle

的 must be used when the modified noun is omitted. For example:

我的孩子象你的（孩子）这样爱好文学。

这种药象那种（药）那么有效。

他的伞象我的（伞）这样好。

（四）表示比较的动词"象"和"有"。

Difference between the verbs 象 and 有 in expressing comparison.

"A象B"表示A跟B相似。"A象B那样C"表示A跟B在C这方面相似。而"A有B这么C"表示A在C方面达到了B达到的程度。例如：

"A 象 B" means that A and B resemble each other. "A 象 B 那样 C" means that A and B resemble in respect of C. But "A 有 B 这么 C" means that A has reached the degree of B in respect of C. Study the following examples:

他象他哥哥那样热情。

（他跟哥哥一样热情）

(He is as warm-hearted as his brother.)

他有他哥哥那么热情。

（他达到他哥哥那样热情的程度）

(He has reached the degree of enthusiasm of his brother.)

（五）"象"和"跟…一样"。

象 and 跟…一样.

"象…"也可以用在"一样"前边构成"象…一样"，表示前后两个事物非常相象；而"跟…一样"表示前后两个事物一样，不只是相象。

"象…" may also occur before 一样 to form the pattern 象…一样, indicating the resemblance of two things while 跟…一样 shows that the two things are the same, not only similar.

练 习 56
Exercise 56

用"象"改写下列句子。

Rewrite the following sentences using 象.

例：　　这本书有三百页，那本书也有三百页。

Model:　　──────→　这本书象那本那么厚。

1. 李华高一米八，王英高一米九。
2. 这种电扇不贵，那种也不贵。
3. 这包糖重两公斤，那包糖重三公斤半。
4. 他喜欢滑雪，我也喜欢滑雪。
5. 我的小孩才三岁，他的小孩也三岁。
6. 这个汉字的笔画多，那个汉字的笔画少。
7. 这两顶帽子又便宜又好看。
8. 弟弟很糊涂，妹妹也很糊涂。
9. 你的学习计划订得很全面，他的也很全面。
10. 他们俩每天都起得很早。

第五节　用"不如"表示比较

Section V　Using 不如 to Express Comparison

一、用"不如"表示比较的意义

The meanings of 不如 in expressing comparison

如要表示某人或某事物比不上另一人或事物，可以用"不如"；前者"不如"后者，就是前者"没有"后者"好"的意思。也可以在"不如…"后面再用其他谓语表示比较的方面或标准。用"不如"表示比较的句子的基本格式有两种：

不如 can be used to show that a person or thing cannot compare favourably with another. When we say A 不如 B, we mean that A is not as good as B. The 不如-phrase (不如 + object) can be used adverbially to modify a predicate that indicates the respect of comparison. There are two basic patterns:

1. 被比较的人或事物——"不如"——比较的人或事物
　　　（主语）　　　（谓语）　　　（宾语）

The person or thing to be compared (subject) —— 不如 (predicate) —— the standard of comparison (object)

例如：

Examples:

> 我不如他。
> 这个报告不如那个报告。
> 坐车不如骑车。
> 你来不如我去。

2. 被比较的人或事物——
　　　（主语）

"不如"——比较的人或事物"那么"——
　　　　　　　（状语）

比较的方面、标准
　　（谓语）

The person or thing to be compared +
　　　　　　（subject）

不如 + the standard of comparison(person or thing) 那么 +
　　　　　　　　（adverbial adjunct）

respect of comparison
　　（predicate）

581

例如：

Examples:

> 我不如他那么刻苦。
>
> 这个报告不如那个报告那么精彩。
>
> 坐车不如骑车有意思。
>
> 你来不如我去合适。

二、用"不如"表示比较的特点

Grammatical features

（一）"不如"前后两个成分的词和词组一般是同类的。例如：

Words or phrases of the two elements before and after 不如 are usually of the same type. For example:

> 他不如你。　　　　　　　（代词）
> 　　　　　　　　　　　　（Pronouns）
>
> 这个球场不如那个球场。　（名词性偏正词组）
> 　　　　　　　　　　　　（Nominal endocentric phrases）
>
> 看电视不如看电影。　　　（动宾词组）
> 　　　　　　　　　　　　（V-O phrases）
>
> 一个人去不如大家一起去。（主谓词组）
> 　　　　　　　　　　　　（S-P phrases）

（二）用"不如"表示比较时，后面也可以有形容词或动词充当的谓语，说明比较的方面。例如：

When 不如 is used to denote comparison, it may be followed by an adjective or verb predicate indicating the respects of comparison. For example:

> 我不如他高。
>
> 这种毯子不如那种软。
>
> 坐船不如坐火车快。
>
> 这里的情况他不如你了解。

谓语前常用"那么"表示程度。例如：

那么 often occurs before the predicate to denote degree.
For example:

> 我不如他那么高。
>
> 我的假日不如你的那么多。

（三）只有否定形式"不如…"，而没有肯定形式"如…"。

The negative form 不如..., has no affirmative form in
Chinese.

三、用"不如"表示比较时需要注意的问题

Points that merit special attention

（一）"不如"前后两个成分是名词性偏正词组，而中心语
相同时，常省略后面的中心语，但定语不能省去。定语如是表示
领属关系的，省略中心语后，一定要用结构助词"的"。例如：

When the two elements before and after 不如 are nominal
endocentric phrases in which the modified nouns are the same,
the one after 不如 can be omitted. But the attributive can
never be omitted. With a possessive attributive, the structural
particle 的 must used when the modified noun is omitted. For
example:

> 这个杯子不如那个（杯子）。
>
> ┌ 我写的文章不如他写的（文章）。
> └ 他们的学习环境不如你们的（学习环境）好。
>
> ┌ 我的计划不如你的（计划）。
> └ 我的计划不如你的（计划）那么详细。

（二）可以充当"不如…"后谓语的动词有一定的限制。常
见的有：

Verbs that can serve as the predicate after "不如…" are
limited to the following two categories:

1. 带程度补语的动词。例如：

Verbs that take complements of degree, as in:

这张照片不如那张照得好。

他外语不如你说得流利。

这个问题不如那个概括得清楚。

2. 前边有助动词的动词。例如：

Verbs that are preceded by auxiliary verbs, as in:

你不如他能吃苦。

我不如你会安排时间。

（三）表示比较的"不如"和"没有"。

Difference between 不如 and 没有 that express comparison.

"不如"可以作谓语，表示"没有…好"的意思，但"没有"不能这样用。例如：

不如 can serve as predicate, meaning "not so good as ..." while 没有 cannot be used this way. For example:

这种收音机不如那种。

这种收音机没有那种好。

不能说"这种收音机没有那种"。

One cannot say 这种收音机没有那种.

"不如…"作状语时跟"没有…"的意思和用法基本相同。

When "不如…" is used as the adverbial adjunct, it is roughly the same as "没有…" in meaning and usage.

练 习 57
Exercise 57

用"不如"改写下列句子。

Rewrite the following sentences with 不如.

例： 这间屋子有十五平方米，那间屋子有十八平方米。

Model: ——这间屋子不如那间大。

1. 这种酒一瓶五块钱，那种酒一瓶四块五。

2. 这张邮票好看，那张邮票不好看。

3. 她毛衣织得不太好，我织得好。

4. 这座楼比那座楼高三层。

5. 我中午十二点到家，他中午十二点二十到家。

6. 她弹钢琴弹得很好，你弹得更好。

7. 这块地有三十亩，那块地有四十亩。

8. 母亲今年五十岁，大姨今年五十二。

9. 新修建的剧场有两千个座位，原来的剧场只有一千二百个座位。

10. 小张高一米六九，小王高一米六八。

11. 你喜欢画画儿，我更喜欢画画儿。

12. 他学汉语比我学得多。

13. 我比他早学一个月汉语。

14. 这本语法书比那本薄得多。

15. 他愿意帮助别人，你更愿意帮助别人。

第六节 用"越来越"表示比较
Section VI Using 越来越 to Express Comparison

一、用"越来越"表示比较的意义

The meaning of 越来越 in expressing comparison

如要表示某人或某事物在某方面的程度是随时间的推移而产生变化的，可以用"越来越"，后面的谓语表示变化的方面。用"越来越"表示比较的句子的基本格式是：

越来越 may be used to show that a certain person or thing changes in a certain respect as the time goes on. The predicate premodified by 越来越 specifies the respect of the change. The basic pattern is:

被比较的人或事物 ── "越来越" ── 变化的方面

（主语）　　　　（状语）　　　（谓语）

The person or thing to be compared (subject) + 越来越
(adverbial adjunct) + aspect of change (predicate)

例如：

Examples：

> 他越来越健康。
>
> 天气越来越冷。
>
> 这里的旅游者越来越多。
>
> 大家的生活水平越来越高了。
>
> 我越来越喜欢我的工作了。
>
> 我们之间越来越了解了。
>
> 这些鸡鸭喂得越来越肥。
>
> 我们的前途越来越有希望。

二、用"越来越"表示比较的特点

Grammatical features

（一）"越来越…"的主语可以是名词、代词、动宾词组或主谓词组等，指某人或某事物。例如：

The subject of 越来越-sentence may be a noun, a pronoun, a V-O phrase, a S-P phrase, etc. referring to a person or thing. For example：

> 生活越来越美好。
>
> 他越来越瘦。
>
> 开展体育运动越来越普遍了。
>
> 那儿环境污染越来越厉害。

（二）"越来越"主要是在谓语前作状语。例如：

越来越 mainly acts as the adverbial adjunct premodifying the predicate. For example：

> 那位老农民的经验越来越丰富。
>
> 雨越来越大了。

这个概念越来越清楚了。

（三）"越来越"后的谓语由形容词或某些能表示程度的动词充当。例如：

The predicate after 越来越 is performed by adjectives or certain verbs of degree. For example:

他的身体越来越坏。

我们的老师越来越严格了。

他越来越关心集体了。

孩子们越来越懂得学习的重要性了。

（四）用"越来越"表示比较的句子末尾常用语气助词"了"表示变化。例如：

The modal particle 了 often occurs at the end of a 越来越-sentence expressing a continuing change. For example:

天越来越黑了。

我们越来越团结了。

这个城市建设得越来越美了。

三、用"越来越"表示比较时需要注意的问题

Points that merit special attention

（一）"越来越"只能在谓语前作状语，而不能放在主语前边。例如：

越来越 can only act as an adverbial adjunct before the predicate, and it can never be placed before the subject. For example:

学习外语的人越来越多了。

这里的工作条件越来越好。

不能说"越来越学习外语的人多了"等。

One cannot say 越来越学习外语的人多了, etc.

（二）用"越来越"表示比较的句子里，谓语后边可以带程度补语，这时，"越来越"要放在程度补语前边，而不能放在谓语前边。例如：

The predicate can take complements of degree in a 越来越-sentence indicating comparison. In this case, 越来越 should be placed before the complement of degree, but not before the predicate. For example:

他长得越来越高了。

我们生活得越来越幸福。

他的房间布置得越来越整齐了。

不能说"他越来越长得高了"等。

One cannot say 他越来越长得高了, etc.

（三）"越来越"后边不能再用表示程度的副词作谓语的状语。例如：

No other adverbs of degree can occur after 越来越 to serve as the adverbial adjunct of the predicate. For example:

这只小猫越来越可爱。

这里的服务人员越来越热情周到了。

不能说"这只小猫越来越很可爱"等。

One can never say 这只小猫越来越很可爱, etc.

练 习 58
Exercise 58

用"越来越"完成下列句子。

Complete the following sentences using 越来越.

例：

Model: 这个公园里的游人<u>越来越多</u>。

1．你的汉语水平_____。

2．我们的身体_____。

3 他们说话的声音_____。

4．这几棵小树_____。

5．他的工作经验＿＿＿＿＿＿＿＿＿＿。

6．你的学习成绩＿＿＿＿＿＿＿＿＿。

7．以前我不太了解这儿的情况，现在＿＿。

8．我开始时不喜欢这个职业，现在＿＿＿。

9．他一直很爱写诗，现在＿＿＿＿＿＿。

10．市场上的新产品＿＿＿＿＿＿＿＿。

附表十： 六种比较方法的简要情况表
Table 10: Six Ways of Expressing Comparison

比较方法 Expressions of comparison	例句 Examples	表示的意义 Meaning	基本格式 Basic patterns	结构特点 Structural features	否定形式 Negative forms	正反式或用"是不是"提问 Affirmative-negative questions or 是不是 question
用"比"	我比你高。	比较两种人或事物的性状、程度的差别 To compare the difference in property or degree be-	被比较的人或事物—"比"—比较对象—比较结果 Person or thing to be compared + 比 + Standard of comparison + Result of comparison 〔A—比—B—C〕	介词结构"比…"作状语，谓语由形容词(或某些动词)充当，谓语能带补语，谓语前可用副词"更，还"或"还要" The 比-phrase is used as adv. adjunct; adjectives (or certain verbs) act as	不比…。	我比（你）不比你高？ 我是不是比你高？

590

	例 Example	用法	结构 Structure	说明	肯定	否定	疑问
		tween two persons or things		the predicate which can take a complement; the adv's 更, 还 or 还要 can be used before the predicate.			跟……一样不一样？ 是不是跟……一样？
用"跟"	我跟你一样（高）。	比较两种人或事物的异同 To illustrate the differences or similarities between two persons or things	被比较的人或事物—"跟"—比较对象—"一样"—（比较的方面） Person or thing to be compared + 跟 + comparison + (Respects of comparison) + 一样 〔A—跟—B—一样（C）〕	介词结构"跟……"作状语，谓语由形容词"一样"等充当；"跟……一样"可作状语、定语或补语 The 跟-phrase is used as adv. adjunct; Adj. 一样 etc. acts as the predicate; 跟……一样 can act as adv. adjunct, attributive, or complement.	跟……一样	跟……不一样 不跟……一样	
用"有"	我有你（这么）高。	比较两种人或事物的相似处（A是否达到了B的程度） To compare	被比较的人或事物—"有"—比较对象—"这么（那么）"—比较的方面 Person or thing to be compared + 有 + Standard of	动宾词组"有……"作状语，谓语由形容词（或某些动词）充当；谓语前常用"这么（那么）"…" The V-O phrase 有…	有……	没有……	有没有……？ 是不是有……？

用"象"

他象你（这么高）。

比较两种人或事物——"象"——比较对象——"这么（那么）"——（比较的方面） 被比较的人或事物—"象"—比较对象—"这么（那么）"—（比较的方面） To state whether two persons or things resemble each other. Person or thing to be compared + 象 + Standard of comparison + "这么（那么）" + (Respect of comparison) comparison + "这么（那么）" + (Respect of comparison) itself; the V-O phrase [A—象—B（这么）—（C）]	"象"可单独作谓语，动宾词组"象…"可作状语，谓语由形容词（或某些动词）充当，谓语前常用"这样（那样）" "象" can act as predicate by itself; the V-O phrase 象… can be used as adv. adjunct. Adj. (or certain verbs) act as the predicate 这样(那样) is often used before the predicate.	象宾不象… 象 不 象 …?

the similarities between two persons or things (if A has reached the degree of B).

comparison + 这么（那么） + Respect of comparison
[A—有—B（这么）—C]

is used as adverbial adjunct; adjectives (or certain verbs) act as the predicate; 这么（那么） is often used before the predicate.

用法	意义	结构	说明	例句
用"不如"	被比较的人或事物没有另一个人或事物好 A person or thing is not as good as another.	"不如"一比较对象一（"那么"）一（比较的方面） "不如" + Standard + (那么) + (Respect of comparison) 〔A一不如一B（那么一C）〕	"不如"可单独作谓语，"不如"和宾语可作状语，谓语由形容词（或某些动词）充当，谓语前常用"那么"。 "不如" can be used as predicate by itself; 不如 and its object can act as an adverbial adjunct; the predicates are often performed by adjectives (or certain verbs). 那么 is often used before the predicate.	我不如你（高）。 不如…（无肯定）形式） 我是不是不如你（高）?
用"越来越"	被比较的人或事物随着时间而变化的程度 The degree of change of a person or thing, as time goes on.	"越来越"一变化的方面 "越来越" + Respect of change 〔A一越来越一C（了）〕	"越来越"作状语，谓语由形容词（或某些动词）充当，句尾常用语气助词"了" "越来越" is used as adverbial adjunct; adjectives (or certain verbs) act as the predicate; the modal particle 了 is often placed at the end of the sentence.	天气越来越冷。 是不是天气越来越冷了?

593

第九章 表示强调的方法

Chapter Nine　Ways of Expressing Emphasis

汉语里表示强调的方法很多，常见的有下面几种：

In Chinese there are many ways of expressing emphasis and the most common ones are as follows:

一、用疑问代词

By using interrogative pronouns

二、用"哪儿…啊"

By using 哪儿…啊

三、用"不是…吗"

By using 不是…吗

四、用"连…都（也）"

By using 连…都（也）

五、用副词"是"

By using the adverb 是

六、用副词"就"

By using the adverb 就

七、用两次否定

By using double negation

八、用"是…的"

By using 是…的

下面分节介绍。

They will be introduced separately in the following sections.

第一节 用疑问代词表示强调

Section I Using Interrogative Pronouns to Express Emphasis

一、用疑问代词表示强调的意义

The meaning of interrogative pronouns to express emphasis

汉语里常在陈述句里用疑问代词"谁、什么、哪、哪儿、怎么"等表示任指，强调任何人或任何事物都不例外；后边常用副词"都"或"也"。例如：

In Chinese interrogative pronouns 谁，什么，哪，哪儿，怎么 are often used in a statement to denote indefinite indication, emphasizing the idea of "no exception." Adverbs 都 or 也 are often used after them. For example:

谁都知道这个消息。　　（任何人，所有的人）
　　　　　　　　　　　（Anyone, all people）

他什么都不吃。　　　　（任何东西）
　　　　　　　　　　　（Anything）

今天他什么地方都不想去了。（任何地方）
　　　　　　　　　　　　　（Anywhere）

哪儿都有公园。　　　　（任何城市，任何地区）
　　　　　　　　　　　（Any city, any district）

哪个公园都很热闹。　　（任何公园，所有的公园）
　　　　　　　　　　　（Any park, all parks）

他怎么要求都不行。　　（用任何方法"要求"）
　　　　　　　　　　　（To demand by any means）

二、用疑问代词表示强调的特点　Grammatical features

（一）疑问代词用于陈述句表示任指，无提问作用，句末用句号。例如：

Interrogative pronouns are used in a declarative sentence to denote indefinite indication without the sense of inquiries. A period is required at the end of the sentence. For example:

> 谁都有自己的理想。
>
> 他什么都懂。

（二）谓语多由动词充当，有时由形容词充当。例如：

The predicate of a sentence with an interrogative pronoun expressing emphasis is usually a verb, but sometimes is an adjective. For example:

> 我们班，谁都喜欢滑冰。
>
> 他什么都想试一试。
>
> 他哪儿都不去。
>
> 哪儿都很安静。
>
> 谁都非常高兴。

（三）表示任指的疑问代词后面要用副词"都"或"也"配合。例如：

The adverbs 都 or 也 are often used after interrogative pronouns expressing indefinite indication. For example:

> 他们班谁都会唱这支歌。
>
> 我怎么也听不懂他的意思。

（四）表示任指的疑问代词用在谓语前边作主语或前置宾语（或主语、前置宾语的定语）。例如：

Interrogative pronouns denoting indefinite indication are used before the predicate, serving as the subject or the fronted object (or attributive of the subject or fronted object). For example:

> 谁都愿意改善工作条件。
>
> （"谁"是主语）
>
> (谁 is the subject)

哪种方法都可以试一下。

（"哪"是主语"方法"的定语）

(哪 is the attributive of the subject 方法)

他谁也没找着。

（"谁"是前置宾语）

(谁 is the fronted object)

刚才我什么声音也没听到。

（"什么"是前置宾语"声音"的定语）

(什么 is the attributive of the fronted object 声音)

（五）重音在表示任指的疑问代词上。全句是降调。

The stress is on the interrogative pronoun denoting indefinite indication. The whole sentence should be read in the falling tune.

（六）否定形式是在"都"或"也"后边、谓语前边用上否定副词"不"或"没有"。例如：

The negative form of a sentence with an interrogative pronoun expressing emphasis is made by inserting the adverb 不 or 没有 after 都 or 也 and before the predicate. For example:

谁也不知道。

昨天我们哪儿也没去。

他什么都不说。

三、用疑问代词表示强调时需要注意的问题

Points that merit special attention

（一）用疑问代词表示强调任指时，后边的"都"或"也"一定不能遗漏，否则全句意思就变成提问了。例如：

When interrogative pronouns are used to emphasize indefinite indication, 都 or 也 after them can never be omitted or else the sentence will become a question. For example:

谁都喜欢这种花。

（强调"任何人"）

(Emphasizing "anyone")

谁喜欢这种花？

（提问"哪个人…？"）

(Raising a question of "which person")

他什么东西也不吃。

（强调"任何东西"）

(Emphasizing "anything")

他什么东西不吃？

（提问"不吃哪种东西？"）

(Raising a question of "what is it he does not eat?)

（二）"也"一般用在否定句中。例如：

Generally speaking, 也 is used in a negative sentence. For example:

谁也不知道这件事。

他什么也没瞒过我们。

（三）强调任指的疑问代词作宾语时只能前置。例如：

As objects, the interrogative pronouns emphasizing indefinite indication are always fronted. For example:

我们哪儿都去了。　　（前置宾语）

(fronted object)

他什么也没有。　　　（前置宾语）

(fronted object)

第一句不能说成"我们都去哪儿了"。第二句如说成"他也没有什么"，意思就变了，"什么"表示虚指，不表示强调。

The first sentence cannot be changed into 我们都去哪儿了, while the meaning of the second sentence will be changed if it is said 他也没有什么 in which 什么 expresses sth. generic but does not indicate emphasis.

598

练 习　59
Exercise 59

用横线标出下列句中表示强调任指的疑问代词。

Underline the interrogative pronouns emphasizing indefinite indication in the following sentences.

例：　　　{ 今天上午他们要去哪儿？
Model:　{ 我听说他们哪儿也不去。

1.{ 请问，去北海怎么走？
　　{ 我们谁都不知道。

2.{ 您要哪种酒？
　　{ 哪种酒都可以。

3.{ 你们需要带什么东西？
　　{ 我们什么东西都不带，谢谢。

4.{ 这种鱼怎么做？
　　{ 这种鱼怎么做都行。

5.{ 你们谁是毕业班的学生？
　　{ 我们谁也不是毕业班的。

6.{ 你们参加谁的婚礼？
　　{ 我们谁的婚礼都参加。

7.{ 你猜着了哪个字？
　　{ 我哪个字都没猜着。

8.{ 你喜欢看什么内容的小说？
　　{ 我什么内容的小说都喜欢看。

9.{ 暑假里你去哪儿旅行？
　　{ 我哪儿都想去。

10.{ 哪儿卖纸？
　　{ 哪儿都卖。

第二节　用"哪儿…啊"表示强调

Section II　Using 哪儿 ... 啊 to Express Emphasis

一、用"哪儿…啊"表示强调的意义

The meanings of 哪儿…啊 in expressing emphasis

如要反驳某情况与实际不相符合,汉语里常在谓语(动词或形容词)前边用疑问代词"哪儿"反问,表示强调。肯定形式强调否定的意思,否定形式强调肯定的意思。例如:

To refute a certain case that is not in keeping with the fact, the interrogative pronoun 哪儿 is often used before the predicate (verb or adjective) to form a rhetorical question expressing emphasis. The negative meaning is emphasized by the affirmative form while the affirmative meaning is emphasized by the negative form. For example:

（一）

反问句 Rhetorical questions	强调的意思 Meaning to be emphasized
我哪儿有工夫啊?	我没有工夫。
他哪儿知道这件事啊?	他不知道这件事。
北京的冬天哪儿冷啊?	北京的冬天不冷。
那个人哪儿是张先生啊?	那个人不是张先生。
她哪儿能来啊?	她不能来。

（二）

反问句 Rhetorical questions	强调的意思 Meaning to be emphasized
他哪儿不知道啊？	他知道。
她哪儿不帮忙啊？	她帮忙。
她哪儿能不来啊？	她能来。

二、用"哪儿…啊"表示强调的特点
Grammatical features

（一）"哪儿…啊"用于反问，句末用问号或惊叹号，不表示提问。例如：

哪儿…啊 is used in a rhetorical question with a question mark or an exclamation mark at the end of the sentence, but it does not indicate any inquiry. For example:

我哪儿会跳舞啊？

今天他哪儿去得了啊？

（二）疑问代词"哪儿"一定要用在所要强调的谓语前边，"啊"用于句末。例如：

The interrogative pronoun 哪儿 must be placed before the predicate that is emphasized while 啊 should be put at the end of the sentence. For example:

他哪儿高啊！

我哪儿记得啊！

（三）"哪儿…啊"中间可以是词或词组。例如：

What is between 哪儿 and 啊 may be a word or a phrase. For example:

今天哪儿热啊？　　　（形容词）

（Adjective）

我哪儿会画画儿啊？（动词性偏正词组）

（Verbal endocentric phrase）

他哪儿不努力啊？　（形容词性偏正词组）

（Adjectival endocentric phrase）

（四）重音在"哪儿"上。

The stress falls on 哪儿。

三、用"哪儿…啊"表示强调时需要注意的问题

Points that merit special attention

（一）用于反问表示强调的"哪儿"一定不能放在谓语动词后面，而且完全不表示处所。

哪儿 in a rhetorical question expressing emphasis can never be put after the predicate verb and it does not indicate locality at all.

（二）用"哪儿"的反问句句末常用语气助词"啊"，表示"使人信服"。例如：

The modal particle 啊 is often used at the end of a rhetorical question with 哪儿, indicating convincingness. For example:

她哪儿能不帮忙啊？（她一定会帮忙的。）

（She will certainly help.）

我哪儿会啊！　　　（我真不会。）

（I really can't.）

他们哪儿忙啊！　　（他们一点儿也不忙。）

（They are not at all busy.）

练 习 60

Exercise 60

用表示反问的"哪儿…啊"改写下列句子。

Rewrite the following sentences using 哪儿…啊 to form

rhetorical questions.

例： 他们没准备好。

Model： ──→ 他们哪儿准备好了啊？

1. 今天真冷。
2. 她很喜欢这个工作。
3. 我现在没看书。
4. 这只鸽子很好看。
5. 暑假里她不想去旅行。
6. 小王没找过你。
7. 哥哥没出国（到国外去）。
8. 他俩不常一起散步。
9. 老马没请他吃饭。
10. 我们没参加过这种活动。
11. 他不了解我的情况。
12. 老师不知道他有病。
13. 我没看见你的手套。
14. 他不知道这个消息。
15. 孩子们快活极了。

第三节 用"不是…吗"表示强调
Section III Using 不是 . . . 吗 to Express Emphasis

一、用"不是…吗"表示强调的意义

The meaning of 不是…吗 to express emphasis

如某情况与已知情况不相符合，汉语里常用"不是…吗"反问，表示强调肯定的意思。例如：

If something is not in keeping with what is already known, then 不是…吗 is often used to form a rhetorical question to stress the meaning of certainty. For example:

他不是明天去北京吗？

（说话人认为"他去北京"的时间是"明天"）

(The speaker holds that the time "he goes to Beijing" is "tomorrow.")

那个图书馆不是早上七点半开门吗？

（说话人认为"那个图书馆开门"的时间是"早上七点半"）

(The speaker holds that the library opens at "7:30 a.m.")

那不是你弟弟吗？

（说话人认为"那个人是你弟弟"）

(The speaker holds that "that person is your younger brother".)

我们不是已经约好了吗？

（说话人认为"我们已经约好了"）

(The speaker thinks that "we have already made an appointment".)

二、用"不是…吗"表示强调的特点　Grammatical features

（一）"不是…吗"用于反问，句末用问号，表示强调。

不是…吗 is used to form a rhetorical question with a question mark at the end of the sentence, expressing emphasis.

（二）"不是"一定要用在所强调的成分前边，"吗"在句尾。例如：

不是 must be placed before the element emphasized, 吗 at the end of the sentence. For example:

他不是来了吗？

（强调的是动词"来"）

(Emphasizing the verb 来)

我不是好了吗？

604

（强调的是形容词"好"）

(Emphasizing the adjective 好)

张老师不是能参加吗？

（强调的是助动词"能"）

(Emphasizing the auxiliary 能)

我们不是已经研究好了吗？

（强调的是副词"已经"）

(Emphasizing the adverb 已经)

他不是请你看过京剧吗？

（强调的是动词"请"）

(Emphasizing the verb 请)

（三）"不是…吗"中间可以是词或词组。例如：

Either words or phrases may be inserted between 不是…吗.

For example:

他不是院长吗？　　　（名词）

(Noun)

你们不是认识吗？　　（动词）

(Verb)

站在门外的不是他吗？（代词）

(Pronoun)

前边那座楼不是你们的宿舍楼吗？

（名词性偏正词组）

(Nominal endocentric phrase)

你明天不是去上海吗？（动宾词组）

(V-O phrase)

你不是星期二动身吗？（动词性偏正词组）

(Verbal endocentric phrase)

这里不是非常安静吗？

（形容词性偏正词组）

(Adjectival endocentric phrase)

（四）重音一般在"不是"后边要强调的成分上。

The stress is generally on the element that is emphasized after 不是.

三、用"不是…吗"表示强调时需要注意的问题

Points that merit special attention

（一）"不是"可以用在主语后边谓语前边，也可以用在主语前边。例如：

不是 may either be used after the subject and before the predicate or be put before the subject. For example:

> 你不是去过我家吗？
>
> > （"不是"在主语"你"后）
> >
> > (不是 is after the subject 你)
>
> 不是你告诉我明天去北京吗？
>
> > （"不是"在主语"你"前）
> >
> > (不是 is placed before the subject 你)
>
> 不是我们都已经报名了吗？
>
> > （"不是"在主语"我们"前）
> >
> > (不是 is before the subject 我们)

（二）"不是"后边的谓语由动词"是"充当时，只能用一个"是"。例如：

When 是 acts as the predicate after 不是, only one 是 can be used. For example:

> 那位不是你的女朋友吗？
>
> 这不是你画的画儿吗？

（三）只有在发现与已知情况不符合的情况时才用"不是…吗"表示反问，用以进一步肯定已知情况，并对新情况提出疑问。例如：

The rhetorical question using 不是…吗 is only used when one finds something is not in keeping with what is already known and wants to make sure further of the information known and

606

to express his doubt about what has happened. For example:

你不是病了吗？

（为什么还来听课呢？）

(Why do you still come to attend class?)

我们不是八点出发吗？

（你怎么七点就去集合地点？）

(Why did you go to the assembly place at 7?)

今天不是星期天吗？

（你为什么不出去玩儿玩儿？）

(Why don't you go out to enjoy yourself?)

练　习　61
Exercise 61

用表示反问的"不是…吗"改写下列句子。

Rewrite the following sentences using 不是…吗 to form
rhetorical questions.

例：　　　他告诉你了。

Model:　　　────→ 他不是告诉你了吗？

1．这是一片树林。

2．这个青年加入进步团体了。

3．他们都买到《实用汉语600句》了。

4．明天下午有篮球比赛。

5．我们已经通过电话了。

6．她特别希望看到老同学。

7．他们为建设祖国贡献了自己的全部力量。

8．我跟他谈过这件事了。

9．她们准备坐飞机去。

10．他下星期回国。

607

11. 病人昏迷过去了。

12. 他对世界地理很有兴趣。

13. 他们俩感情很好。

14. 他讲课讲得很生动。

15. 他从小就喜欢思考。

第四节　用"连…都（也）"表示强调
Section IV Using 连 … 都（也）to Express Emphasis

一、用"连…都（也）"表示强调的意义

The meaning of 连…都（也）in expressing emphasis

汉语里常用介词"连"引出要强调的成分，表示所强调的对象尚且这样，其他情况更不言而喻了。

In Chinese, the conjunction 连 is often used to introduce the element that is to be emphasized, showing that even what is emphasized is so, to say nothing of other cases.

（一）突出强调主语。例如：

Emphasizing the subject. For example:

连孩子们都很讲礼貌。

（强调人人都讲礼貌，甚至"孩子们"也这样）
(Emphasizing that everyone is courteous, even "children")

现在连他也常去图书馆了。

〔强调现在去图书馆的人很多，甚至平时不常去图书馆的人（"他"）也常去了〕
(Emphasizing that nowadays many people go to the library, even those who used not to go there like "him", now often go too.)

连他都戴帽子了。

（强调外边很冷，以至平时不戴帽的人——"他"也戴上了）

(Emphasizing that it is very cold outside, so even "he" — who does not wear a hat usually, is now wearing one.)

这样好的节目，连我都想看了。

（节目太好了，以至平时很少看的人——"我"也想看了）

(The performance is so good that even "I" — who seldom watch them—want to watch it now.)

（二）突出强调前置宾语。例如：

Emphasizing the fronted object. For example:

他连角落里的灰都扫掉了。

（强调他扫屋子扫得很干净，甚至"角落里的灰"也扫掉了）

(Emphasizing that he sweeps the room very clean, even 角落里的灰 is swept away.)

他们连饭也没吃，就去医院了。

（强调情况紧急，到吃饭时间也顾不上吃）

(Emphasizing that it is so urgent that he has no time to eat even when it is meal time.)

（三）突出强调谓语动词。例如：

Emphasizing the predicate verb. For example:

这件事，他连考虑一下也不考虑。

（强调不愿意考虑，不同意这件事）

(Emphasizing that he does not agree to the matter, so he does not want to give it any consideration.)

昨天他连看也没看，就把书还给我了。

（强调"没有"，不愿看这本"书"）

(Emphasizing 没有, i.e. he did not want to read the 书.)

二、用"连…都（也）"表示强调的特点 Grammatical features

（一）介词"连"的宾语可以是词或词组。例如：

Objects of the conjunction 连 can either be words or phrases. For example:

连老师都已经来了，你怎么才来。（名词）
                                    (Noun)

连他都会修理打字机。   （代词）
                                    (Pronoun)

他连碰也没碰。   （动词）
                                    (Verb)

连抽屉里都找了，哪儿也没有。   （方位词组）
                                    (Locality phrase)

我们班同学连一个也不知道这件事。（数量词组）
                                    (N-Mw-phrase)

他连下星期六的飞机票都买好了。（名词性偏正词组）
                                    (Nominal endocentric phrase)

（二）所要强调的成分要放在"连…都（也）"的中间。

The emphasized elements should be placed between 连…都（也）.

（三）介词"连"后边是名词、代词或名词性偏正词组时，常是要强调一般句式中的主语或宾语。例如：

The conjunction 连 means to emphasize the noun, pronoun or nominal endocentric phrase that follows it as the subject or object of an ordinary sentence. For example:

连老人都参加了这次庆祝活动。

（"老人"是主语）

(老人 is the subject.)

连床都搬走了。

（"床"是表示被动意义的"受事主语"）

(床 is the recipient subject in the passive.)

他连手套都戴上了。

（"手套"是谓语动词"戴"的受事者，前置宾语）

(手套 is the fronted object and receiver of the verb 戴.)

他连我都不认识了。

（"我"是谓语动词"认识"的受事者，前置宾语）

(我 is the fronted object and receiver of 认识.)

我们连明天的课都准备好了。

（"明天的课"是谓语动词"准备"的受事者，是前置宾语）

(明天的课 is the fronted object and receiver of the predicate verb 准备.)

（四）介词"连"后边是动词或动宾词组时，谓语多是否定形式或是表示遗忘一类的动词。例如：

When the preposition 连 is followed by verbs or V-O phrases, the predicate is, most often, a negative one, or is a verb like 'forget', etc. For example:

他连讨论都忘了。

他连游泳都不会。

他连洗衣服都没时间。

（五）"连…"后边一定要用副词"都"或"也"。

The adverb 都 or 也 must be preceded by 　"连…"

（六）重音在"连"后边要强调的成分上。

The stress is on the element to be emphasized after 连.

三、用"连…都（也）"表示强调时需要注意的问题

Points that merit special attention

（一）"连…都（也）"中的介词"连"可以省略不用，但后边的副词"都"或"也"一定不能遗漏。例如：

The preposition 连 in 连…都（也）can be left out while the adverb 都 or 也 can never be omitted. For example:

（连）他都参加锻炼，我们更应该参加了。

他（连）门也没关，就出去了。

他（连）看报都没时间，哪儿有时间看小说啊？

一定不能只用介词"连"而不用副词"都"或"也"。不能说"连他参加锻炼…"、"他连门没关"或"他连看报没时间"等。

One can never use the preposition 连 by itself without using the adverb 都 or 也. One cannot say 连他参加锻炼…，他连门没关，他连看报没时间，etc.

（二）如要强调宾语，宾语要提到谓语动词前边，成为前置宾语。例如：

The object to be emphasized, should preposition the the predicate, thus it becomes a fronted object. For example:

他连话也不想说。

我们连本子都买来了。

（三）谓语和"连"后的宾语如果是同样的动词，谓语动词都是否定形式。例如：

If the predicate and the object of 连 are one and the same verb, then the predicate verb must be in the negative. For example:

对这种事，他连想也没想过。

这样的东西，我连看也不看。

（四）"连一…也（都）"常省去介词"连"，而形成"一…也（都）"，汉语里常用来表示甚至连"一"这个最小的数量

612

都达不到，以强调"没有"，谓语是否定形式。重音在"一"字上。例如：

The preposition 连 in 连——…也（都）is often omitted
and the construction becomes ——…也（都）which is often used
to show that the amount is even less than — —— the smallest
number, emphasizing 没有. The predicate is in the negative
form and the stress is on —, e.g.

屋子里（连）一个人也没有。

他（连）一支笔也不买。

这项工作，我们（连）一天也没耽误。

还常用"一点儿"或"一会儿"表示强调。例如：

一点儿 or 一会儿 are also often used to express emphasis.
For example:

他一点儿也不害怕。

我们在那儿一会儿也没闲着。

练 习 62

Exercise 62

用"连…都（也）"改写下列句子（强调带横线的部分）。

Rewrite the following sentences using 连…都（也）
(emphasizing the underlined parts).

例：　来中国以前，我不会说中国话。

Model：——→ 来中国以前，我连一句中国话也不会说。

1. 这位老人高兴得唱起来了。

2. 这些小学生都积极参加了这次有益的活动。

3. 屋前屋后都种了一些树。

4. 你没问他，怎么知道他没去！

5. 他没穿大衣就走了。

6. 现在他会开<u>拖拉机</u>了。
7. 以前我<u>没</u>想<u>过</u>能来北京。
8. 他新买的提包还<u>没</u>用<u>过</u>就不见了。
9. 他的<u>孩子</u>也会弹钢琴了。
10. 我们<u>没</u>订<u>计划</u>。

第五节 用副词"是"表示强调
Section V Using the Adverb 是 to Express Emphasis

一、用副词"是"表示强调的意义
The meaning of the adverb 是 in expressing emphasis

汉语里常在谓语（动词或形容词）前用副词"是"表示证实，强调后边的情况是确实的，"是"要重读。例如：

In Chinese, the adverb 是 is often used before the predicate (verb or adjective) to indicate confirmation, emphasizing that what follows is doubtless. 是 is stressed in reading or speaking. For example:

<blockquote>
他是去过欧洲。   这种看法是片面。

他是进会场了。   他的身体是不错。

这碗汤是淡。   这位老人的脸色是好。
</blockquote>

二、用副词"是"表示强调的特点
Grammatical features

（一）表示强调的"是"后边可以是动词、形容词或以动词、形容词为主的词组。例如：

What follows the adverb 是 may be a verb, an adjective, a verbal phrase or an adjectival phrase. For example:

<blockquote>
他是去。   （动词）

                (Verb)
</blockquote>

他是在那个研究所工作。（动词性偏正词组）
(Verbal endocentric phrase)

他是搞研究工作。（动宾词组）
(V-O phrase)

他是工作得很好。（动补词组）
(V-C phrase)

他是来过一次。（动补词组）
(V-C phrase)

他是不想离开。（动词性偏正词组）
(Verbal endocentric phrase)

她是漂亮。（形容词）
(Adjective)

她是非常认真。（形容词性偏正词组）
(Adjectival endocentric phrase)

她是高多了。（形补词组）
(Adjective-Complement phrase)

她是瘦了一点儿。（形补词组）
(Adjective-Complement phrase)

（二）表示强调的"是"后边的谓语动词可以有不同的状态。例如：

The predicate verb after 是 indicating emphasis may have various aspects. For example:

他是在写信。（动作正在进行）
(The action is going on.)

她是去图书馆了。（动作已完成）
(The action is finished.)

我们是要走了。（动作将要发生）
(The action will take place.)

她们是找过我。（过去的经历）
(The action is a past experience.)

桌子上是放着一封电报。

　　　　（动作结果处于持续状态）

　　　（The result of the action continues.)

　　（三）表示强调的"是"可以用在肯定形式或否定形式前边，都表示证实后边的情况（肯定的或否定的）。例如：

The predicate modified by the emphatic adverb 是 may be affirmative or negative and in either case, 是 functions to confirm what follows it. For example:

　　　　　他是买了一件大衣。

　　　　　（证实"买了"这个肯定情况）

　　　　　（Confirming the affirmative case of 买了)

　　　　　他是没买大衣。

　　　　　（证实"没买"这个否定情况）

　　　　　（Confirming the negative case of 没买)

　　　　　我是吃了饭了。

　　　　　（证实"吃了"这个肯定情况）

　　　　　（Confirming the affirmative case of 吃了)

　　　　　我是没吃饭呢。

　　　　　（证实"没吃"这个否定情况）

　　　　　（Confirming the negative case of 没吃)

　　（四）表示强调的"是"应重读。

是 indicating emphasis should be stressed in pronunciation.

三、用副词"是"表示强调时需要注意的问题

Points that merit special attention

　　（一）"是"字句里如果要表示强调证实的意思，只需把"是"字变成重读，而不能再加一个"是"字。例如：

If the predicate of a 是-sentence is emphasized for confirmation, one needs only to stress the verb 是 before which the adverb 是 is never used. For example:

他是我们的朋友。

我们是这个学院的学生。

这座楼是电报大楼。

不能说"他是是我们的朋友"等。

One cannot say 他是是我们的朋友 etc.

（二）强调证实的副词"是"本身不能用于否定形式。不能说"他不是买了大衣"等。

The adverb 是 emphasizing confirmation does not have the negative form, so one can never say 他不是买了大衣, etc.

练 习 63
Exercise 63

用表示"确实"的副词"是"改写下列各句。

Rewrite the following sentences using the adverb 是 indicating "doubtlessness".

例：　　　这个问题比较复杂。

Model:　　────→ 这个问题是比较复杂。

1. 这支钢笔五块钱。

2. 他的家在广州。

3. 要下雪了。

4. 台上坐着不少科学家。

5. 谢力今天特别高兴。

6. 那位是张老师的爱人。

7. 玛利去过中国。

8. 这个问题大家已经解决了。

9. 他们不想在这儿过圣诞节。

10. 他没用过这种照相机。

11. 我有点儿不舒服。

12. 他不准备在历史系学习了。

第六节 用副词"就"表示强调
Section VI Using the Adverb 就 to Express Emphasis

一、用副词"就"表示强调的意义

The meaning of the adverb 就 in expressing emphasis

汉语里常在谓语动词前用副词"就"表示强调,而且可以表示不同的强调意义,常见的有:

In Chinese, the adverb 就 is often used before the predicate verb to indicate emphasis of various implications, of which the common ones are as follows:

（一）强调"正是"后边的情况,而不是别的。例如:

Emphasizing the meaning of "precisely", "none other than", as in:

他就是王院长。

我哥哥就是那个戴眼镜的。

（二）强调"立刻、马上"的意思。例如:

Emphasizing the meaning of "immediately", "at once", as in:

我就来。

他就给你送去。

（三）强调"只"的意思。例如:

Emphasizing the meaning of "only", as in:

这儿就有两把椅子。

我们班就有一个中国人。

他们就来两个代表。

（四）强调"坚决"的意思。例如:

618

Emphasizing the meaning of "resolution", as in:

> 我就看。
>
> 他就不来。
>
> 她们就不肯这么做。

二、用副词"就"表示强调的特点 Grammatical features

（一）表示强调的"就"常用在谓语前边。例如：

就 indicating emphasis often occurs before the predicate. For example:

> 饭菜就熟。
>
> 大家就选了一个代表。
>
> 您就吃这么一点儿？
>
> 那就是他最近的创作。

（二）表示强调的"就"后边的谓语一般由动词充当。例如：

The predicate emphasized by the adverb 就 is usually a verb. For example:

> 八十五号就是他家。
>
> （请等一下，）他就翻译完那首诗。
>
> 他们就租三辆车。
>
> 她就不采取措施。

（三）表示强调的副词"就"应重读。

The adverb 就 indicating emphasis should be stressed in pronunciation.

三、用副词"就"表示强调时需要注意的问题

Points that merit special attention

（一）副词"就"没有否定形式。

The adverb 就 does not have a negative form.

（二）副词"就"表示强调"只"的意思时，谓语动词后边常带数量词组。例如：

When the adverb 就 emphasizes the meaning of "only", the predicate verb often takes a N-Mw phrase. For example:

他就有一本汉语语法书。

我们就去三天。

（三）副词“就”一般都用在肯定形式的谓语前边，只有表示“坚决不”、“偏不”的意思时，可以用在否定形式“不…”前边。例如：

The adverb 就 usually occurs before the predicate in the affirmative form. Only when indicating the meaning of "resolutely not", "simply not", can it occur before the negative form "不…". For example:

我就不干。

他就不写。

练　习　64
Exercise 64

指出下列各句中副词“就”强调的意义。

State the meanings that the adverb 就 emphasizes.

例：

Model: 他就是昨天刚到的汉语老师。（正是）

1．老马就有一个女孩子。

2．我们就路过那儿一次。

3．这位就是冠军。

4．他就不喜欢穿那种样子的上衣。

5．张先生就下楼来。（您稍等一下。）

6．那儿就是颐和园。

7．就要下雨了。（赶快把衣服收进来。）

8．我就看过一次中国的京剧。

9．火车就要进站了。

10．我就不告诉你一个人。

第七节 用两次否定表示强调

Section VII Using Double Negation to Express Emphasis

一、用两次否定表示强调的意义

The meaning of double negation in expressing emphasis

汉语里常在一个句子里用两次否定的形式来表示肯定，强调肯定的程度是不容置疑的。常见的用两次否定形式强调肯定的格式有：

Double negation is often used in a sentence to indicate affirmation, emphasizing that the degree of affirmation is beyond any doubt. Common patterns of emphasizing affirmation with double negation are as follows:

（一）"不…不…"

他不应该不来。

（强调"应该来"）

(Emphasizing 应该来)

我们不得不这么做。

（强调得(děi)这么做）

(Emphasizing 得 (dei) 这么做)

大家不能不表示自己的态度。

（强调"一定要表示"）

(Emphasizing 一定要表示)

这个任务今天不能不完成。

（强调"一定要完成"）

(Emphasizing 一定要完成)

（二）"没有…不…"

我们学校没有人不戴手套。

（强调"人人都戴"）

(Emphasizing 人人都戴)

他们家没有人不喜欢音乐。

（强调"全家人都喜欢"）

(Emphasizing 全家人都喜欢)

我们班没有一个人不及格。

（强调"每个同学都及格"）

(Emphasizing 每个同学都及格)

他没有一天不游泳。

（强调"每天都游泳"）

(Emphasizing 每天都游泳)

（三）"不…没有…"

我们家不能没有你。

（强调"必须有你"）

(Emphasizing 必须有你)

每个学生都不能没有教科书。

（强调"必须有教科书"）

(Emphasizing 必须有教科书)，

她不应该没有时间复习。

（强调"应该有时间"）

(Emphasizing 应该有时间)

（四）"没有不…"

我们没有不能解决的问题。

（强调"所有问题都能解决"）

(Emphasizing 所有问题都能解决)

他没有不想看的节目。

（强调"所有节目他都想看"）

(Emphasizing 所有节目他都想看)

她房间里没有不需要的东西。

（强调"房里所有东西都需要"）

(Emphasizing 房里所有东西都需要)

世界上没有克服不了的困难。

（强调"所有困难都克服得了"）

(Emphasizing 所有困难都克服得了)

二、用两次否定表示强调的特点　Grammatical features

（一）否定副词"不"或"没有"可以同时出现在一个句子里，构成"不…不…"、"没有…不…"、"不…没有…"或"没有不…"等两次否定的格式。例如：

The negative adverb 不 or 没有 may occur in one sentence at the same time, forming the double negative 不…不…，没有…不…，不…没有… or 没有不…. For example:

他不会不来。

这批机器没有一台不符合标准。

这座办公大楼里不可能没有电梯。

我们几个人没有不喜欢游泳的。

（二）否定副词"不"或"没有"可以连用，也可以分开用。例如：

The negative adverbs 不 and 没有 can other be used either in combination or separately. For example:

我们这里没有不知道这件事的人。

（连用）

(Used in combination)

这个车间没有一台机器不是新的。

（分开用）

(Used separately)

（三）否定副词"不"或"没有"后边可以是词或词组。例如：

Either words or phrases may follow the negative adverb 不 or 没有. For example:

你们不能不考虑。

他们班没有人不报名。

这里不能没有医院。

三、用两次否定表示强调时需要注意的问题

Points that merit special attention

（一）否定副词"没有"和"不"的连用形式只能是"没有不"，而不能说"不没有"。

The form of the negative adverbs 没有 and 不 used in combination, can only be 没有不 and not 不没有.

（二）用两次否定表示强调的句子里，谓语多由动词充当，少数用"不"的地方后面也可以用形容词作谓语。例如：

In a sentence of double negation expressing emphasis, the predicate is usually a verb, and in a few cases 不 can be followed by an adjective predicate. For example:

这个院子里没有不干净的房间。

她没有一天不高兴。

（三）在两次否定的格式"没有…不"中间常用带有数词"一"的数量词组，强调"没有例外"。例如：

A N-Mw phrase in which N is 一 is often inserted into the double negation pattern 没有…不 emphasizing the meaning of "without exception". For example:

我们三个人没有一个不爱打乒乓球。

他们没有一天不踢足球。

这个车间没有一个月不提前完成任务。

（四）用两次否定表示强调的句子里，否定副词后边的谓语一般不能再受程度副词修饰。不能说："她没有一天不很高兴"。

In a sentence of double negation indicating emphasis, the predicate after the negative adverb normally cannot be modified by an adverb of degree. One cannot say 她没有一天不很高兴, etc.

624

练 习 65

Exercise 65

把下列句子改成用两次否定表示强调的句子。

Rewrite the following sentences using double negation indicating emphasis.

例： 他们一定能来参加这个重要的会议。

Model: ——→ 他们不能不来参加这个重要的会议。

1. 我们应该准备雨衣。
2. 他们人人都讲究卫生。
3. 这个地区必须有个青年俱乐部。
4. 这场比赛不能缺少你。
5. 这个村子的人都会编这种筐。
6. 这次他一定考得很好。
7. 我们几个人都非常细心。
8. 人人都懂得这是一种外交礼节。
9. 这个问题今天必须解决。
10. 各种体育运动他都喜欢。

第八节 用"是…的"表示强调

Section VIII Using 是 ... 的 to Express Emphasis

一、用"是…的"表示强调的意义

The meanings of 是…的 in expressing emphasis

如要特别强调一个已完成动作发生的时间、地点或方式，可以用"是…的"表示。

是…的 may be used to emphasize particularly the time, locale or manner of a completed action.

（一）强调动作发生的时间。例如：

Emphasizing the time when the action took place, as in:

> 我们是八点出发的。
>
> 他是去年来的。

（二）强调动作发生的地点。例如：

Emphasizing the locale where the action took place, as in:

> 她是在上海遇见他的。
>
> 我是从美国来的。

（三）强调动作的方式。例如：

Emphasizing the manner in which the action was carried out, as in:

> 我是跟父母一起来的。
>
> 他们是坐船走的。

二、用“是…的”表示强调的特点

Grammatical features

（一）表示强调的“是…的”中间一般是动词性偏正词组。例如：

Verbal endocentric phrases generally occur between 是…的 indicating emphasis. For example:

> 我是早上去的。
>
> 他是在食堂吃的。
>
> 我们是骑车来的。

（二）“是”要放在所要强调的时间、地点或方式的词语前边，“的”一般放在句尾。例如：

是 precedes the word of time, place or manner to be emphasized and 的 is usually at the end of the sentence. For example:

> 我们是昨天晚上看的。
>
> 他们是在北京语言学院学习的。

她是坐车来的。

（三）表示强调的"是…的"中间如果是动宾词组，"的"在宾语前边或句尾都可以。例如：

When a V-O phrase is emphasized by 是…的, 的 can be placed either before the object (O) or at the end of the sentence. For example:

我们是昨天晚上看电影的，

他们是在北京语言学院学的汉语。

她是坐车来我这儿的。

（四）肯定形式中如有主语可不用"是"；否定形式为"不是…的"，"是"不能省去。例如：

In an affirmative sentence where the subject is present, 是 is optional, however, in the negative form of such a sentence 是 cannot be omitted, i.e. 不是…的 is the formula. For example:

我（是）早上去的，不是下午去的。

他（是）在饭馆吃的，不是在家里吃的。

我们不是坐车来的。（是骑车来的）

姐姐不是跟朋友一起去的。（是一个人去的）

（五）重音在所强调的时间、地点或方式状语上。

The stress falls on the adverbial adjunct of time, place or manner which is emphasized.

三、用"是…的"表示强调时需要注意的问题

Points that merit special attention

（一）在强调已完成动作发生的时间、地点或方式的句子里，"是…的"不能跟表示完成的动态助词"了"并用。例如：

In sentences emphasizing the time, place or manner of a completed action, 是…的 cannot go together with the aspectual particle 了 indicating completion. For example:

我们是去年九月开始学习汉语的。

我祖母是在南京病死的。

不能说"我们是去年九月开始学习了汉语的"或"我祖母是在南京病死了的"等。

One cannot say 我们是去年九月开始学习了汉语的 or 我祖母是在南京病死了的, etc.

（二）"是…的"中间是动宾词组，而宾语是人称代词，或者动宾词组后带有趋向补语时，"的"要放在句尾。例如：

的 must be at the end of a sentence when 是…的 is used to emphasize a V-O phrase which is followed by a directional complement or in which the object (O) is a personal pronoun. For example:

我是上星期五看见他的。

他是下午从城里到这儿来的。

练 习 66
Exercise 66

把下列句子改成用"是…的"表示强调的句子。

Rewrite the following sentences using 是…的 indicating emphasis.

例：　　　前年他毕业了。

Model:　　　——→　他是前年毕业的。

1．一九八〇年张文去日本学习。

2．我们都用汉语谈话。

3．小王什么时候回去了？

4．她在汽车站等我。

5．他们骑车去公园了。

6．您在哪儿遇见马老师了？

7．你怎么知道我住院了？

8．我母亲从上海回来了。

9. 他上星期离开北京了。
10. 他昨天坐飞机走了。

附表十一： 八种表示强调方法的简要情况表
Table 11: Eight Ways to Express Emphasis

表示强调的方法 Expressions of emphasis	例 句 Examples	表示的意义 Meanings	结 构 特 点 Structural features
用疑问代词 Using interrogative pronouns	谁都知道这个消息。 他什么也不吃。 哪儿都有公园。 哪个公园都很好。 他怎么要求都不行。	表示任指，强调任何人或事物都不例外 Showing indefinite indication, emphasizing "no one or nothing is an exception."	用于陈述句，句尾用句号；疑问代词可作主语、前置宾语、状语或定语，谓语动词（或形容词）前要用副词"都"，重音在疑问代词上。 Used in statement with a full stop at the end. Interrogative pronouns act as subject, fronted object, adverbial adjunct or attributive. 都 is used before the predicate verb (or adjective). Stress is on the interrogative pronoun.

用法	例句	意义	说明
用"哪儿…啊" Using 哪儿…啊	他哪儿睡了？ 我哪儿不高兴啊	表示反问，肯定形式强调否定的意思，否定形式强调肯定的意思 Indicating rhetorical questions. Negation is emphasized by affirmative form while affirmation is emphasized by negative form.	不表示提问，句尾用问号，"哪儿"要用在所强调的成份前边，"啊"用在句尾；重音在"哪儿"上。 Question mark at the end of a sentence without indicating inquiry 哪儿 used before element emphasized 啊 used at the end of a sentence. 哪儿 is stressed.
用"不是…吗" Using 不是…吗	你不是明天去吗？ 我们不是约好了吗？	表示反问，强调肯定的意思 Indicating rhetorical questions; emphasizing certainty.	不表示提问，句尾用问号，"不是"一定要用在所强调的成份前边，"吗"用在句尾 A period at the end of a sentence without indicating inquiry 不是 must be used before the element emphasized. 吗 is put at the end of a sentence.

用法 Usage	例 Examples	意义 Meaning	说明 Notes
用"连…都(也)" Using 连…都(也)	连孩子们都很讲礼貌。 他连饭也没吃，就走了。 他连想也没想。	表示某情况尚且如此，其他情况不言而喻 Showing that even what is emphasized is so, to say nothing of other cases.	"连"的宾语可以是词或词组，"连"要放在所强调的成份前边，"连…"后边要用副词"都"或"也" Object of 连 may be words or phrases. 连 is placed before the element emphasized. 都 or 也 must occur after "连…".
用副词"是" Using the adverb 是	她是演员。 他是笑出。 我是不知道这件事。	强调后边的情况是确实的 Emphasizing the following case is doubtless.	副词"是"常用在谓语形容词或动词前边， "是"可用在肯定形式或否定形式前， "是"要重读。 是 is often used before the predicate adjective or verb. 是 occurs before either the affirmative or the negative form. 是 is stressed.
用副词"就" Using the adverb 就	他就是王院长。 我就来。 她就有一本词典。 他就要看。	强调"正是"，"只"或"坚决"的意思 Emphasizing the ideas "precisely", "at once", "only", or "resolution".	副词"就"常用在谓语动词前边， "就"要重读。 就 is often used before the predicate verb and is stressed.

			否定副词"不"和"没有"可在同一句子里构成"不…不"，"没有…不"，"不…没有"或"没有不"等格式；只有"没有不"这种连用形式，其他都应分开用	不 and 没有 may occur in the same sentence to form 不…不, 没有…不, 不…没有 or 没有不, etc. 没有不 is the only combined form of double negation.
用两次否定 Using double negation	他不应该不来。 他没有一天不游泳。 每个学生都不能没有书。 我们没有不能解决的问题。	强调肯定的意思 Emphasizing affirmation		
用"是…的" Using 是…的	他是去年来的。 他是从法国来的。 我们是坐船来的。	强调已完成动作发生的时间、地点或方式 Emphasizing the time, place or manner of a completed action.	"是"要放在所强调的时间、地点或方式状语前边，"的"可放在宾语后或句尾，否定形式是"不是…的"；"是…的"中不能用表示完成的动态助词"了"	"是" should be placed before the adv. of time, place or manner that is emphasized. 的 can be placed either before the object or at the end of a sentence. The negative form is 不是…的. The aspectual particle 了 indicating the completion of an action cannot occur between 是…的.

633

第十章 复 句
Chapter Ten Complex Senetences

一、什么是复句 Definition

由两个或两个以上单句构成的、有完整意义和一定语调的句子叫复句，复句所包括的单句叫分句。例如：

Sentences consisting of two or more simple sentences, expressing a complete meaning and spoken in a certain intonation, are called complex sentences. Simple sentences contained in a complex sentence are called clauses. For example:

他是冠军，我是亚军。

老马刚走，小王来了。

风停了，雨也不下了。

如果他们来，我就在家等着。

虽然天气不好，他们也要去。

二、复句的特点

Grammatical features

（一）复句包含两个或两个以上的分句，分句和分句之间有较小的语音停顿，书面上用逗号"，"或分号"；"表示，全句末尾有一个较大的语音停顿，书面上用句号、问号或感叹号表示，整个句子有一个完整的语调。

A complex sentence contains two or more clauses between which there is a pause when spoken and the pause is indicated by a comma (,) or sometimes by a semicolon (;) in writing. When the whole sentence is spoken, there should be a stop which is indicated in writing by a full stop (.), a question mark(?) or an exclamation mark (:). The sentence is spoken intonationally as a complete whole.

（二）复句中各个分句可以是各种主谓句，如果各分句的主语相同，也可以只用一个主语。例如：

The clauses in a complex sentence may be various kinds of S-P sentences. If the clauses share the same subject, then the subject does not have to be repeated, e.g.

她会英文，她会法文，她也会日文。

（每个分句都有主语，都是"她"）

(Each clause has a subject and they are all 她.)

这本小说没意思，我不想看了。

（每个分句都有主语，但不一样）

(Each clause has a subject, but they are not the same.)

他今天很忙，（他）不能陪你出去。

（两个分句只用一个主语"他"）

(Two clauses share one subject 他.)

（三）复句中各分句之间可以有各种不同的关系，常需要用关联词表示。例如：

In a complex sentence clauses have various relations which are often denoted by correlatives. For example:

因为今天星期日，所以公园里的人特别多。

不但他们要去那儿避暑，而且我们也准备去。

既然你不舒服，就在家休息吧。

（四）关联词是一些能连接分句的连词和具有关联作用的副词。关联词可按分句之间的不同关系放在前边或后边的分句里，有的在主语前边，有的在主语后边。例如：

Correlatives are 1) conjunctions that connect clauses and 2) adverbs that have the function of connection. Correlatives can be put either in the first or second clause according to different relations between clauses. Some correlatives are used before the subject and others after it. For example:

> 他又喜欢踢足球，又喜欢听音乐。
>
> 要是你有兴趣，我们就去参观博物馆。
>
> 你与其坐船去，不如坐火车去。
>
> 他今天有事，所以不能来了。
>
> 虽然天气不太好，他们也要去游览长城。

有些关联词必须配合使用，有些可以单用。

Some of the correlatives must be used together while others can be used individually.

（五）复句中各分句可以是各种结构的谓语句。例如：

Clauses in a complex sentence may have various kinds of predicates. For example:

> 今天星期一，明天星期二。
>
> （名词谓语句）
>
> (Sentence with predicate)
>
> 只要有决心，就有成功的希望。
>
> （动词谓语句）
>
> (Sentence with verbal predicate)
>
> 与其他去，不如我去。
>
> （动词谓语句）
>
> (Sentence with verbal predicate)
>
> 不论天气怎么冷，他都要洗凉水澡。
>
> （形容词谓语句）
>
> (Sentence with adjectival predicate)

三、复句的种类

Types of complex sentences

复句中分句和分句之间的关系非常复杂，但总括起来，大致可以分成并列复句和偏正复句两大类。这两类复句又可分别表示各种不同的关系。现将简单情况列表如下：

In a complex sentence relationships between clauses are quite complicated. To put it briefly, complex sentences can be roughly divided into two types: coordinate complex sentences and subordinate complex sentences. They, again, be divided into subclasses in terms of the relationships of their clauses. Below is a table showing the different relationships of the clauses in complex sentences:

复 句
Complex sentence

并列复句
Coordinate complex sentence

- 联合关系
  Coordinative relation
- 承接关系
  Successive relation
- 递进关系
  Progressive relation
- 选择关系
  Alternative relation

偏正复句
Subordinate complex sentence

- 转折关系
  Adverse relation
- 因果关系
  Causative relation
- 条件关系
  Conditional relation
- 假设关系
  Hypothetical relation
- 目的关系
  Purposive relation
- 取舍关系
  Preference relation

另外还有一种紧缩复句，是介乎单句和复句之间的一种句子，也将在本章介绍。

This chapter will introduce another type of sentence called contracted complex sentence which is a form between the simple sentence and the complex sentence.

下面分节介绍。

The various types of complex sentences will be introduced in turn in the following sections.

第一节　并列复句

Section I　Coordinate Complex Sentences

一、什么是并列复句　Definition

由表示并列关系的分句构成的复句，叫并列复句。并列复句中分句之间的意义关系是平等的，相互之间没有主次的区别。例如：

Complex sentences formed of clauses indicating coordinate relations are called coordinate complex sentences.　In a coordinate complex sentence, the clauses are equal in meaning and there is no difference in importance between them. Here are some examples:

这是卧室，那是书房。

他一边喝茶，一边听音乐。

您（还是）在新闻界工作，还是在教育界工作？

二、并列复句的种类

Types of coordinate complex sentences

并列复句中分句之间可以表示下列各种不同的关系。

The relationships between the clauses of a coordinate complex sentence are as follows:

（一）联合关系

Coordinative relation

几个分句分别说明或描写几件事，或者说明同一事物的几个方面。例如：

The clauses explain or describe several things respectively or explain the different aspects of one thing. For example:

> 他学习音乐，我学习舞蹈。
>
> 她一方面工作，一方面还要帮徒弟学习文化。
>
> 这种帽子又好看、又便宜、又适合你的年龄。
>
> 不是我不想来，而是没有时间。

（二）承接关系

Successive relation

几个分句按动作的先后或相互的关系排列顺序，各分句之间的意思是连贯的。例如：

The clauses are arranged according to the sequence of actions or to the relations between them. The meanings of the clauses are coherent. For example:

> 你先选好题目，然后再商量怎么写。
>
> 下了课，我就去你那儿。
>
> 太阳一出来，就暖和了。

（三）递进关系

Progressive relation

后边的分句比前边分句的意思更进一层。例如：

The second clause goes further in meaning than the first one. For example:

> 这道数学题对不对，还要算一下。
>
> 那种火车不但设备好，而且速度快。

（四）选择关系

Alternative relation

几个分句分别叙述的几件事或几种情况不能同时并存，需要在其中选择一件或一种。例如：

The clauses state different things that are alternatives, and only one of them is chosen. For example:

　　您（还是）明天动身，还是后天动身？

　　（或者）当工人，或者当战士，他都愿意。

　　那本新词典不是哥哥买的，就是姐姐买的。

三、并列复句的特点　Grammatical features

　　（一）在结构上，可以包含两个或两个以上的分句。例如：

Structure: A coordinate complex sentence contains two or more than two clauses. For example:

　　这件事可以这样处理，也可以那样处理。

　　他有错，你也有错，我们都有错。

　　（二）在分句的次序上，表示联合关系和选择关系的分句一般可以对调而不影响意思，而表示承接关系和递进关系的分句不能任意颠倒。例如：

The order of clauses: Generally speaking, the order of the clauses of coordinative relation and alternative relation can be changed without affecting the meaning. But the order of the clauses of successive relation and progressive relation cannot be reversed at will. For example:

　　　他一边弹琴，一边唱。
　　　他一边唱，一边弹琴。

　　　　（联合关系）
　　　　(Coordinative relation)

　　　或者是红的，或者是蓝的，都可以。
　　　或者是蓝的，或者是红的，都可以。

　　　　（选择关系）
　　　　(Alternative relation)

　　　他不但会开车，而且会修车。
　　　他不但会修车，而且会开车。

（递进关系）

(Progressive relation)

（不能说成"他而且会修车，不但会开车"等）

(One cannot say 他而且会修车，不但会开车.)

他一高兴，就唱起来了。

（承接关系）

(Successive relation)

（不能说成"他就唱起来，一高兴"）

(One cannot say 他就唱起来，一高兴.)

（三）在使用关联词上，表示递进关系和选择关系的并列复句一般都要用关联词；而表示联合关系和承接关系的，不一定都要用关联词。例如：

The use of correlatives: Normally, clauses of progressive and alternative relations should be connected by correlatives, but with those of coordinative and successive relations, correlatives are not always necessary. For example:

不但他喜欢游泳，我也喜欢。

（递进关系）

(Progressive relation)

院子里（还是）种花，还是种树?

（选择关系）

(Alternative relation)

昨天晴天，今天阴天。

（联合关系）

(Coordinative relation)

他一说完，就走了。

（承接关系）

(Successive relation)

我讲，你们记。

（承接关系）

(Successive relation)

（四）关联词在并列复句中的位置

Positions of correlatives in a coordinate complex sentence.

1. 前后分句的主语相同时，多在句首用一个主语，连词"不但"、"还是"、"或者"等都要放在主语后边。例如：

When the subjects of the two clauses are identical, the second usually does not occur and the first comes at the beginning of the whole sentence. The conjunctions 不但，还是，或者，etc. should be placed after the subject. For example:

我们不但是同学，而且是好朋友。

你（还是）明天手术，还是后天手术？

2. 前后分句的主语不同时，连词"不但"、"而且"、"还是"、"或者"等都要放在主语前边。例如：

When the subjects of the two clauses are different, the conjunctions 不但，而且，还是，或者，etc. should be put before the subject. For example:

不但我和他是同学，而且我妹妹和他也是同学。

3. 副词都要放在主语后边。例如：

All adverbs should be put after the subject. For example:

你们先休息一下，下午再谈。

我们一下课，他就到了。

四、使用并列复句时需要注意的问题

Points that merit special attention

（一）表示联合关系和选择关系的关联词"又"、"一边"、"一面"、"一方面"、"不是"、"还是"、"或者"都可以连用两次以上。例如：

Correlatives indicating coordinative and alternative relations 又，一边，一面，一方面，不是，还是，或者 can all be used in more than two clauses in a sentence. For example:

他又奇怪，又高兴，又感激。

我一边听录音，一边朗读，一边记录。

不是你去，也不是我去，而是他去。

我们还是听音乐，还是打扑克牌，还是聊天？

（二）分句之间的关系很清楚时，不需要用关联词，更不能在两个分句之间用连词"和"。例如：

When the relationships between clauses are fairly clear, correlatives are not necessary and the conjunction 和 can never be used between clauses. For example:

哥哥在银行工作，姐姐在医院工作。

（联合关系）

(Coordinative relation)

你们说，我们听。

（承接关系）

(Successive relation)

不能说"哥哥在银行工作，和姐姐在医院工作"或"你们说，和我们听"等。

We can never say 哥哥在银行工作，和姐姐在医院工作 or 你们说，和我们听, etc.

（三）"不是…而是…"后边的分句是不能调换的，否则意思就变了。如果把"不是我们去，而是他们去"说成"不是他们去，而是我们去"，意思就完全相反了。

The order of the clauses introduced by 不是…而是… cannot be changed, otherwise the meaning will be changed, 不是我们去，而是他们去 and 不是他们去，而是我们去 are opposite in meaning.

五、并列复句中常用的关联词，列表如下：

Listed below are correlatives frequently used in coordinate complex sentences:

	联合关系 Coordinative relation	又…，又… 一边…，一边… 一面…，一面… 一方面…，一方面… 不是…，而是…
并列复句 Coordinate complex sentence	承接关系 Successive relation	（先）…然后（再，接着）… …，就… 一…，就…
	递进关系 Progressive relation	…，还… 不但…，而且（还、也、又）…
	选择关系 Alternative relation	（还是）…，还是… 或者…，或者… 不是…，就是…

下一节将具体介绍关联词的用法。

Uses of correlatives will be introduced in detail in the following section.

第二节　并列复句和关联词

Section II　Coordinate Complex Sentences and Correlatives

一、表示联合关系的关联词

Correlatives of coordinative relation

（一）关联副词 "又…又…" 的用法。

Uses of the correlative adverb 又…又….

1. "又…又…" 常前后配合使用，表示几种情况、性质、动作同时存在。

"又…又…" is often used to indicate the simultaneous existence of several cases, properties or actions.

2．"又"后边的谓语一般由动词或形容词充当。例如：

Normally verbs and adjectives serve as the predicates after each 又. For example:

> 他又是我的老师，又是我的朋友。（动词）
>
> (Verbs)
>
> 时间又短，任务又重。（困难很多）（形容词）
>
> (Adjectives)
>
> 这个青年又会踢足球，又会画画儿。（动宾词组）
>
> (Verb-object phrase)

3．注意："又…又…"连接的词或词组一般是同一种类型的。例如：

Note: Words or phrases joined by "又…又…" are generally of the same type. For example:

> 时间又短，任务又重。（困难很多）（形容词）
>
> (Adjectives)

一般不能说："时间又短得很（补充词组），任务又非常重（偏正词组）。"

Generally one cannot say 时间又短得很（补充词组），任务又非常重。（偏正词组）。

（二）关联副词"一边…一边…"的用法。

Uses of correlative adverb "一边…一边…".

1．"一边…一边…"总是配合使用，表示两个或两个以上的动作同时进行。例如：

"一边…一边…" is often used in coordination indicating two or more actions going on simulatneously. For example:

> 我们一边走，一边谈。
>
> 他一边听电话，一边记内容。
>
> 我一边收拾房间，一边跟他聊天。

他们一边划船，一边唱歌，高兴极了。

2．"一边"后边的谓语由动词充当，动词谓语后边可以带宾语和动态助词"着(zhe)"。例如：

The predicate following 一边 is a verb which can take an object as well as the aspectual particle 着 (zhe). For example:

他一边听（着）音乐，一边写（着）信。

我们一边喝着咖啡，一边听着新闻广播。

3．注意：

Notes:

（1）谓语是单音动词时，"一边"可以简略为"边"。例如：

When the predicate is a monosyllabic verb, 一边 can be shortened as 边. For example:

他边写，边念。

我们可以边干，边学。

（2）"一边…一边…"常用于口语。

"一边…一边…" is often used in speaking.

（三）关联副词"一面…一面…"的用法。

Uses of the correlative adverb "一面…一面…".

1．"一面…一面…"总是配合使用，表示两个或两个以上的动作同时进行。例如：

"一面…一面…" is always used in coordination, indicating two or more actions going on simultaneously. For example:

他们一面走，一面唱。

主人一面倒茶，一面跟客人谈话。

他一面推着自行车，一面向我介绍情况。

欢迎队伍一面前进，一面高喊欢迎口号。

2．"一面"后的谓语由动词充当，谓语动词可带宾语和动态助词"着"。

The predicate following 一面 is a verb which can take an

646

object as well as the aspectual particle 着.

3. 注意："一面…一面…"和"一边…一边"的用法基本相同，而"一面…一面…"还可以连接表示抽象意义的动词。例如：

Note: "一边…一边…" and "一面…一面…" are used basically in the same way, only "一面…一面…" can also join verbs of abstract meaning. For example:

> 我们一面积极主张节约，一面努力发展生产。
>
> 我一面工作，一面学习。
>
> （指在一段时间里）
>
> (Refer to a certain period of time)

（四）关联词"一方面…一方面…"的用法。

Uses of correlative "一方面…一方面…".

1. "一方面…一方面…"总是配合使用，常连接两个相互关联的情况，或同一件事的两个方面。例如：

"一方面…一方面…" is always used in combination, connecting two cases related to each other, or connecting two aspects of one thing. For example:

> 大家一方面努力工作，一方面抓紧时间学习外语。
>
> 厂长一方面要了解职工的要求，一方面要帮助他们解决困难。

2. "一方面"后的谓语由动词充当，动词谓语多是表示抽象意义的，可带宾语。

The predicate following 一方面 is usually a verb expressing abstract meaning and it can take an object.

3. 注意：

Notes:

（1）后一个"一方面"的前边可加副词"另"，后边可用副词"也"、"还"或助动词"要"。例如：

The second 一方面 can be premodified by the adverb 另 and after it the adverb 也，还 or the auxiliary verb 要 can be used. For example:

> 我们一方面要肯定成绩，另一方面也要指出缺点。
>
> 我们一方面虚心学习人家的工作经验，另一方面还注意总结自己的经验。

（2）"一方面…，一方面…"很少连接具体的动作。

"一方面…，一方面…" rarely connects verbs indicating concrete actions.

（五）连词"不是…，而是…"的用法。

Uses of the conjunctions "不是…，而是…".

1．"不是…，而是…"连接两个分句，表示否定前者，肯定后者。例如：

"不是…，而是…" connects two clauses, indicating the negation of the former and the confirmation of the latter. For example:

> 他不是空军军官，而是陆军军官。
>
> 他们不是中午来的，而是傍晚来的。
>
> 不是我悲观，而是你太乐观了。

2．"不是"用在前边的分句里，"而是"总用在后边的分句里。

不是 is used in the first clause while 而是 always in the second.

3．注意：

Notes:

（1）"不是"和"而是"都不能单独使用。

Neither 不是 nor 而是 can be used alone.

（2）"不是"和"而是"后边的分句次序是固定的，不能前后对调。

The order of the clauses introduced by 不是 and 而是 is fixed and the clauses cannot be exchanged.

二、表示承接关系的关联词

Correlative of successive relation

（一）"（先）…，然后…"、"（先）…，再…" 和 "（先）…，接着…" 的用法。

Uses of "（先）…，然后"，"（先）…，再…" and "（先）…，接着…"。

1. 这三组关联词都表示第二件事发生在第一件事之后。例如：

All these three groups of correlatives indicate that the second event takes place after the first one. For example:

代表团先到北京，然后到上海、广州。

大家先准备好意见，再讨论。

她先发言，接着大家都谈了自己的看法。

2. 关联副词 "先" 用在第一个分句的主语后边，"然后"、"再" 和 "接着" 都只能用在第二个分句里。

The correlative adverb 先 is used in the first clause to be more exact, after its subject, while 然后，再 or 接着 can only be used in the second clause.

3. 注意：有时可不用 "先"，只用 "然后"、"再" 或 "接着" 表示动作的先后。例如：

Note: Sometimes 先 can be left out and the sequence of actions is only indicated by 然后，再 or 接着. For example:

她梳好头发，然后把梳子放到抽屉里。

她看了当天的报，接着写了一封信。

但第一个分句里要有表示动作已进行的词语，如第一句的结果补语 "好" 和第二句的动态助词 "了"。

But when 先 is absent, there should be other element to indicate the completion of the action, e.g. the complement of result 好 in the first sentence and the aspectual particle 了 in the second sentence.

（二）关联副词 "…就…" 的用法。

Uses of the correlative adverb "…就…".

1. "就"常用在第二个分句里，表示前后两件事发生的时间接得很紧。例如：

就 is often used in the second clause to indicate that the first and second events take place in close succession. For example:

他来了，您就告诉他。

我们商量完，就去找你。

他看完排球比赛，就回家了。

2. 前后两个分句的主语可以相同，可以不同，主语不同时，"就"要放在第二个分句的主语后边。例如：

The subjects of both clauses may either be identical or different. When they differ, 就 should be put after the subject of the second clause. For example:

电影散了，他们就回宿舍了。

3. 注意：关联副词 "就" 一定不能放在主语前边。一定不能说 "他来了，就您告诉他" 或 "电影散了，就他们回宿舍了" 等。

Note: The correlative adverb 就 can never be put before the subject. One can never say 他来了，就您告诉他 or 电影散了，就他们回宿舍了, etc.

（三）关联副词 "一…，就…" 的用法。

Uses of the correlative adverb "一…，就…".

1. "一…，就…" 表示前后两件事在时间上接得很紧。例如：

"一…，就…" indicates that the first event is closely followed by the second. For example:

早上他一起床，就去打太极拳。

他们一到，我们就出发。

代表们一下飞机，就受到热烈的欢迎。

2. "一…，就…" 连接的谓语由动词充当。

The predicates connected by "一…就，…" are two verbs.

650

3. 注意："一"和"就"都要放在主语后边。例如：

Note: Both 一 and 就 should be put after the subject. For example:

他腿一软，就跪在地上了。

他一说，我们就明白了。

一定不能说"一他腿软，…"或"一他说，就我们明白了"等。

One can never say 一他腿软，… or 一他说，就我们明白了 etc.

三、表示递进关系的关联词

Correlatives of progressive relation

（一）关联副词"还"的用法。

Uses of the correlative adverb 还.

1. "还"常用在第二分句里，表示进一层的意思。例如：

还 is often used in the second clause, indicating the meaning of a step further. For example:

光说不行，还得干。

办完这件事，他还要去人民公社参观。

这个计划不错，不过还要修改一下。

2. 前后两个分句的主语可以相同，也可以不相同。例如：

The subjects of two clauses may either be identical or different. For example:

他缺少一本汉英词典，还缺少一张世界地图。

这些交通规则很重要，新来的司机还要仔细研究一下。

3. "还"一定要放在主语之后。

还 must be placed after the subject.

（二）连词"不但…而且…"的用法。

Uses of the conjunctions 不但…而且….

1. "不但…而且…"表示在第一个分句所说的前提情况下重

点提出第二层意思。例如：

"不但…而且…" shows that further meaning is focused on the premise mentioned in the first clause. For example:

> 他不但会打乒乓球，而且获得了全国冠军。
>
> 学校不但要对学生进行爱国主义的教育，而且要对学生进行国际主义的教育。
>
> 学习外语不但要多听、多会话，而且要多看书，多写字。

2. "不但"总用在第一个分句里，"而且"总用在第二个分句里。分句主语相同时，"不但"要放在主语后边；分句的主语不同时，"不但"和"而且"都要放在主语前边。例如：

不但 is always put in the first clause while 而且 always in the second. When the subjects in the two clauses are identical, 不但 should be put after the subject. When the subjects in the two clauses are different, both 不但 and 而且 should be put before the subject. For example:

> 这本书不但内容有意思，而且很容易懂。
>
> 他不但工作认真，而且办事也很谨慎。
>
> 不但老马是我忠实可靠的朋友，而且老张也是我忠实可靠的朋友。
>
> 不但他喜欢说笑话，而且他妻子也喜欢说笑话。

3. 注意：

Notes:

（1）"不但"不能单用，后边分句里一定要用"而且"或者副词"还"、"也"。例如：

不但 cannot be used alone, and 而且 or the adverb 还 or 也 must be used in the second clause to go in concert with it. For example:

> 他不但努力目标很明确，行动也很坚决。
>
> 她不但脾气好，还肯帮助人。

不但这片游览区吸引人，那片游览区也同样吸引人。

一定不能说"他不但来，他朋友来"或者"不但你来，他来"等。

One can never say 他不但来，他朋友来 or 不但你来，他来, etc.

（2）"而且"可以单独用在第二个分句里，"而且"后边常用"也"或"还"。例如：

而且 can be used alone in the second clause, and it is often followed by 也 or 还. For example:

《现代汉语词典》已经出版了，而且也很好买。

这个盲人没有失去信心，而且还鼓励别的盲人战胜困难。

四、表示选择关系的关联词

Correlatives of alternative relation

（一）连词"（还是）…还是…"的用法。

Uses of the conjunction "（还是）…还是…".

1.用"（还是）…还是…"可以构成表示选择的疑问复句。例如：

"（还是）…还是…" is used to form alternative questions. For example:

你（还是）喜欢文学，还是喜欢历史？

你觉得（还是）汉语的语音难学，还是语法难学？

你（还是）欣赏西方音乐，还是欣赏东方音乐？

那（还）是导弹，还是原子弹，还是氢弹？

2."还是"一般要用在要求选择的成分前边。例如：

还是 should be normally used before the alternative elements. For example:

现在你（还是）休息，还是工作？

（谓语前边）

(Before the predicates)

（还是）你介绍，还是他介绍？

（主语前边）

(Before the subjects)

你们（还是）明天，还是后天去实习？

（时间状语前边）

(Before the adverbial adjuncts of time)

这首诗（还）是你写的，还是他写的？

3．注意：第一个"还是"常省去不用。

Note: The first 还是 is often omitted.

（二）连词"或者…或者…"的用法。

Uses of the conjunction "或者…或者…"

1．"或者…或者…"用于陈述句，表示选择。例如：

"或者…或者" is used in a declarative sentence, indicating alternation. For example:

他或者用筷子，或者用刀叉，都行。

每人都要经过考试，或者参加口试，或者参加笔试。

或者让他去科学院，或者让他去大学，他都愿意。

2．"或者"一般要放在要求选择的成分前边。例如：

或者 is generally put before the alternatives. For example:

这份资料，或者打字，或者印，或者抄写，都可以。

（谓语前边）

(Before the predicates)

或者你接待，或者我接待，地点就在二层客厅。

（主语前边）

(Before the subjects)

你或者今天来取这本书，或者明天来取，最迟不要超过后天。

（时间状语前边）

(Before the adverbial adjuncts of time)

3．注意："或者…或者…"不能用在表示选择的疑问句里。

654

不能说"你或者吃点心，或者吃米饭？"等。

Note: "或者…或者…" cannot be used in alternative questions, e.g. one can never say 你或者吃点心，或者吃米饭？ etc.

（三）连词"不是…就是…"的用法。

Uses of the conjunctions "不是…就是…".

1. "不是…就是…"表示前后两者必居其一。例如：

"不是…就是…" indicates the meaning of "it must be one or the other". For example:

今天晚上，我们不是出席一个朋友的告别宴会，就是参加一个朋友的婚礼。

他不是这个单位的领导，就是这个单位的工程师。

不是你们拜会部长，就是他们拜会总理。

2. "不是"用在第一个分句里，"就是"总用在第二个分句里。

不是 is always used in the first clause while 就是 in the second.

3. 注意：

Notes:

（1）"不是"和"就是"都不能单独使用。

Neither 不是 nor 就是 can be used by itself.

（2）"不是"和"就是"后边的分句可以前后对调，不影响意思。例如：

Clauses introduced by 不是 and 就是 can be exchanged without affecting the meaning. For example:

不是他来看你，就是你去看他。
不是你去看他，就是他来看你。

第三节 偏正复句

Section III Subordinate Complex Sentences

一、什么是偏正复句 Definition

由表示偏正关系的分句构成的复句叫偏正复句。偏正复句中各分句之间的意义有偏有正，有主有次，正句是主要的意思，偏句是陪衬。例如：

Complex sentences formed by clauses of subordinate relations are called subordinate complex sentences. In a subordinate complex sentence, the clauses are not equally important in terms of meaning — the main clause carries the main idea while the subordinate clause only helps to make the sentence. For example:

> 不管是什么颜色，我都喜欢。
>
> > （"不管是什么颜色"是偏句，"我都喜欢"是正句。）
> >
> > (不管是什么颜色 is the subordinate clause while 我都喜欢 is the main clause.)
>
> 因为他来电话了,所以咱们得等他。
>
> > （"因为他来电话了"是偏句,"所以咱们得等他"是正句。）
> >
> > (因为他来电话了 is the subordinate clasue while 所以咱们得等他 is the main clause.)
>
> 虽然衣服样子不少，但是没有他要的那种。
>
> > （"虽然衣服样子不少"是偏句，"但是没有他要的那种"是正句。）
> >
> > (虽然衣服样子不少 is the subordinate clause while

但是没有他要的那种   is the main clause.)

二、偏正复句的种类

Types of subordinate complex sentences

偏正复句中分句之间可以表示下列各种不同的关系。

The clauses in a subordinate complex sentence may be of different relationships as follows:

（一）转折关系　Adversative relation

后一个分句是正句，跟前一个分句（偏句）的意思相反或相对。例如：

The second clause is the main clause which is opposite or stands in contrast to the first clause (the subordinate clause) in meaning. For example:

> 这场球赛虽然卖出了一万张票，但是很多人还是没买到。
>
> 尽管他住得比较远，却来得最早。

（二）因果关系　Causative relation

一个分句（偏句）说出原因或前提，另一个分句（正句）说出结果或根据前提作出的推断。例如：

One clause (the subordinate clause) states the reason or premise while the other clause (the main clause) states the result or inference drawn from the premise. For example:

> 因为他病了，所以不能参加这次大型演出活动。
>
> 由于他太高兴了，没注意外边发生的情况。
>
> 你既然病了，就别参加这次大型演出活动了。

（三）条件关系　Conditional relation

一个分句（偏句）提出条件，另一个分句（正句）说明在这条件下产生的结果。例如：

One clause (the subordinate clause) puts forward a condition, the other clause (the main clause) states the resulting action. For example:

不管前排后排的票，你都替我买一张。

只要是星期天，我就有时间。

只有努力工作，才不辜负人民的培养。

我一感冒，就发烧。

（四）假设关系　Suppositive relation

一个分句（偏句）提出一个假设的情况，另一个分句（正句）说明由假设情况产生的结果或推论。例如：

One clause (the subordinate clause) puts forward an assumption while the other one (the main clause) states the result or inference drawn from the assumption. For example:

要是你们有兴趣，我就陪你们去公园。

大家如果有意见，就提出来。

即使我病了，也一定参加这次大型的演出活动。

（五）目的关系　Purposive relation

一个分句（偏句）表示为达到某种目的的行为，另一个分句（正句）表示这种行为达到的目的。例如：

One clause (the subordinate clause) indicates an action for a purpose which is expressed by other clause (the main clause). For example:

他努力学习，为的是取得好的成绩。

我们应该早点儿告诉他，好让他放心。

（六）取舍关系　Preference relation

一个分句（偏句）提出一种较极端的作法，另一个分句（正句）提出经过比较要选择的另一种作法；即舍弃一种作法，选取另一种作法。例如：

One clause (the subordinate clause) puts forward an extreme course of an action while the other clause (the main clause) indicates another course of action that will be adopted after comparison, i.e. to prefer one course to the other. For example:

他宁可在家呆着，也不去看球赛。

我宁可不看足球比赛，也要写完这篇文章。

与其看足球比赛，不如写完这篇文章。

三、偏正复句的特点　Grammatical features

（一）在结构上，表示偏正关系的复句一般由两个分句构成。

Complex sentences of subordinate relations are generally formed of two clauses in structure.

（二）在分句的次序上，一是通常的偏句在前，正句在后的形式，一是正句在前，偏句在后的形式。后一种形式多有补充说明的意味。例如：

The order of the clauses normally goes with the subordinate clause preceding the main clause. But sometimes it goes with the main clause coming first. In this case, it suggests additional explanation. For example:

前一个分句——偏句 The first or the subordinate clause	后一个分句——正句 The second or the main clause
虽然今天是晴天，	但是气温比较低。
因为今天是晴天，	所以气温比较高。
只有晴天，	他才出去。
就是今天晴天，	她也不出去。
他希望星期日是晴天，	好去爬山。
与其爬山，	不如划船。

前一个分句——正句	后一个分句——偏句
The first or the main clause	The second or the subordinate clause
我明天不能来，	因为我得去医院。
他不想打架，	虽然并不怕打架。
我想喝点咖啡，	如果你们有的话。

（三）偏正复句一般都要用关联词。例如：

Generally speaking, correlatives are necessary in a subordinate complex sentence. For example:

尽管今天是晴天，他也不出去。

既然今天是晴天，咱们就去爬山吧。

不管晴天阴天，他都去北京图书馆。

要是明天晴天，咱们就去划船。

（四）关联词在偏正复句中的位置。

Positions of correlatives in a subordinate complex sentence.

1. 连词"虽然"、"尽管"、"因为"、"由于"、"既然"、"不管"、"不论"、"无论"、"只要"、"只有"、"除非"、"要是"、"如果"、"假如"、"假使"、"即使"、"就是"、"宁可"、"与其"等通常都用于前一个分句（偏句）；

连词"但是"、"所以"、"因此"、"好"、"为的是"、"不如"和关联副词"反而"、"却"、"都"、"也"、"就"、"才"等都用于后一个分句（正句）。例如：

Conjunctions often used in the first clause (subordinate clause) are: 虽然、尽管，因为，由于，既然，不管，不论，无

论，只要，只有，除非，要是，如果，假如，假使，即使，就是，宁可，与其。

Conjunctions 但是，所以，因此，好，为的是，不如, and correlative adverbs 反而，却，都，也，就，才, etc. are used in the second clause (main clause). For example:

除非你去，我才去。

即使你去，我也不去。

他宁可晚睡，也要把这篇文章改完。

今天刮大风，他反而不戴帽子了。

她把头发剪短了，为的是节省一些时间。

2. 前后分句的主语相同时，主语多在句首，关联词"虽然"、"由于"等多在主语后边。例如：

When the subjects of the two clauses are identical, they are often put at the beginning of the sentence. The correlative words 虽然，由于, etc. are often used after the subject. For example:

她虽然很想去看那个话剧，但是实在没有时间。

我们尽管费了半天工夫，也没说服他。

你既然不能参加，就别勉强了。

3. 前后分句的主语不同时，关联词一般在前一个分句的主语前边。例如：

When the subjects of the two clauses differ, correlatives are normally put before the subject of the first clause. For example:

由于大家努力抢险，一场可怕的灾难避免了。

假如我碰到这样的困难，你们也会帮助我的。

4. 关联副词"却"、"都"、"才"等都要放在主语后边谓语前边。

The correlative adverbs 却，都，才 etc. should be put after the subject and before the predicate.

四、使用偏正复句时需要注意的问题

Points that merit special attention

（一）分句之间的关系很清楚时，前一分句中的关联词（连词）常省去不用，而后一分句中的关联词一般不能省去。例如：

When the relationship between the clauses is fairly clear, the correlative in the first clause is often omitted. But the correlative in the second clause normally cannot be omitted. For example:

（虽然）今天下雪，但是天气不太冷。

（就是）今天不下雪，他也不出去。

（除非）你也去，我才去。

不能说"虽然今天下雪，天气不太冷"、"就是今天不下雪，他不出去"或"除非你也去，我去"等。

One cannot say 虽然今天下雪，天气不太冷，就是今天不下雪，他不出去 or 除非你也去，我去, etc.

（二）关联副词一定不能用在主语前边。例如：

Correlative adverbs can never be used before the subject. For example:

要是你不能来，我就去你那儿。

尽管今天不冷，他也戴手套。

不能说"要是…，就我去你那儿"或"尽管…，也他戴帽子"。

One cannot say 要是…就我去你那儿 or 尽管…，也他戴帽子

五、偏正复句中常用的关联词，列表如下：

Listed below are correlatives commonly used in subordinate complex sentences:

转折关系 Adversative relation	⎧ ⎨ ⎩	虽然…，但是… 尽管…，但是… ……，反而… ……，却…
因果关系 Causative relation	⎧ ⎨ ⎩	因为…，所以… 由于…，…… ……，因此… 既然…，就…
条件关系 Conditional relation	⎧ ⎨ ⎩	不管…，都（也）… 不论…，都（也）… 无论…，都（也）… 只要…，就… 只有…，才… 除非…，才… 一…，就…
假设关系 Suppositive relation	⎧ ⎨ ⎩	要是…，就… 如果…，就… 假如…，就… 假使…，就…
目的关系 Purposive relation	⎧ ⎩	……，好… ……，为的是…
取舍关系 Preference relation	⎧ ⎩	宁可…，也… 与其…，不如…

偏正复句
Subordinate complex sentence

下一节将作具体介绍。

More detailed introduction will be given in the following section.

第四节　偏正复句和关联词

Section IV　Subordinate Complex Sentences and the Correlatives

一、表示转折关系的关联词

Correlatives of adversative relation

（一）连接"虽然…，但是…"的用法。

Uses of the conjunctions 虽然…，但是….

1. 连词"虽然"和"但是"常配合使用，表示先承认某事实，然后转入主要意思。"虽然"用于偏句，"但是"用于正句。例如：

The conjunctions 虽然 and 但是 are often used in combination to indicate the admission of a certain fact then turning to the main idea. 虽然 occurs in the subordinate clause, 但是 in the main clause. For example:

> 虽然他最近很忙，但是每天都按时锻炼。
>
> 虽然他们进行了几次试验，但是都没有成功。
>
> 虽然我们很久没见到你，但是常听到你的消息。
>
> 她虽然不是北方人，但是能说一口标准的普通话。
>
> 大家虽然都这么说，但是他还是不相信。

2. 正句中也可以用表示转折的连词"可是"、"不过"或关联副词"却"等。例如：

The adversative conjunctions 可是，不过 or the correlative adverb 却, etc. can also be used in the main clause. For example:

> 虽然那两个国家之间的战争已经结束了，可是战争留
> 下的问题还没完全解决。
>
> 虽然世界人民都喜欢和平，可是战争还经常发生。

虽然每个人都能唱歌，不过唱得特别好的人比较少。

他的病虽然相当重，他的情绪却很好。

3．注意：

Notes:

（1）"虽然"和"但是"一般成对使用，当表示转折的程度较轻时，常只在正句中用"但是"。例如：

虽然 and 但是 are generally used in pairs. But when adversation is not particularly emphasized, 但是 is often used alone in the main clause. For example:

虽然天气很冷，但是他还要坚持跑步锻炼。

（成对使用）

(In pairs)

他虽然特别喜欢滑冰，但是今天没去。

（成对使用）

(In pairs)

（虽然）他不知道这件事，但是他来了。

（单用）

(Alone)

他们（虽然）有条件编基础汉语教材，但是不知道哪儿能给出版。

（单用）

(Alone)

"但是"可简略为"但"。但是 can be shortened as 但.

（2）在偏句在后，正句在前的句式中，只能在偏句中使用连词"虽然"，不能在正句中同时使用"但是"。例如：

In the case of the main clause preceding the subordinate, one can only use the conjunction 虽然 in the subordinate clause. 但是 can never be used at the same time in the main clause. For exemples:

他把仅有的一点食物送给了别人，虽然他两天两夜没吃东西。

我心里总觉得没尽到责任，虽然他已长成了大人。

（二）连词"尽管…，但是…"的用法。

Uses of the conjunctions 尽管…，但是….

1. 连词"尽管…，但是…"的意思相当于"虽然…，但是…"，用法也基本相同，但用"尽管"时语气比"虽然"重些。例如：

The conjunctions 尽管…，但是… are equivalent to 虽然…，但是… in meaning and their uses are about the same. However, 尽管 carries a stronger tone than 虽然. For example:

尽管已经到下班时间了，但是他还在工作。

尽管他感冒了，但是还陪我们去公园了。

大家尽管觉得路比较远，但是都去了。

2. 后一个分句中也可以用表示转折的关联副词"却"、"仍然"、"还"或"也"等。例如：

The correlative adversative adverbs 却，仍然，还，也，etc. can also be used in the second clause. For example:

尽管他每天工作很紧张，生活却很有规律。

尽管他已经离开我们单位了，仍然关心我们大家。

3. 注意：

Notes:

（1）"尽管"和"但是"一般要成对使用，也可以只在正句中用"但是"。例如：

Generally speaking, 尽管 and 但是 are used in pairs. Sometimes, 但是 can also be used alone in the main clause. For example:

尽管又渴又热，但是大伙儿还是坚持走完了这段路。

（成对用）

(In pairs)

尽管困难重重，但是这件事毕竟成功了。

（成对用）

(In pairs)

他学习最用功，但是考试成绩总不理想。

（单用）

(Alone)

我给他讲了很多次，但是他就是听不进去。

（单用）

(Alone)

（2）在偏句在后、正句在前的句式中，只能在偏句中使用连词"尽管"（不能与"但是"成对使用）。例如：

When the main clause precedes the subordinate, 尽管 can be used only by itself in the subordinate clause (not in pairs with 但是). For example:

这些事我都知道，尽管他一点儿也不透露。

他来的很准时，尽管外边雨下得很大。

（三）关联副词"反而"的用法。

Uses of the correlative adverb 反而.

1．"反而"是用在后边分句里起转折作用的关联副词，表示某种现象不合乎常情。例如：

反而 is a correlative adversative adverb used in the second clause indicating a certain phenomenon that does not stand to reason. For example:

春天到了，反而下起雪来了。

小王住得最远，反而来得最早。

风不但不停，反而刮得更大了。

2．"反而"要用在第二个分句的主语后边谓语前边。例如：

反而 should be used after the subject and before the predicate in the second clause. For example:

他一再提醒我带入场券，他自己反而忘了。

他平时很少去商店，今天下雨他反而去了两次。

3. 注意：

Note:

"反而"可以和"不但"配合使用，"不但"后边的谓语应是否定形式。例如：

反而 can be used in combination with 不但，however, the predicate after 不但 should be in the negative form. For example:

他父亲的病不但没好，反而更重了。

这个星期天，他不但不能休息，反而比平时更忙。

（四）关联副词"却"的用法。

Uses of the correlative adverb 却.

1. "却"总是用在后边分句里表示转折。例如：

却 is always used in the second clause to indicate adversativity. For example:

他对你很热情，你对他却没有一点表示。

东郭先生救了狼，狼却要吃东郭先生。

外面冰天雪地，屋里却温暖如春。

2. "却"要用在表示转折的正句中主语后边谓语前边。例如：

却 should be used after the subject and before the predicate in the main clause indicating adversativity. For example:

他的文化基础差，进步却很快。

这个电影的缺点很明显，他却看不出来。

3. 注意：

Note:

表示转折的分句里用了"但是"，后边还可再用"却"。例如：

When 但是 is used in an adversative clause，却 can still be used after it. For example:

天气虽然很冷，但是我心里却感到很温暖。

盲人眼睛不起作用，但是手却很巧。

二、表示因果关系的关联词

Correlatives of causative relation

（一）连词"因为…，所以…"的用法。

Uses of the conjunctions 因为…，所以….

1. 连词"因为"和"所以"常配合使用，表示原因和结果。例如：

The conjunctions 因为 and 所以 are often used in combination to denote cause and effect. For example:

老王因为身体不太好，所以不能来看你。

因为他们准备得很充分，所以会开得不错。

因为节日快到了，所以很多人都忙着买礼物。

2. 注意：

Notes:

（1）"因为"可以单独用在前一个分句里。例如：

因为 can be used alone in the first clause. For example:

因为他临时有事，提前走了。

因为我们招待得不够周到，向您表示歉意。

（2）"所以"也可以单独用在后一个分句的句首。例如：

所以 can also be used alone at the beginning of the second clause. For example:

这张画是他父亲留给他的，所以不能卖掉。

我的好朋友明天结婚，所以我明天不能跟你们去长城了。

"所以"不能放在主语后边。不能说"…，我所以明天不能跟你们去长城了"。

所以 cannot be put after the subject. One can never say "…，我所以明天不能跟你们去长城了"

（3）在偏句在后，正句在前的句式中，可以只在偏句中使用"因为"，也可以正句中用"（之）所以"偏句中用"是因为"。例如：

In the form of the main clause preceding the subordinate, one can either use 因为 in the subordinate clause only, or put 之所以 in the main clause and 是因为 in the subordinate. For example:

> 这个讨论会我不能按时到，因为我有个多年不见的老
> 朋友来了。
> 他（之）所以能这么快就掌握了汉语，是因为他学习
> 非常刻苦。

（二）连词"由于"的用法。

Uses of the conjunction 由于.

1．"由于"一般用于前一个分句，表示原因。例如：

由于 is generally used in the first clause to denote cause. For example:

> 由于我们没经验，这次试验失败了。
> 由于时间不多了，我们下次再商量吧。
> 由于天气不好，飞机没有按时到达。

2．"由于"可以单独用于前边表示原因的分句，也可以和连词"因此"或"所以"配合使用。例如：

由于 can either be used by itself in the first clause denoting cause or be used in combination with the conjunction 因此 or 所以. For example:

> 由于领导很重视，因此工程进展得很快。
> 由于他们俩的生活环境不同，所以性格也不一样。

3．注意：

Notes:

（1）在一般的情况下，"由于"可以省略。例如：

In most cases, 由于 can be omitted. For example:

> 我们的准备工作做得不够充分，因此试验失败了。
> 今天天气不好，所以飞机没有按时到达。

670

（2）在偏句在后，正句在前的句式中，可只在偏句中用"由于"。例如：

In the case of the main clause preceding the subordinate, 由于 can be used alone in the subordinate clause. For example:

> 工程进展得这么快，这都是由于领导的重视。

> 这场比赛很顺手，主要是由于大家配合得好。

（3）"由于"一般用于书面语。

Generally speaking, 由于 is used in written Chinese.

（三）连词"因此"的用法。

Uses of the conjunction 因此.

1. "因此"总用在后一个分句句首，表示结果。例如：

因此 is always used at the beginning of the first clause and indicates effect. For example:

> 大家都知道这件事，因此不需要重复了。

> 那个司机不遵守交通规则，因此受到了批评。

> 我们在一起工作了很多年，因此互相都很了解。

2. "因此"可以单独用在表示结果的正句里，也可以和"由于"配合使用。例如：

因此 can either be used alone in the main clause indicating effect or be used in coordination with 由于. For example:

> 我们是老朋友了，因此谈话比较随便。

> 由于事情办得很顺利，因此大家感到十分满意。

3. 注意：

Notes:

（1）表示结果的"因此"要用在后边的分句句首，而不能用在前边分句里。例如：

因此 indicating effect should be used at the beginning of the second clause and it can never be used in the first clause. For example:

> 我们学习都很努力，因此学校非常满意。

不能说"因此学校非常满意，我们学习都很努力。"

One cannot say 因此学校非常满意，我们学习都很努力.

（2）"因此"多用于书面语。

因此 is mostly used in written Chinese.

（四）"既然…，就…"的用法。

Uses of 既然…，就….

1．"既然…，就…"表示根据前提得出某种结论。连词"既然"用在前边提出前提的分句里，关联副词"就"用在后边表示结论的分句里。例如：

既然…，就… indicates a certain conclusion drawn from a premise. The conjunction 既然 is used in the first clause where the premise is put forward, while the correlative adverb 就 is used in the second clause indicating conclusion. For example:

> 既然大家都同意这个设计，咱们就通过了。
>
> 既然你们都了解长城的历史，我就不介绍了。
>
> 你既然一定要走，我就不留你了。
>
> 他既然答应了，就让他辛苦一趟吧。

2．后边表示结论的分句里除了常用副词"就"以外，也常用"也"或者"还"，这些副词一定要放在主语后边谓语前边。例如：

Besides the adverb 就, 也 or 还 is also frequently used in the second clause indicating conclusion. These adverbs should be put between the predicate and the subject. For example:

> 你既然不舒服，就好好休息吧。
>
> 既然你对这个活动有兴趣，你也来参加吧。
>
> 既然他已经知道了，还给他打电话吗？

3．注意：Note:

前后两个分句之间可以用连词"那么"，表示后边分句是从前边分句的前提引出来的结果。例如：

The conjunction 那么 may be used between two such clauses to show that the second clause is the conclusion drawn from the premise put forward by the first. For example:

> 你既然明天有约会，那么，我一个人在宿舍吧。
>
> 既然他的病已经完全好了，那么，我们可以接他 出院了。

三、表示条件关系的关联词

Correlatives of conditional relation

（一）"不管（不论、无论）…，都（也）…" 的用法。

Uses of 不管（不论，无论）…，都（也）…"

1. "不管…，都…" 表示虽然条件不同，但是作法不变。连 词 "不管（不论、无论）" 用在前一个分句里表示条件，"都 （也）" 用在后一个分句的主语后边，表示主要意思。例如：

"不管…，都…" indicates that the ways of doing something remain the same although conditions vary. The conjunction 不管（不论，无论）is used in the first clause to denote condition while 都（也）is used after the subject of the second clause to express the main idea. For example:

> 不管有多少困难，我们都能克服。
>
> 不论怎么忙，他每天都要看一小时报纸。
>
> 无论刮风下雨，明天都按原计划进行活动。
>
> 不管你来不来，我们也要讨论。

2. "不管（不论，无论）" 后边一定要有疑问代词或并列 词组。例如：

不管（不论，无论）must be followed by an interrogative pronoun or a coordinative phrase. For example:

> 不管我们谁有困难，他都热情帮助。
>
> 不论哪个公园，我都喜欢去。
>
> 无论人们怎么逗那只猴子，它也没有反应。
>
> 不管白天黑夜，医院里都有大夫。

无论如何，在这个问题上，我们会起促进作用的。

无论他多么忙，也要坚持打半小时的球。

不能说"不管我们有困难，他都热情帮助"或"无论他忙，也要坚持打半小时的球"等。

One cannot say 不管我们有困难，他都热情帮助 or 无论他忙，也要坚持打半小时的球，etc.

"不管（不论、无论）"后边的并列词组之间可以用"还是"连接。

Coordinative phrases after 不管（不论，无论） can be connected by 还是.

3．注意：

Notes:

（1）表示结论的分句中不能不用"都"或"也"。不能说"不管什么地方，我想去看看"或"无论下雨不下雨，他去听技术讲座"等。

都 or 也 can never be absent from the clause indicating conclusion. One cannot say 不管什么地方，我想去看看 or 无论下雨不下雨，他去听技术讲座，etc.

（2）"不管"多用于口语，"无论（不论）"多用于书面语。

不管 is mostly used in speaking while 无论（不论） is mostly used in writing.

（二）"只要…，就…"的用法。

Uses of "只要…，就…".

1．"只要…，就…"表示在某种条件下产生某种结果。连词"只要"用在前一个表示条件的分句里，关联副词"就"用在后一个表示结果的分句里（主语后边）。例如：

"只要…，就…" expresses the idea that a certain result is produced under a certain condition. The conjunction 只要 is used in the first clause which indicates the condition while

674

the correlative adverb 就 is used in the second clause (after the subject) which indicates the result. For example:

只要您同意，我就立刻去您那儿。

只要对人民有好处，我们就应该做。

我们只要努力，就能取得好成绩。

你只要安静地躺一会儿，就会好起来。

2．"只要"后边的分句除了用"就"配合使用外，还可以用表示判断的"一定"或"是…的"等。例如：

Besides 就 which is used in coordination with 只要, 一定 or 是…的, etc. that indicate judgement, can also be used in the second clause. For example

只要你热爱这个工作，是会做出贡献的。

我们只要多想办法，工作中的困难（就）一定能克服。

3．注意：

Note:

"只要"后边的条件不是唯一的条件。例如：

The condition after 只要 is not the only one. Study the following examples:

只要你来，我就高兴。

只要大家高兴，我就高兴。

只要孩子们健康，我就高兴。

（三）"只有…，才…"的用法。

Uses of "只有…，才…"

1．"只有…，才…"表示没有前边的条件，是不能达到后边的结果的。连词"只有"用在前一个表示条件的分句里，关联副词"才"用在后一个表示结果的分句里（主语后边）。例如：

"只有…，才…" expresses the meaning that a result cannot be attained without the condition given in the first clause. The conjunction 只有 is used in the first clause which indicates the condition, the correlative adverb 才 in the second clause

675

which indicates the result (after the subject). For example:

只有大家团结起来，才有力量。

只有不怕困难，才能战胜困难。

只有刻苦钻研，才能掌握一门外语。

她只有手术，才能继续活下去。

2．"只有"后边可以是名词、动宾词组、主谓词组等。例如：

只有 can be followed by nouns, V-O phrases, S-P phrases, etc. For example:

只有老张，才有条件参加比赛。

只有修好这部机器，才能进一步增加生产。

只有国家富强，人们的生活水平才会提高。

3．注意：Notes:

（1）"只有"后边的条件是指定的唯一的条件，表示结果的分句如果含有"可能"的意思，"才"后边一般要用"能"。例如：

The condition introduced by 只有 is the only one. If the clause expressing result implies the meaning of possibility, 才 should be followed by 能. For example:

只有他，才能解决这个问题。

只有多听、多说、多看、多写，才能学好一种新的
语言。

不能说"只有他，才解决这个问题"等。

One cannot say 只有他，才解决这个问题, etc.

（2）表示条件的"只有"分句不能用在表结果的分句之后。

The 只有 clause which indicates condition can not follow the clause of result.

（四）"除非…，才…"的用法。

Uses of "除非…，才…".

1．"除非…，才…"表示如果没有前边的条件，就不会得到

后边的结果。连词"除非"用在前边表示条件的分句里，关联副词"才"用在后边表示结果的分句里（主语后边）。例如：

"除非…，才…" indicates that the result cannot be achieved without the condition given in the first clause where 除非 is used. The correlative adverb 才 is used in the second clause which indicates the result (after the subject). For example:

除非明天下大雨，运动会才推迟。

除非我有重要会议，才不去你那儿。

2. 注意："除非"后边的条件是推断出的唯一的条件。后一个分句中的"才"是不能漏用的，而前一个分句里的"除非"有时可以省略不用。例如：

Note: The condition after 除非 is the only condition inferred. 才 in the second clause can never be absent, while 除非 sometimes can be left out. For example:

（除非）大家都有诚意，才能达成协议。

你（除非）病了，才会让别人照顾你。

不能说"除非大家都有诚意，能达成协议"等。

One cannot say 除非大家都有诚意，能达成协议，etc.

（五）关联副词"一…，就…"的用法。

Uses of the correlative adverbs "一…，就…".

1. "一…，就…"表示在前边分句的条件下，一定会产生后边分句的情况，例如：

"一…，就…" indicates that under the condition given in the first clause, a result as stated in the second clause will surely be brought into being. For example:

鱼一离开水，就会死。

他一紧张，就脸红。

气温一到零摄氏度，水就结冰。

2. 表示条件的关联副词"一"后边的谓语由动词或形容词充当。

Verbs or adjectives can act as the predicate after the correlative adverb — indicating condition.

3．注意：Note:

关联副词"一"和"就"都必须放在主语后边，而不能用在主语前边。不能说"一鱼离开水，…"或"太阳一出来，就天气暖和"等。

Both the correlative adverb — and 就 must be placed after, not before, the subject. One can never say 一鱼离开水，… or 太阳一出来，就天气暖和，etc.

四、表示假设关系的关联词

Correlatives of supposative relation

（一）"要是（如果、假如、假使）…，就…"的用法。

Uses of "要是（如果，假如，假使）…，就…"

1．连词"要是"、"如果"、"假如"和"假使"都表示假设，用在前边分句里，关联副词"就"用在后边分句里，说明由假设情况产生的结果。例如：

The conjunctions 要是,如果，假如，and 假使 all indicate supposition and are all used in the first clause. The correlative adverb 就 is used in the second clause to indicate the result produced from the supposition. For example:

要是你不愿意坐火车，就坐船。

如果他不愿意参加，就不要叫他了。

假如她写不完，就让她明天交。

假使我们都会汉语，就能用汉语谈话了。

大家要是同意，就这样决定吧。

他如果有时间，我们就去他那儿。

你假如寄航空信，下午就能收到。

他们假使来调查这件事，我们就把这些情况都告诉他们。

2．"要是（如果、假如、假使）"可以单独用在前边分句里，后边分句不用"就"。例如：

要是（如果，假如，假使）can be used in the first clause alone without 就 being used in the second clause. For example:

> 要是你不能去，我去。

> 你如果不去，他还去吗？

要表示在某种假设情况下会产生某种结果时，也可以只在后边分句里用"就"。例如：

就 may be used by itself in the second clause to indicate that a certain result may be produced from a supposed condition. For example:

> 你有意见，就提出来。

> 你实在有困难，就别勉强了。

3. 注意：

Notes:

（1）用"要是（如果、假如、假使）"表示条件关系时，两个分句之间可以用连词"那么"。例如：

When 要是（or 如果，假如，假使）is used to indicate conditional relation, the conjunction 那么 can be used between the two clauses. For example:

> 如果你们都去，那么我也去。

> 你们假如真想学画画儿，那么我可以教你们。

"那么"一定不能用在后一分句的主语后边。不能说"如果你们都去，我那么也去"等。

那么 can never be used after the subject of the second clause. One cannot say 如果你们都去，我那么也去, etc.

（2）"要是（如果）"多用于口语；"假如（假使）"多用于书面语。

要是（如果）is mostly used in speaking, 假如（假使）in writing.

（二）"即使（就是）…，也…"的用法。

Uses of "即使（就是）…，也…".

1. 连词"即使"和"就是"都用于前边表示假设的分句里，提出比较极端的情况，关联副词"也"用在后一分句里，说明结果。例如：

The conjunction 即使 or 就是 is used in the first clause expressing an extreme supposition, and the second clause, where the correlative adverb 也 is used, gives the consequence. For example:

即使你不愿意参加，也没关系。

我们即使获得冠军，也要坚持练习。

就是明天阴天，我也要去看他。

我就是知道这个情况，也不会改变自己的看法。

2. 有时可以只在后一分句里用"也"。例如：

Sometimes the adverb 也 alone is enough to indicate the suppositive relation, i.e. 即使 or 就 is absent from the first clause. For example:

你现在赶到机场，也晚了。

她不装饰，也很好看。

3. 注意：

Note:

"就是"多用于口语，"即使"多用于书面语。

就是 is mostly used in speaking, 即使 in writing.

五、表示目的关系的关联词

Correlative words of purposive relation

（一）连词"好"的用法。

Uses of the conjunction 好.

1. 连词"好"总是用在第二个分句里，表示后边分句是前边分句要达到的目的。例如：

The conjunction 好 is always used in the second clause to introduce the purpose of the action expressed by the first clause.

For example:

你要坚持治病，好早一点恢复健康。

我们都应该抓紧时间准备，好顺利地通过毕业考试。

2．两个分句的主语不同时，连词"好"用在后边分句的主语后边。例如：

When subjects of the two clauses differ, the conjunction 好 is placed after the subject of the second clause, for example:

你回头一定来，咱们好一起去看芭蕾舞。

3．注意：

Note:

连词"好"不能用在主语前边。一定不能说"你回头一定来，好咱们一起去看芭蕾舞。"

The conjunction 好 cannot precede the subject, so one can never say 你回头一定来，好咱们一起去看芭蕾舞.

（二）连词"为的是"的用法。

Uses of the conjunction 为的是.

1．"为的是"总是用在后边分句里，表示后边分句是前边分句要达到的目的。例如：

为的是 is always used in the second clause to introduce the purpose of the action expressed by the first clause. For example:

你要坚持治病，为的是早一点儿恢复健康。

他正在积极准备，为的是顺利地通过毕业考试。

他已经来了，为的是跟咱们一起去看芭蕾舞。

2．"为的是"一定要用在后一个分句句首，主语前边。

为的是 must be placed at the beginning of the second clause or before the subject when there is one.

3．注意：

Notes:

（1）"为的是"不能用在主语后边。

为的是 cannot be used after the subject of the second clause.

（2）前边分句可表示过去、现在或将来发生的动作。

The first clause may indicate actions which either happened in the past, are going on at the moment or will happen in the future.

六、表示取舍关系的关联词

Correlatives indicating preference relation

（一）"宁可…，也…"的用法。

Uses of 宁可…，也….

1. "宁可…，也…"表示经过比较，为了得到后边的结果而选择了前边的动作。例如：

"宁可…，也…" expresses the idea that after comparison, the action indicated in the first clause is chosen in order to achieve the result indicated in the second. For example:

他宁可少休息一会儿，也要写完这篇文章。

（意思是为了"写完这篇文章"，他选择了前者"少休息一会儿"；不愿意为了多休息而写不完文章）

(Meaning: In order to 写完这篇文章, he chooses 少休息一会儿. He does not want to leave the article unfinished in order to have more rest.)

我宁可明天再来一趟，也不愿再等了。

（意思是"明天再来一趟"比"再等"好）

(Meaning: 明天再来一趟 is better than 再等.)

2. 连词"宁可"一般用在第一个分句里，副词"也"要用在第二个分句前边，"也"后边常用"要"或"不"。例如：

The conjunction 宁可 is generally used in the first clause, while the adverb 也 which is often followed by 要 or 不, should be used at the beginning of the second clause. For example:

大家宁可累一点儿，也要争取当天完成任务。

他宁可饿着肚子，也不愿意麻烦别人。

3. 注意："宁可"可以单用。例如：

Note: 宁可 can be used by itself. For example:

我们安排工作要慎重，宁可先把困难考虑得多些。

（二）连词"与其…不如…"的用法。

Uses of "与其…，不如…".

1. "与其…不如…"表示在前后两件事物中还是选择后者好些。例如：

"与其…，不如…" indicates that of the two things, the second is preferred to the first. For example:

我们与其在这儿等他，不如去他家找他。

与其明天还要来，不如再等一会儿。

2. "与其"一般用在第一个分句里，"不如"用在第二个分句里，"不如"前还可加"还"、"倒"或"真"。例如：

与其 is generally used in the first clause while 不如, which is often preceded by 还, 倒 or 真, occurs in the second. For example:

与其他去，不如我去。

与其种麦子，还不如种稻子。

与其在外边冻着，倒不如另外找个地方。

与其在屋子里开电扇，真不如出去走走。

3. 注意："与其"不能单用。

Note: 与其 cannot be used by itself.

第五节 紧 缩 句
Section V The Contracted Sentence

一、什么叫紧缩句 Definition

用单句形式表达复句内容的句子叫紧缩句。例如：

A contracted sentence is one which, in the form of a simple sentence, expresses what is normally expressed by a complex sentence. For example:

他越跑越快。

（意思是：他跑的速度不断加快）

(Meaning: His speed of running accelerated.)

这件事非他处理不行。

（意思是：这件事如果不让他处理，就处理不好）

(Meaning: Unless he attends to this matter, it cannot be properly handled.)

你不想去也得去。

（意思是：你就是不想去，也得去）

(Meaning: You must go, even if you are unwilling.)

二、紧缩句的特点 Grammatical features

（一）紧缩句和主语。

The contracted sentence and the subject.

前后两个谓语成分同属一个主语。例如：

The two predicates share one subject, as in:

我非亲自去一趟不可。

他一接到电报就动身了。

（二）紧缩句的两个谓语成分之间一般可表示并列、选择、递进、假设、原因、条件和承接等关系。例如：

The relation between the two predicates of a contracted sentence may be coordinative, alternative, progressive, suppositive, causative, conditional or successive. For example:

她越想越生气。

（表示递进关系）

(Progressive relation)

路不修不平。

（表示假设关系）

(Suppositive relation)

（意思是：路如果不修，就不平）

(Meaning: If the road is not repaired, it will be uneven)

他有事晚点儿来。

（表示因果关系）

(Causative relation)

（意思是：他因为有事，所以晚点儿来）

(Meaning: Since he has got something to do, he will come later)

（三）紧缩句的谓语成分多由动词、动宾词组、动补词组、动词性偏正词组或形容词等充当。

The predicate elements in contracted complex sentences are often performed by verbs, V-O phrases, V-C phrases, verbal endocentric phrases or adjectives.

（四）紧缩句的两个谓语成分都很简短，结构紧凑，常用于口语，中间一般没有语音停顿，书面上一般也不用逗号或分号。

Both the predicate elements in a contracted complex sentence are brief and compact. This kind of structure is often used in speaking without any pause in between. In writing, normally no comma or semicolon is used.

（五）紧缩句和关联词。

Contracted complex sentences and correlatives.

有些紧缩句要用关联词，有些不用。例如：

Correlatives are needed in some of the contracted complex sentences, while in others they are not necessary. For example:

他们越谈越高兴。

（表示递进关系）

(Progressive relation)

明天你非来参加不可。

（表示条件关系）

(Conditional relation)

她病了没来。（因为她病了，所以没来）

（表示因果关系）

(Causative relation)

你想听就听。（如果你想听，你就听）

（表示假设关系）

(Suppositive relation)

三、紧缩句中常用的关联词

Common correlatives used in contracted complex sentences

（一）关联副词"越…越…"的用法。

The uses of the correlative adverb "越…越…".

1. 副词"越"用在谓语（动词或形容词）前边作状语，表示后者的程度是随着前边条件的发展而发展变化的。例如：

The adverb 越 comes before each predicate (a verb or an adjective) as an adverbial adjunct to show that the degree of the second action or state changes proportionally to the changes of the first. For example:

这孩子越长越漂亮。

（"漂亮"的程度随着"长"大的过程而增加）

(The degree of 漂亮 increases in course of 长大)

大雨越下越大了。

（"大"的程度随着"下"的时间延长而增加）

(The degree of 大 increases with the duration of the action 下)

大家越说越兴奋。

2. 前边的谓语成分多由动词充当；后边的谓语成分多由形

容词或能表示程度的动词充当。例如：

The first predicate is mostly a verb and the second an adjective or a gradational verb.　For example:

他的画儿越画越有特色。

这个城市越建设越美。

3．注意：

Notes:

（1）后边的"越"和谓语成分之间不能再用表示程度 的 副词。例如：

No adverbs of degree occur between the second 越 and the predicate.　For　example:

这种花越开越香。

这对小猫她越看越喜欢。

不能说"这种花越开越很香"等。

One cannot say 这种花越开越很香, etc.

（2）重音一般在第一个"越"字上。

In general, the first 越 is spoken with a stress.

（二）关联副词"一…就…"的用法。

The uses of the correlative adverbs　"一…就…".

1．副词"一"和"就"用在谓语前边作状语，可以表示动作的承接关系。例如：

When the adverbs — and 就 are used as adverbial adjuncts before predicates, they may denote the successive relation of actions.　For　example:

我们一接到电话就出发了。

他一进门就脱了大衣。

还可以表示条件关系。例如：

— and 就 may also indicate conditional relation. For example:

他一看书就睏。

她一看见狗就害怕。

2．副词"一"、"就"后的谓语成分多由动词充当；表示条件的"一"后的谓语成分也可由形容词充当。例如：

The predicates respectively following — and 就 are mainly verbs; however, the predicate after — denoting conditional relation may be an adjective. For example:

他一不小心就摔倒了。

天气一凉快，就好了。

3．注意：

Notes:

（1）"一…就…"构成的紧缩句有时中间可以稍有停顿，形式上更接近于一般包含两个分句的复句；表示承接关系的属并列复句，表示条件关系的属偏正复句。

Sometimes there may be a short pause in a contracted sentence formed of "一…就…". Then it is, in form, more like an ordinary complex sentence containing two clauses. In that case, contracted sentences denoting successive relation belong to coordinate complex sentences whereas those denoting conditional relation belong to subordinate complex sentences.

（2）重音一般在前边的副词"一"字上。

In general, the stress is on the first adverb 一.

（三）关联副词"非…不…"的用法。

The uses of the correlative adverbs "非…不…".

1．"非…不…"是双重否定的格式，表示强调"如果不…，就不行"、"一定要…，才…"的意思。例如：

"非…不…" is the pattern of double negation, showing emphasis of the meaning "如果不…"就不行，"一定要…，才…".For example:

这件事非你不行。

（意思是：这件事如果不让你办，是办不好的）

(Meaning: If you do not do this ,it cannot be done well.)

明天你非来不可。

（意思是：明天你不来是不行的；你一定要来）

(Meaning: It will not do if you do not come tomorrow; You must come.)

2．"非"后边的谓语成分可由动词、名词、代词或词组充当；"不"后边的谓语成分多由单音词"可"或"行"等充当。例如：

The predicate following 非 may be a verb, a noun, a pronoun or a phrase, and that following 不 is often a monosyllabic 可，行， etc. . For example:

他非走不可。

这个会非张主任出席不行。

这件事非找他不可。

他们非骑车去不成。

中午我非睡会儿不行。

3．注意：

Notes:

（1）"非"和"不"后边的谓语成分一般都指尚未实现的事。

The predicate elements after 非 and 不 normally refer to things that have not yet come true.

（2）重音一般在前边的"非"字上。

Generally speaking, the stress is on 非.

练 习 67
Exercise 67

（一）指出下列各句是哪类复句（并列、偏正、紧缩）。

Point out types of the following complex sentences

(coordinate, subordinate, contracted).

例：　　　要是你明天不能来，就给我打个电话。（偏正）

Model:　　　　　　　　　　　　　　　　　(subordinate)

1. 今天非下雨不可。

2. 他一进来就开灯。

3. 她们有办法，我们也有办法。

4. 我在国内学习，我哥哥在国外学习。

5. 这里不但是游览胜地，而且也是避暑的好地方。

6. 他俩越走越慢。

7. 这种药你不吃不行。

8. 这次他们一下飞机，就到旅馆去了。

9. 我越学习越觉得需要多学习。

（二）在下列句中括号内填上适当的关联词。

Fill in the brackets with proper correlatives in the following senteces.

1. 张明（　　　）会弹钢琴，（　　　）会画画儿。

2. 他常常（　　　）吃饭，（　　　）听音乐。

3. 下午我（　　　）办点儿事，（　　　）去你那儿。

4. （　　　）你要研究世界历史，（　　　）他要研究？

5. 一年来，他（　　　）虚心学习，（　　　）刻苦钻研，收获很大。

6. 您别着急，张先生（　　　）今天下午到，（　　　）明天上午到。

7. 我（　　　）自己多用些时间，（　　　）不愿意打扰别人。

8. 他是专家，这个专业会议（　　　）我去，（　　　）他去。

9. 你们（　　　）买这个牌子的，（　　　）买那个牌子的，两种质量都不错。

10 她在工作中，（　　　）干，（　　　）学，提高得很快。

690

11. （　　　）没有工夫，你（　　　）别来了。

12. 我们（　　　）有决心，（　　　）一定能学会这种技术。

13. （　　　）今天他有点儿不舒服，（　　　）我代替他。

14. 那里的生活条件（　　　）再好，我（　　　）不想去。

15. 她（　　）长（　　）象她母亲。

16. （　　　）他已经承认错误了，（　　　）应该原谅他。

17. 明天（　　　）天气怎么样，我们的活动（　　　）照常进行。

18. 大家（　　　）多练习，（　　　）能把汉语学好。

19. （　　　）困难再大，我们（　　　）不怕。

20. 他（　　　）走进教室，上课铃（　　　）响了。

（三）改正下列病句。

Correct the mistakes in the following sentences.

1. 他们几个人一方面走，一方面谈。

2. 那位老师不但教本国学生，而且不教外国学生。

3. 不但她想去欧洲旅行，而且还要去亚洲旅行。

4. 这本画报不是是我的，而是他的。

5. 与其骑车去，还是坐车去。

6. 我们一下课，他才走了。

7. 要是明天下雪，就我不去了。

8. 还是买床单，还是买窗帘，都要漂亮一点儿的。

9. 不管唱歌跳舞，都她很喜欢。

（四）指出下列句中的对句（划"✓"）和错句（划"×"）并改正错句。

Mark the correct sentences with a tick "✓" and the wrong ones with a cross "×" and correct them.

1. 要是你们都赞成，就开这个会。

2. 只有下午，才他有时间。

3. 不论他唱，别人也必须唱。

4. 他虽然同意这样做了，他爱人但是不同意。

5. 不管飞机什么时候到，我们都去接他。
6. 只要每个人抽出半小时，就可以搞完了。
7. 就是他病了，也我们要按时完成这项工程。
8. 因为他就要毕业了，我们所以没有选他作学生会主席。
9. 他既然通过了毕业考试，应该发给他毕业证书。
10. 我们快把房间打扫干净，好接待客人。

语 法 术 语 表
Grammatical Terms

B

把字句	bǎzìjù	把-sentence
被字句	bèizìjù	被-sentence
宾语（宾）	bīnyǔ	Object (O)
并列复句	bìngliè fùjù	Coordinate complex sentence
补语	bǔyǔ	Complement
补充词组	bǔchōng cízǔ	Complementary phrase

C

陈述句	chénshùjù	Declarative sentence (statement)
程度补语	chéngdù bǔyǔ	Degree complement
词序	cíxù	Word order
词组	cízǔ	Phrase
存现句	cúnxiànjù	Existential sentence

D

代词（代）	dàicí	Pronoun (pron.)
单宾语	dān bīnyǔ	Single object
单部句	dānbù jù	One-member sentence
单句	dānjù	Simple sentence
的字结构	de zì jiégòu	的-phrase

定语（定）	dìng yǔ	Attributive (attrib.)
动宾词组	dòng bīn cízǔ	Verb-object (V-O) phrase
动补词组	dòng bǔ cízǔ	Verb-complement (V-C) phrase
动词（动）	dòng cí	Verb (V)
动词性词组	dòng cíxìng cízǔ	Verbal phrase
动词性联合词组	dòngcíxìng liánhé cízǔ	Verbal coordinative phrase
动词谓语	dòngcí wèiyǔ	Verbal predicate
动词谓语句	dòngcí wèiyǔjù	Sentence with a verbal predicate
动量补语	dòng liàng bǔyǔ	Complement of frequency
动量词	dòng liángcí	Verbal measure word
动态助词	dòngtài zhùcí	Aspectual particle
独语句	dúyǔjù	One-word phrase/sentence

F

方位词	fāngwèicí	Noun of locality
方位词组	fāngwèi cízǔ	Phrase of locality
非主谓句	fēi zhǔwèijù	Non-subject-predicate (Non-S-P) sentence
否定式	fǒudìngshì	Negative form
复合趋向补语	fùhé qūxiàng bǔyǔ	Compound directional complement
复句	fùjù	Complex sentence
副词（副）	fùcí	Adverb (adv.)

G

感叹号	gǎntànhào	Exclamation mark
感叹句	gǎntànjù	Exclamatory sentence
固定词组	gùdìng cízǔ	Set phrase
关联词	guānliáncí	Correlative word

J

兼语句	jiānyǔjù	Pivotal sentence
简单趋向补语	jiǎndān qūxiàng bǔyǔ	Simple directional complement
简略句	jiǎnlüèjù	Elliptical sentence
降调	jiàngdiào	Falling tone
结构助词	jiégòu zhùcí	Structural particle
介词（介）	jiècí	Preposition (prep.)
介词结构	jiecí jiégòu	Prepositional phrase
紧缩句	jǐnsuōjù	Contracted sentence
句号	jùhào	Full stop, period

K

肯定式	kěndìngshì	Affirmative form

L

连词（连）	liáncí	Conjunction (conj.)
连动结构	liándòng jiégòu	Verbal constructions in series
连动句	liándòngjù	Sentence with verbal constructions in series
联合词组	liánhé cízǔ	Coordinative phrase
量词	liàngcí	Measure word

695

M

名词（名）	míngcí	Noun (N.)
名词性偏正词组	míngcíxìng piānzhèng cízǔ	Nominal endocentric phrase
名词性谓语	míngcíxìng wèiyǔ	Noun predicate
名词谓语句	míngcí wèiyǔjù	Sentence with a noun predicate
名量补语	míngliàng bǔyǔ	Complement of nominal measure
名量词	míngliàngcí	Nominal measure word

P

偏句	piānjù	Subordinate clause
偏正词组	piānzhèng cízǔ	Endocentric phrase
偏正复句	piānzhèng fùjù	Subordinate complex sentence

Q

其他成分	qítā chéngfèn	Other element
祈使句	qíshǐjù	Imperative sentence
前置宾语	qiánzhì bīnyǔ	Fronted object
趋向补语	qūxiàng bǔyǔ	Directional complement

R

人称代词	rénchēng dàicí	Personal pronoun

S

升调	shēngdiào	Rising tone
声调	shēngdiào	Tones

时间词	shíjiāncí	Time noun
时量补语	shíliàng bǔyǔ	Complement of duration
是字句	shìzìjù	是 -sentence
数词（数）	shùcí	Numeral (num.)
数量补语	shùliàng bǔyǔ	Complement of quantity
数量词组	shùliàng cízǔ	Numeral-measure word (N-Mw) phrase
双宾语	shuāng bīnyǔ	Double objects
双部句	shuāngbùjù	Two-member sentence

T

同位词组	tóngwèi cízǔ	Appositive phrase

W

谓语（谓）	wèiyǔ	Predicate (P)
谓语部分	wèiyǔ bùfen	Predicate section
谓语动词	wèiyǔ dòngcí	Predicate verb
问号	wènhào	Question mark
无主句	wúzhǔjù	Subjectless sentence
无主兼语句	wúzhǔ jiānyǔjù	Subjectless pivotal sentence

X

象声词	xiàngshēngcí	Onomatope
形容词（形）	xíngróngcí	Adjective (adj.)
形容词谓语句	xíngróngcí wèiyǔjù	Sentence with an adjectival predicate
修饰语	xiūshìyǔ	Modifier
选择式疑问句	xuǎnzéshì yíwènjù	Alternative interrogative sentence (Alternative

Y

疑问代词	yíwèn dàicí	Interrogative pronoun (interrog. PN)
疑问句	yíwènjù	Interrogative sentence (question)
有字句	yǒu zì jù	有-sentence
语调	yǔdiào	Intonation
语气助词	yǔqì zhùcí	Interjection

Z

正反疑问句	zhèngfǎn yíwènjù	Affirmative-negative question
正句	zhèngjù	Main clause
指示代词	zhǐshì dàicí	Demonstrative pronoun
中心语	zhōngxīnyǔ	Modified word
重音	zhòngyīn	stress
主语（主）	zhǔyǔ	Subject (S)
主语部分	zhǔyǔ bùfen	Subject section
主谓词组	zhǔwèi cízǔ	Subject-predicate (S-P) phrase
主谓句	zhǔwèijù	Subject-predicate (S-P) sentence
主谓谓语句	zhǔwèi wèiyǔjù	Sentence with an S-P phrase predicate
助词（助）	zhùcí	Particle (P)
助动词（助动）	zhùdòngcí	Auxiliary verb (Aux. V)
状语（状）	zhuàngyǔ	Adverbial Adjunct (adv. adjunct)

练 习 答 案
KEY TO EXERCISES

第 二 章

练习 1

一、1，4，5，8，9，10——（✓）

2，3，6，7，——（×）

二、1.里（边）　2.旁边　3.里（边），外边　4.里（边）

5.上（边）〔或：下（边）〕6.前边，后边

三、1，2，4，6，9，10，12，14，15，17，18，19，20

四、1.记者　2.教室里黑板　3.银行　4.邮局银行西边

5.动物园 6.操场 7.地址 8.壶 9.信 10.妹妹头发

练习 2

一、1.汉语，英语　2.树，花　3.饭　4.电视　5.衣服，脸

6.家，祖国　7.祖国，国家　8.足球　9.代表　10.问题

二、1.打，踢 2.学习 3.看 4.去 5.喝 6.收拾 7.画

8.听 9.安装，修理 10.参观

三、1，3，5，8 ——（是）

2，6，9 ——（在）

4，7，10 ——（有）

四、1. 他们不是工人。　　2. 我没有中文书。

3. 她在朋友那儿。　　4. 我们分析分析。

5．他谈了谈意见。　　6．学校前边是研究所。

6．学校前边有研究所。　　6．研究所在学校前边。

7．他去图书馆。　　8．他在朋友家。

9．我是教师。　　10．你看一看我的书房。

练习 3

一、1.会　2.想　3.要　4.要　5.应该　6.会，会　7.肯
8.得 (děi) 9.可以　10.敢

二、1.能，可以　　2.要　　3.必须，应该，可以，能　　4.会
5.应该，必须　6.应当，要　7.要，应该　8.会，能
9.可以，能　10.要

三、1．明天他不想请客。　　2．我们不能做这个试验。

3．我不想请教他。　　4．我们不应该选他。

5．领导不可能表扬他。　　6．他不愿意发表声明。

7．我们不用限制时间。　　7．我们不要限制时间。

8．大家不该相信他。　　9．我哥哥不会开飞机。

10．他们不肯参加。

练习 4

一、2，3，5，6，8，10 ——（ ✓ ）

二、1，3.红,黄,蓝,白,黑,绿　2.新,旧,大,小

4.大,小,新鲜　　5.好,坏,新,重要

6.大,小,新,旧,长,方　7.蓝,红,黑

8.瘦,肥,新鲜　　9.正常,好

10.厚,薄,大,小,新,旧

三、1.早,晚,快　　2.努力,认真,刻苦

3.多,热情地,高兴地,满意地　4.早,晚,快,慢

5.积极,坚决,热情　　6.仔细,认真,多

7.及时,快,迅速,彻底　　8.热烈,热情

9.早,快,认真,积极　　10.少,多,快

练习 5

一、1. 二　　　　　　　　　　　　2. 二十二
　　3. 一百一十五　　　　　　　　4. 三千四百七十八
　　5. 十　　　　　　　　　　　　6. 六万一千九百一十二
　　7. 三百零八　　　　　　　　　8. 七千零五
　　9. 五万零四百九十　　　　　　10. 三十八万
　　11. 五分之二　　　　　　　　　12. 九分之七
　　13. 百分之八十　　　　　　　　14. 百分之二十九
　　15. 千分之五

二、1.八　2.二八　　3.二二八　　4.九六〇七　　5.九〇〇一
　　6.一〇〇〇二　　　7.五六四三〇　　　8.八九九九二二
　　9.一二〇五〇　　10.五〇四〇三〇

三、1.两　　2.两　　3.两　　4.十二　　5.二十　　6.二十二
　　7.六十二　8.一百二十　9.二百二十二　10.一百八十二

练习 6

一、1, 2, 3, 4, 5, 6, 7, 8, 9, 10——两

二、1.架　2.封　3.件　4.座　5.个　6.块（或：毛，分）
　　7.公斤　8.米　9.副　10.根

三、1.一块（钱）　　　　　2.两块两毛二（分钱），两块二毛二
　　3.四块五（毛钱）　　　4.九块九（毛钱）
　　5.三块三毛五（分钱）6.七块八毛六（分钱）
　　7.十块零五分（钱）　　8.三十二块三毛一（分钱）
　　9.一百零五毛（钱）　　10.一百二十一块一毛二（分钱）

四、1.一点四十八（分），差十二分两点
　　2.两点二十（分）
　　3.九点三十（分），九点半
　　4.三点四十五（分），三点三刻，差一刻四点
　　5.四点零五（分）

6．六点十分

7．十点十五（分），十点一刻

8．八点三十七（分）

9．七点零一分

10．五点五十九（分），差一分六点

五、1．一九八〇年十二月二十五日星期四

2．一九四九年十月一日

3．一九六四年五月十日

4．一九八一年三月八日星期日

5．一九七二年六月七日

练习7

一、1．哪儿　2．什么　3．谁　4．哪　5．怎么样　6．怎么

二、1，5——人称代词　2，6——指示代词　3，4——疑问代词

三、1．我们　2．她们　3．这些　4．哪些　5．那些　6．你们

四、1．个　2．本　3．号　4．个　5．辆　6．块（或：毛，分）

五、1．你们去哪儿？　　　　　　2．这是什么？

3．谁有《汉英词典》？　　　　4．这套房间怎么样？

5．你怎么回答他的问题？　　　6．这个句子怎么分析？

练习8

一、1．都，也，不，特别　　　　2．常常，也，不

3．也，不　　　　　　　　　4．特别，也，不

5．不，特别　　　　　　　　6．马上

二、1．我的兴趣很广泛。　　　　2．他的理想终于实现了。

3．这件事给我的印象非常深。　4．他能按时完成这项工作。

5．你可以随时来我的办公室。　6．最近一连下了三天雨。

三、1．他也许不来。　　　　　　1．他也许没有来。

2．他不可能接见我们。　　　2．他可能不接见我们。

3．我们也不准备出席。　　　4．他们不常组织晚会。

702

5．这些孩子不瘦。　　　　　6．他的技术不太熟练。

四、1．他们也都参加谈判。　　　2．这件事已经公布了。

　　3．我一直反对这种作法。　　4．我们都从事文艺工作。

　　5．他今天多么激动啊！　　　6．我明天再搞。

五、1．大家都买。　　　　　　　2．他也是作家。

　　3．我就来。　　　　　　　　4．她常常锻炼。

　　5．她们不唱。

练习9

一、1，5，15，18——从　　　　2，13——给

　　3，6，11，16——对　　　4，14，17，19，20——在

　　7.离　8.向，往　9.除了　10.跟　12.为　14.沿着

二、1．在花园散步　　　　　　　2．从朋友那儿来

　　3．往西走　　　　　　　　　4．按原则办

　　5．对人热情　　　　　　　　6．在老师家听音乐

　　7．为大家办事　　　　　　　8．跟我讨论

　　9．给学生讲课　　　　　　　10．跟运动员谈话

练习10

一、1.和　2.和（跟）　3，7——而（和）　4，5——并（和）

　　6.和（及）　8，10——还是　9.或者

二、1．白粉笔和彩色粉笔都在黑板旁边。

　　2．主人跟客人都进了客厅。

　　3．他这个月搜集并整理这些资料。

　　4．我们应该迅速而准确地完成这个计算任务。

　　5．他要进行全面、详细和深入的分析。

　　6．主任要了解情况并且解决困难。

　　7．我打排球或者打乒乓球。

　　8．他们去长城还是去十三陵？

三、1．科学与艺术　　　　　　2．我和你

3．勤劳而勇敢　　　　　4．认识并改正错误
5．仔细阅读并且进行分析　6．数量和质量
7．简单而明确　　　　　8．发明和创造
9．坚强还是软弱？　　　10．具备还是不具备条件？

练习 11

一、1，2，5，6，9——的
　　3，8——地
　　4，7，10——得

二、1，10——吗（吧）　　2.啊　　3，7，8——呢（啊）
　　4，9——吧　5.吧　6.呢

三、1．他正喝着凉开水。
　　2．他对大家点了点头。
　　3．他们曾经安装过这种机器。
　　4．她翻译了一本小说。
　　5．昨天我买了三套明信片。
　　6．我在朋友那儿听过那只歌。
　　7．父亲正穿着大衣。
　　8．孩子嘴里含着糖。
　　9．我们村子里没发生过这类事情。
　　10．这张画儿存在着不少毛病。

第 三 章

练习 12

一、1，2，5，6，10，11，14，17——名词
　　3，8，9，18——动词
　　4，7，12，15——形容词
　　13，16——代词

二、1，2，7，9——的

　　　3，5，6，　——地

　　　4，8，10　——得

练习 13

一、

名词	形容词
1.变化	小
3.颜色	深
6.路	窄
8.距离	大
11.心	好
12.座位	远
13.答案	正确
15.情绪	稳定
16.衣服	薄
17.关系	密切
19.基础	好
20.皮肤	白，

名词	动词
2.老虎	叫
4.命令	取消
5.技术	交流
7.记者	报道

代词	动词
9.他	设计
10.我们	反对

代词	形容词
14.这里	安静

名词	代词
18.效果	怎么样

二、1.外边冷　2.猫叫　3.他很糊涂　4.他反对　5.阳光充足

　　6.身体健康

三、1.我们爬，的　　　2.态度坚决，地　　　3.满头大汗，得

　　4.学校邀请，的　　　5.我们刚打，的　　　6.心急，地

　　7.我请，的　　8.语气柔和，地　　9.我都快不认识了，得

　　10.意志坚强，地

练习14

一、代词——1.谁   14.大家   19.我们

　　名词——2.差别   4.觉   5.日记   8.话   9.马   11.语法

　　　　　　12.商场   13.老人   16.长城   17.学习   18.汗

　　形容词——3.为难   20.安静

　　动　词——6.辩论   7.批评   10.表演   15.参观

二、1. 买机床——定语　　　　　　2. 吃中国饭——宾语

　　3. 缺乏经验——主语　　　　　　4. 流眼泪——补语

　　5. 个别交换意见——定语　　　　6. 参加晚会——定语

　　7. 表演节目——宾语　　　　　　8. 符合实际——补语

　　9. 用左手——状语　　　　　　 10. 喝着茶——状语

　　11. 有计划——状语　　　　　　 12. 锻炼身体——主语

　　13. 完成任务——定语　　　　　 14. 符合标准——补语

　　15. 含着眼泪——状语

三、1，2，5，7，9——一点儿

　　3，4，6，8，10——有一点儿

练习15

定语——1.大   2.这只   4.三个   5.儿童   8.外交   9.狡猾

　　　　11.绿   12.很多   13.山   15.熟练   16.祖国   18.白

　　　　20.那些   21.圆   23.必要   24.关键   28.一切

　　　　29.全国   30.村子

状语——3.后天   6.及时   7.很   10.临时   14.真   17.公开

　　　　19.突然   22.个别   25.十分   26.怎么   27.非常

练习16

一、1.一年，十二个月   2.一间   　　3.一米，三市尺

　　4.三月，二十五号   5 一次   　　6.八十块

　　7.一双一双　　　　 8.一个一个　 9.十分

10.一趟

二、1，3，4，5，8，9，11，13，15，16——（√）

2，6，7，10，12，14 ——（×）

2.五条裤子　　6.一篇一篇地阅读　　7.一支一支的笔

10.那两位先生　12.三本字典　14.两把剪子

习练17

一、词——1.妥当　2.平　3.很　5.清楚　6.开　7.满　11.熟

12.准　13.来　15.很　20.伤

词组——4.极了　8.三遍　9.半小时　10.出来　14.很高

16.一天　17.进去　18.极了　19.很正确

二、1．清楚极了；　　　　　清楚——形容词

2．听完；　　　　　　听——动词

3．织好；　　　　　　织——动词

4．结实得很；　　　　结实——形容词

5．休息一天；　　　　休息——动词

6．幸福得很；　　　　幸福——形容词

7．选得很合适；　　　选——动词

8．吃得太饱；　　　　吃——动词

9．写得很有水平；　　写——动词

10．学得会；　　　　　学——动词

练习18

一、1，5，12，16，20——时间

2，7，10，17，19——数量

3，4，6，8，9，11，13，14，15，18——处所

二、1.两天以后　　2.手上　　　3.路东

4.圣诞节以前　5.箱子里　　6.墙上

7.三个月以内　8.一个星期左右　9.他的右边（他右边）

10.十二点左右　11.五百公斤以上　12.六十岁上下

练习 19

一、1. 我们学校北京语言学院——主语
　2. 一份杂志《旅游》　　——宾语
　3. 小马他　　　　　　　——定语
　4. 第一、第二两本　　　——定语
　5. 张文、谢明两位老师　——宾语
　6. 我们自己　　　　　　——主语
　7. 你们俩　　　　　　　——宾语
　8. 钱民同学　　　　　　——定语
　9. 我们大家　　　　　　——主语
　10. 我的朋友王刚　　　　——主语

二、1. 自己　2. 他们　3. 先生　4. 那天　5. 张文　6. 俩

练习 20

　1，7，13——在　　　　2，8，14，19——从
　3，12——给　　　　　4，16——往（向）
　5，17——对　　　　　6，11——比
　10，20——除了
　9. 被　15. 向　16. 往　18 为

练习 21

一、宾语——1. 新建立的　2. 你的，他的　3. 彩色的，黑白的
　　　　　　5. 石头的　6. 我自己织的，买的
　　　　　　8.（那位）戴眼镜的　10. 今天的
　主语——3. 我买的　7. 他拿的　9. 男的，女的
　谓语里主谓词组中的"主"——4. 吃的、穿的

二、1. 我送你的——礼物（东西）
　　2. 穿花裙子的——人
　　3. 中文的，英文的——书

708

4．蓝的——毛衣

5．跑步的——人

第 四 章

一、1.这个词　　　　2.风　　　　　3.工人们

4.月亮　　　　　5.咱们大家　　　6.五的五倍

7.这样做　　　　8.访问中国　　　9.明天

10.汽车　　　　11.骆驼和象　　　12.客厅的灯

13.呼吸新鲜空气　14.生活幸福

二、名词——1.今天　　3.儿童　　5.经理　　6.印象　　8.弟弟

9.颜色　10.文学家　11.损失

动词——2.模仿

代词——4.我们

动宾词组——7.听新闻广播　15.遵守交通规则

联合词组——12.赞成或者反对　13.治病救人　14.电灯和电扇

一、1. 舍不得离开这儿　　　2. 是石油工人

3. 很关心同学　　　　　4. 都想参观那个画展

5. 包括主语部分和谓语部分　6. 送我们许多礼物

7. 引起了广大群众的注意　8. 是十分必要的

9. 哭得真伤心　　　　　10. 都是老朋友

二、形容词——1.方便　4.好

动词——2.是　3.给　5.出　6.说　10.解决

联合词组——7.谦虚谨慎

主谓词组——8.意见一致

偏正词组——9.两块钱

709

练习 24

一、名词——1.狮子　　2.汽车　　6.月　　8.作家　　9.眼睛
　　　　　　10.钢笔

　　动词——4.祝贺

　　联合词组——3.风俗习惯　　7.排球篮球

　　主谓词组——5.那个城市不太大

二、

主语	宾语	
1.妹妹	护士	（名词）
2.拖拉机	人民公社的	（的字结构）
3.工厂	医生	（名词）
4.看病	职业	（名词）
5.售货员	经验	（名词）
6.光线太强	好处	（名词）
7.人	常识	（名词）
8.他	下星期比赛	（偏正词组）
9.他	同学们已经出发了	（主谓词组）
10.我	他妹妹是护士	（主谓词组）

练习 25

一、

定语	主语
2.我和他	想法
3.哪间	屋子
5.人民	利益
6.雄伟壮观	长城
7.爱好艺术	同学
8.那些高大	建筑
9.为人民牺牲	英雄们

定　　语	宾　　语
1.一个多民族	国家
4.新出版	中国青年
8.一个	研究所的
10.这个鼓舞人心	消息

二、1. 你看看挂在墙上的照片。

2. 这座楼是学生吃饭的地方。

3. 去上海的旅客从这边上车。

4. 刚才来的客人是我权权。

5. 这已经是三年前的事了。

6. 那座大楼是研究环境保护的地方。

7. 我刚接到朋友寄来的信。

8. 人们都穿着干干净净的衣服。

9. 我买了三张下星期三的电影票。

10. 他真是一个很热情的人。

练习 26

1. 暂时（副词），在这儿（介词结构）

2. 昨天（名词），突然（副词）

3. 热烈（形容词）

4. 常（副词），为电影里的人物的命运（介词结构）

5. 对这种雕刻艺术（介词结构），非常（副词）

6. 任何时候（偏正词组），都（副词），应该（助动词）

7. 都，非常（副词）

8. 原来，比较（副词）

9. 最近（名词）；实在，太（副词）

10. 应该，能（助动词）

11. 明天(名词)，一定(副词)，要(助动词)，早(形容词)

12. 顺利（形容词）

13. 往热水瓶里（介词结构）

14. 不要（副词），那样（代词）

15. 上星期四（偏正词组），对我（介词结构）

16. 到底（副词），明天下午（偏正词组）

17. 今天（名词），能（助动词）

18. 从很远的地方，给我们（介词结构）

练习 27

一、动词——1.住 2.给 3.到 5.完 6.见 8.开 9.懂

　　形容词——4.干净 7.错 10.坏

二、1. 我打通电话了。

　　2. 昨天晚上没找到小高。

　　3. 我们决心学好汉语。

　　4. 大家都打开书了。（或者：大家都打开了书。）

　　5. 我没看清楚布告上的字。

　　6. 病人睁开眼睛。

　　7. 这个笑话真笑死（了）人了。

　　8. 孩子们都睡着了。

　　9. 他能翻译对这些句子。

　　10. 老师已经讲到第八课了。

练习 28

一、1. 很慢，很快　　　　　　　　2. 很晚，太晚了

　　3. 不错，很好　　　　　　　　4. 非常漂亮

　　5. 很流利，不太流利，也很流利　6. 很高，好极了

　　7. 不太好，比较好　　　　　　8. 特别好看，很合适

　　9. 很多，饱极了　　　　　　　10. 好极了，很好，很好吃

二、1. 我们每天都起得很早。

　　2. 他念课文念得（很）流利。

3．他穿得太多了。

4．他对我关心得很。

5．他搜集资料搜集得很完全。

（或者：资料他搜集得很完全。

他资料搜集得很完全。）

6．他考虑问题考虑得十分全面。

（或者：他问题考虑得十分全面。

问题他考虑得十分全面。）

7．这个电影有意思极了。

（或者：这个电影有意思得很。）

8．我们说汉语都说得不太好。

（或者：汉语我们都说得不太好。）

我们汉语都说得不太好。）

9．这间屋子打扫得不干净。

10．他们俩打乒乓球打得都很好。

（或者：他们俩乒乓球都打得很好。）

乒乓球他们俩都打得很好。）

练习 29

一、名量补语　1．一点　9．一百米

动量补语　2．一遍　3．两次　4．一下儿　7．三遍

时量补语　5．一年　　6．半个小时　8．一上午，五个小时

10．四年

二、1．跳一个晚上舞　（或者：跳舞跳一个晚上）

2．访问两次作家　（或者：访问作家两次）

3．碰到他一次

4．已经订婚三年

5．在南方旅行一个半月

6．打一下午网球　（或者：打网球打一个下午）

7．看一个晚上电视　（或者：看电视看一个晚上）

8．打一次电话

9．翻译半年小说 （或者：翻译小说翻译半年）

10．踢一场足球

练习 30

一、1，2，4，6，10，——（去）

3，5，7，8，9，——（来）

二、1，2，3，6，7，13，14，15，——（起来）

4，5，8 ——（下去）

9，11 ——（出来）

10，12 ——（下来）

三、1．回宿舍来

2．进剧场去

3．带来一瓶醋 （或者：带一瓶醋来）

4．走进俱乐部来

5．买回来一件红毛衣 （或者：买回一件红毛衣来）

6．抬出去一个书架 （或者：抬出一个书架去）

7．唱起歌来

8．走起路来

9．寄回去一包衣服 （或者：寄回一包衣服去）

10．走上楼去

练习 31

一、1．上得去　　　　2．数不完　　　　3．找不到

4．称得对　　　　5．推得出去　　　　6．挂不上去

7．说得清楚　　　　8．听不懂　　　　9．挡得住

10．看得见

二、1，6，10——动（了）

2，3，5，7，9——下（了）

4，8——了

714

练习 32

一、结果补语——1.在　6.走

程度补语——2.极了　3.很早　4.又唱又跳　9.多

动量补语——5.三遍

可能补语——7.动　8.到

趋向补语——10.出来

二、

补　语		宾　语	
1.很快	（偏正词组）	马	（名词）
2.下来	（补充词组）	苹果	（名词）
3.一个钟头	（偏正词组）	棋	（名词）
4.一下儿	（数量词组）	他	（代词）
5.进去	（补充词组）	火车	（名词）
6.完	（动词）	作文	（名词）
7.了	（动词）	计划	（名词）
8.出来	（补充词组）	血	（名词）
9.两天	（偏正词组）	病假	（名词）
10.一下儿	（数量词组）	意见	（名词）

第 五 章

练习 33

一、

动词谓语	宾　语	动词谓语	宾语
1.喝	牛奶	2.倒	茶

3．开	窗户	4．有	花瓶
5．买	鱼	6．看	杂志
7．爱	姑姑	8．信任	你
9．用	筷子和叉子	10．打	羽毛球
11．介绍介绍	情况	12．获得	解放
13．钻研	问题	14．赞成	建议
15．打算	去风景优美的南方		

二、1．向窗户外边　　　　　2．有一点儿
　　3．最近，更　　　　　　4．明天，要，重新
　　5．替我　　　　　　　　6．一连
　　7．都，必须　　　　　　8．都，提前
　　9．关于那次战争的情况　10.对这些奇怪的现象，一定，要

三、程度补语——1.很顺利　6.很不错　8.楼上的人都听见了
　　结果补语——2.好　3.开　4.完
　　可能补语——5.下　9.完
　　趋向补语——7.进去
　　动量补语——10.一趟

练习34

一、1．今天天气不凉快。　　　2．今天的客人不（太）多。
　　3．他们俩不亲密。　　　　4．这个客厅不（太）干净。
　　5．那个孩子不诚实。　　　6．他刚买的那件衬衫不贵。
　　7．这里的交通不方便。　　8．这儿的空气不新鲜。
　　9．这个号码不对。　　　　10．这课的语法不难。

二、1.非常　2.特别　3.比较　4.很　5.十分　6.相当　7.太
　　8.特别　9.最　10.太

三、程度补语——1.极了　3.很　4.多了　5.多了
　　　　　　　　　7.一个人提不动　8.极了　9.多

数量补语——2.三公尺　6.一点儿　10.一点儿

练习 35

一、1，3，5，6，7，10——（✓）

二、1．今天不是星期五。

2．他们都不是阿拉伯人。（或者：他们不都是阿拉伯人。）

3．这件大衣不是二百五十块钱。

4．后天不是开斋节。

5．现在不是夏天。

6．今年他不是五十五岁。

7．今天不是复活节。

8．今年不是一九八一年。

9．这不是一千块钱。

10．他不是炊事员，我不是服务员。

练习 36

一、1.颜色　2.他　3.钥匙　4.哥哥　5.结构　6.水平　7.用法

8.我　9.胳臂　10.态度

二、1．昨天他背受伤了。　　　　2．他代表资格取消了。

3．我头有一点儿晕。　　　　4．这个青年工作非常吃苦。

5．这个地方气候很不错。

练习 37

1，3，4，10，13，16，20——动词谓语句

2，5，15，17——名词谓语句

8，9，11，12，——形容词谓语句

6，7，14，18，19——主谓谓语句

练习 38

一、　1，2，7，8——无主句

4，10——独语句

二、 1.咱们 2.大家 3.衣服是我的 4.今天 5.最近学习 6.他

练习39

主 要 特 点	回　　答
1．吗	是。（他在电视台工作。）
	不。（他不在电视台工作。）
2．坐　不坐	坐。
	不坐。
3．大　不大	大。
	不大。
4．哪	我喜欢这种方式。
	我喜欢那种。
5．是　不是	是，很大。
	不，（雾）不大。
6．吗	会来。
	不会来。
7．是　不是	是。
	不是。
8．有　没有	我有，他也有。
	我没有，他也没有。
9．多（长）	有十五米长。
10．好　不好	好。
	不好。
11．还是	我吃米饭。（我吃馒头。）
12．多大	（我）六十岁了。
13．是　不是	是。（他已经给我买了火车票了。）
	没有。（他没有给我买火车票。）

14 吗	是。（那位是新来的校长。）
	不，那位不是。
15．还是	船票容易买。（飞机票容易买。）
	都容易买。
	都不容易买。（都不好买。）
16．漂亮　不漂亮	很漂亮。
	不（太）漂亮。
17．谁	我朋友
18．是　不是	是。（比较难。）
	不。（不太难。）
19．呢	我也休息。
	我不休息。
20．还是	我在家准备。
	我去图书馆。

练习 40

一、1．她不是上海人。

　　2．他在自己的房间听音乐。

　　3．他很高。

　　4．大家都没有这样的信封。

　　5．他进食堂去了。

　　6．我们都不去机场。

　　7．下星期日同学们都来我这儿。

　　8．他每天睡觉睡得很早。

　　9．他从家里搬到学生宿舍去了。

　　10．我们的作业本都在老师那儿。

　　11·明年八月我们就要回国了。

　　12．这是他写的书。

　　13．这是什么地图？

14. 他不是政府官员。

15. 朋友们都从别的城市来了。

16. 他今天起得很早。

17. 他能听懂那个报告。

18. 你妹妹在哪儿？

19. 他送我一块手绢。

20. 下雪了。

21. 你去不去植物园？　　　　21. 你去植物园吗？

22. 这句话应该怎么说？

23. 这只公鸡是你家的吗？

24. 我们都没有那样的车。

25. 他已经回宿舍来了。

26. 北京冬天很冷吗？　　　　26. 北京冬天是不是很冷？

27. 谁是玛丽？　　　　　　　27. 玛丽在哪儿？

28. 你是哪国人？

30. 请坐下！

二、 造句，无标准答案。如读者有兴趣，欢迎把这项练习寄给
　　编者，作为修改本书的参考。

第 六 章

练习 41

一、1. 我们在喝咖啡。　　　2. 他在尝我做的点心。

　　3. 那个演员在唱歌。　　4. 我朋友在打电话。

　　5. 他们在踢足球。

二、1. 那位老师正在辅导学生。

　　2. 我们正在商量克服困难的办法。

　　3. 他正在安排课外活动。

720

4. 国家领导人正在检阅军队。

5. 我们正在建设自己的国家。

三、1. 我正在切菜呢。

2. 他正在海关联系呢。

3. 那位老师傅正在介绍经验呢。

4. 她们正在体育馆里比赛呢。

5. 他们正在慰问受伤的战士呢。

四、1. 对。（他正在打字。）

2. 对。（我在画画儿。）

3. 对。（他们正在听录音。）

4. 对。（孩子们正在游泳。）

5. 对。（记者正在写访问报道。）

五、1. 没有。（他们没在搬家。）

2. 没有。（老师没在讲语法。）

3. 没有。（我没在预习新课。）

4. 没有。（工人们没在砍树。）

5. 没有。（运动员没在练基本动作。）

六、1. 他没在吃饭，他在休息。

2. 他们正在写总结。

3. 我们正在实验室做实验。

4. 他去操场了。

5. 我们都喜欢这种山水画。

6. 大家常常思考您提出的问题。

7. 刚才我没对照这两本外文书。

8. 那个售货员没在包点心。

9. 我正在翻译这篇稿子呢。

10. 他有一个收音机。

练习42

一、1. 屋子里开着电扇。

2．院子里种着两棵树。

3．她们挑选着合适的礼物。

4．他和朋友快乐地唱着歌。

5．公路旁边停着三辆小汽车。

6．他肩上杠着一个箱子。

7．下雨的时候我们都打着伞。

8．那个翻译同志穿着一套灰衣服。

9．我叫他的时候，他正在抄写着一篇散文。

10．我进屋的时候，妹妹正念着一首诗。

二、1．书架上摆着很多书和词典。

2．箱子里收着他的一件新雨衣。

3．他嘴里含着一块糖。

4．他手里拿着一盒火柴。

5．床上放着一对绣花枕头。

6．墙上挂着一张气象记录表。

7．碗里盛着米饭。

8．旅馆门口停着许多汽车。

9．桥上站着许多人。

10．他戴着一副黑边眼镜。

三、1．喝着　2．拍着　3．带着　4．听着　5．鼓着

练习 43

一、1．他听（了）广播了。

2．我预先通知他了。

3．运动员们上场了。

4．他丢了一副手套。

5．他给我们介绍了沙漠地区的情况。

6．她在五年里掌握了三种外语。

7．明天他下了课（以后）去你那儿。

8．我上月在上海认识了一位老知识分子。

9．他跟他爱人一起写出了一本三十万字的小说。

10．那个研究所为国家培养了一批年轻的研究工作人员。

二、1．他出院了没有？

　　　没有。（他没出院。）

2．她脱了厚毛衣没有？

　　　没有。（她没脱厚毛衣。）

3．你敲门了没有？

　　　没有。（我没敲门。）

4．他在银行存了一些钱没有？

　　　没有。　（他没在银行存钱。）

5．那个偷东西的人逃走了没有？

　　　没有。（那个偷东西的人没逃走。）

6．昨天他画了山水画没有？

　　　没有。（昨天他没画山水画。）

7．他向你道歉了没有？

　　　没有。（他没向我道歉。）

8．你们交换了对这件事的看法没有？

　　　没有。（我们没交换对这件事的看法。）

9．他们座谈了学习方法的问题没有？

　　　没有。（他们没座谈学习方法的问题。）

10．他们搜集了有关森林的资料没有？

　　　没有。（他们没搜集有关森林的资料。）

三、1．他去（了）医院了。

2．他们下（了）课了。

3．他在我宿舍坐了坐。

4．去年夏天我们游泳了。

5．上次美国留学生没看足球比赛。

6．我们没买那种瓷器。

7．昨天我们在友谊宾馆没看节目。

8．他们俩已经翻译完了那篇文章。

9. 明天下午他看了朋友再买东西。

10. 明天我们去公园。

练习 44

一、1. 他要发言了。

2. 我们要迟到了。

3. 他们学校七月要放假了。

4. 他们要回来了。

5. 码头工人要卸货了。

6. 音乐会要结束了。

7. 队伍马上要出发了。

8. 明天上午中央民族歌舞团要到北京了。

9. 五分钟以后我们要登上山顶了。

10. 欢迎新同学的晚会要开始了。

二、1，3，4，5，10——就

2，6，7，8，9——快，就

三、1. 下星期一她就要来北京了。

2. 他明年九月就要当中学教师了。

3. 报名日期月底就要截止了。

4. 这条重要新闻七点就要广播了。

5. 那座办公大楼下星期就要盖好了。

6. 那两个国家今年十二月就要正式建交（建立外交关系）了。

7. 全市人民代表大会五月六日就要召开了。

8. 他父亲写的那本书下半年就要出版了。

9. 参加这次国际会议的代表们明天就要到了。

10. 那个国家的驻华（中国）大使馆三天以后就要正式办公了。

练习 45

一、1. 他一直没有失望过。

2．两年以前他姐姐在中国工作过。

3．那个工厂去年生产过这种药。

4．这位著名的医生给我父亲治过病。

5．那个地区有过这种传染病。

6．他十三岁的时候在这个中学学习过。

7．去年我看过两次国际乒乓球比赛。

8．他写博士论文的时候参考过这几本书。

9．我哥哥在小学学过英语，在中学学过日语，在大学学过西班牙语。

10．他们学校的爬山运动员受到过严格的训练。

二、1．他没在农村劳动过。

2．别人没批评过他。

3．他没拒绝过他朋友的邀请。

4．他没观察过这儿的地理状况。

5．上星期我没请过事假。

6．他们没测量过这条河。

7．老师没给我们讲过这个学校的历史。

8．我们没征求过他对这次试验的意见。

9．那位教授没指导过新来的研究生。

10．我们学院上星期一没举行过学术报告会。

三、1．他在农村劳动过没有？

2．别人批评过他没有？

3．他拒绝过他朋友的邀请没有？

4．他观察过这儿的地理状况没有？

5．上星期你请过事假没有？

6．他们测量过这条河没有？

7．老师给你们讲过这个学校的历史没有？

8．你们征求过他对这次试验的意见没有？

9．那位教授指导过新来的研究生没有？

10．你们学院上星期一举行过一次学术报告会没有？

第 七 章

练习 46

一、1. 那不是广播站。

2. 这个消息不是我们听到的。

3. 这辆电车不是去北海的。

4. 这不是一个秘密。

5. 这两张船票不是那位先生的。

6. 排球队的队员都不是南方人。

排球队的队员不都是南方人。

7. 他不是外科大夫。

8. 跳远比赛的冠军不是他。

9. 那个录音机不是他刚买的。

10. 广场南边不是历史博物馆。

11. 我后边不是张明。

12. 这个主意不是他出的。

13. 今天不是星期二。

14. 高方不是我妹妹。

15. 滑雪不是他的爱好。

二、1. 那是不是广播站？

2. 这个消息是不是你们听到的？

3. 这辆电车是不是去北海的？

4. 这是不是一个秘密？

5. 这两张船票是不是那位先生的？

6. 排球队的队员是不是南方人？

7. 他是不是外科大夫？

8. 跳远比赛的冠军是不是他？

9. 那个录音机是不是他刚买的?

10. 广场南边是不是历史博物馆?

11. 你后边是不是张明?

12. 这个主意是不是他出的?

13. 今天是不是星期二?

14. 高方是不是你妹妹?

15. 滑雪是不是他的爱好?

三、1. 这不是豆子。

2. 这句话不是他说的。

3. 他在我旁边。

4. 俱乐部在体育馆西边。

5. 球场北边不是游泳池。

6. 今天不是星期天。

7. 电影院在旅馆东边。

8. 那件事情不是关于他的。

9. 那几位旅客是日本人。

10. 这是那位老人的皮帽子。

练习 47

一、1. 明天没有雨。

2. 小李现在没有事。

3. 他们没有证明。

4. 我家没有这种花。

5. 她没有日记。

6. 他叔叔没有儿子。

7. 他们都没有这种鞋。

8. 这个学校没有游泳池。

9. 那个运动员没有二十几岁,只有十八岁。

10. 他们组没有十二个人,只有十个人。

二、1. 明天有没有雨? 明天有雨没有?

2．小李现在有没有事？小李现在有事没有？

3．他们有没有证明？他们有证明没有？

4．你家有没有这种花？你家有这种花没有？

5．她有没有日记？她有日记没有？

6．他叔叔有没有儿子？他叔叔有儿子没有？

7．他们有没有这种鞋？他们有这种鞋没有？

8．这个学校有没有游泳池？这个学校有游泳池没有？

9．那个运动员有没有二十几岁？　那个运动员有二十几岁没有？

10．他们组有没有十二个人？他们组有十二个人没有？

三、1．他外祖父是不是有一些珍贵的资料？

2．他是不是有一个美好的理想？

3．一斤这样的西红柿是不是有五个？

4．那位老大爷是不是有两个孙女？

5．学校旁边是不是有一个商店？

6．那个俱乐部是不是有二十个工作人员？

7．电影院对面是不是有个邮局？

8．你的老师是不是有很多外国学生？

9．前边那条小河上是不是没有桥？

10．明天上午是不是有四节课？

四、1．我没有世界地图。

2．明天没有体育课。

3．他没有小汽车。

4．桌子上没有铅笔和尺。

5．他爸爸没有六十岁。

6．这些苹果没有十斤。

7．一个学年（里）有两个学期。

8．弟弟没有照相机。

9．墙上有画儿没有？没有。

10．外边有树没有？有两棵。

练习 48

一、1. 我把今天的家庭作业做完了。

　　2. 他把毕业论文写完了。

　　3. 鸡把地上的米吃光了。

　　4. 弟弟把爸爸看的报撕破了。

　　5. 大家都把耳机戴上了。

　　6. 他已经把大衣穿好了。

　　7. 妈妈把刀子和叉子拿出来了。

　　8. 他把奖学金领来了。

　　9. 工人们把那条公路修好了。

　　10. 那只猴子把小朋友给的花生拿走了。

二、1. 我没把今天的家庭作业做完。

　　2. 他没把毕业论文写完。

　　3. 鸡没把地上的米吃光。

　　4. 弟弟没把爸爸看的报撕破。

　　5. 大家都没把耳机戴上。

　　6. 他没把大衣穿好。

　　7. 妈妈没把刀子和叉子拿出来。

　　8. 他没把奖学金领来。

　　9. 工人们没把那条公路修好。

　　10. 那只猴子没把小朋友给的花生拿走。

三、1.干净　　　2.大家　　　　3.走　　　　4.上

　　5.上　　　　6.来　　　　7.地上　　　8.黑板上

　　9.我（朋友）10.妈妈（她）11.外边　　12.地上

　　13.桌子上　14.花瓶里　15.衣架上　16.干净

　　17.中文　　18.一下　　19.我们（朋友）20.来

四、1. 他把面包吃了。

　　2. 我把不懂的地方写在一张纸上了。

　　3. 我朋友把我的信带来了。

729

4．他把存在银行里的钱取出来。

5．我把墙上的画儿拿下来了。

6．他把自己的名字写在本上了。

7．我把"本子"写成"木子"了。

8．同学们能把这些资料看完。

9．我们把这些点心放在盘子里。

10．我昨天没把那封信寄出去。

11．他没把那块绸缎送给别人。

12．他一定能把这个问题解决。

13．弟弟把他的脏衣服藏在床底下。

14．那个技术员把这种机器改成新的了。

15．他把要洗的衣服放在洗衣机里了。

练习 49

一、1．敌人被我们打败了。

2．电视机被他弄坏了。

3．这几棵菜被虫子咬坏了。

4．暖水瓶被她打碎了。

5．广告被大风刮破了。

6．这张画儿的颜色被我涂坏了。

7．屋子里的东西都被他弄乱了。

8．院子里的雪被我们扫到一边去了。

9．那些枪被战士们运走了。

10．那些小椅子被孩子们搬到院子里去了。

二、1．排球没被人拿走。

2．那只狼没被人捉住。

3．那条黑狗没被人打死。

4．树上的叶子没被风刮下来。

5．那条路没被那些工人铺好。

6．那个村子没被占领。

7．我们的申请没被批准。

8．那个售货员没被商店经理叫去。

9．那个沙漠地区没被征服。

10．我的脖子没被蚊子咬着(zháo)。

练习 50

一、1．旅行（玩，参观）　　2．看足球比赛(看朋友，买东西)

3．请教（问）一个问题　4．去展览馆

5．看电影　　　　　　6．寄信

7．谈话　　　　　　　8．看

9．喝　　　　　　　　10．写字（写文章，写信）

11．参加（这个晚会）　12．去看你

二、1．他们没去公园玩儿。

2．我们没去游泳池游泳。（我们不去游泳池游泳。）

3．老师没去他们班讲课。（老师不去他们班讲课。）

4．我没去图书馆还书。（我不去图书馆还书。）

5．我没找他们下棋。

6．咱们不买汽水喝。

7．我们没有地方踢球。

8．他没时间打网球。

9．我没兴趣滑冰。

10．他没有打电话通知我。

11．这儿没有椅子坐。

12．他每天不用盐水漱口。

13．我屋里没有箱子放衣服。

14．现在他没有工作做。

15．他跟中国朋友没用汉语聊天。　（他不跟中国朋友用汉语
聊天。）

16．我母亲没去大使馆参加宴会。

17．我朋友不常用圆珠笔写信。

18. 我没开汽车去北京（飞）机场。〔我开汽车没去北京（飞）机场。〕

练习 51

一、1. 老师叫<u>你们两个人</u>快走。

2. 我们国家的大使请<u>我们留学生</u>去大使馆看电影。

3. 我请<u>那几位同志</u>告诉我去天安门的路。

4. 他们在外边叫<u>我</u>跟他们一起打乒乓球。

5. 我有<u>一个好朋友</u>是医生。

6. 他有<u>三支钢笔</u>都是黑色的。

7. 宿舍楼前面有<u>好几个中国学生</u>在托排球。

8. 医院南边有<u>一个小商店</u>晚上开门。

9. 我从前有<u>一个同学</u>唱歌唱得特别好。

10. 我们有<u>一位外国老师</u>教我们阿拉伯语。

二、

兼　语	主谓词组作宾语
1. A 我们	B 我们爱听音乐
2. A 朋友	B 他很喜欢看电影
3. B 一个哥哥	A 他哥哥是（一个）医生
4. A 我们	B 我们在这儿比赛
5. B 他们的爱情	A 他们的爱情被破坏

练习 52

1. 后边开来了几辆卡车。

2. 教室里走出来几个同学。

3. 地上放着一堆黄瓜。

4. 公园门口蹲着两个石狮子。

5. 俱乐部门前站着很多人。

6.病房里推出来一个病人。

7.我们楼里搬走了一对青年夫妇。

8.刚才死了一只鸭子。

9.飞机上下来几个军官。

10.车间里出来十几个工人。

第 八 章

练习 53

1.这座山比那座山高两千米。

　这座山比那座山矮两千米。

2.这个礼堂比那个礼堂多三百个座位。

　那个礼堂比这个礼堂少三百个座位。

3.这篇短文比那篇多五百字。

　那篇短文比这篇少五百字。

4.他父亲比他母亲大两岁。

　他母亲比他父亲小两岁。

5.这条路比那条路长六公里。

　那条路比这条路短六公里。

6.昨天气温比今天低两度。

　今天气温比昨天高两度。

7.这间屋子比那间窄一米半。

　那间屋子比这间宽一米半。

8."大"字比"夫"字少一笔。

　"夫"字比"大"字多一笔。

9.他日语说得比你差。

　你日语说得比他好。

10.我画中国画比他差得多。

他画得比我好得多。

11. 晚上我比我朋友晚睡半个小时。

我朋友比我早睡半个小时。

12. 我们比他们早到一刻钟。

他们比我们晚到一刻钟。

13. 中午这个食堂比那个食堂早开一刻钟饭。

那个食堂比这个食堂晚开一刻钟饭。

14. 谢力比李华多买了两本《汉英小词典》。

李华比谢力少买了两本《汉英小词典》。

15. 张英比马明在大学多学了一年。

马明比张英在大学少学了一年。

练习 54

一、1. 李华跟马明一样想去旅行。

　　2. 这条路跟那条路一样长。

　　3. 我跟他一样想学化学。

　　4. 他父亲跟我父亲一样大。

　　5. 这块玻璃跟那块一样，都很厚。

　　6. 她买的书跟我买的一样，都是中文(版)的。

　　7. 他跟我们一样在考虑这个问题。

　　8. 他们俩跟我们俩一样来往很密切。

　　9. 这个措施跟那个一样，都很具体。

　　10. 这种拖拉机跟那种一样，都是中国制造的。

二、1. 这个信封跟那个不一样。

　　2. 这个箱子的颜色跟那个不一样。

　　3. 马明跟李华学的不一样。

　　4. 老张跟老马不一样大。

　　5. 他们学习的地方跟我们的不一样。

　　　（他们跟我们不一样。）

　　6. 他跟你的职业不一样。

7. 这个公园跟那个公园不一样。

8. 你们用的分析方法跟他们用的不一样。

9. 我跟弟弟起床的时间不一样。

10. 他的中文杂志跟我的不一样多。

练习 55

1. 订这种报的人没有订那种（报）的（人）多。

2. 我的女儿有他的女儿那么大。

3. 今年的夏天有去年那样热。

4. 这座桥没有那座桥那么长。

5. 这间客厅的光线没有那间的好。

6. 那个城市的人口没有这个城市的人口多。

7. 我每天晚上工作的时间没有他那么长。

8. 这个游泳池有那个那么深。

9. 他没有你写得这么整齐。

10. 你们俩打网球没有他们俩打得好。

11. 大使开车没有司机开得快。

12. 那本书没有这本书这么厚。

13. 那本小说没有这本（小说）这么有意思。

14. 颐和园没有友谊宾馆离我们学校近。

15. 今天气温没有昨天高。

练习 56

1. 李华不象王英那样高。

2. 那种电扇象这种这样便宜。

3. 这包糖不象那包那样重。

4. 我象他那样喜欢滑雪。

5. 我的小孩象他的小孩那样大。

6. 那个汉字不象这个汉字的笔画这么多。

7. 这顶帽子象那顶那样又便宜又好看。

8．妹妹象弟弟那样糊涂。

9．他的学习计划订得象你的那么全面。

10．每天他都象他朋友起得那么早。

练习 57

1．那种酒不如这种贵。

2．那张邮票不如这张好看。

3．她毛衣织得不如我（织得好）。

4．那座楼不如这座（楼）高。

5．他中午不如我早到家。

6．她不如你弹得好。

7．这块地不如那块（地）大。

8．母亲不如大姨大。

9．原来的剧场不如新修建的大。

10．小王不如小张高。

11．你不如我喜欢画画儿。

12．我学汉语不如他学得多。

13．他（学汉语）不如我学得早。

14．这本语法书不如那本厚。

15．他不如你这么愿意帮助别人。

练习 58

1．越来越高

2．越来越好（越来越健康）

3．越来越大（越来越小）

4．越来越高

5．越来越丰富，越来越多

6．越来越好

7．越来越了解了

8．越来越喜欢了

9.越来越有兴，趣越来越喜欢，越来越爱写了

10.越来越多了（越来越丰富了）

第 九 章

练习 59

1, 5, 6——（谁）　　　　　2, 7——（哪）

3, 8　——（什么）　　　　4　——（怎么）

9, 10　——（哪儿）

练习 60

1. 今天哪儿暖和啊？

2. 她哪儿不喜欢这个工作啊？

3. 我现在哪儿看书了？

4. 这只鸽子哪儿不好看啊？

5. 暑假里她哪儿想去旅行啊？

6. 小王哪儿找过你啊？

7. 哥哥哪儿出国了？

8. 他俩哪儿常一起散步？

9. 老马哪儿请他吃饭了？

10. 我们哪儿参加过这种活动？

11. 他哪儿了解我的情况啊？

12. 老师哪儿知道他有病啊？

13. 我哪儿看见你的手套了？

14. 他哪儿知道这个消息？

15. 孩子们哪儿不快活啊？

练习 61

1. 这不是一片树林吗？
2. 这个青年不是加入进步团体了吗？
3. 他们不是都买到《实用汉语600句》了吗？
4. 明天下午不是有篮球比赛吗？（不是明天下午有篮球比赛吗？）
5. 我们不是已经通过电话了吗？
6. 她不是特别希望看到老同学吗？
7. 他们不是为建设祖国贡献了自己的全部力量吗？
8. 我跟他不是谈过这件事了吗？（我不是跟他谈过这件事了吗？）
9. 她们不是准备坐飞机去吗？
10. 他不是下星期回国吗？
11. 病人不是昏迷过去了吗？
12. 他不是对世界地理很有兴趣吗？
13. 他们俩感情不是很好吗？
14. 他讲课不是讲得很生动吗？
15. 他不是从小就喜欢思考吗？

练习 62

1. 连这位老人也高兴得唱起来了。
2. 连这些小学生都参加了这次有益的活动。
3. 连屋前屋后都种了一些树。
4. 你连问也没问他，怎么知道他没去！
5. 他连大衣也没有穿就走了。
6. 现在他连拖拉机也会开了。
7. 以前我连想也没想过来北京。
8. 他新买的提包连用还没用过就不见了。
9. 连他的孩子也会弹钢琴了。
10. 我们连计划也没订。

练习 63

1. 这支钢笔是五块钱。
2. 他的家是在广州。
3. 是要下雪了。
4. 台上是坐着不少科学家。
5. 谢力今天是特别高兴。
6. 那位是张老师的爱人。
7. 玛莉是去过中国。
8. 这个问题大家是已经解决了。
9. 他们是不想在这儿过圣诞节。
10. 他是没用过这种照相机。
11. 我是有点儿不舒服。
12. 他是不准备在历史系学习了。

练习 64

1，2，8——（只）　　　3，6——（正是）
4，10　——（坚决）　　5，7，9——（马上，立刻）

练习 65

1. 我们不应该不准备雨衣。
2. 他们没有人不讲究卫生。
3. 这个地区不能没有个青年俱乐部。
4. 这场比赛不能没有你。
5. 这个村子没有人不会编这种筐。
6. 这次他不会考得不好。
7. 我们没有一个人不细心。
8. 没有人不懂得这是一种外交礼节。
9. 这个问题今天不能不解决。
10. 没有一种体育运动他不喜欢。

练习66

1. 张文是一九八〇年去日本学习的。
2. 我们都是用汉语谈话的。
3. 小王是什么时候回去的?
4. 她是在汽车站等我的。
5. 他们是骑车去公园的。
6. 您是在哪儿遇见马老师的?
7. 你是怎么知道我住院的?
8. 我母亲是从上海回来的。
9. 她是上星期离开北京的。
10. 他是昨天坐飞机走的。

第 十 章

练习67

一、1, 2, 6, 7, 9——紧缩句
　　3, 4, 5,　　——并列复句
　　8.　　　　　——偏正复句

二、1. 又…, 又…
　　2. 一边…, 一边…
　　3. 先…, 再…
　　4. 还是…, 还是…
　　5. 不但…, 而且…
　　6. 不是…, 就是…
　　7. 宁可…, 也…
　　8. 不是…, 而是…
　　9. 或者…, 或者…

10. 边…，边…

11. 要是…，就…

12. 只要…，就…

13. 因为…，所以…

14. 就是…，也…

15. 越…越…

16. 既然…，就…

17. 不管（不论）…，也（还）…

18. 只要…，就…

19. 即使（就是）…，也…

20. 一…，就…

三、1. 他们几个人一边走，一边谈。

2. 那位老师不但教本国学生，而且（还，也）教外国学生。

3. 她不但想去欧洲旅行，而且还要去亚洲旅行。

4. 这本画报不是我的，而是他的。

5. 与其骑车去，不如坐车去。

6. 我们一下课，他就走了。

7. 要是明天下雪，我就不去了。

8. 或者买床单，或者买窗帘，都要漂亮一点儿的。

9. 不管唱歌跳舞，她都很喜欢。

四、1，5，6，10——（✓）

2. 只有下午，他才有时间。

3. 不论他唱不唱，别人也必须唱。

4. 他虽然同意这样做了，但是他爱人不同意。

7. 就是他病了，我们也要按时完成这项工程。

8. 因为他就要毕业了，所以我们没有选他做学生会主席。

9. 他既然通过了毕业考试，就应该发给他毕业证书。

参 考 文 献

Reference Books

中国现代语法	王 力	中华书局	1955年
中国语法理论	王 力	中华书局	1951年
中国文法要略	吕叔湘	商务印书馆	1957年
现代汉语语法讲话	丁声树等	商务印书馆	1961年
汉 语	张志公主编	人民教育出版社	1956年
语法和语法教学	张志公主编	人民教育出版社	1956年
现代汉语	胡裕树主编	上海教育出版社	1979年
现代汉语	黄伯荣 廖序东	甘肃人民出版社	1981年
现代汉语语法研究	朱德熙	商务印书馆	1980年
语法讲义	朱德熙	商务印书馆	1982年
汉语口语语法	赵元任（吕叔湘译）	商务印书馆	1979年
现代汉语词典	中国社会科学院语言研究所词典编辑室	商务印书馆 1979年	
现代汉语虚词例解	北京大学中文系汉语专业	湘潭地区教师辅导站 1976年	
现代汉语八百词	吕叔湘主编	商务印书馆	1980年
基础汉语课本	北京语言学院编	外文出版社	1980年

责任编辑：贾寅淮
封面设计：李士伋

外国人实用汉语语法

*

©华语教学出版社
华语教学出版社出版
（中国北京百万庄路 24 号）
邮政编码 100037
电话: 010-68995871 / 68326333
传真: 010-68326333
电子信箱: hyjx @263.net
北京外文印刷厂印刷
中国国际图书贸易总公司海外发行
（中国北京车公庄西路 35 号）
北京邮政信箱第 399 号　邮政编码 100044
新华书店国内发行
1988 年（大 32 开）第一版
2003 年第五次印刷
（汉英）
ISBN 7-80052-067-6 / H · 50(外)
9－CE－2046P
定价：45.00 元